Urban Design Since 1945

Urban Design Since 1945
A Global Perspective

David Grahame Shane

A John Wiley and Sons Ltd, Publication

The author and the publisher gratefully acknowledge the people who gave their permission to reproduce material in this book. While every effort has been made to contact copyright holders for their permission to reprint material, the publishers would be grateful to hear from any copyright holder who is not acknowledged here and will undertake to rectify any errors or omissions in future editions.

Front cover images:
London Street, St. Paul's, After Air Raid © Bettmann/Corbis
Aerial View of Downtown Manhattan © Charles E. Rotkin/Corbis

This edition first published 2011
© 2011 John Wiley & Sons Ltd

Registered office
John Wiley & Sons Ltd, The Atrium, Southern Gate, Chichester, West Sussex, PO19 8SQ, United Kingdom

For details of our global editorial offices, for customer services and for information about how to apply for permission to reuse the copyright material in this book please see our website at www.wiley.com.

Executive Commissioning Editor: Helen Castle
Project Editor: Miriam Swift
Assistant Editor: Calver Lezama

ISBN 978-0-470-51525-9 (hb)
ISBN 978-0-470-51526-6 (pb)

Cover design by Parent Design
Page design and layouts by Artmedia, London
Printed by Everbest, China

Contents

This book is dedicated to Regina Wickham, my wife, and our children Ben, Rachael and Michael; also to my mother Irene Shane-Diederichsen and her husband Jürgen Diederichsen.

Acknowledgements

I am grateful to Helen Castle, my editor at John Wiley & Sons Ltd, who asked me four years ago: 'Do you have another book?' Helen's small addition of the phrase 'in a global perspective' to my proposed title transformed this work.

I am also grateful to Dean Tony Vidler at Cooper Union, who asked me to shift my Town Planning course there towards a global perspective at about the same time, giving me much support and encouragement. Together these two requests provided the impetus for the current book aimed at undergraduates.

Early and generous support from the Graham Foundation of Chicago, headed by Sarah Herder, encouraged me enormously. Conversations and emails with my friend Leon van Schaik, Innovation Professor at RMIT Melbourne, helped me form the global perspective for the book. I am also grateful for the continued support over many years of my friend Professor Colin Fournier at the UCL Bartlett's Urban Design programme.

Throughout the entire process I have benefited enormously from the comments of my two best 'readers'; Professors Brian McGrath and Victoria Marshall of Parsons The New School for Design in New York. Their unwavering support for this project and continual critical stance, not to mention patience with the innumerable variations, helped me through every chapter. I am especially grateful to Professor McGrath for enriching my knowledge of Asian megacities and Bangkok in particular.

The early support of the Graham Foundation enabled me to imagine a book with a large number of colour plates and wide range of illustrations, from stock photographs to specially redrawn analytical plans and sections. I am grateful to Caroline Ellerby, the photo editor, for her drive, energy and toughness in the acquisition and organisation of images.

I am grateful to many professional friends from around the world who helped me with images, suggested sites and commented on chapters. The list is enormous, but without this network of generous friends this book would not have had the scope that it has.

The Graham Foundation grant also enabled me to hire a series of wonderful assistants who helped create this book. I am grateful to Masha Panteleyeva who started me on this process, and to Angie Hunsaker who saw me through at the end. Angie's wit and precision made the final tasks, when all hope seemed lost, a miracle of just-in-time delivery.

In addition, the Graham Foundation allowed me to work with the young architect Uri Wegman who was my steady companion, drawing, drawing, drawing and redrawing plans and sections until we reached some kind of clarity. I am deeply grateful for his patience, steadiness, skill and vision.

I am grateful to the Wiley team in London and Oxford – Calver Lezama and Miriam Swift, working with Helen Castle – for efficiently bringing this effort to fruition.

Finally I must acknowledge the support of my family, my wife Regina Wickham, our children Ben, Rachael and Michael. All at one time or another leant their shoulder to the wheel of production or supported this troubled author through his book fantasies or anxieties. I am a lucky man and I deeply appreciate my family's support and kindness.

St Paul's Cathedral, London, amongst the ruins of the City of London, UK (photo 1945)
London, like Berlin and Tokyo, was badly damaged in the Second World War. These cities faced an uncertain future as the USA and USSR emerged as global superpowers, replacing the old imperial system in the Cold War. (Photo © Keystone/Stringer/Getty Images)

After the Second World War, urban design emerged as a separate professional activity in both Europe and America. Patrick Abercrombie and John Henry Forshaw were the first modern authors to use the term 'urban design' in their 1943 *County of London Plan* for rebuilding the city after the wartime Blitz.[1] This new term was in part a response to the necessity of addressing war damage, but also as a result of the perceived need to plan ahead for the automobile (by 1950 over 342,000 cars were registered in Greater London, more than in all of Italy).[2] A series of international conferences helped to define the field and the British architect and new town designer Frederick Gibberd provided an excellent early manual in his *Town Design* (first published in 1953, revised 1959).[3]

Abercombie was a prominent British town planner who was used to working with architects like Gibberd, but also saw the need for a new field between the two disciplines. In 1945 city planners worked at a large scale, completing a survey of the town, then making an analysis, before projecting solutions according to their theories, whether Beaux-Arts, garden city or modern (segregating all the functions of urban life into separate zones). Architects normally dealt with a single building. There had always been architects who designed at a larger scale, making what Kevin Lynch called 'city designs', like the Baroque plans of Rome or Washington, or the standardised grid plans of the Spanish colonial cites (with their central square containing cathedral, governor's palace, market place, prison and gallows).[4] These designs formed part of the European tradition of urban design that had no technical name, but appeared in Italian Renaissance architectural treatises such as Sebastiano Serlio's *Five Books of Architecture*, published in Venice in the 1530s and 1540s and associated with the development of single-point perspective.[5] This European tradition continued into the 19th century at the Beaux-Arts School in Paris, forming the standard of professional excellence against which modern architects measured themselves. Although Baroque and Beaux-Arts plans appear large and do interact with the landscape, none of the European cities of 1700 contained a million people and all were smaller than Ancient Rome.

By 1945 the largest cities containing the world's urban population (which the United Nations estimated at under 30 per cent of the 3 billion global total) were located in Europe and a few large American cities, like New York or Chicago with 5 to 7 million people. Asian cities like Beijing, for centuries the world's largest city, still maintained a population of 1 million, while Tokyo in 1945 had shrunk to 4 million.[6] During the 18th and 19th centuries the European *metropolis* had grown larger via industrialisation and trade routes from colonies around the world. London merchants, for instance, built the West India Dock for the Caribbean sugar trade in 1802 and the East India Dock for the tea trade from Asia in 1806.[7] In 1945 these London docklands and much of the City of London business centre lay in ruins. There were millions of homeless refugees in both Europe and Asia, some cared for later by the United Nations Relief and Rehabilitation Administration (UNRRA), as the victorious Allied leaders redrew their global 'spheres of influence' at the Yalta Conference of 1945.[8] Two other great imperial capitals, Berlin and Tokyo, also suffered severe damage with people living in temporary shanties at the city centre; Moscow and many Soviet cities barely survived the war intact.[9]

European architects dreamt of controlling every facet of the great metropolitan centres, as well as the subsidiary cites in the imperial system, the colonial administrative capitals, ports and towns that stretched back into the global, imperial hinterland. Urban design in that imperial age was a grand affair of Beaux-Arts axes, or modernist towers in the park, designed from the top down by the master builder. The British architects Edwin Lutyens and Herbert Baker, for instance, planned and built the new colonial capital of India along Beaux-Arts and Garden City lines in the 1920s (completed 1931), while in the 1930s and 1940s Le Corbusier projected his car-based vision on the French colonial port of Algiers (hypothetical designs that influenced his conception of urban design at Chandigarh (see chapter 4)). In contrast to these imperial cities, the New York of the City Commissioner and then highway czar Robert Moses, represented the modern metropolis containing a population of 8 million, with the compact Rockefeller Center as its paradigmatic urban design (see chapter 3).

By the end of the 20th century this picture had changed completely. In 1945 most people in the world still lived in agricultural settlements. By 2007 the UN estimated that more than 50 per cent of the world's population would live in cities, 3 billion urban people, with one third in informal settlements. The location of the world's urban population had also changed. While the New York–Newark conurbation was still in the top three, none of the European imperial metropolitan centres was in the top ten. The centre of gravity of the urban world had shifted to Asia, with Mumbai, Shanghai and Jakarta appearing so that the list included many poor and middle-income cities.[10]

The form of the city had also changed. Unlike the rich, compact metropolis of 1945, the *megacity* of 2005 stretches across enormous territories including informal and formal developments, central business parks and malls, markets and bazaars, dense enclaves and open spaces, agricultural and recreational parklands, connected by high-speed communications and complex infrastructure systems. No single person, let alone one architect, could think of designing this enormous territory in all its complexity. Tokyo stood as the richest and largest Asian megacity with 32 million inhabitants, but many others rivalled this size without the wealth or technological resources.

This book is structured around four themes that all ran concurrently through the period under study from 1945 to 2010. Each theme is treated in one section, in a sequence of metropolis, megalopolis, fragmented metropolis and then megacity/metacity. This sequence is not intended to indicate a temporal sequence; contemporary urban actors could use any one of these themes, or hybridise them, in the same period, even in the same city. Each theme section is made of a pair of chapters. The first chapter outlines the theories associated with each theme, with relatively few illustrations. The second chapter in each section is an illustrated chapter of case studies, often of built projects, but sometimes of unbuilt theoretical projects, such as competition entries. In the section on the metropolis, for example, the first chapter will outline the competing theories of the metropolis from 1945 onwards and their influence on urban design, while the second will illustrate many projects built using the metropolitan model at various times during the last 60 years. The second chapter of each section will usually include a heterotopic element like a world's fair or Olympic Games, that gives an indication of changing urban design thinking in a particular period.

The next chapter will illustrate how different urban actors in different periods during the last 60 years worked to create different urban models, using the basic urban elements of *enclave*, *armature* and *heterotopia*. Urban design played a complex and shifting role in this process from metropolis to megacity, and these three urban elements form the basis of all the following sections and paired chapters.

Notes

NB: See 'Author's Caution: Endnote Sources and Wikipedia', towards the end of this book.

1   Patrick Abercrombie and John Henry Forshaw, *County of London Plan*, Macmillan & Co (London), 1943.

2   For a history of urban design as a fragmentary practice, see: Urban Design Group, http://www. udg.org.uk/?document_id=468 (accessed 27 September 2009). For statistics on European automobiles, see: Tony Judt, *Postwar: A History of Europe Since 1945*, Penguin (New York), 2006, p 342 (available on Google Books).

3   Frederick Gibberd, *Town Design*, Architectural Press (London), 1953, revised 1959.

4   For a general history of city design, see: Kevin Lynch, *A Theory of Good City Form*, MIT Press (Cambridge, MA), 1981, pp 73–9.

5   For an English translation of Serlio, see: Sebastiano Serlio, *The Five Books of Architecture*, Dover (New York), 1982.

6   For UN statistics of world population 1950–2003, see p 13 of 'World Urbanization Prospects: The 2003 Revision', http://www.un.org/esa/population/publications/wup2003/WUP2003Report. pdf (accessed 27 September 2009).

7   For London Docks history, see: http://www.portcities.org.uk/london/ (accessed 27 September 2009).

8   For refugees and UNRRA, see Judt, *Postwar*, pp 28–32.

9   For European war damage including that in Berlin, ibid pp 13–18. For Tokyo, see: Tokyo Metropolitan Government, *A Hundred Years of Tokyo City Planning*, TMG Municipal Library No 28 (Tokyo), 1994, pp 44–8.

10   See UN diagrams in: 'UN-HABITAT Secretary General's Visit to Kibera, Nairobi, 30–31 January, 2007', UN-HABITAT website, http://www.unhabitat.org/downloads/docs/Press_SG_visit_ Kibera07/SG%205.pdf (accessed 27 September 2009).

CHAPTER 1

Urban Design – An Overview

The intense urbanisation of the planet in the last 60 years has been the accidental by-product of an equally astonishing industrialisation of the globe that produced both great wealth and great poverty. Oil provided the new energy source for this massive industrialisation process, and small petroleum-powered engines transformed the lives of millions of rich and poor people both in cities and in the countryside. As the 21st century opens, the costs of this dependence on the easy energy of oil are becoming clearer in terms of global warming and human-induced climate change. This change threatens many of the new Asian megacities built in great river estuaries (as well as their European and American equivalents).

Americans led the way in this oil-based revolution but were not very efficient in their consumption since oil was cheap and plentiful, and oil companies received indirect government subsidies to keep it that way. All the elements of the city, such as department stores, libraries, churches, cinemas and restaurants moved out to the suburban shopping strips of postwar America, like Wilshire Boulevard, Los Angeles. Here owners relocated their stores in isolated pavilions surrounded by parking lots (see chapter 5). The result is that the USA is less energy efficient than its rivals, and Americans today consume 10 times as much energy as the global average per person.[1] As in earlier oil booms, the high prices of energy after the 9/11/2001 terrorist attacks on the World Trade Center in New York benefited oil producers enormously, who then invested in cities in the Middle East, Latin America and across Russia and its ex-satellite states. In such territories where oil is still cheap, early American urban forms based on the automobile continue to expand. But most other oil consumers face higher prices in the long term that will result in changes in their lifestyle and shrinking cites, as remote suburbs are abandoned. This presents great opportunities for creative urban designers to re-conceive patterns of life in the city, perhaps learning from Asian economies that operate with one thirtieth of the American consumption of energy per capita.

Urban Design Since 1945: A Global Perspective tells the story of this global shift and transformation, highlighting the role of architects, urban designers, planners and their changing clients: central governments, local governments, communities, non-governmental organisations (NGOs), developers and world institutions. The global perspective means that the traditional Eurocentric narrative no longer works and new urban actors enter. The transformation of the imperial metropolis into the global megacity inevitably involves many urban design innovations from both Europe and America, whose early post-war wealth sponsored experiment. American mall architects like Victor Gruen, for example, developed key features of what became the global standard, pioneering the interior, two-level, air-conditioned, regional shopping centre in the 1950s (see chapter 6).[2]

Much revolves around the application of such urban innovations, first inside the imperial colonial system, then inside the emerging independent nation states, and then in the new fragmented global economy based on global corporations exploiting Asia and Africa, Latin America, Europe and the Middle East. Gruen, for instance, planned the expansion of oil-rich Tehran, Iran, in the 1960s.[3] This narrative of innovation meant the rapid transformation of modernist prototypes and their hybridisation with local cultures and climates in a two-way process. By the end of the 20th century the old metropolitan cities in Europe and the USA were importing new urban innovations from their former colonies, such as Renzo Piano's 2000 Shard at London Bridge, London. This is a typical Hong Kong, mixed-use, hybrid tower with a vertical, interior, urban mall at its base connected to a railway station and, below ground, a London Underground station (see chapter 8).

The shift in the global centre of urban population from Europe to Asia and the shrinking of the European percentage of the urban global population has accompanied the rise of India and China as urban giants, with very different urban design strategies. In broad terms China appears to cherish the modernist metropolitan model of Robert Moses at a new, unprecedented scale, with its megablocks, towers, superhighways and centralised planning. India does not have the same degree of top-down coordination or state control of landownership, and supports a far more diverse, and slower developing, bottom-up pattern with many more self-built city sectors like Dharavi, Mumbai. The Indian state invests mainly in infrastructure in a hybrid model of state planning, whereas the Chinese state has a more comprehensive range of control. Both face enormous urban design problems as barely a third of each country's population has moved to the cities.[4]

In addition the cities built in the USA, Canada and Latin America in the 1960s and 1970s, when oil was cheap and plentiful, face a crisis of their own as this resource may become far more expensive, threatening their dispersed spatial logic that made public transportation uneconomical. The ex-imperial metropolitan cities of Europe face their own version of this crisis, as they too have expanded across vast territories to become miniature versions of Asian megacities, with the vast 'Blue Banana' of urbanism stretching across the EU from London, through Holland and Germany to Milan. Europeans are pioneering an ecological approach, initiated in the USA but then neglected, attempting to learn from the lower carbon footprints of Asian cities. Europeans imported ideas such as central area congestion pricing to Stockholm and London from Singapore. At the same time European designers are providing eco-city models for the Asian megacities of the future (like the proposed Dongtan Eco-City, outside Shanghai, China: see chapter 10).

Global urban actors, patterns and models
In order to tell the story of the transformation of the European metropolis into the Asian megacity, the narrative highlights some themes that run through the period like threads in a vast tapestry. The first theme is that urban actors – people, groups, associations – and their beliefs build cities. Despite the seemingly out-of-control growth of cities, human actors and their belief systems contribute their energy and organisational skills to building even the most

random-looking city. This ostensibly chaotic swarming instinct is in fact the result of many individual choices and actions made by urban actors following what they believe is their best interest. There may be many unintended consequences stemming from such actions, especially if repeated on a massive scale. Urban actors need to cooperate not only in building the city, but then to maintain it and regenerate it, to modify it and transform it. Cities are about people living together, and this requires organisation and skills in managing the affairs of the local community and larger city.[5]

As cities have grown, so has the need for organisation that leads to the second theme of cybernetics: urban modelling and self-organisation. In the 20th century the development of cybernetics – the art and science of managing information flows through sorting and feedback mechanisms including computers – enabled urban actors to process far more information than before, looking for self-organising, iterative patterns and emergent conceptual models in the complexity of cities in the 1960s. At first these models were exercises in number crunching for economic models, social trends or traffic flows, but by the 1990s computer animation programs like Director (1987) and 3-D programs like Form Z (1991) emerged that could help urban designers model the physical city and study its complex feedback systems over time in three dimensions. Traditional urban codes that controlled the appearance of the city could be fed into these 3-D models, so that urban designers could set up codes for small urban fragments and model them in virtual space before building them. By the year 2000, urban designers using personal computers could create complex urban renderings, as well as find repetitive patterns in seemingly random urban assemblies such as the self-built housing in Latin-American *favelas*.[6]

The third thread in this story of urban transformations is the idea that urban actors manipulate a limited set of urban elements in building their urban models and cities. Urban actors organise urban elements to make urban models that work for them in a particular time and place. The next chapter will elaborate further on three important urban elements – the enclave, the armature and the heterotopia – as key elements employed by urban actors in constructing cities.[7] The enclave is a more or less bounded space, like a field in the countryside, a piece of urban property with a wall around it or an open space like a square at the centre of a city surrounded by buildings. The Rockefeller Center, for instance, is an enclave inside New York under single ownership with a distinctive architectural presence, like the Forbidden City at the heart of Beijing. An armature is a linear spatial organising device, like a street or highway with sequential, numbered houses or exits. Urban actors often use armatures as the approach to an enclave, to cut through enclaves or as the link between two attractors. Baron Haussmann, the Prefect of Paris from 1853 to 1870, used great street armatures like the Boulevard Saint-Germain and Boulevard Saint-Michel cutting across the south bank of the old city to modernise Paris, creating a ring and radial boulevard system that led out to the periphery and parks. Finally the heterotopia is a specialised urban element, an enclave that has multiple interior subdivisions that can hold conflicting urban activities in the same place at the same time (often in section). It is an important place of urban experimentation and change, handling nonconforming urban activities and

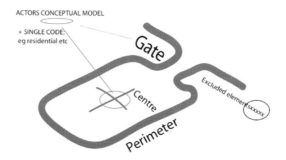

Single Centre Enclave

Actors establish a conceptual model that controls single code for an enclave
self-centering system, feed-back reinforces the centre

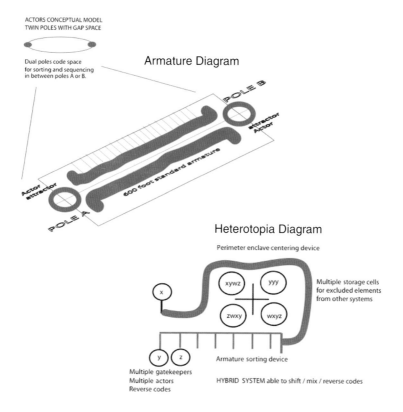

City diagrams

Diagrams of three urban elements
(Diagrams © David Grahame Shane, 2009)

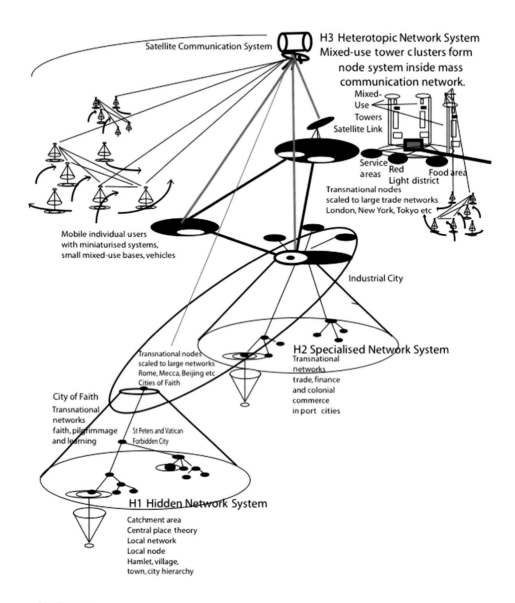

Satellite Communication System

H3 Heterotopic Network System
Mixed-use tower clusters form node system inside mass communication network.

Mixed-Use Towers

Satellite Link

Service areas   Red   Food area
Light district

Transnational nodes
scaled to large trade networks
London, New York, Tokyo etc

Mobile individual users
with miniaturised systems,
small mixed-use bases, vehicles

Industrial City

Transnational nodes
scaled to large networks
Rome, Mecca, Beijing etc
Cities of Faith

H2 Specialised Network System
Transnational networks
trade, finance and colonial commerce in port cities

City of Faith
Transnational networks
faith, pilgrimmage and learning

St Peters and Vatican
Forbidden City

H1 Hidden Network System

Catchment area
Central place theory
Local network
Local node
Hamlet, village,
town, city hierarchy

City diagrams

Cities are composed of basic organisational units: the enclave, armature and heterotopia. Urban actors combine these urban elements into different urban systems. This diagram shows three urban systems operating as layers simultaneously in a city territory. The first system has a single power centre, the second extends this to a new satellite city and the third is a multicentred city overlaid on both of the others with mobile urban actors who can communicate to each other in real time. (Diagrams © David Grahame Shane, 2009)

contributing to the overall stability of the city through its capacity to host change. The term is borrowed from French philosopher Michel Foucault's writing and is examined further in the next chapter. Foucault pointed to prisons, hospitals, clinics, asylums, courthouses and clinics as heterotopias of 'deviance' that helped give birth to the modern city by removing people who were ill, could not work or did not fit in the city, accelerating the shift to a modern, efficient, industrial society.[8]

The fourth thread involves the ability of urban actors to reflect on their work, reorganise elements and transform models to fit local circumstances and times. This ability to reflect, adapt, discuss and change is very important to the continual creation of new urban forms and the adaptive reuse of old ones. The last 60 years has been a period of enormous changes. Global European empires broke down into independent nation states dominated by two superpowers of the Cold War from 1945 to 1991 (the USSR and the USA). In this period American and Russian urban models had a privileged status. The Russian urban model focused on the *metropolis* at the heart of empire with satellite states and cities that were miniature clones of the original. The American model involved the *megalopolis*, a linear network of cities, originally linked by rail and coastal plain, but then cemented together into a network city by highways and the mass ownership of automobiles in the 1960s. Europeans and their shrinking empires straddled between these two models, making new hybrids based on the safety net of the welfare state, but slowly introducing American features like mass automobile ownership and commercial media, advertising and mass consumption merchandise in large supermarkets. Japan and the Asian Tigers (small nation states on the Pacific Rim around China, like Thailand and colonial city-states like Hong Kong) created a different hybrid model, with stronger, more centralised governments, creating the *fragmented metropolis*. Latin American nations developed their own characteristic urban model that included a non-industrialised informal housing sector where urban immigrants built their own homes as best they could in megacities with *favelas*. While the American model proved triumphant by 1991, based on the easy energy of plentiful cheap oil supplies, it is now under question as its true ecological, financial and social costs become apparent and Asian *megacities* emerge as an alternative model.

This book is organised around these four models: the *metropolis*, the *megalopolis*, the *fragmented metropolis* and the *megacity/metacity*. As explained in the Introduction, each model is the subject of one section made up of two chapters, the first chapter detailing the urban design features of each model and the second providing illustrative examples and case studies. The short global narrative above indicates that urban actors watch each other's work and compete for the best model and best city, creating new hybrids that work for them in their local situation. As global financial institutions replaced both the international aid agencies and nation-states as sources of capital for urban development, this inter-city competition intensified. The narrative weaves together these four models over the last 60 years and maps their interactions as different urban actors came to prominence, ending with the global financial crisis of 2008 (when the G8 states rescued the system and changed the rules).

The metropolitan model

The first model, the metropolis, is ancient, belonging to imperial systems throughout the ages. A succession of imperial cities and cultures marks the migration of early human settlements out of the East African Rift Valley up to Jericho 11,000 years ago, on to the agricultural settlements of the 'fertile crescent' stretching from the Nile to the Euphrates, and then beyond to the Asian landmass, Europe and the Americas.[9] In the metropolitan system there is one privileged, central, mother city at the heart of a surrounding spider's web of towns, villages and hamlets that form the agricultural hinterland to this imperial capital. The highly structured hierarchical organisation of Beijing, with its enclaves within enclaves as in the Forbidden City and axial approach armature, exemplifies the archaic form of metropolitan urban design. For centuries Beijing was a giant among cities, with over a million people. Every detail of urban life was ordered, with the majority of the Chinese population living as agricultural peasants tied to the land, waiting on the elite, which they could only join through a complex exam system. The hierarchical urban design system of grid cities with imperial compounds at the centre matched the social and bureaucratic organisation that survived until the Communist Revolution of 1949.[10]

In 1945, most of the world's urban population lived in large European capital cities – Berlin, Brussels, London, Madrid, Paris, Rome, Vienna – that had served as metropolitan capitals of 19th-century global empires (Tokyo being the equivalent Asian example). The coal-fired industrial base of these empires enabled them to operate at a new scale, with improved communications and transportation links, and new social organisation based on the factory and on mass consumption of mass-produced goods. The governmental shift from monarch of European nation state to Emperor of a global colonial system was often accompanied by grandiose urban design projects to transform the national capital, with great Beaux-Arts axial approaches to palaces, networks of urban boulevards, railways linking to ports and ships to empires. In the 19th century, London became the largest city in the world with a population of 7 million, but it remained a disorganised, fragmented metropolitan model compared to Paris, where Haussmann's ring and radial network of modern boulevards provided the ideal metropolitan model for several generations.

After two devastating world wars, with concentration camps, blitzkrieg bombing of civilian populations and firebombing of cities, the Europe of 1945 could no longer claim the privilege of culture and world leadership in urban design. It is estimated that there were 20 million homeless refugees in Europe (including camp survivors and displaced persons) and another 20 million refuges in Asia as a result of the war against Japan, the Chinese Revolution and the Korean War.[11] Huge parts of London, Berlin and Tokyo lay in ruins – not to mention Hiroshima, Nagasaki or the many Russian cities devastated in the war. Moscow continued the French Beaux-Arts metropolitan model incorporated in Stalin's plans from the mid-1930s as the Soviet ideal, supported by linear industrial cities as great centres of innovation, new towns where Russian peasants would transform into modern Soviet industrial workers. The goal of these urban designs and the associated state central planning was rapid industrialisation to catch up with Europe. Architects and planners had a big role in this top-down, central control system.

Baron Haussmann, Avenue Ledru-Rollin, Paris, France, 1860 (photo 1990s)
Well-ordered Paris rather than chaotic London represented the ideal metropolis of the 19th century,
the ideal imperial capital with its public monuments, broad armatures and great squares, capable of
accommodating grand military parades. Haussmann's landscape architect Jean-Charles Alphand designed
every aspect of the street, from boulevard layout and paving surfaces to cast-iron street furniture and
selecting species of trees. (Photo © David Grahame Shane)

The success of this metropolitan model encouraged the Russians to export it to satellite
countries across central Europe, to their allies in China, even to African and Indian allies and
to Cuba. Stalin's metropolitan model, with its web of ring and radial roads as well as satellite
new towns in green belts, also included skyscrapers modelled on New York in the 1920s and
1930s. Wedding-cake skyscrapers based on the American city's 1916 setback laws appeared
on the skylines of Moscow, Warsaw and even, scaled down, in Beijing. These giant heterotopic
structures included living quarters, offices, hotels, restaurants, recreational facilities, cinemas
and theatres as well as shops, forming miniature modern cities inside their host city.

New York in 1945 represented the modern metropolis for many Europeans. Le Corbusier
had argued that New York skyscrapers were too close together in *When the Cathedrals Were
White* (1947), but the Rockefeller Center provided the model 'community centre' for the modern
architect and critic Sigfried Giedion in *Space, Time and Architecture* (1941).[12] For many
European and Asian urban designers the skyscraper city combined with Robert Moses' parks,
parkway system and public housing blocks provided a new vision of the modern American
metropolis free of the imperial armatures and palatial enclaves of the past. Here the repetitious,
fractal pattern of skyscraper centres, inner-city urban renewal and satellite new towns,
whether private or publicly planned, created a powerful, iterative fractal system (see p 20).

Dmitry Chechulin, Kotelnicheskaya Embankment Skyscraper, Moscow, Russia (photo 1952)
After 1945, Moscow represented a metropolis not based on capitalism or private property. Stalin's plan of the 1930s built on the city's ring–radial pattern, adding green belts and new towns. Stalin planned an enormous monument to Lenin at the centre and other 'wedding-cake' skyscraper buildings at important junctions around the inner ring road, including this elite apartment complex beside the Kremlin. (Photo © Dmitry Azovtsev, http://fotki.azovtsev.com)

The modern metropolis: New York, USA
In 1945, downtown New York represented the image of the modern, commercial metropolis. Urban designers were fascinated by the power of the skyscraper to concentrate the city. Commercial cities around the globe like Hong Kong or Shanghai have replicated this scheme, while many cities created mini-Manhattan skyscraper zones, like La Défense, Paris (1958). (Photo © Henry Groskinsky/Time & Life Pictures/Getty Images)

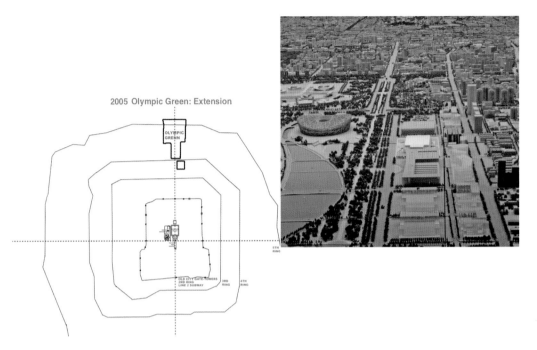

2005 Olympic Green: Extension

Sasaki Associates, Olympic Green, Beijing, China, 2008 (photo 2008)
The Beijing Olympic Park aligned with the great north–south axis of the imperial Forbidden
City, demonstrating the continued power of the metropolitan model in the contemporary
city. Modern designers have also tried to create similar powerful, metropolitan axes like Le
Corbusier's design for Chandigarh, India and Auguste Perret's design for Le Havre, France in
1958. (Photo and plan © David Grahame Shane, 2008)

The metropolitan dream proved very powerful and adaptable. Highways leading to
skyscraper clusters at the centre of the city replaced the imperial boulevards, but the centre
as central business district (CBD) still dominated. In Paris in the 1950s the imperial east–
west axis from the Louvre to the Arc de Triomphe was extended out to the new La Défense
skyscraper district. Le Corbusier's design at Chandigarh from the 1950s, like Oscar
Niemeyer's 1960 design for Brasilia, also demonstrates the continuity of Beaux-Arts imperial
planning moves, including huge axes and giant palaces, within modernism. Architects had
the illusion of power, while nearby shantytowns housed the construction workers, becoming
unplanned, informal cities in their own right. The Olympic planning for Beijing in 2008 shows
the persistence of the metropolitan ideal and its imperial axis. The main cluster of Olympic
sports facilities is built to the north of the Forbidden Palace, extending the imperial axis into
the modern metropolis of Beijing, with its ring and radial roads, peripheral developments
and satellite towns.

The megalopolis model

The second model is the megalopolis, a city based on a new distribution system and energy source, oil and petroleum, that sprawls beyond the confines of the metropolis and has no single centre. The French geographer Jean Gottmann coined the term in his book *Megalopolis: The Urbanized Northeastern Seaboard of the United States* (1961), an area that included metropolitan New York.[13] He pointed to an enormous scale jump that had occurred in an urban agglomeration stretching from Boston to Washington that contained 32 million people. Gottmann analysed a set of cities in transition as car-based suburban tracts spread out from old urban centres, but the Dwight D Eisenhower Defense Highway System, with its limited-access, multilane carriageways and grade separated interchanges (initiated 1956), had not been completed. Gottmann's megalopolis included large tracts of forested land across several watershed basins, as well as agricultural land that fed the cities, and water, rail and electrical supply infrastructures. Gottmann still dreamt that planners and engineers could control the megalopolis, but the administration of the American East Coast corridor stretched over thousands of governmental organisations, some organised from the top down (in the metropolis) but most organised from the bottom up following local variations of federal regulations, creating local village codes.

The mathematician Alan Turing had predicted in 1952 that twin dominant satellite cities would emerge on either side the metropolis, creating a three-centre, linear dynamic across the ring system.[14] A similar logic of linear armature growth out from the centre formed the basis of the influential Greek planner Constantinos Doxiadis's 'ecumenopolis'.[15] This global city encompassed all forms of human settlement including informal developments like Latin American *favelas* (there were also shantytowns in Europe at this time, in Athens and Rome). In modelling this new city, Doxiadis pioneered the use of computers and mathematical models that forecast the growth of the world's urban population. His estimates of global population growth laid the basis for the first UN-HABITAT meeting in Vancouver (1976). This meeting marked the shift from the government-controlled metropolis to a megalopolitan model including bottom-up non-governmental organisations (NGOs) in informal settlements (see chapter 9).

In the 1970s, Tokyo emerged as a model megalopolis just as New York had formed the ideal metropolis. After the firebombing of Tokyo in the Second World War and official plans for a very low-density, green, semi-rural city, architects and urban designers dreamt of a much denser city. In 1960 the winner of the 1947 Hiroshima Peace Memorial Park Competition, Kenzo Tange, imagined huge new residential structures built in giant A-frames above a highway grid stretching out above Tokyo Bay. Meanwhile the city expanded along railway lines, with small-scale construction enforced by earthquake regulations across an enormous area, showing minute local variations around each railway station. Highways were later built 18 metres (60 feet) above central Tokyo for the 1964 Olympics, setting in place an Asian pattern copied in Seoul, Taipei and Bangkok. Huge oil installations in Saudi Arabia and across the Middle East powered this Asian growth, just as Israeli planners created a modern, miniature megalopolis city-state in the 1960s.

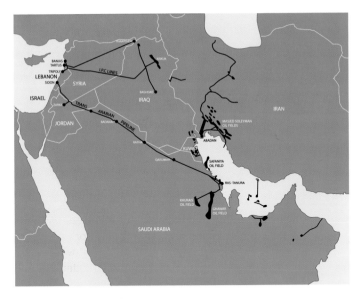

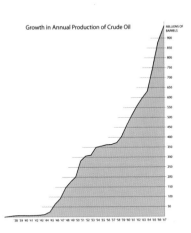

Growth in Annual Production of Crude Oil

Growth in World Oil Production

Middle East oil installations and production, 1945–67
Middle East oil production took off after the Second World War, powering the reconstruction of Europe and Asia. Saudi Aramco built the ill-fated Trans-Arabian Pipe Line (Tapline) to supply Europe, stretching from Ras Tanura refinery (the world's largest) to the Lebanon. Oil replaced coal as the energy source of the modern megalopolis, allowing further extensions based on automobiles and telecommunications networks (phones, radios, televisions). (Diagrams © Uri Wegman and David Grahame Shane, redrawn from Aramco, *The Tap Line*, 1968; photo © Bettmann/Corbis)

Kenzo Tange, Tokyo Bay Scheme, Japan, 1960
Tokyo rapidly became Asia's first megalopolis during the Korean War, recognised by Jean Gottmann in 1961. Tokyo was short of land because of the surrounding mountains and valuable rice-producing terrain. To solve this problem Tange, the designer of the Hiroshima Memorial Park in 1947, proposed enormous new A-frame megastructures built over elevated highways above Tokyo Bay. (Photo © Kawasumi architectural photograph office)

Fumihiko Maki, a member of the Japanese Metabolist Group, distinguished between small-scale 'group forms' that covered the landscape and megastructural forms that rose above, proposing an enormous intervention for Shinjuku, Tokyo, at the junction of several suburban railway lines (1960).[16] The 1968 Tokyo City Plan included a ring of five such mega-centres along the inner-city ring railway line, including Shinjuku, with a green belt further out and new towns stretching down the high-speed bullet train rail armature towards Osaka.[17] Later Tange planned an enormous City Hall complex at Shinjuku (1975). Gottmann went on to study global megalopolitan 'constellations' in Asia (recognising the Tokyo–Osaka corridor) and in Europe (identifying the Rhine–Ruhr industrial corridor).[18]

In the 1960s it seemed logical to urban designers that the new urban nodes should scale up to match the megalopolis, producing giant megastructures. The Archigram group of young architects in London dreamt of futuristic megacities in the 1960s, while the French state built megastructural housing projects for aviation workers at the new town of Toulouse-Le Mirail (Georges Candilis and Shadrach Woods, 1968). HOK planned the Galleria mall as a megastructure, the first megamall, with offices and hotels in oil-rich Houston, Texas (1967). Singapore pioneered such megadevelopments in Asia (see chapter 5). Paul Rudolph designed a huge but unbuilt A-frame structure of housing and offices to cover a Robert Moses highway heading towards the World Trade Center (WTC) in New York (Minoru Yamasaki, 1968) through the historic district of SoHo. Reyner Banham featured this design on the cover of his book, *Megastructure: Urban Futures of the Recent Past* (1976).[19]

The linear form of the megalopolis based on highways for automobiles and trucks powered by oil, easily accommodated airports and container ports for global trade. Cheap and plentiful oil supplies encouraged the development of global corporations and global commerce. Old villages and local bottom-up codes were easily included in the large-scale network of highways as small urban patches, as at the Mark III British New Town of Milton Keynes (1967). Reyner Banham described the nonplan, top-down and bottom-up megalopolitan ideal in his *Los Angeles: The Architecture of Four Ecologies* (1971).[20] The Robert Venturi, Denise Scott Brown and Steven Izenour team described the stretched armature design of the automobile strip, with its giant signs, in *Learning from Las Vegas* (1972).[21] Banham stressed the top-down logic of the Los Angeles highway engineers in scaling their armatures from highway, to feeder road, to boulevard, allowing a bottom-up, participatory freedom in local patches. This enabled an 'art of the enclave' that also created pedestrian environments in shopping malls, theme parks and nature trails. The flexibility of this system equally allowed planners to protect natural landscape features in parks and green belts, while also planning central business districts, residential areas and industrial parks as at Shenzhen, the first Chinese Special Economic Zone (SEZ, 1990) outside Hong Kong. The problem with this system was that the megalopolis defied control: the scale of the development, its speed and dispersion of controls, meant that no one thought of the overall built environment, its ecological setting or human costs.

The fragmented metropolis

The third model, the fragmented metropolis, is a combination of the top-down control of the metropolis applied to a small urban patch and set in the large networks of the megalopolis. It takes advantage of the small-scale, local flexibility of the sprawling megalopolis and provides local areas of architectural and urban design control in urban villages. Jonathan Barnett described this urban design condition in his *The Fractured Metropolis* (1996).[22] Barnett's metropolis grows in fits and starts through history and ends up being a series of fragments. Barnett wrote from experience. This urban design model emerged when Metropolitan governments were losing their economic tax base as people moved into the megalopolitan sprawl. New York, for instance, almost went bankrupt in 1975 (it was saved by the local teachers' union pension fund).[23] After the Second World War, New Yorkers moved to the suburbs, like Levittown, where cheap, new, mass-produced housing was available, with GI loans for returning soldiers, resulting in a loss of population and income from the metropolis.

Barnett was part of the urban design team that pioneered the fragmented metropolis model as the solution to New York's problems. The team reinvented the New York City zoning 'Special District', originally created in 1916 to recognise the existence of earlier Wall Street skyscrapers. The Urban Design section of New York City Planning Department extended this approach in the early 1970s, writing Special District codes to protect Chinatown and Little Italy, as well as the Broadway theatre district and midtown's Fifth Avenue street corridor. Alexander Cooper (another member of the team) and Stanton Eckstut's winning design for Battery Park City (1978) extended the downtown street grid across the new

**Fragmented Metropolis
Cooper Eckstut & Associates,
Battery Park City, New York, USA, 1978**
As the finances of the shrinking metropolis became more
challenging, urban designers found that they could create
Special Districts where they could control the image
of the city inside a small urban fragment, re-creating
the traditional street-and-block system for a specific
community. This photograph shows the residential and
commercial components of Cooper Eckstut's design
for the new town-in-town at Battery Park City, New York
(1978) that pioneered this approach. (Plan © Cooper,
Robertson & Partners; photo © David Grahame Shane)

development and introduced urban design guidelines, reinforcing the traditional 1916 street
wall and setback formula. Cesar Pelli designed the World Financial Center (WFC, 1985–8),
a shopping mall and office tower complex at the centre of the new residential enclave.
The urban design guidelines of Battery Park City took the best elements from the New
York zoning code of 1916 and modernised them to create a powerful new streetscape that
was attractive, but clearly different from the old city; so returning suburbanites could feel
comfortable in the new hybrid.

The fragmented metropolis urban design model also had the advantage of flexibility,
allowing the incorporation of feedback from local urban actors in urban village communities
like Chinatown, or associations formed to resist building megalopolitan infrastructure in
London, Paris, New York or Tokyo. In New York Jane Jacobs, author of *The Death and Life of
Great American Cities* (1961), participated in the fight against Robert Moses.[24] Jacobs argued
that Moses' giant highways were for suburban drivers and that they were destructive of the
old city. She championed the small-scale bottom-up 'choreography' of the street armature

in Greenwich Village against highways. In Paris, Brussels, London, San Francisco and Tokyo large infrastructural projects, such as highways or airports, were delayed or blocked by local protest movements. In Copenhagen in 1964, the city government began the pedestrianisation of the historic core, gradually extending it across the whole centre. In New York or London, special zoning districts like the historic district declared in Covent Garden in the 1970s could also serve preservation purposes and block development. Disruption in oil supplies, due to Middle East wars or OPEC embargoes, also impacted the megalopolis, just as it triumphed over the metropolis. In the 1980s of Margaret Thatcher and President Reagan, the triumph of oil, the closings of coalmines and railway lines, strikes and high inflation set in motion the shrinking of cities in huge rust-belt industrial areas in Europe and the USA. The rise of the Asian Tigers (Hong Kong, Singapore, South Korea and Taiwan), financed in part by recycled oil profits from Africa, Latin America and the Middle East, began to alter the global distribution of industry and population.[25] Asian cites outpaced Latin American cities' expansion in the 1980s.[26]

London emerged as the exemplary fragmented metropolis in the 1980s, as the British Prime Minister Margaret Thatcher took apart the democratically elected Greater London Council (GLC), giving more power to locally elected municipalities and removing all planning controls in the decaying imperial dockyards of London's East End (replaced by container ports on deep water channels elsewhere). In the 17th and 18th centuries, London had had a long fractal tradition of developing large, single-landowner enclaves, called the 'Great Estates' by John Summerson in *Georgian London* (1945).[27] This system was extended in the 19th century to the industrial East End where large dock companies acted like the landlords

Downtown Copenhagen, Denmark (photo 1990s)
Beginning in the 1960s, Copenhagen City Council created a large pedestrian and car-free zone over 20 years, also providing new street surfaces and signs, plus modern street furniture, lighting and policing methods. Public transportation and investment strategies were linked to this pedestrianisation, creating student housing and apartments for seniors and families in surrounding blocks. (Photo © David Grahame Shane)

of the 'Great Estates' of the West End, controlling huge areas of the city within restricted boundaries (in the East End often surrounded by 12-metre- (40-foot-) high walls). Here 100 years later the American Special District system was imported in a tightly controlled urban experiment, a developer's dream. Mrs Thatcher personally invited the developers of the New York WFC to initiate Canary Wharf (1988–91), a huge urban fragment with a street armature leading to a high office tower (like the Rockefeller Center). Despite the later bankruptcy of the developers at Canary Wharf, such centres succeeded in capturing the administrative offices for the new global corporations that replaced the imperial powers. These financial corporations often moved to recycled imperial docks, waterfronts and railway stations in the metropolis, as they became the dominant global urban actors.

Other European states also followed this fragmented metropolis model of giant urban patches, examples including Rem Koolhaas and OMA's Euralille project (1991–4), or Renzo Piano's Potsdamer Platz in Berlin (mid-1990s). 'World financial centres' proliferated as a global brand of office tower and mall complexes in Tokyo, Hong Kong, Singapore, Mumbai, Shanghai and Beijing. By the 2000s these giant urban fragments transformed into transit-oriented developments (TODs) such as the Hong Kong International Financial Centre 2 (IFC2) mall, tower and hotel complex above the new station linked to the airport (2003). In Tokyo the Shinjuku commercial node had always been above railway lines. Other examples include the huge railway station reconstructions for the Eurostar at Berlin's Hauptbahnhof (2006) or London's St Pancras (2008), or the proposed Transbay station complex, San Francisco (2008). These megaprojects represent a return to the metropolitan ideal inside a giant fragment, in anticipation of probable higher energy prices in future. The British Olympic bid for 2012 continued this tradition, scattering Olympic sites as urban fragments across the city, especially around Stratford East megamall and towers complex in London's East End, above a new Eurostar high-speed rail station (see chapter 8).

Urban design theorists like Colin Rowe and Fred Koetter had anticipated the breakdown of the metropolis and megalopolis in their *Collage City* (1978), which examined the combinatorial logic of a city of urban fragments – some historic, some modern, some postmodern – themed to accommodate urban actors' dreams, like Disneyland (1954).[28] The American New Urbanism movement developed this thematic fragment approach in large suburban subdivisions in the 1980s and 1990s, as part of the historic housing boom that included many peripheral, gated communities. While Rowe and Koetter stressed the political dimension of the system in terms of freedom and choice, they were vague about the methods of coordinating such fragments. In *Fractal Cities* (1996), Michael Batty and Paul Longley highlighted how urban actors used the geometric quality of urban design fragments to make iterative patterns in cities that were never the same twice, especially within well-defined enclaves.[29] But they also showed how armatures had their own fractal geometries of bifurcations, tree structures and hierarchies, connecting together enclaves in monocentric, binary and multicentric cities. At a smaller scale their colleague at London University, Bill Hillier, showed in *Space is the Machine* (1996) how pedestrian flows also created networks between urban fragments in the city.[30]

The megacity/metacity territory

Like the fragmented metropolis, the final model, the *megacity*, recombines elements from the metropolis and megalopolis. In Rotterdam in 1997, in the first Megacities Lecture (an annual event delivered to the Megacities Foundation and Congress), Peter Hall, the British urban planner, credited city planner Janice Perlman with the invention of the term 'megacity' in her PhD studies of Rio *favelas* in the early 1970s (published 1976).[31] Perlman left academia to found the Mega-Cities Project to fight for the rights of officially unrecognised informal settlements that made up some 60 per cent of Latin American cities.[32] Perlman stressed something that was invisible to officials, outside their plans and in between their spaces. Like John Turner at UN-HABITAT I in 1976, Perlman highlighted the sea surrounding the urban designers' islands of order, the spaces between the urban fragments that constituted the megacity and its territory.[33] In the 1990s the UN accepted the term for a city of 8 million, then 10 million and, by 2005, 20 million, accentuating the scale change at the UN-HABITAT III conference in Vancouver (2006). There are perhaps 30 megacities in the world, mainly in Asia, housing 8 per cent of the global urban population.[34]

Despite its name, the megacity model is not just about a scale jump; it is also about reversing codes in the city. Previously invisible urban actors and spaces become visible. The pioneering Scottish ecologist Patrick Geddes in *Cities in Evolution* (1915) took the topography of the city into account, stressing the hills, heaths and especially the 'valley section' as part of a river basin and watersheds linking land and sea.[35] The space inside the valley, its gradient and the flow of the watershed helped shape the city, where its food and water supplies came from, where the settlement was established, its sewage disposal system and communications with the outside world. During the Second World War many cities had allotment garden systems where citizens grew their own vegetables as part of the war effort (including London, Amsterdam and Copenhagen). Emergency housing, slums and refugee camps were often located in these in-between, invisible valley spaces, which often also contained the new oil refineries, tank farms and distribution centres. Later Buckminster Fuller and John McHale drew attention to the unequal distribution of world resources and population on 'Spaceship Earth', leading to the impossibility of sustainable development, in their *World Resources Inventory* and *World Game* (1969).[36] By the 1990s Vancouver, Canada, the host city of the first UN-HABITAT in 1976, had become a leading Eco-city and home to William Rees, co-author of *Our Ecological Footprint: Reducing Human Impact on the Earth* (1996).[37]

British post-war urban designers, like Frederick Gibberd in his *Town Design* (1953), learning from Geddes, proposed a 'space body' concept to help design the space between buildings.[38] Gibberd applied the concept in a valley of gardens leading to the town hall at Harlow New Town (1947). Later Ian McHarg in *Design With Nature* (1969) advanced Geddes' concept of the watershed and landscape containing the city, using computers to make layered maps of the city territory, identifying valuable ecological sites and farmland, in order to pinpoint sites for development.[39] The in-between space became important as the American Landscape Urbanism movement of the 1990s extended this mapping approach to deal with shrinking cities, like Detroit, and brownfield industrial and waste sites. James

Corner and Field Operations' winning Freshkills Park design for Staten Island (2001) built on McHarg's systematic layering to propose a long-duration time frame for the remediation of the brownfield site for recreational uses. Throughout the world, urban designers and landscape urbanists began to convert waterside industrial areas, covered streams, old metropolitan airfields and steel mills into park enclaves and armatures, as in Seoul's Cheonggyecheon Park (2005).

Most contemporary megacities are in middle-income or poor countries with large populations that use far less energy per capita than industrialised nations. Urban designers turned a blind eye to the global informal city built by peasants moving into the cities of Latin America, Asia and Africa for the last half of the 20th century as a result of European de-colonialisation. These megacity shanty settlements were sometimes on public land zoned as green belts or parks (as in Caracas, Venezuela), or built with the collusion of landlords (who collected rents secretly) on land zoned as agricultural (as in Bogotá, Colombia), or on riverbeds, marshlands or dangerous flood plains (as at Dharavi, Mumbai). In the 1970s and 1980s the World Bank experimented with 'Sites and Services' projects to incorporate the self-build activities of urban settlers into the formal economy, with limited success (such areas tended to become gentrified). In the 1990s the controversial Peruvian economist Hernando de Soto advocated giving landownership to squatters to achieve the same participatory goal, a policy that is currently being tested in Rio and Sao Paolo, as well as in Bangkok.[40]

Bogotá, Colombia, has provided under two progressive mayors an exemplary, low-energy, megacity model, expanding on the low-cost ecological blueprint for slum upgrading and linkages by bus lines offered by the relatively wealthy city of Curitiba, Brazil in the 1980s. In Bogotá urban designers took advantage of earlier plans by Le Corbusier and JL Sert to create in the 1990s a new system of linear armatures of garden parkways that linked the pedestrianisation of downtown, express bus lanes and local community upgrading with a new water supply, hospitals and schools (with internet access) and allotment gardens in the parks.

Social organisations on the Internet, like Shack/Slum Dwellers International (SDI) or the World Social Forum (WSF), established virtual networks for the interchange of ideas and best practices. Founded to provide a bottom-up counter to the top-down Davos World Economic Forums, the anti-globalisation WSF provides an Internet platform for NGOs from small-scale, local and emergent communities to be able to learn from each other, while also attracting academics like Noam Chomsky, the linguist and political activist, and Joseph Stiglitz, the former Chief Economist of the World Bank to annual international meetings held initially in Porto Alegre, Brazil (2001–5).[41] Across Asia, Africa and Latin America, urban designers are learning to talk to the inhabitants of the self-organising system of *favelas* and are using remote satellite sensing systems, like Google Earth and hand-held GPS devices, to map these areas. At the UN-HABITAT III in Vancouver (2006), David Satterthwaite of the International Institute for Environment and Development (IIED), London, noted that the megacities hold only 8 per cent of the global urban population. He sees this as a reason for hope because NGOs and local municipalities have a better chance of improving urban conditions in the smaller city constellations of 1 million plus, where feedback from, and participation of, inhabitants can be

Transmilenio Bus, Bogotà, Colombia 2000 (photo 2000)
Following the example of Curitiba in Brazil, two mayors of Bogotà fought during the 1990s to bring
water to isolated, peripheral, self-built housing districts via greenways, containing parks and gardens,
along with new schools and libraries. This photograph shows the Transmilenio (which translates as
'Transmillennium') bus route linking from the peripheral *favelas* down the greenway to the old city centre
that is pedestrianised. (Photo © Aaron Naparstek)

more effective. Food is also close by as agricultural areas still surround these smaller cities.
In Africa and Asia more than half the population still lives in agricultural settlements that now
have links to the city facilitated by cellphone service.[42]

Based on a similar analysis of the Veneto, Italy as an urban constellation, Paola Viganò
hypothesised a 'reverse city' in her *La Città Elementare* (1999), where the spacing between
urban elements in the landscape became the subject of urban design, deriving from earlier
regional studies with Bernardo Secchi that emphasised the ecological aspects of landscape
designs.[43] As in the Asian megacities, Secchi and Viganò highlighted the contours of the
productive agricultural landscape embedded within the fabric of the sprawling city as a
positive, valuable force, a 'reverse city' code that should be a part of the overall design.
Other European theorists, like Rem Koolhaas (*S,M,L,XL* (1995)) and Xaveer De Geyter (*After-
Sprawl* (2002)) pursued megacity growth across rural landscapes, while their friends MVRDV
documented the global emergence of the 20 million-plus megacity in *Metacity/Datatown*

(1999).[44] Thomas Sieverts, the coordinator of the German IBA Landschaftspark in the Rhine–Ruhr corridor (1999) theorised a new form of half city, half countryside, the 'in-between-city', in his *Cities without Cities* (1997; English translation 2003).[45]

These theorists inside the wealthy European Union dealt with hybrid landscape conditions similar to the lower-income situations of Indonesian *desa-kota* (town–village hybrid) or Bangkok urban–rural fringes, where agriculture and urbanism mixed in strange combinations. Some American theorists faced this reality, pursuing a renewed rural–urban fringe with organic, urban agriculture that will once again feed cities locally (as in the work of Brian McGrath and Victoria Marshall of the Parson's New School, New York for the Baltimore *Ecosystem Study* (BES) 2006).[46] More typical of the metropolitan response is Dickson Dupommier's proposed strange new 'sky farm' green skyscrapers that grow food in the centre of the city; while in Italy, home of the Slow Food Movement, designers like Carlo Petrini imagined the 'Cittaslow', 'Slow City', producing its own food locally in the voids in and around cities.

Conclusion: urban archipelagos

It is tempting to see the four urban design models as part of a sequence of urban development covering a 60-year span, each model dominating a period of 15 years approximately. After the Second World War, a period of reconstruction followed using the metropolitan model based on the crumbling European imperial system. During this period of the Cold War a new world system emerged based on two superpowers, the USSR and USA. America developed a new megalopolitan model based on oil instead of coal, and exported this model to Europe and Asia after 1960 in what the historian Eric Hobsbawm called the 'Golden Age', lasting until the early 1970s.[47] This system became unstable as a result of a series of oil shocks, setting in motion the fragmented metropolis model with its more stable smaller urban patches financed by global corporations. As the century ended, this global system reached its limits and by 2008 suffered a global financial meltdown, as the global urban population shifted to low- and middle-income Asian-style megacities.

While this temporal sequence has its appeal, the lesson of *Urban Design Since 1945: A Global Perspective* is that all these models – the metropolis, megalopolis, fragmented metropolis and megacity – are separate but related patterns of urban development. They are all present at once as patches in most cities, forming a network of interrelated fragments that have symbiotic relations with each other. We can view such cities of fragments as urban archipelagos, clusters of urban islands, with privileged links between the patches or islands and the sea separating or connecting them. Many great cities like Amsterdam, Bangkok, Hong Kong, Stockholm, Tokyo and Venice are literal archipelagos, built on small islands, but the model now extends far beyond these coastal examples. In the archipelago city, all models are simultaneously co-present in a constellation of patches where people have the ability to live together with all their differences, offering hope for the planet and future.

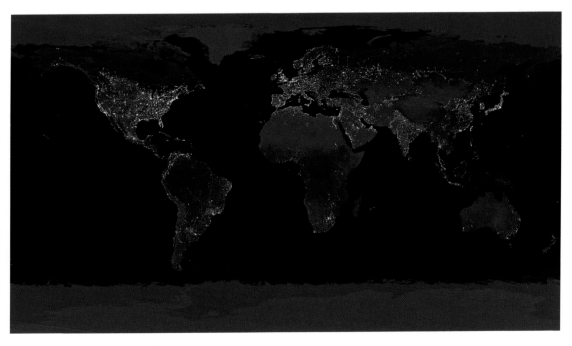

NOAA night image urban constellation (photo 2009)
Remote sensing equipment on board earth-orbiting satellites provides one of the few ways of envisioning the vast scale of the global urban revolution of the last 60 years. An equivalent image in 1945 would have shown a few cities in Europe with Moscow and New York, Chicago and a few major American cities lit at night. (Photo © NASA)

Notes
NB: See 'Author's Caution: Endnote Sources and Wikipedia', towards the end of this book.

1   On US and global oil use, see: Paul Roberts, *The End of Oil: On the Edge of A Perilous New World*, Houghton Mifflin (New York), 2004, p 15.

2   For malls, see: Victor Gruen, *The Heart of Our Cities: The Urban Crisis – Diagnosis and Cure*, Simon & Schuster (New York), 1964.

3   On Tehran master plan, see: Wouter Vanstiphout, 'The Saddest City in the World: Tehran and the legacy of an American dream of modern town planning', 2 March 2006, http://www. thenewtown.nl/article.php?id_article=71 (accessed 1 April 2010); and: Jeffrey M Hardwick, *Mall Maker: Victor Gruen, Architect of an American Dream*, University of Pennsylvania (Philadelphia), 2004, pp 220–23.

4   For global population shift, see UN diagrams in: 'UN-HABITAT Secretary General's Visit to Kibera, Nairobi, 30–31 January, 2007', UN-HABITAT website, http://www.unhabitat.org/ downloads/docs/Press_SG_visit_Kibera07/SG%205.pdf (accessed 27 September 2009).

5   On cellular automata cities, see: Juval Portugali, *Self-Organisation and the City*, Springer-Verlag (Berlin), 2000, pp 65–8 (available online at Google Books).

6   Brian McGrath, *Digital Modelling for Urban Design*, John Wiley & Sons (London), 2008, p 19.

7   For enclave, armature and heterotopia, see: DG Shane, *Recombinant Urbanism: Conceptual*

Modeling in Architecture, Urban Design and City Theory, Wiley-Academy (Chichester), 2005.

8   See Michel Foucault, 'Of Other Spaces', in Catherine David and Jean-Francois Chevrier (eds), *Documenta X: The Book*, Hatje Cantz (Kassel), 1997, p 262, also available at http://foucault.info/documents/heteroTopia/foucault.heteroTopia.en.html (accessed 29 September 2009).

9   For early migrations, see: Alan Weisman, *The World Without Us*, Thomas Dunne Books St Martin's Press (New York), 2007, pp 48–9.

10   On Beijing history, see: Stephen G Haw, *Beijing – A Concise History*, Routledge (London; New York), 2006; also: http://en.wikipedia.org/wiki/Beijing (accessed 28 March 2010).

11   Tony Judt, *Postwar: A History of Europe Since 1945*, Penguin (New York), 2006, p 17.

12   Le Corbusier had argued that New York skyscrapers were too close together in *When the Cathedrals Were White* (1947), but the Rockefeller Center provided the model 'community centre' for the modern architect and critic Sigfried Giedion in *Space, Time and Architecture* (1941).

13   Jean Gottmann, *Megalopolis: The Urbanized Northeastern Seaboard of the United States*, Twentieth Century Fund (New York), 1961.

14   On Turing, see: Paul Krugman, *The Self-Organizing Economy*, Blackwell (Oxford), 1996, pp 22–9, 48–9.

15   Constantinos Doxiadis, *Architecture In Transition*, Oxford University Press (New York), 1963.

16   Fumihiko Maki, 'Some Thoughts on Collective Form', in Gyorgy Kepes (ed), *Structure in Art and Science*, George Braziller (New York), 1965, pp 116–27.

17   For the 1968 Tokyo City Plan, see: *Tokyo Metropolitan Government, A Hundred Years of Tokyo City Planning*, TMG Municipal Library No 28 (Tokyo), 1994, pp 56 and 74.

18   For Gottmann on Tokyo, see: Jean Gottmann and Robert A. Harper (eds), *Since the Metropolis: The Urban Writings of Jean Gottmann*, Institute of Governmental Studies, University of California (Berkeley, CA), 1990, p 19.

19   Reyner Banham, *Megastructure: Urban Futures of the Recent Past*, Thames & Hudson (London), 1976.

20   Reyner Banham, *Los Angeles: The Architecture of Four Ecologies*, Harper & Row (New York), 1971.

21   Robert Venturi, Denise Scott Brown and Steven Izenour, *Learning from Las Vegas: The Forgotten Symbolism of Architectural Form*, MIT Press (Cambridge, MA), 1972.

22   Jonathan Barnett, *The Fractured Metropolis: Improving The New City, Restoring The Old City, Reshaping The Region*, HarperCollins (New York), 1996.

23   On New York City near bankruptcy in 1975, see: Ralph Blumenthal, 'Recalling New York at the Brink of Bankruptcy', *The New York Times*, 5 December 2002, http://www.nytimes.com/2002/12/05/nyregion/recalling-new-york-at-the-brink-of-bankruptcy.html?pagewanted=1 (accessed 15 February 2010).

24   Jane Jacobs, *The Death and Life of Great American Cities*, Vintage Books (New York), 1961.

25   For oil profits, see: Peter, R Odell, *Oil and World Power: A Geographical Interpretation*, Penguin (Harmondsworth), 1970, pp 65–94.

26   For UN population figures, see: 'World Urbanization Prospects: The 2003 Revision', http://www.un.org/esa/population/publications/wup2003/WUP2003Report.pdf (accessed 27 September 2009).

27   John Summerson, *Georgian London*, Pleiades Books (London), 1945.

28   Colin Rowe and Fred Koetter, *Collage City*, MIT Press (Cambridge, MA), 1978.

29   For fractal patterns, see: Michael Batty and Paul Longley, *Fractal Cities: A Geometry of Form and Function*, Academic Press (San Diego, CA), 1996, pp 10–57.

30   For connections between fragments, see: Bill Hillier, *Space is the Machine*, Cambridge University Press (Cambridge), 1996, pp 149–82.

31   For Peter Hall, see 1997 lecture in archive at: Megacities Foundation website, http://www.megacities.nl/ (accessed 27 September 2009). For Perlman's PhD thesis, see: Janice Perlman, *The Myth of Marginality: Urban Politics and Poverty in Rio de Janeiro*, University of California Press (Berkeley, CA), 1976.

32   For Janice Perlman and megacities, see: Mega-Cities Project website, http://www.
        megacitiesproject.org/ (accessed 27 September 2009).

33   See: John FC Turner, *Housing by People: Towards Autonomy in Building Environments*, Pantheon
        Books (New York), 1977.

34   For global urban population, see: United Nations Human Settlements Programme (UN-
        HABITAT), *The State of the World's Cities 2006/7*, Earthscan (London), 2006, pp 4–12.

35   Sir Patrick Geddes, *Cities in Evolution: An Introduction to the Town Planning Movement and to
        the Study of Cities*, Williams & Norgate (London), 1915.

36   Buckminster Fuller and John McHale's *World Resources Inventory* and *World Game*, Southern
        Illinois University (Carbondale, IL) 1969.

37   William Rees and Mathis Wackernagel, *Our Ecological Footprint: Reducing Human Impact on the
        Earth*, New Society Publishers (Gabriola Island, BC), 1996.

38   Frederick Gibberd, *Town Design*, Architectural Press (London), 1953, revised 1959.

39   Ian McHarg, *Design with Nature*, published for the American Museum of Natural History
        (Garden City, NY), 1969.

40   See: Hernando de Soto, *The Other Path: The Invisible Revolution in the Third World*,
        HarperCollins (New York), 1989.

41   For SDI and WSF, see: David Satterthwaite, 'The Scale of Urban Change Worldwide 1950–2000
        and its Underpinnings', International Institute for Environment and Development (IIED) Human
        Settlements Programme Discussion Paper, Urban Change 1 (London), 2005, pp 19–23.

42   For cellphones and the city, see: Brian McGrath and DG Shane (eds), *Sensing the 21st-Century
        City – Close-up and Remote*, *Architectural Design*, vol 75, issue 6, November/December 2005,
        pp 4–7, 26–49.

43   Paola Viganò, *La Città Elementare*, Skira (Milan; Geneva), 1999.

44   Rem Koolhaas and Bruce Mao, *S,M,L,XL: Office for Metropolitan Architecture*, Monacelli Press
        (New York), 1995; Xaveer De Geyter (ed), *After-Sprawl: Research for the Contemporary City*,
        NAi (Rotterdam) and Kunstcentrum deSingel (Antwerp), 2002; MVRDV, *Metacity/Datatown*, 010
        Publishers (Rotterdam), 1999.

45   Thomas Sieverts, *Cities Without Cities: An Interpretation of the Zwischenstadt*, Spon Press
        (London; New York), 2003 (original work published 1997).

46   See: Brian McGrath and Victoria Marshall, 'Operationalising Patch Dynamics', in Michael Spens
        (ed), *Landscape Architecture*, *Architectural Design*, vol 77, issue 2, March/April 2007, pp 52–9.

47   Eric Hobsbawm, *The Age of Extremes: The History of the World, 1914–1991*, Vintage Books
        (New York), 1996.

CHAPTER 2

Illustrated Urban Elements

Urban designers have always worked with urban elements, and the last 60 years is no exception. In the modern metropolis the designers of the Rockefeller Center, for instance, combined an armature and enclave within a double block nested in the New York City grid. The standard facade design hid multiple uses and actors inside the superblock that was crossed by a pedestrian street leading to the skating rink. The list of hidden elements is long: the underground parking enclave; the sunken skating rink enclave and shopping arcade; the entry to the subway and truck access. Within the GE (formerly RCA) Building tower there is the large public lobby at ground level and a public roof deck, not to mention the Rainbow Room restaurant and bar. The surrounding approach buildings have roof gardens. The super-block section also included heterotopias of illusion, a movie theatre, radio studios, later TV studios and the great Radio City Musical Hall showcase theatre for spectacles.[1]

Asian meganodes at the end of the 20th century continued this heterotopic tradition of combining multiple urban elements within one more or less porous enclave. In this case the urban actors wrapped all their complex sectional functions around a compressed, vertical mall armature, with food courts, multicinema complexes, and interior atria as attached enclaves, stretching up between towers and roof gardens above. Tokyo, Hong Kong and Bangkok all provide examples of such complex heterotopic enclaves with elaborate sectional armatures, escalators ascending through guarded public spaces. Some grew by accretion, as in Bangkok, but others were planned from the start, as in the case of Hong Kong new towns.

This chapter examines the evolution of three urban elements over the last 60 years: the enclave, armature and heterotopia. Urban actors combine urban elements inside urban ecologies, sets of relationships that can change over time, resulting in shifts in the design of urban elements. The actors who created the Rockefeller Center, for instance, were different from the civic authorities in Hong Kong that created the enormous transport exchanges with malls attached, like Kowloon Central Railway Station megablock with its roof garden, cinemas, food courts and attached towers (see chapter 11).

Urban actors create networks of urban institutions in a city that help organise and maintain the city, creating an urban ecology. Here an ecology means a more or less stable set of relationships that can be maintained over time and give order to the city, people's relationships and the flow of goods and ideas. Actors may begin desiring one set of relationships, favouring enclaves for instance, but over time decide they would prefer another set of relations, creating a new ecology or organisation of relationships around armatures. Actors use heterotopias as places of experiment in making these changes. Heterotopias play an important role in aiding the shift between urban ecologies or organisational systems.

Preliminary definitions of urban elements

In the previous chapter the enclave, armature and heterotopia were briefly described as organisational devices employed by actors in urban design ecologies. The enclave is a space defined by a perimeter with one or more entries and a clearly defined centre, with Beijing's Forbidden City and the Rockefeller Center given as examples. As an organisational device, the enclave serves as a collecting point for people, objects or processes that fall within the purview of a single urban actor who controls the space, its contents and its perimeter. Hierarchical systems of control and top-down command structures radiate out from this dominant actor, who nests many enclaves within enclaves to aid sorting and memory. This nesting of enclaves within enclaves can scale up to encompass a whole city, as in imperial Beijing, focusing symbolically on the Forbidden City. Urban actors altered the role of the enclave when they paid more attention to flow and process in the city, so the enclave became a stationary point in the system, where people, goods or services could be temporarily located and stored in places like hotels, warehouses or storage yards, docks and containers. Later still, enclaves became containers for urban fantasies and imagery, a means of way-finding, attraction and identification for different areas of the city, as in Kevin Lynch's *The Image of the City* (1961).[2]

The armature, by contrast, is a linear space containing and sorting flows. It is a linear sequencing device controlling space and time inside a linear, logical process. An armature may also be hierarchical, making dendric, tree-like structures, as in rivers flowing to an estuary or roads leading to a highway entrance. The standard urban pedestrian armature for many centuries has been a five-minute walk, about 200 metres (600 feet), a unit found in Greek and Roman city plans, medieval towns, the Manhattan grid and modern shopping mall design. Standard armatures are for people on foot. Stretched armatures imply a transportation system. Large-scale armatures, like rivers and highways, stretch across the city territory. In addition there is the compressed armature. This involves stacking or spiralling armatures one on top of another, so in three floors, for instance, 600 metres (1,900 feet) can occupy a small footprint of 200 metres (600 feet). Shopping mall designers took advantage of this compression, but Trajan's Market in Ancient Rome and countless bazaars across the ancient global trading networks like the Silk Route from Europe to Asia applied the same principle of compression.[3]

Urban actors and designers use heterotopias to combine enclaves and armatures, making new hybrids that they hope will have special advantages and accommodate change or difference in the city. Michel Foucault, the French philosopher who introduced the term to architects in the 1960s, was especially interested in the heteteropias used to bring modernism into traditional societies not based on modern science, organised by custom, magic or belief in different hierarchical systems. Foucault emphasised that heterotopias were often miniature models of an urban ecology, a small city within a city. Also the actors in charge often reversed significant codes inside the heterotopia. If the city was chaotic, for instance, then actors sought order, calm and control within the perimeter of the heterotopia. The other distinguishing characteristic of the heterotopia was its multiple actors, each with their own spaces and codes, all within one perimeter. This contrasted with a modern enclave that tended to be monofunctional – a business park, for instance, without other uses. Multiple actors could interact inside the heterotopia, try new combinations and experiment, without disturbing the whole urban ecology.[4]

Foucault recounted how urban actors who sought a modern scientific basis for society created 'heterotopias of deviance', where people who did not conform to modern society were marked and segregated as deviants, to be reformed and re-educated. Because of their nonpunitive nature, Foucault called the earlier system of handling people in transition or stress situations 'heterotopias of crisis'.[5] People could voluntarily come and go from these special spaces without penalty or stigma. In the heterotopias of deviance, urban actors such as asylum doctors or prison officials set rigid rules and punished all deviance, locking people away until their term was served or the authorities deemed them cured. The 18th-century social theorist Jeremy Bentham designed a circular Panopticon prison. The jailer hidden in the centre observing all cells on the periphery, symbolised the heterotopia of deviance (another variant was the star-shaped prison with the jailer in the central junction).[6]

Foucault also listed a third order of 'heterotopias of illusion' that had fast-changing rules and codes and involved fashion and aesthetics, reversing all the codes of the heterotopia of deviance that was devoted to work. These pleasure palaces and temples of consumption did not interest Foucault as much, although he listed many urban components, such as shopping arcades, department stores, museums, theatres, cinemas and brothels in this category.

Three urban elements:
enclave, armature and heterotopia
Urban actors employ these three urban elements to construct urban ecologies in the city, shaping urban space to their needs. (Diagrams © David Grahame Shane, 2009)

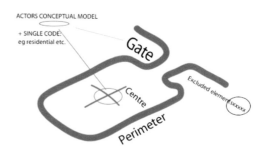

ACTORS CONCEPTUAL MODEL

+ SINGLE CODE
eg residential etc.

Gate

Centre

Excluded elements xxxxx

Perimeter

Single Centre Enclave
Actors establish a conceptual model that controls single code for an enclave self-centering system, feed-back reinforces the centre.

Urban actors have always used models of urban design ecologies to guide their work. In the previous chapter four models were reviewed: the metropolis, the megalopolis, the fragmented metropolis and the megacity/metacity. These models relate back to a long tradition. In 2001 the young planners' group of ISOCARP (International Society of City and Regional Planners) renewed this tradition based on the British architect Cedric Price's three 'breakfast models' of the city – the hard-boiled egg, the fried egg and the scrambled egg – from his Taskforce Project of 1982.[7]

The young planners called the hard-boiled egg the *archi-città*, because architects had a big role in building the city in stone to last for ages in a feudal society organised around warlords or powerful clerics. The city was an enclave with a hard shell, the city wall. Inside the wall the urban fabric of wooden or mud houses for peasants and merchants formed the egg white. The castle and cathedral of the great lord (with dungeons included) formed the urban core, the yellow yoke at the centre of the hard-boiled egg. In Cedric Price's fried-egg model new urban actors, merchants, bankers and engineers built roads, canals or railways out from the hard-boiled egg, creating linear armatures or corridors of growth, making a star-shaped formation with an irregular edge, beyond the city walls. At the centre of the fried egg a special enclave of skyscraper density formed, represented by the bubble of the fried egg's yoke. The young planners called this city the *cine-città*, because of the linear nature of its expansion and the invention of the cinema, a new form of mass media that shaped how the city was seen in movement. Finally urban actors dissolved the city's boundaries with the countryside, forming the scrambled-egg model that the young planners called the *tele-città*, because of the role of television in holding the dispersed city together. This city diagram consists of a system of fragments spread across the countryside, some with one centre, some with two centres, some with none, forming a city archipelago or fragmented metropolis.[8]

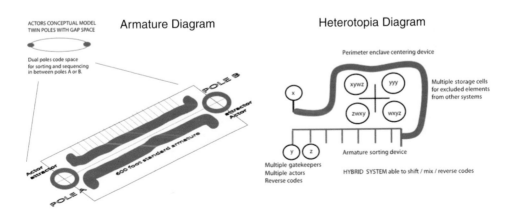

In this book these three city ecologies or sets of relationships are renamed and a fourth model or urban design ecology added. The *archi-città* becomes the *metropolis*, the historic imperial capital city, of ancient empires. By 1945 this model had become overlaid with elements of the industrial city, linking around the world to European colonial empires. In contrast New York represents the pure modern commercial and industrial metropolis, with its skyscrapers displaying the power of corporations. The *cine-città* becomes the modern *megalopolis*, the extended linear city containing many millions stretching along coastal plains or up river valleys, originally linked by rail but later by highways and automobiles. The *tele-città* with its mass communications becomes the *fragmented metropolis*, representing the breakdown of the old metropolis centre under the impact of the auto-age megalopolis, but also the re-centering of the megalopolis with multiple urban fragments of density.[9]

In addition the Swiss urban designer Franz Oswald suggested a fourth category, the *frittata*, an omelette that contains large chunks and also gaps in its fabric, that stretches like the megalopolis over very large areas.[10] In this book the *frittata* is called the *megacity* or *metacity*, to recognise its enormous scale and potential to include agricultural development, as well as mass mobility and modern communications systems. These four models or ecologies of urban relationships are all present in patches in cities today and interact with each other, forming a dynamic patchwork city, where the outcome of interactions between urban actors is unpredictable. The result is that cities change and shift over time, in nonlinear sequences, where planned outcomes do not always come to pass and unexpected outcomes often appear.

Archi-Città	Cine-Città	Tele-Città
Walled city	Centre + agglomeration	Periurbanisation
Agricultural production	Industrial production	Informational production
Muscular movement	Mechanical movement	Light-speed communication
Feudal government	Democratic government	
Architect	Physical planner	Spatial development manager ...?
Local scale	Regional / national scale	.....knowledge+info./airports
Architecture, boulevards	Land use, infrastructure	IT infra ..?
Projects	Plans	strategies / actions ...?

Urban design ecology models
Urban actors combine the three basic urban elements – enclave, armature and heterotopia – to build different city models. ISOCARP identified the city types in 2001 (*archi-*, *cine-* and *tele-città* models). (Diagrams courtesy of ISOCARP, 2009)

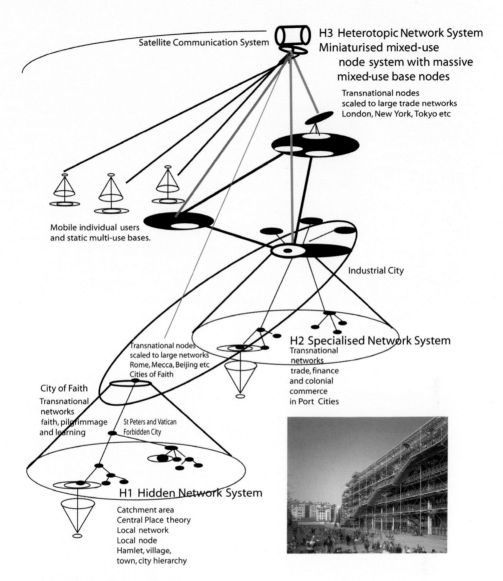

Satellite Communication System

**H3 Heterotopic Network System
Miniaturised mixed-use
node system with massive
mixed-use base nodes**

Transnational nodes
scaled to large trade networks
London, New York, Tokyo etc

Mobile individual users
and static multi-use bases.

Industrial City

Transnational nodes
scaled to large networks
Rome, Mecca, Beijing etc
Cities of Faith

H2 Specialised Network System
Transnational
networks
trade, finance
and colonial
commerce
in Port Cities

City of Faith
Transnational
networks
faith, pilgrimmage
and learning

St Peters and Vatican
Forbidden City

H1 Hidden Network System
Catchment area
Central Place theory
Local network
Local node
Hamlet, village,
town, city hierarchy

Urban networks and systems diagram

The diagram shows a city formed from three sets of urban actors and urban models overlaid on each other, creating a complex, layered, interactive system. Richard Rogers and Renzo Piano's Pompidou Centre is inset as a heterotopic art gallery installed by the eponymous French President in central Paris in 1971–7 that triggered the transformation of the surrounding area. (Diagram © David Grahame Shane, 2005)

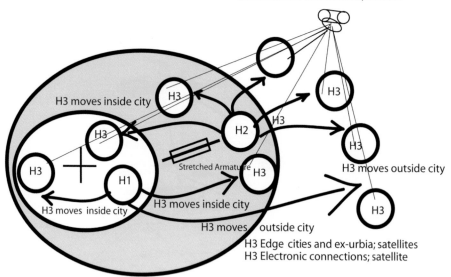

H3 Electronic connections; satellite

H3 moves inside city

H3 moves outside city

H3 moves inside city

H3 moves outside city

H3 Edge cities and ex-urbia; satellites
H3 Electronic connections; satellite

H2 Binary in Industrial City and satellite suburbs

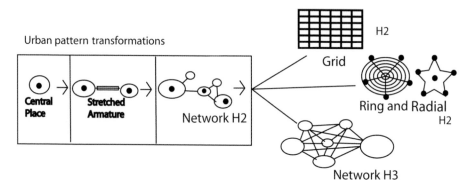

Urban pattern transformations

Central Place → Stretched Armature → Network H2

Grid

H2

Ring and Radial
H2

Network H3

Heterotopic systems diagram
Modern urban actors have traditionally migrated to the edge of the city to seek more open space for their activities, often housed in innovative, heterotopic designs. This diagram tracks this outward movement and then the feedback into the city of innovative social institutions, through new insertions in the centre and edge. It shows how innovative institutions, like a hospital or prison in the 19th century, or new towns in the 20th century, moved to the outside of the city and then became integrated into the city fabric with later growth. (Diagram © David Grahame Shane, 2005)

Cities have changed in the last 60 years. All the wealth, design skills and innovations used to be concentrated in the imperial capitals of Europe, with New York representing the commercial metropolis. Where the European metropolis offered grand vistas along great armatures to vast plazas, perfect for military displays, New York offered a well-regulated street grid with skyscrapers in city block enclaves. The Rockefeller Center, as a miniature city within a city, occupied several blocks. With a miniature street and plaza in front of a very tall skyscraper, it represented the new future combination of armature, enclave and skyscraper inside a double block. By 2010 the American metropolitan model has triumphed, as Asian cities vie for the tallest skyscraper and largest business centre, but urban designers have transformed the model. The block has expanded to the megablock, the towers now include business, residential and hotel facilities, the street is enclosed as a multilevel shopping mall, and public transportation, including bullet trains and skytrains, connects into the commercial podium, as in Bangkok or Hong Kong (see chapters 10).

In 1945 the European or American metropolitan model presumed a dense city core and compact urban development surrounded by green belts or truck-farming agricultural areas that provided food to the city. The two largest cities, London and New York, contained about 7 million people.[11] Aqueduct armatures brought water from distant hills to be stored in reservoir enclaves, hidden pipes beneath the street armature conveyed sewage to treatment plant enclaves to be sent out to sea. Railway armatures served the city centre and ports, sending out tentacles into the suburbs. Industrial activities and heating with coal generally polluted the city air, even though by tradition industrial enclaves were located downwind and downstream, to the east of the centre in the northern hemisphere. Food and resources from all over the world flowed to the metropolitan warehouses that commanded a global trade network.

The metropolis contained an array of highly specialised enclaves, an advanced version of the traditional city's sorting of activities.[12] Some enclaves were about display and consumption, like department stores, shopping arcades, grand hotels, theatres, museums and art galleries. Others were about business, areas for finance, insurance, shipping, the stock market and lawyers. Others were reserved for industrial production, occupying riverfront properties near the port and railway armatures. Hidden from view were ghetto enclaves containing poor minorities, homosexuals, red-light districts and areas controlled by organised crime. The continuity of the block system masked these many differences and many enclaves under an apparent uniformity. Active police work maintained these differences, as did street gangs associated with new immigrant groups, creating differences often sanctioned by law – such as the racial segregation of the American South or the South African apartheid regime.

The metropolitan theory of enclaves, as described by the modernist Chicago School sociologists Ernest Burgess and Robert Park in the 1920s, connected urban enclaves into an ecology, a set of spaces and relationships forming an urban 'metabolism'.[13] New immigrants progressed from poverty in the ghetto to suburban respectability in the surrounding suburbs, like fish swimming up a stream to enclaves of greater wealth, education and social status. Each step of the way involved a different urban neighbourhood, a distinct social and economic patch, with a distinct built form reflecting a person's economic status. Decaying walk-up tenements housed poor immigrants in the inner-city ghetto patches, houses with a rental apartment for income filled the next patch, where small single-family suburban houses marked ascension into the middle class, leading to larger houses and then great millionaires' mansion estates on the periphery. Modern architects altered this ecology by proposing a diversion away from the single-family suburban house outside the city centre to large slab or tower apartments set in superblock parkland enclaves. Modern planners also proposed to move the specialised urban enclaves containing offices, factories, shopping or recreation to garden city locations.

The ecology of enclaves in an Asian megacity like Bangkok, Beijing, Shanghai or the Pearl River Delta is far more complex than the simple model of the Chicago School. Urban migrants are just as likely now to move to work in a suburban factory as move into inner-city ghettos. The megalopolis exploded the metropolis into a new urban design ecology of mass suburban developments, creating a vast city territory that was a patchwork of differentiated residential enclaves. A grid of feeder access roads framed these new enclaves in megascaled cellular blocks. This new ecology of patches had attendant shopping mall enclaves and service strips with gas stations, repair shops, fast food depots and medical facilities in small pavilions. In the American version of the megalopolis new support facilities, oil tank depots, truck distribution warehouses, sewage works, waste disposal dumps and other undesirable enclaves filled in the cheap land between housing enclaves, polluting swamps or river valleys liable to flooding. Urban actors later added business centres with skyscrapers, megamalls or large institutional campuses as dense urban fragments within this ecology, creating the fragmented metropolis with its large enclaves. The Asian megacity, as an even further extended city territory, includes all these ecologies of urban fragments, but also has space to accommodate traditional urban agricultural practices in patches. Cheap mass communication and personal mobility systems greatly enlarge the city territory, freeing rivers and valleys, allowing designers to work with the water of the city in park ribbons and enclaves (see Conclusion).

Diagrams of enclaves, blocks, neighbourhood units, superblocks, megablocks and city skylines
(Diagrams © David Grahame Shane, 2010)

Enclaves and Patches

Small
Micro
courtyard / row house

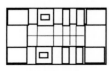

city block

Enclave
inside
enclave

Medium
Urban Village
city blocks

neighbourhood unit
with school

Enclave
inside
enclave

Large
Super
modern super block

neighbourhood unit
with school

Enclave
inside
enclave

Large Patches
superblocks

Suburban
residential
enclave

Office
industrial
enclave

Mall
enclave

Mega= Extra Large

Megablock 1km x 1km

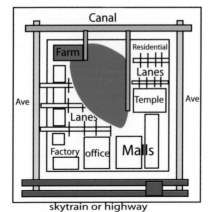

Desa-kota
mixed-use
patch

Beijing Bowl

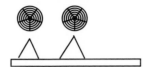
Manhattan Twin Cluster

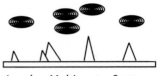
London Multicentre Scatter

Enclave Patches and City Skylines

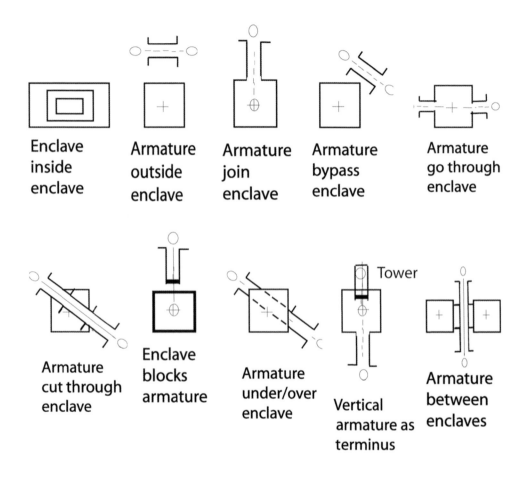

Enclave
inside
enclave

Armature
outside
enclave

Armature
join
enclave

Armature
bypass
enclave

Armature
go through
enclave

Armature
cut through
enclave

Enclave
blocks
armature

Armature
under/over
enclave

Tower

Vertical
armature as
terminus

Armature
between
enclaves

Enclave and armature combinations diagram
(Diagram © David Grahame Shane, 2005)

Lakeside pavilions and stream system enclave

Hutong historic fabric preservation area enclave courtyards and lanes

Forbidden City Enclave

Tiananmen Square enclave

Chang'an Boulevard approach armature

The Forbidden City enclave at the centre of
the Beijing City Model in the Beijing Planning
Museum, Beijing, China (photos 2009)
(Photos © David Grahame Shane)

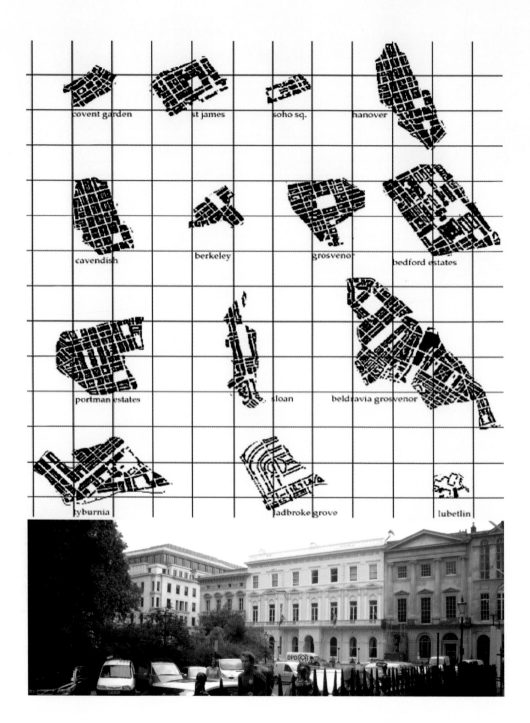

covent garden   st james   soho sq.   hanover

cavendish   berkeley   grosvenor   bedford estates

portman estates   sloan   beldravia grosvenor

tyburnia   ladbroke grove   lubetlin

**Drawings of London estates
and St James Square enclave,
London, UK (photo 2009)**
(Drawings © David Grahame
Shane, 1971; photo © David
Grahame Shane)

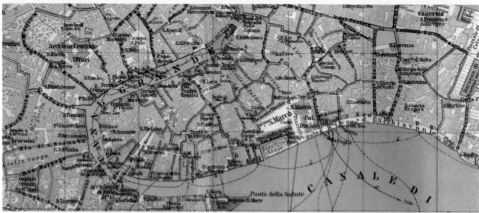

Piazza San Marco enclave, Venice, Italy – night, day, map and distant views (photos 2009)
Opposite (Photos © David Grahame Shane, map courtesy David Grahame Shane)

Kohn Pedersen Fox, remodelled atrium of The Landmark Shopping Mall enclave, Central, Hong Kong, 2002–6 (original structure 1983) (photo 2009)
Above (Photo © David Grahame Shane)

Like squares and enclaves, streets and armatures have served urban designers for centuries. In 1945 Soviet urban designers and many of their Beaux-Arts colleagues were deeply committed to the linear organisation of the armature as a basic structuring device in the city. Stalin's plan for Moscow and Mao's for Beijing both created a spider's web of broad boulevards to tie their vast city expansions together. Planners and architects in New York and London had their own versions of such plans, which all derived from Haussmann's imperial plans for Paris and its ring and radial boulevards in the 19th century. These boulevards would either skirt or cut through existing villages, setting up a hierarchy of streets and bypasses for local and long-distance traffic. Haussmann regulated the architecture of these armatures, their scale, width and setbacks, as well as their planting and street furniture. The introduction of automobile highways as stretched armatures in the megalopolis disrupted this clear system and metropolitan hierarchy.

The design of small village streets and lanes was an urban preoccupation of those who opposed modern design, like British architectural critic and designer Gordon Cullen, American writer and community activist Jane Jacobs, and the American Contextualists or New Urbanist designers. Local streets might be dead ends, as in the Islamic cities of the Middle East or European medieval cities (or postwar suburban subdivisions with their 'lollipop' layouts). Local streets might also extend through the block to connect with surrounding arteries. In Beijing and Shanghai there were many such small lanes within the block stretching from edge to edge. In Bangkok these small lanes ended in cul-de-sacs called 'soi', resulting in a green heart to the block with tall towers on the periphery. While historic preservation activists saved some village streets from disappearing, in the late 20th century street and lane design also became a prerequisite of high-density megamalls and complex sectional casinos catering to tourists from suburban nations. With the vast expansions of the megalopolis and megacities, many old city centres and villages, with their narrow streets and lanes, have found new uses also as entertainment centres and leisure centres. Examples include the elegant redevelopment of the miniblocks around the Temple Bar and Meeting House Squares, Dublin in the 1990s or the *hutongs* of Beijing repurposed as pedestrian shopping areas in the 2000s.[14]

Traditionally village main streets or 'high streets' were self-organising systems created by merchants to serve the inhabitants of cities. By 1945 some modernists like Le Corbusier saw the street as a major obstacle and dangerous place because of the invasion of cars in the metropolis. Le Corbusier advocated raised highways as stretched armatures for automobiles in the city centre, leaving the ground theoretically free for pedestrians in parkland. In practice in Chandigarh and many other proposals Le Corbusier sank the cars below the main pedestrian level in cuttings. Other modern French architects like Auguste Perret in Le Havre (see chapter 4) sought to modernise the street, extending the lessons of Haussmann, to develop the street section with car parking below. The Team X architects suggested moving pedestrians up one level onto walkways and bridges, like the 1957 Berlin Haupstadt project (see chapter 3) by British architects Alison and Peter Smithson. British town planner Colin Buchanan gave the impression of advocating the application of these ideas to central London during the 1960s and influenced the planning of the upper-level walkway system in

Central, Hong Kong (see chapter 10).[15] Buchanan also argued that subways would be a better transport solution than highways, an idea also applied in Hong Kong. In many historic cities urban activists like Jane Jacobs opposed highways and upper level pedestrian schemes.

The successful multiyear pedestrianisation of Copenhagen in the 1960s led to the establishment of car-free armatures in many European cities, where mall development was restricted. In American and Asian cities the proliferation of stretched armatures, multilane highways and private automobiles created conditions where it was difficult for pedestrians to cross a street that might be over 40 metres (120 feet) wide. The development in the 1990s of street crossings with air-conditioned escalators up to air-conditioned bridges on the Las Vegas Strip demonstrates one luxurious solution to this problem. Many miserable underground corridors illustrate a more common, but less successful answer. Urban actors moved all the functions of the city into isolated pavilions alongside these stretched armatures in 1950s America. Low-rise or high-rise strip development along the side of such multilane highways created linear corridors of disconnected big box malls, stores and towers, behind which low-rise development might be located within the megablock (as in Los Angeles, Houston, Bangkok or Beijing).

In the megalopolis there is a constant stretching and compressing of armatures. City extensions require new stretched armatures along highways for access and at the same time need compressed armatures stacked inside malls to re-centre the suburban experience for social and commercial purposes. Legislation effecting mall finance in the USA meant that developers could build new and more luxurious malls every five years, making the previous generation out of date. In this process urban designers compressed the armature of the mall so that it became a complex, three-dimensional layered space that could be themed or beautifully proportioned as a glass enclosed 'galleria'. These structures developed in the suburbs but also entered the heart of the city when urban actors sought to create new attractors in the centre, as at the World Financial Center in New York in the 1980s (see chapter 7).

Urban designers like Victor Gruen, Welton Becket and IM Pei played an important role in suburban mall development. Later American offices like Jon Jerde's pioneered complex interior and exterior sections that learnt from the experiments of the Deconstructivists, like Zaha Hadid's unbuilt Peak Project in Hong Kong (see chapter 7). Mall designers sought to make their interior armatures more street-like, creating design guidelines, and these in turn were one inspiration for urban designers seeking to re-create the street as at Battery Park City (1978, see chapter 7).

A similar interior–exterior armature interplay drove mall owners in central Bangkok to turn their malls inside out to connect to the elevated SkyTrain when it arrived in the early 2000s (see chapter 10). Casino owners in Las Vegas in the same period reversed their designs, bringing urban elements out on the Strip and hiding the car parking at the back of the block. The complexity of these interactions is thrown into high contrast in the Mid-Levels in Hong Kong, where the city government inserted a raised and covered escalator system climbing up the hill in the open armature of the street corridor, completely changing the character of the neighbourhood. The street corners by the escalator suddenly became alive and super active, as developers slipped in sliver towers and condominiums along this striking, slinky, sectional armature (see Conclusion).

Armature Sectional Positions and Plans

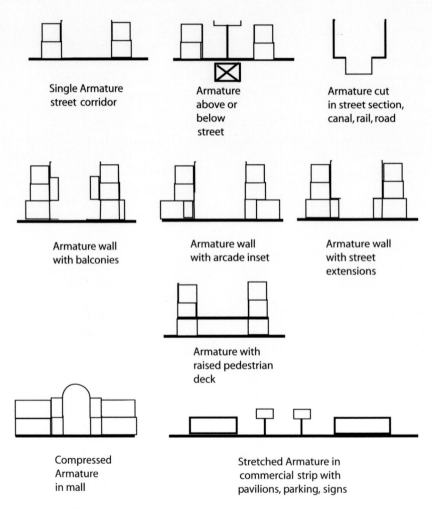

Single Armature
street corridor

Armature
above or
below
street

Armature cut
in street section,
canal, rail, road

Armature wall
with balconies

Armature wall
with arcade inset

Armature wall
with street
extensions

Armature with
raised pedestrian
deck

Compressed
Armature
in mall

Stretched Armature in
commercial strip with
pavilions, parking, signs

Armature sections
(Diagram © David Grahame Shane, 2009)

Stretched and compressed armature diagrams and Giorgio Vasari's Uffizi Museum armature, Florence, Italy, 1566 (photo 1990s)
(Diagram © David Grahame Shane, 2005; photo © David Grahame Shane)

STRETCHED ARMATURE DIAGRAMS

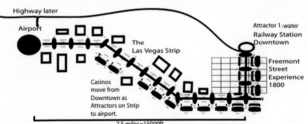

LAS VEGAS STRIP; the REVERSE CITY: Casinos as isolated pavilions. PARKING LOTS REPLACE TUILERIES GARDENS

COMPRESSED ARMATURE DIAGRAM

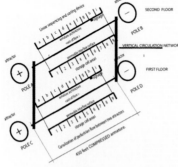

STANDARD ARMATURE DIAGRAM

Stretched and compressed land and water armatures in Venice, Italy (photos 2009)
Note railway and highway approach across lagoon. (Photos © David Grahame Shane)

**Stretched automobile armatures in Los Angeles, USA (photos 2008)
and multilevel highways Taipei, Taiwan (photo 2009)**

(Photos © David Grahame Shane)

**Stretched automobile armatures and compressed
pedestrian armatures in Los Angeles, USA (photos 2008)**
(Photos © David Grahame Shane)

Stretched high-speed rail armatures in Spain, and Asian mixed-use shop–house street armatures accommodating bikes and automobiles (photos 2008)

(Photos © David Grahame Shane)

High-speed rail armature, and pedestrian armatures:
Pedestrian armature of Las Ramblas and Barceloneta Beach, Barcelona (photos 2007)
top and centre (Photos © David Grahame Shane)

Taiwanese Bullet train (photo 2009)
above (Photo © David Grahame Shane)

James Corner and Field Operations High Line Park pedestrian armature, New York (photos 2009)
top and centre (Photos © David Grahame Shane)

**Taiwanese rur-urban landscape of coastal plain, with factories,
housing, fish farms and rice paddies (photo 2009)**
above (Photo © David Grahame Shane)

Pedestrian armatures
Compressed armatures are shown here in the Passage des Panoramas, Paris, France (1819)
(above left) and in Eaton's Mall, Toronto, Canada (above right), while stretched armatures are
illustrated by the upper-deck pedestrian system of Central, Hong Kong (opposite top) and the
SkyTrain, Bangkok, Thailand (opposite bottom). (Photos © David Grahame Shane)

Michel Foucault, the French philosopher, when he wrote about heterotopias in the 1960s imagined three primary categories with many variations, making his 'heterotopology'.[16] There were heterotopias of crisis that helped people grow and change, hidden in plain sight, amongst the community. There were heterotopias of deviance that prepared people for and enforced the application of the codes of modernity, usually located outside the old city in a separate enclave. Then there were heterotopias of illusion that accommodated virtual and fleeting worlds, changing fast and manipulating information, giving the impression of freedom. Foucault did not develop this category so much in his essay as the computer and information age was just beginning as he wrote. Nonetheless he spoke of information systems, flows, bits and bytes of information as a potent force for change in the city. Foucault specifically excluded Nazi death camps from his analysis, since his heterotopias involved changes in people's lives, not the state deliberately planning the death of its citizens and plundering their property.[17]

Foucault's three categories form a useful basis for charting the evolution of heterotopias in the last 60 years since 1945. His first category of heterotopias of crisis, where people in transition take refuge from life crises, have continued. Foucault mentioned places for the instruction of boys approaching puberty, menstrual huts for women in tribal encampments, boarding schools, military barracks, wedding weekend places, motels, medieval almshouses and hospitals in cities, student or migrant hostels, old-age homes and nursing homes integrated in society. This category could be extended to the *favelas* and informal settlements where people voluntarily move in order to take advantage of urban life compared to rural subsistence. The invisibility of these settlements on official maps, and yet their obvious presence adding to the city, conforms to the 'hidden in plain sight' characteristic of the medieval almshouses for instance, and distinguishes them from the refugee camps and internment camps that involve coercion and force. This inclusion allows the category to evolve into a vast system of informal settlement patterns, NGOs and bottom-up self-organising groups – sometimes cooperating with the state and global forces, as in the oil booms in Latin America in the 1950s and 1960s in Caracas, Venezuela, and other times resisting as at Dharavi, Mumbai (see chapter 10).

At the same time, heterotopias of crisis appeared in shrinking cities of the northern hemisphere as urban designers plan expanded facilities to house and care for an aging population on a voluntary basis, as distinct from state-supported facilities. A key characteristic of these heterotopias is their voluntary, collective and cooperative nature, creating a place where people go for a time without penalty or punishment. People are free to leave and re-emerge when they feel ready. These spaces are part of a larger social process accommodating personal changes and circumstances within a community. Religious foundations and charitable organisations have often supported these urban shelters from modernity, including homeless shelters, food pantries, homes for battered women, ex-prostitutes, runaway children, orphans and other outcasts, like AIDS victims in gay health centres and clinics in the 1970s and 1980s. In the past, many of these organisations maintained an institution in the metropolis or on its periphery to house those in need. While these buildings remain in use, many institutions have shifted to a more widely distributed system to serve people's needs, finding families or homes willing to accept orphans, distributing housing vouchers to homeless people so they do not have to live in a shelter, trying to prevent homelessness through outreach programmes making better information available to people on the verge of losing their house.

Throughout the last 60 years, war, famine, natural disasters and economic and political folly have constantly created new refugee camps and temporary cities. Some, like Gaza or Soweto, became permanent settlements; others, like Kowloon's Walled City, were demolished. Many of these settlements were indistinguishable from the many shantytowns that developed around oil-rich cities like Caracas in Latin America, Lagos in Africa or Jakarta in Indonesia. Millions of people participated in this mass urban design experiment without professional help. As described by David Sattherthwaite, professionals arrived late with plans for upgrades and modern insertions, bringing heterotopias from Foucault's list of state communal institutions, such as schools, libraries, hospitals, sports clubs, parks and sewage systems (see chapter 9).[18]

Over the years, the scale of the self-built heterotopic settlements, so often overlooked and unmapped, has grown incrementally as in the case of Dharavi, Mumbai, which Mike Davis branded as a megaslum (see chapter 10). Such settlements even exist inside planned new towns like the urban villages of Shenzhen, China. The UN estimates that one third of the urban population of 3 billion lives in shantytowns in 2010, meaning that these heterotopic, temporary structures are continuing to house a billion people. In some cities such self-built city extensions approach the 50 per cent tipping point where they become the new norm, not the exception.[19]

Much of Foucault's research concerned the shift from the heterotopia of crisis to the heterotopia of deviance, as the modern state created a safety net for its citizens after the Great Depression of the 1930s. Foucault concentrated his research on the emergence of the modern state and its repressive institutions in the 19th century, writing during the 1960s when the European states created vast social welfare systems in competition with Khrushchev's USSR. European states rapidly built new schools, universities, mass social housing estates, hospitals, asylums, clinics and other welfare facilities for their citizens in what Eric Hobsbawm called the 'Golden Age'.[20] As the European states lost their global empires, their governments concentrated their resources at home, modernising and vastly expanding the old state equipment to educate and serve the children of the postwar baby boom as they became adult citizens.[21] Architects redesigned universities, schools, hospitals and prisons for modern times. Urban designers worked on new towns as solutions to the housing crisis.

It is worth pausing briefly in this review of Foucault's heterotopias to examine in detail an outstanding example of such state urban design: the Swedish new town of Vällingby, outside Stockholm, much visited by later generations of urban designers. Vällingby was planned by Sven Markelius on one of the new subway lines leading out to the fjords and Hässelby Strand beaches.[22] The exit from the train opens onto a central square, with a shopping complex on two sides, the station on the third and a theatre on the fourth opening up to the hillside. Buses and taxis wait on the other side of the station, where there is also a church building. The main

Sven Markelius, Vällingby New Town, Stockholm, Sweden, 1952 (photos 2003)
The Swedish welfare-state government built heterotopic new towns to modernise and urbanise Swedish society after the Second World War. Vällingby town centre included a cinema, a cultural area, and housing towers close to the subway station. (Photos © David Grahame Shane, diagram courtesy David Grahame Shane)

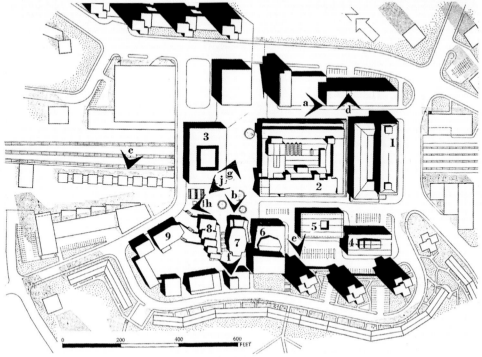

pedestrian shopping armature runs from beside the station back towards downtown on a platform built over the train tracks and maintenance yard. A small cross-axis of shopping leads towards freestanding restaurants next door to the theatre. Behind these low buildings, further up the hill, housing in towers looks down on the central plaza. With buildings designed by architects Sven Backström and Leif Reinius, the new town centre became a showpiece for modern commercial design, visited by mall designers from America, such as Victor Gruen, in search of new ideas. The standard of finishes was very high and impressed these American visitors, another of whom was San Francisco landscape architect Lawrence Halprin. Halprin had pioneered 'festival malls' like San Francisco's Ghirardelli Square (1962), in which pieces of the historical city centre were converted into mall-like complexes based on the sales logic and pedestrian traffic patterns of suburban malls. In his notebooks, he recounts his surprise at the quality of Vällingby.[23] In particular he liked the coordinated design control that allowed variety and colour. He sketched the incorporation of steps up the hillside, landscape features and fountains, even the lighting fixtures. The paving pattern by Erik Glemme delighted him with its circles and swirls. Here he learnt a valuable lesson about the importance of street furniture and quality for urban design compared to utilitarian first-generation malls in America, lessons he would use in his creation of the second-generation American 'festival mall'.

Foucault also fought against the rigid rules and brutal, utilitarian standardisation enforced in the rapid re-modernisation of the state institutions of Europe. Vällingby represented the best that the European welfare state had to offer. But Foucault also recognised that passage through this phase, however painful, was a necessary prelude to modern life. Many of these state institutions have changed enormously in the years since Foucault wrote in the 1960s, in part because of criticism of their rigidity from the left-wing politicians, in part because of complaints about their high cost from right-wing politicians wanting to reduce the state and cut taxes. The impact of this double campaign about heterotopias could be devastating in a city. In New York, for instance, the homeless population reached over 70,000 people in the 1980s as the state authorities shut mental hospitals and shelters in an effort to lower costs without providing any alternative place to live. Combined with the introduction of crack cocaine, this resulted in the breakdown of security on the streets, where crack addicts might rob people at gunpoint and steal cars (symptoms of urban distress still prevalent in many Latin American, Asian and African cities).[24]

After the loss of population and tax base to the suburbs and megalopolis, the New York City government finally restructured its economy and provided a safety net in the city, investing in the police force, enforcing strict gun laws and developing a system of 'Special Districts' that encouraged redevelopment in the city via tax breaks for corporations. The fragmented metropolis relied on the renovation of old metropolitan heterotopias. Draconian Rockefeller drug laws were part of this solution, involving the construction of a system of new super prisons across the state, where young men from New York City (primarily African-Americans) are still sent for petty crimes, costing the city millions of dollars annually (as documented by Laura Kurgan and her research partner's work on the 'Million Dollar Blocks' of Brooklyn). It would be cheaper to send the young men to Harvard University.[25]

This brief history of New York heterotopias in the 1980s illustrates the impact of heterotopias in a city and their role in handling change. The failure of the Reagan–Thatcher cuts in social welfare and privatisation of public assets, such as transportation systems, resulted in further transformations in heterotopias. Private contractors ran many public facilities like prisons, hospitals and railways, altering their priorities from care to profit. From the perspective of a state emerging from the Soviet sphere of influence and rigid central governmental control, this might seem an improvement. From a European shrinking-city perspective, this cut in services and resources might represent the loss of hospital care, rail service, pension funds, public housing or post office service.

New communication technologies introduced in this period also altered the method of delivery of basic services and altered the role of heterotopias in the provision of welfare state services.[26] With the widespread availability of televisions, and then personal computers, universities took to the airwaves, like the Open University in Britain, supplementing traditional means of education. After 2007 Wikipedia became available on smart phones anywhere there is cell service, making a universe of information available. Prisons could also be replaced by house arrest or parole systems using ankle bracelets to report via satellite to computers monitoring the parolee's movements. Doctors developed new microsurgery techniques that allowed patients to go home from hospital as outpatients, where they could nurse themselves under the supervision of their doctor, always available via cellphone. In special cases, remote sensing equipment could monitor a patient's heartbeat from their home, again communicating via satellite to their doctors. New drugs enabled doctors to treat mental patients who might once have been locked up for depression or violent behaviour in an asylum, releasing them to return to their homes and communities. Instead of building housing estates, housing associations could give vouchers to the homeless to find housing in the city, while having spaces for those in transition, from prison or mental institutions. In a horrific but ironic twist, prison has become the subject of a top-ranking 'reality show' on American television, just as schools and hospitals were earlier the subject of soap operas in suburbia.

As the European states have abandoned their empires, urban designers have worked on the conversion of colonial infrastructures to new uses, in old docklands, waterfronts, abandoned railway stations, railway shunting yards, old warehouse districts, slaughterhouses, stables, wholesale markets, barracks, hospitals, prisons and rubbish dumps. Christiania, for instance, the disused military base occupied by hippies in Copenhagen in the early 1970s represented a heterotopic conversion (see chapter 4). Camden Market in north London provides another example where a disused canal basin, railway stable blocks and warehouses have all coalesced into a youth centre, with nightclubs, street markets, sellers of used books and clothing, antique flea markets, restaurants, pubs and bars, with high-end restaurants starting to appear in new buildings. The Greater London Council (GLC) converted Covent Garden, the old London central fruit and vegetable market, into a 'festival market' the 1980s. In 2007 the Hong Kong Architecture and Urbanism Biennale converted the disused colonial police headquarters into temporary galleries, including the cell blocks.[27]

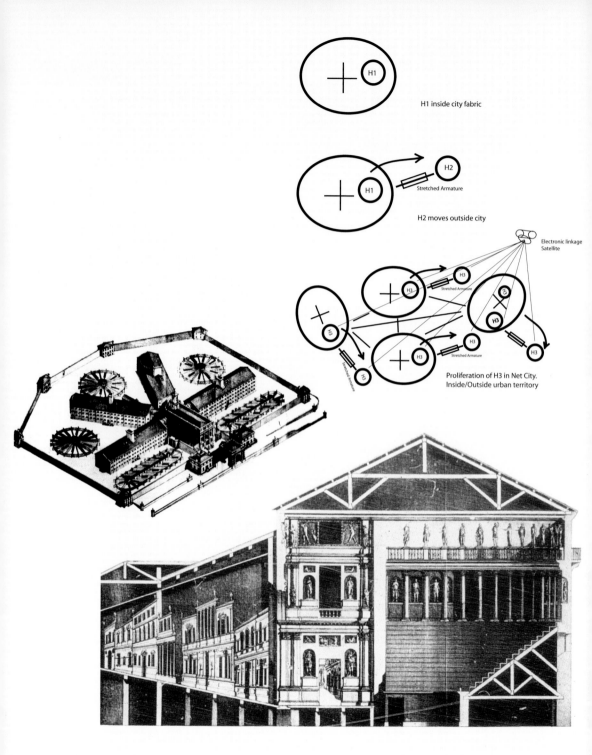

H1 inside city fabric

H2

Stretched Armature

H1

H2 moves outside city

Electronic linkage
Satellite

H3

Stretched Armature

H3

H3

H3

H3

H3

H3

Stretched Armature

H3

Stretched Armature

Proliferation of H3 in Net City.
Inside/Outside urban territory

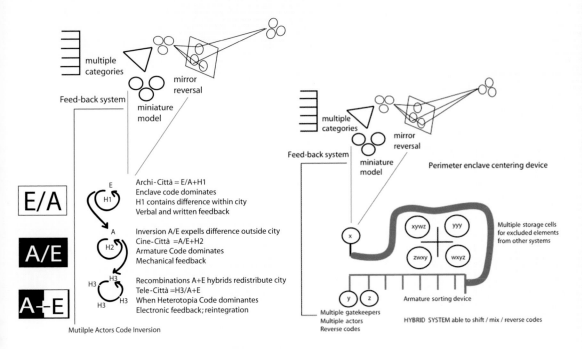

E/A

Archi-Città = E/A+H1
Enclave code dominates
H1 contains difference within city
Verbal and written feedback

A/E

Inversion A/E expells difference outside city
Cine-Città =A/E+H2
Armature Code dominates
Mechanical feedback

A–E

Recombinations A+E hybrids redistribute city
Tele-Città =H3/A+E
When Heterotopia Code dominantes
Electronic feedback; reintegration

Multiple categories

Feed-back system

mirror reversal

miniature model

Mutilple Actors Code Inversion

Perimeter enclave centering device

Multiple storage cells for excluded elements from other systems

Armature sorting device

Multiple gatekeepers
Multiple actors
Reverse codes

HYBRID SYSTEM able to shift / mix / reverse codes

The heterotopia's shifting functions and positions, with built examples

Heterotopias reflect their host systems, compressing them into miniature models, as their urban actors reverse normal codes in the system. Urban actors seeking change have either hidden inside the city (Palladio's Teatro Olimpico, Vicenza, lower left), sought refuge outside its boundaries (Pentonville Prison, London, middle left), or today sought comfort in speed and mobility as at the interior Grand Canal in the Venetian casino, Las Vegas (lower right). (Diagrams and photos © David Grahame Shane, 2005).

Many military bases in the metropolises and colonies became available for alternative uses. Military camps evolved and shrunk as national armies outsourced services to private contractors and secret services employed either private contractors, client militias or local warlords to advance their objectives. The story of al-Qaeda told in the investigation of the 9/11 terrorist attacks on New York in 2001 revealed the role of remote, hidden, CIA-backed training camps in the 1980s anti-Soviet war in Afghanistan in creating the terrorist organisation. In reaction, the American invasion of Iraq created the ultimate gated community in the fortified Green Zone in the heart of Baghdad, just as US military camps spread across the country close to oil fields. Private contractors such as Blackwater had their own bases and logistical centres hidden around the city, outnumbering the American army. The US secret service also operated a system of 'black sites' and secret air flights, conveying terrorist suspects in body bags to interrogation centres across the globe. From the exterior these military prisons might be nearly identical to the big box retail centres and malls across the street as in suburban Aman, Jordan.[28]

The conversion of military bases to parks and playgrounds represents a further shift in Foucault's heteropology, from deviance to illusion. He criticised the rigid codes of the prison or heterotopia of deviance, and pointed to their opposite, the flexible codes that seemed to promise freedom in heterotopias of illusion. These structures accommodated the dreams and fantasies of urban actors, whether in palaces of consumption, like department stores or gallerias, or theatres, cinemas, museums or red-light-district bordellos. From department stores to malls is a small step, and from malls to multilevel megamalls like Langham Place, Hong Kong (2005, see p 78) is the result of the scaling up of mass communications and easy transport access via subway and automobile. Steven Holl's Linked Hybrid (2003–9; see chapter 10) in Beijing, China also shows the impact of the megacity in a megablock, experimenting with new public spaces in high-level links between towers on the site of an old work brigade factory. In urban terms, temporary exhibitions and world's fairs played a great role as places of experiment, as at the Brussels World's Fair of 1958 (see chapter 4), or Osaka in 1970 (see chapter 6). World's fairs meant that entire cities became the subject of design, as the host city upgraded itself for the occasion.[29] Similarly the Olympics came to have a heterotopic and transformative effect after the 1964 Tokyo Olympics, followed most successfully by the Barcelona Olympics of 1992 and the Beijing Olympics of 2008 (see chapter 8), with London in 2012 (see chapter 8). Arts-led development, whether from the bottom up as in the artists' studios of New York's SoHo (1970s) or Chelsea (1980s), or top down, as at the Pompidou Centre in Paris (1971–7) or Bilbao Guggenheim Museum (1997), could also have a similar effect in a small urban area.[30]

The evolution of a university town
Starting with a small house contained a scholar and students, later combined around a courtyard to produce a college, a line of which produce a new town extension along the High Street. This diagram the traces the addition of 19th century industry and railways, followed by the mobility of the automobile age and highway expansion into a city region with research parks. (Diagram © David Grahame Shane, 2005)

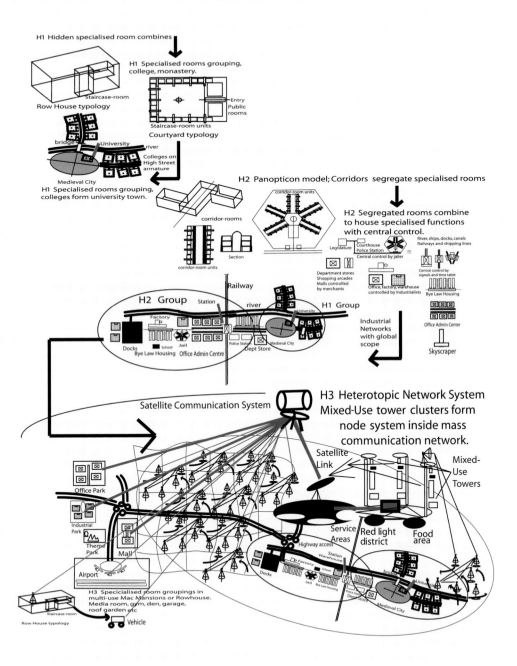

H1 Hidden specialised room combines

Row House typology

Staircase-room

H1 Specialised rooms grouping, college, monastery.

Staircase-room units

Courtyard typology

Entry Public rooms

bridge

University

river

Colleges on High Street armature

Medieval City

H1 Specialised rooms grouping, colleges form university town.

corridor-rooms

corridor-room units

Section

H2 Panopticon model; Corridors segregate specialised rooms

corridor-room units

Central control by jailer

H2 Segregated rooms combine to house specialised functions with central control.

Legislature

Courthouse Police Station

Department stores Shopping arcades Malls controlled by merchants

Office, factory, warehouse controlled by Industrialists

River, ships, docks, canals Railways and shipping lines

Central control by signals and time table

Bye Law Housing

Office Admin Center

Skyscraper

Railway

H2 Group

Station

river

University

H1 Group

Factory

Docks

School

Jail

Police Station

Medieval City

Bye Law Housing

Office Admin Centre

Dept Store

Industrial Networks with global scope

Satellite Communication System

H3 Heterotopic Network System Mixed-Use tower clusters form node system inside mass communication network.

Satellite Link

Mixed-Use Towers

Office Park

Industrial Park

Theme Park

Mall

Airport

Service Areas

Red light district

Food area

Highway access

Station Warehouse

Docks

Factory

School

Jail

Bye Law Housing

Police Station

Dept Store

bridge

University

Medieval City

H3 Specicialised room groupings in multi-use Mac Mansions or Rowhouse. Media room, gym, den, garage, roof garden etc

Row House typology

Staircase-room

Vehicle

Heterotopic City Sections

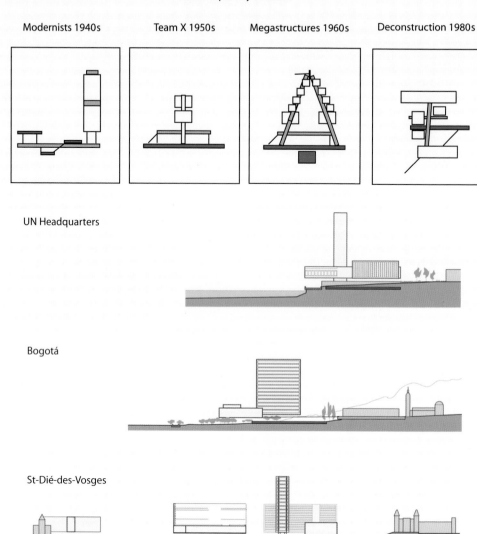

Modernists 1940s   **Team X 1950s**   **Megastructures 1960s**   **Deconstruction 1980s**

UN Headquarters

Bogotá

St-Dié-des-Vosges

Heterotopic city section diagrams

Each successive architectural movement – the CIAM Modernists in the Ville Radieuse, 1935; Team X c 1958; the Metabolists in the early 1960s; Archigram in the late 1960s; and the Deconstructivists in the 1980s – altered the relationship between the car level (indicated in red) and pedestrians (shown in yellow). Examples shown include Le Corbusier's projects for St-Dié-des-Vosges, France, the United Nations Headquarters, New York, USA, and Bogotá, Colombia, 1947 to early 1950s. (Diagrams © David Grahame Shane and Uri Wegman, 2010)

PLANO 26: UDU 10.85-SAN MIGUEL.
CONSTRUCCIONES EXISTENTES

Caracas *ranchos* as self-built, unofficial new towns, Venezuela (photo 2002)
The analysis is of the San Miguel district of steep hillside development. The photograph shows
Carlos Raúl Villaneuva's 23 de Enero modernist blocks invaded by the informal construction
of *ranchos*. (Caracas Growth Maps © Alfredo Brillembourg and Hubert Klumpner/U-TT, 2003;
aerial view of 23 de Enero © Pablo Souto/U-TT)

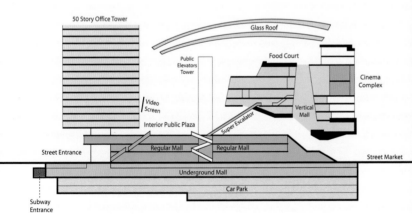

The Jerde Partnership, Langham Place Mall, Mongkok, Kowloon, Hong Kong, 2005: section (redrawn by the author, 2010)
(Redrawn section © David Grahame Shane and Uri Wegman, 2010. Photo © David Grahame Shane)

Steven Holl Architects, Linked Hybrid, Beijing, China, 2003–9 (photos 2009)

(Photos © and courtesy David Grahame Shane)

Conclusion: co-existent models and timeline

The timeline attached at the end of this chapter gives some sense of the chaotic nature of the interaction of the different urban ecologies over the past 60 years, mapping the interaction of urban actors from the metropolis, megalopolis, fragmented metropolis and megacity. Actors evolved and combined urban elements within these urban ecologies as the balance between the ecologies shifted over time, empires crumbled and global corporations emerged. How actors would make these combinations could not be predicted exactly as it depended on the particular place, its combination of patches and balance between players. The outcome of such experiments was not fixed or immutable; it was unknown, despite precedents. Urban actors work in a nonlinear situation; their actions may have a certain logic, but how the complex situation of the multiple urban systems, ecologies and models in a city will react is unknown. There is no one logic and actors cannot predict the outcome of interactions or needs. Actors use heterotopias as a way to deal with this uncertainty. These useful organisational devices recombine as needed, layering parts from different models in different patches within one perimeter, holding different organisational systems together in a trial relationship for a time. While there might have seemed a compelling logic to an actor in one system at one time, the move viewed from a parallel system at the same time might appear to have no logic. Different impulses and different urban actors shaped different places at different times, making a vast panoply of urban designs worldwide. The automobile had been invented 40 years before 1945 and some cities like Houston, Detroit or Los Angeles in America, for instance, pioneered experiments involving architects and urban designers. The linear sequence of the chapters that follow does not indicate a clear historical sequence or precedence. All the four urban ecologies were present at once, even if not dominant or clearly obvious, as the timeline indicates. Urban actors wove together elements from the different models to meet their needs in small patches as time went by, evolving new urban combinations of elements to meet their needs as their urban ecologies changed.

Notes

NB: See 'Author's Caution: Endnote Sources and Wikipedia', towards the end of this book.

1   For the Rockefeller Center, see: Rem Koolhaas, *Delirious New York: A Retroactive Manifesto for Manhattan*, Oxford University Press (New York), 1978, pp 150–67.

2   Kevin Lynch, *The Image of the City*, MIT Press (Cambridge, MA), 1961. For a fuller treatment of enclaves, see: DG Shane, *Recombinant Urbanism: Conceptual Modeling in Architecture, Urban Design and City Theory*, Wiley-Academy (Chichester), 2005, pp 176–98.

3   For a further discussion of armatures, see Shane, *Recombinant Urbanism*, pp 198–218.

4   For a further discussion of heterotopias, see ibid pp 231–314.

5   For Foucault, see: Michel Foucault, 'Of Other Spaces', in Catherine David and Jean-François Chevrier (eds), *Documenta X: The Book*, Hatje Cantz (Kassel), 1997, p 265; also http://foucault. info/documents/heteroTopia/foucault.heteroTopia.en.html (accessed 29 September 2009).

6   For Bentham's Panopticon, see: R Evans, 'Bentham's Panopticon: an incident in the social history of architecture', in *Architectural Association Quarterly*, vol 3, no 2 (Spring 1971), pp 58–69); also: http://en.wikipedia.org/wiki/Panopticon (accessed 29 September 2009).

7   Samantha Hardingham (ed), *Cedric Price: Opera*, John Wiley & Sons (London), 2003, pp 222–5.

8   See: International Society of City and Regional Planners (ISOCARP) Conference, 'Honey I

City Model Timelines.

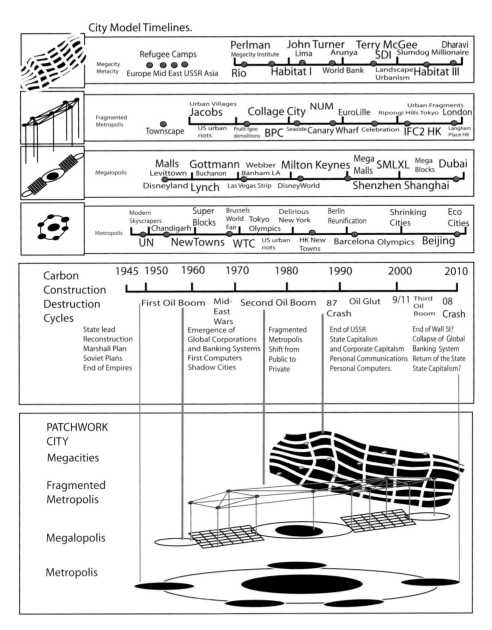

Megacity / Metacity
Refugee Camps
Europe Mid East USSR Asia
Rio
Perlman — Megacity Institute
John Turner — Lima
Arunya
Terry McGee — SDI
Slumdog Millionaire
Dharavi
Habitat I
World Bank
Landscape Urbanism
Habitat III

Fragmented Metropolis
Townscape
US urban riots
Pruitt-Igoo demolitions
BPC
Urban Villages
Jacobs
Collage City
Seaside
NUM
EuroLille
Canary Wharf
Celebration
Ripongi Hills Tokyo
IFC2 HK
Urban Fragments
London
Langham Place HK

Megalopolis
Levittown
Disneyland
Malls
Lynch
Buchanon
Gottmann
Banham LA
Webber
Las Vegas Strip
Milton Keynes
DisneyWorld
Mega Malls
Shenzhen
SMLXL
Shanghai
Mega Blocks
Dubai

Metropolis
UN
Modern Skyscrapers
Chandigarh
NewTowns
Super Blocks
Brussels World Fair
Tokyo Olympics
WTC
US urban riots
Delirious New York
HK New Towns
Berlin Reunification
Barcelona Olympics
Shrinking Cities
Beijing
Eco Cities

Carbon Construction Destruction Cycles

1945	1950	1960	1970	1980	1990	2000	2010

First Oil Boom
Mid-East Wars
Second Oil Boom
87 Crash
Oil Glut
9/11
Third Oil Boom
08 Crash

State lead
Reconstruction
Marshall Plan
Soviet Plans
End of Empires

Emergence of
Global Corporations
and Banking Systems
First Computers
Shadow Cities

Fragmented
Metropolis
Shift from
Public to
Private

End of USSR
State Capitalism
and Corporate Capitalsm
Personal Communications
Personal Computers.

End of Wall St?
Collapse of Global
Banking System
Return of the State
State Capitalism?

PATCHWORK
CITY
Megacities

Fragmented
Metropolis

Megalopolis

Metropolis

Four urban design ecologies timeline and diagram
Each urban design ecology runs parallel with the others,
taking precedence with the ascendance of particular urban
actors. (Diagrams © David Grahame Shane, 2010)

Shrank the Space', 2001, keynote address by Luuk Boelens, http://www.isocarp.org/pub/events/congress/2001/keynotes/speech_boelens/sld001.htm (accessed 7 July 2010).

9   For fragmented metropolis, see: Jonathan Barnett, *The Fractured Metropolis*, HarperCollins (New York), 1995.

10   Author's notes at Franz Oswald 'Seligmann Lecture' at Syracuse University, New York, 2005.

11   For NYC population as 7,454,995 in 1940, see: Campbell Gibson, 'Population of the 100 Largest Cities and Other Urban Places in the United States: 1770 to 1990', June 1998, Table 1, US Census Bureau website, http://www.census.gov/population/www/documentation/twps0027/twps0027.html (accessed 7 July 2010). For London, see: Patrick Abercrombie and John Henry Forshaw, *County of London Plan*, Macmillan & Co (London), 1943.

12   On specialisation, see Shane, *Recombinant Urbanism*, pp 261–2.

13   See Robert E Park and Ernest W Burgess, 'The Growth of the City: An Introduction to a Research Project' (1925), reprinted in Richard T Le Gates and Frederic Stout (eds), *The City Reader*, Routledge (London), 1996, pp 94–6.

14   For Dublin's Meeting House Square and Temple Bar, see: http://www.templebar.ie/home.php (accessed 2 April 2010). For Beijing *hutong*, see: Michael Sorkin, 'Learning from the *Hutong* of Beijing and the Lilong of Shanghai', *Architectural Record*, July 2008, http://archrecord.construction.com/features/critique/0807critique-1.asp (accessed 15 March 2010).

15   For the Buchanan Report, see: Great Britain Ministry of Transport, *Traffic In Towns*, HM Stationery Office (London), 1963.

16   See: Michel Foucault, 'Of Other Spaces', in Catherine David and Jean-Francois Chevrier (eds), *Documenta X: The Book*, Hatje Cantz (Kassel), 1997, p 262, also available at http://foucault.info/documents/heteroTopia/foucault.heteroTopia.en.html (accessed 29 September 2009).

17   For Foucault text on concentration camps, see Foucault, 'Of Other Spaces'.

18   David Satterthwaite on slum upgrading: http://stwr.org/megaslumming and http://vimeo.com/9880676 (accessed 2 April 2010).

19   For UN urban population statistics and estimates, 1950–2030, see p 13 of 'World Urbanization Prospects: The 2003 Revision', http://www.un.org/esa/population/publications/wup2003/WUP2003Report.pdf (accessed 27 September 2009).

20   For the Golden Age, see: Eric Hobsbawm, *The Age of Extremes: The History of the World, 1914-1991*, Vintage Books (New York), 1996.

21   On the welfare state, see: Tony Judt, *Postwar: A History of Europe Since 1945*, Penguin (New York), 2006, pp 330–36.

22   On Vällingby, see: Frederick Gibberd, *Town Design*, Architectural Press (London), 1953, revised 1959, pp 162–5.

23   See: Lawrence Halprin, *Lawrence Halprin Notebooks 1959–1971*, MIT Press (Cambridge, MA), 1972.

24   For homelessness in New York, see: Christopher Jencks, *The Homeless,* Harvard University Press (Cambridge, MA), 1995 (available on Google Books).

25   For Million Dollar Blocks, see: Laura Kurgan and Justice Mapping Centre, http://www.justicemapping.org/archive/9/this-article-is-a-test/ (accessed 1 April 2010).

26   For heterotopias of discipline/deviance, see: http://www.bbcprisonstudy.org/ (accessed 2 April 2010).

27   For the use of the HK Police Compound for the 2007 Hong Kong Shenzhen Bi-City Biennale, see Venue History at http://www.hkszbiennale.asia/ (accessed 2 April 2010).

28   See Deborah Natsios, 'Security in the Global City', in Part 8 of: C Greig Crysler, Stephen Cairns and Hilde Heynen (eds), *SAGE Handbook of Architectural Theory*, SAGE Publications (London), to publish in 2011.

29   For world's fairs as heterotopias, see: Foucault, 'Of Other Spaces'.

30   For the Pompidou Centre and the Bilbao Guggenheim, see: David Grahame Shane, 'Heterotopias of Illusion From Beaubourg to Bilbao and Beyond', in: Michiel Dehaene and Lieven De Cauter, (eds), *Heterotopia and the City: Public Space in a Postcivil Society*, Routledge (Abingdon), 2008, pp 259–74.

**Steven Holl Architects,
Linked Hybrid,
Beijing, China, 2003–9
(photo 2009)**
(Photo © David
Grahame Shane)

Raymond Hood, Rockefeller Center, New York City, USA, 1939 (photo 2009)
The complex, built by the wealthy oil family, represented the modern, commercial metropolis for many European theorists in the 1940s and 1950s, as well as for Rem Koolhaas in 1978. The approach armature slopes down to a central enclave at the foot of the GE Building, miniaturising an ancient urban design arrangement from the imperial metropolis. (Photo © David Grahame Shane)

CHAPTER 3

The Metropolis

In 1945 the USA and USSR emerged as two new global superpowers, replacing the European and Japanese empires, whose public symbolism fell into disgrace as a result of Hitler's megalomaniac plans for Berlin. Both superpowers seemed determined to break the power of the old empires, the USA because of its own ex-colonial history, and the USSR in the name of the peasants and industrial proletariat enslaved under the old empires. The metropolis remained a potent symbol of the global city, intense, busy, fast, dense and at the centre of world affairs. Both the USA and the USSR attempted to redefine the image of the metropolis to suit their own purposes in their political spheres after the Second World War. New York and Moscow became the metropolitan urban design models of choice on either side of the Iron Curtain and Bamboo Curtain during the Cold War years from 1945 to 1990.[1]

The concept of the metropolis, the mother city, is antique, relating back to ancient empires in Egypt, the Middle East and China, and later to Europe in Athens, Rome, Paris, Venice, Amsterdam, London and Moscow. Metropolitan cities are always giant, busy hubs that presume an imperial hinterland, containing a hierarchy of smaller cities that support their mother city paying tribute and taxes.[2] This fundamental, organisational hierarchy is built into the English dictionary definition of a city as part of an urban system that descends from the mother city, the metropolis, to a city with a cathedral, to a town with several churches and a market, to a village with a church, to the humble hamlet (a village without a church). This urban ladder represents a top-down social organisation where orders come from the imperial centre and descend to the majority of the population, the serfs and peasants who work the land in the countryside and provide the food.

Urban design in early metropolitan complexes often consisted of a monumental approach to the singular centre of power and authority, as well as an assembly point before this centre of power, all within a clearly defined enclave. This schema of approach axis and terminal square before the place of power can be found throughout the ancient world, from the Forbidden City of Beijing in Asia to the temple tombs on the shores of the Nile in Africa, to the Mayan and Aztec temple–palace complexes of ancient Meso-American empires. Armatures, linear approaches, and enclaves, sacred central enclosures, formed the twin elements of this urban design system.[3] Echoes of this ancient pattern can even be seen in modern designs like the Rockefeller Center, New York from the 1930s.

Few of the early metropolitan cites reached one million, Beijing remained for centuries the largest global metropolis until 1800. In that period many big secondary cities accommodated around 10,000 people, representing the limit of the organisational capacity of the agricultural system to sustain and maintain city functions. Industrialisation reshaped the image of the metropolis as a monstrous machine, as in Fritz Lang's film *Metropolis* (1928). But this mechanical image remained a phantasm that did not touch most people's lives globally. Even in Europe, where most of the world's urban population lived in 1945, Italy, France, Spain, Belgium and many Scandinavian countries, as well as the USSR, still had the majority of their population working the land as agricultural peasants.[4]

A new dawn seemed to be breaking in 1945. The establishment of the United Nations (UN) in New York placed the spotlight on this city as a prime example of the modern metropolis. Meanwhile the USSR provided an alternative Communist metropolitan model copied throughout Eastern Europe and in Beijing. Western Europe had to go back to the drawing board. This chapter ends with a comparison of two competition projects for the reconstruction of West Berlin in 1958 as a new European metropolis. Both looked forward to the age of the automobile, but with very different attitudes towards the scale and organisation of the city and state.

New York enclaves: the modern commercial metropolis

The American metropolis differed from earlier models in its emphasis on commercial interests and civil society rather than imperial displays of state or religious power. Such displays were reserved for the national capital Washington DC or for state capitals. The image of the city of 7 million with skyscrapers seen from the New York harbour and Hudson River mesmerised European urban designers in the 1920s and 1930s. New York, like Chicago, appeared to be a commercial city machine that never stood still and was constantly changing. Its rapid growth and unique form seemed unprecedented, creating a new model for the future of the city.[5]

At the symbolic centre of this intense city machine lay a new kind of public space that was privately owned and operated, like the great public foyer inside Grand Central Station (1912). This space was distinct from the city's traditional assembly points, on the steps in front of City Hall downtown, or in Union Square or Madison Square further north on Broadway. The modernist historian and friend of Le Corbusier, Sigfried Giedion, writing in 1941, recognised the Rockefeller Center as the 'ideal community center'.[6]

The Rockefellers, whose wealth derived from their early monopoly in the American oil industry (broken apart into the 'Five Sisters' – Standard Oil, Esso (Exxon), Chevron, Texaco and Mobil – by the Federal government in 1911), could afford to build this cluster of skyscrapers in the depth of the Great Depression. Their products (oil, kerosene, lubricants, synthetic rubber, tarmac, etc) facilitated the development of the automobile and they also invested in new communication companies such as the Radio Corporation of America (RCA).[7] The architect Raymond Hood's design symbolised the metropolitan ideal, both by its central planning focused on the plaza and by the density of its surrounding towers.

The Rockefeller Center's central plaza and small approach street from Fifth Avenue aligned with the RCA skyscraper tower on axis to provide a miniature version of the ancient metropolitan ideal of an armature-and-enclave approach to the seat of power. The effectiveness of this compressed reconfiguration was not lost on urban designers. John

Graham, the pioneer American regional mall architect and urban designer of the 1950s, spent his apprenticeship working there in the 1930s.[8] He later attested to the influence of the Center's 200-metre-long (600-foot) approach armature and central plaza on his early designs, as well as the hidden, underground truck and parking service levels in the complex section.

The central axis of the Rockefeller Center attached to Fifth Avenue, a north–south spine of Manhattan, leading to Frederick Law Olmsted's Central Park. This wide avenue of high-end shops, offices and apartments, with St Patrick's Cathedral across the street, formed the approach armature to the new centre of the metropolis, just as the Champs Elysées led from the Louvre to the Arc de Triomphe in Paris. From Central Park the height of the RCA tower amongst the forest of Midtown skyscrapers branded the city skyline with the RCA corporate logo, its red neon, modern, sans-serif letters symbolising the new metropolis at night.

American comic books captured the dynamic of this new metropolis, integrating it into the urban mythology and poetry of the fictitious Gotham City. Comic book illustrators portrayed Gotham as a city of skyscrapers inhabited by Superman, Batman, Wonder Woman and other such urban heroes (all urban mutants with specialised powers). Later, Hollywood films reproduced this imagery on screen. Superman battles the forces of evil to clean up the city. Unlike Goethe's *Faust* (1808), he never falls into the hands of the devil or dark side, betraying the citizen's trust and demolishing beloved parts of the city.[9] Instead, Superman triumphs through his ability to fly and experience the city in three dimensions, offering young readers a tantalising promise of future aerial mobility in the complex, layered metropolis.[10]

Besides building the new symbolic centre of the American metropolis, the Rockefeller Brothers Fund also supported the research of the New York Regional Plan Association (RPA) in the 1930s, when the City Planning Department did not have the resources or manpower to plan the future of the metropolis.[11] The RPA imagined a linear city region stretching up the Hudson Valley to the state government capital in Albany, and then westwards towards Chicago. This reorganisation of the hinterland would provide water, food, industrial locations and recreational opportunities for Gotham's citizens, with access provided by high-speed railway lines to the centre.

A more detailed RPA hinterland study of the New York City region in 1939 showed a series of ring and radial roads around the metropolis, linking New Jersey and Connecticut into its orbit and creating a Garden City region of suburbs. The plan proposed to move the main pedestrian level of the city up one floor above the traffic in Midtown and around dense transport hubs like Grand Central. Hugh Ferris drew these hubs as gigantic skyscraper clusters tapering towards their peaks.[12] Robert Moses would later use this plan as his guide in equipping the metropolis and its hinterland for the auto age. In his case, he proposed elevating the highways as they cut through the buildings of the city centre and ran around Manhattan's waterfront edge.[13]

In the background to these huge metropolitan clusters portrayed by Ferris lay the basic elements of New York City, the grid planned by the City Commissioners in 1811, coupled with the New York City 'setback' Zoning Code of 1916. The grid building massing was controlled by setback regulations linked to the width of the street, to ensure sunlight and daylight penetration (modelled on Parisian boulevard codes). Skyscrapers were exceptional elements in this urban fabric, occupying a Special District under the 1916 New York Zoning Code around Wall Street. Most of the city grid housed low- and mid-rise residential districts, where the new urban immigrants developed social organisations and associations through work, leisure, church and politics to replace lost rural or national community links.[14]

With in the grid, New York neighbourhoods, like those surveyed by the pioneering urban sociologists Robert Park and Ernest Burgess in Chicago in the 1920s, developed strong local characteristics, both ethnic and functional, as part of the specialisation and segregation that powered such great cities. The metropolis ironically thus housed a linked system of neighbourhoods or urban villages, each with their social services, schools, commercial centre and parks, often concentrated around a street armature. Park and Burgess described an 'ecology' of immigrant flows in the city, as groups moved in orderly succession through neighbourhoods up the social ladder to respectability and suburban lives as middle-class citizens.[15]

Robert Moses, as City Parks Commissioner in the 1930s, had added innumerable small parks to both rich and poor city neighbourhoods. He had also begun a Parkway system of auto-only highways leading out to wealthy garden suburb settlements, like Riverdale in the Bronx, as well as Jones Beach, Long Island (a huge public beach resort for the metropolitan masses, only reachable by car). By the 1950s Moses, as Commissioner of the independent New York Bridge and Tunnel Authority, was ideally positioned to add to this road system with Federal Highway and Slum Clearance grants. He modelled his schemes on the modernist housing blocks of Le Corbusier, reduced by budget cuts to minimal, utilitarian towers and slab blocks.[16] Garment industry union leaders shared this ideal, building Co-op City, a gigantic new town of 35 slab and tower blocks in the Bronx (1968–71).[17]

Stretched armatures: Moscow as a global metropolis in 1945

In 1945 there was a competing global model of the metropolis, that of Stalin's Moscow. This city was badly damaged in the war but possessed a clear master plan with a distinctive, Communist layout, without skyscraper clusters (or private property). In the West the Moscow model and the Soviet system is relatively unknown because of the legacy of the Cold War. The Soviet metropolis was an important beacon for many newly formed independent nations emerging from the control of European empires and their capitalist economies.

As in the imperial past, the new Soviet metropolis required appropriate symbolic representation at its heart in Moscow, its world capital, replacing St Petersburg in 1918. In the 1930s Stalin enlarged the symbolic, central, ceremonial square of Moscow, Red Square, building Lenin's Tomb along with widening the approach street. On Gorky Street, buildings were moved back on rollers and new apartments above stores created for the administrators of the new state apparatus, leading down to Red Square (which itself sloped down to the river). This 70-metre-wide (200-foot) approach street was modelled on Napoleon's Champs Elysées in Paris, with its wide sidewalks and long traffic islands separating different traffic flows.[18]

In Stalin's eyes its greater length, size and width showed the triumph of the Soviet proletariat over the old corrupt bourgeoisie. Hitler's unbuilt scheme for Berlin had a similar architecture, scale and logic as designed by Albert Speer.[19] The same formal approach could be found in Western Europe in the Beaux-Arts tradition, though at a reduced scale, as in Auguste Perret's work in Le Havre that we will examine in the next chapter. Many Western European Social Democrats and Communists looked to the USSR for urban models, like the young Aldo Rossi in Italy. In addition, after the Yalta Pact in 1945 the whole of Eastern Europe came under the Soviet sphere of influence, so the Moscow model took on a new relevance in East Berlin, Warsaw, Prague, Budapest and Bucharest.[20]

The Soviet metropolis represented the Communist ideal of urban design without private property, theoretically freeing people from care though extensive social welfare programmes, with free education and health care, as well as heavily subsidised housing. The city's master planners coordinated with the planners of the national economy so theoretically everyone had everything they needed and was free to enjoy their leisure. Because of efficient state planning and good infrastructure, including a monumental underground metro system, there would be no need to have dense clusters of skyscrapers and everyone would have access to sunlight, parks and clean air in carefully designed new superblock neighbourhood units. Skyscrapers would serve symbolic state purposes and be placed at intervals on ring roads, housing universities, hotels or ministries. The Soviet war dead, who numbered in many millions, would be commemorated in big public statues on hills outside strategic cities, such as Mother Russia at St Petersburg (Leningrad), Volgograd (Stalingrad) or Kiev in the Ukraine, all built in the 1950s and 1960s.[21]

Soviet urban designers in 1945 followed the rigid directives of the Communist Party about the correct symbolic displays of power in the city and their proper distribution, using stretched armatures, wide boulevards and subways as connectors. The urban designs adhered to the Moscow ring-and-radial plan, with its green belts and satellite new towns, following the Ebenezer Howard Garden City model, but at far higher densities. Later, Khrushchev-era mass-produced six- or eight-storey slab blocks continued this pattern.[22] Soviet designers constructed these new 'microdistrict' (microraion, with 8,000 to 12,000 population) superblock neighbourhoods on the periphery of many central European cities as well as Moscow.[23] As well as building the palatial Moscow Metro system for Stalin, Khrushchev was intimately involved in this effort to quickly improve Soviet urban living conditions, his modernising efforts showing in the modern towers of the Novy Arbat Street development, Moscow (1968). Each new neighbourhood was theoretically self-contained, with social services, schools and hospitals, workers' clubs, factories and offices, a police station, fire station, sewage system, water supply, parks and playgrounds scaled to its population. Zelenograd (1958) a 'closed', secret science city built just outside Moscow as the Soviet answer to Silicon Valley, contains 15 microdistricts.[24]

The 'microdistrict (superblock enclave concept) could also be applied to historic cities and neighbourhood as in Warsaw, for instance, a city whose centre was blown up by the retreating Nazis. After the war the local Communist party decided to rebuild the old city

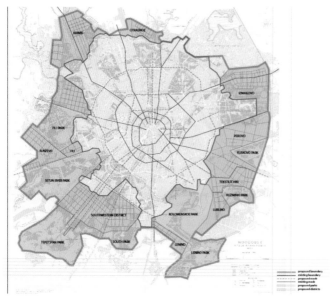

Joseph Stalin, Ring–Radial Plan, Moscow, Russia, 1935, revised 1957
Stalin's plan combined Ebenezer Howard's Garden City plan for London (1896) with Haussmann's Beaux-Arts Paris boulevards from the 1860s, to transform Moscow into a Communist metropolis. This hybrid of grand boulevards, green belts and satellite new towns became an attractive, anti-capitalist model for many nations emerging from the European colonial system to independence in the 1950s and 1960s. (Drawing © David Grahame Shane and Masha Panteleyeva)

Joseph Stalin, Red Square, Moscow, Russia, 1930s (photo 1963)
Stalin enlarged Red Square to become the central, symbolic place for the Soviet Revolution, replacing the old capital in St Petersburg and setting Lenin's Tomb as a reviewing stand for Soviet Army parades below the imperial Kremlin Castle walls. The Cathedral of Christ the Saviour, at the lower end of the slope to the Moskva River, was demolished in 1931 for this project and has since been rebuilt (2000). (Photo © Central Press/Stringer/Getty Images)

Novy Arbat Street, Moscow, Russia (photo 2009)
Stalin's ring–radial plan for Moscow called for new avenues to be cut from the centre, following the
example of Gorky Street from the 1930s. In 1956 Krushchev denounced Stalinist architecture, allowing
the introduction of modern residential and commercial skyscrapers above a continuous, commercial
podium in the Novy Arbat radial boulevard and microdistrict (completed 1968). (Photo © David
Grahame Shane, courtesy of class members 'CiudadLab: Utopia in Moscow' (www.ciudadlab.com),
ArqPOLI: School of Architecture, Polytechnic University of Puerto Rico)

core using paintings from the 1800s as a guide, since all the city plans had been destroyed.[25]
At the same time, the urban designers decided to run a new highway and streetcar system
under the new centre, creating a concrete platform on which all the new-old facades would
be set with modern construction behind. The new highways and streetcars along broad
armatures led out to a new government district on the edge of the centre, where Stalin's gift of
a wedding-cake skyscraper as a science and cultural centre symbolised Poland's dependent
relationship with Moscow. Similar schemes could be found in East Berlin, focusing on Karl
Marx Allee leading to the old centre, or in Dresden where the old central square was built at a
new scale, eradicating the old city plan. In all these cities the majority of the urban population
lived in the new 'microdistrict' neighbourhoods in Krushchev slab blocks set in parkland on
the surrounding ring roads.

Market Square (Rynek Starego Miasra), Warsaw, Poland (photo 1994)
The retreating Nazi army dynamited the historic core of Warsaw in 1945, but the Polish Communist Party decided to rebuild the central square and castle as a national symbol in 1947. This photograph shows the central square closed to protest unchecked extortion and intimidation by organised crime gangs in 1994. (Photo © Chris Niedenthal/Getty Images)

Lev Rudnev, Palace of Culture and Science, Warsaw, Poland, 1952–4 (photo 2000)
Stalin gave this wedding-cake skyscraper to Poland as a 'gift', placing it on the new ring road around the old city. This photograph shows the 1960s Khrushchev-era boulevard across the street with modern towers above a continuous commercial podium, one of the towers being converted into a giant Coca-Cola billboard in 2000. (Photo © Laski Diffusion/Getty Images)

Nowa Huta New Town, Poland, 1956
The Polish Communist Party built the Nowa Huta steel mill, which became the largest in Europe,
to rapidly transform peasants into modern industrial workers housed in Stalinist boulevards. The
plant – now owned by an Indian conglomerate – and new town were intended to represent the
new socialist society at its best. (Photo © Adam Golec/Agencja Gazeta)

Microdistricts also played a prominent role housing peasants from Eastern Europe, who
were moved to work in new industries within new towns that were required to modernise
the state and rapidly raise living standards. Communist planners sought to break the hold
of the Catholic Church and feudal landlords by moving the Eastern European peasantry to
giant factory complexes to become modern workers, following the example of Magnitogorsk
in Russia in the 1930s. This rapid industrialisation model had in turn been modelled on the
19th-century American steel boom town of Pittsburg. Stalinstadt (Eisenhüttenstadt) in East
Germany and Nowa Huta in Poland near Kiev (Ukraine) were prime examples of this heavy
industry new-town strategy. The steel mill at Nowa Huta grew to be the largest in Europe.[26]
Propaganda films of the period praised the young 'Volunteers' who moved to the city to
build the Stalinist housing blocks laid out along grand avenues, stretched armatures leading
to a central square. Andrzej Wajda's film of the champion bricklayer of the period, *Man of
Iron* (1980), looks back at the human costs of this effort and the Party's cynical manipulation
of workers. Few people knew the repressive nature of the Soviet regime despite the tanks
putting down rebellions in public squares in East Berlin (Germany) in 1953, in Budapest
(Hungary) in 1956 and in Prague (Czechoslovakia) in 1968.[27] The secret police, gulags and
work camps were hidden from view.[28] In plain view the broad avenues of Nowa Huta and new
housing, changing to Krushchev slab blocks in the 1960s, represented a considerable urban
achievement and rapid modernisation of society.

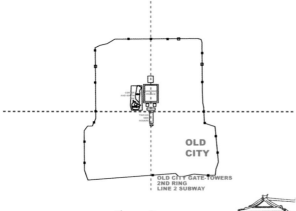

Liang Sicheng, city-wall-park, plan for Beijing, China, 1951
Soviet and Central European advisors planned for a ring-and-radial pattern of development in Beijing, with an east–west axis of industrial development in the south. This new city district was designed to counter the imperial north–south axis of power and to house the new industrial proletariat. Liang Sicheng proposed instead a city-wall-park, 1951, and a new administrative district to the west (not shown). (Plan © Sy Lyng Yong)

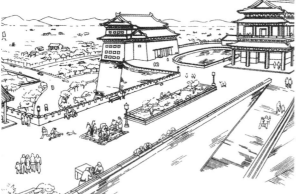

Liang Sicheng, proposed city-wall-park, Beijing, China, 1951
Mao decided against this linear wall-top proposal and an associated plan for a new administrative city to the west of Beijing. Instead the walls were demolished for a ring road and subway. Liang Sicheng went on to become the champion of traditional Chinese architecture and historic preservation in Beijing. (Photo © Lin Zhu)

Mao Zedong, Tiananmen Square, Beijing, China, remodelled 1954 (photo 2007)
This photograph shows Mao's view of Tiananmen Square, which he enlarged for mass demonstrations and military parades so that it would be larger than Red Square, Moscow. The Great Hall of the People and the National Museum of China frame Mao's Mausoleum (inserted in 1977) near the site of an old imperial gate. (Photo © Zeng Li)

The Soviet metropolitan and new-town satellite model not only dominated Eastern Europe after 1945, it was also exported around the world to sympathetic states that wanted to modernise quickly, celebrate their freedom from colonial status and show their opposition to capitalist economic development. Mao Zedong greatly admired Stalin and after the Communist Revolution in 1949 adapted the Soviet schemes to Beijing. Beijing planners created a ring–radial plan radiating out from the Imperial Palace in the Forbidden City, which became a museum. Tiananmen Square was enlarged to be five times larger than Red Square. The University of Pennsylvania-trained Chinese architect Liang Sicheng advised Mao and the Communist party, drawing up a scheme for a new satellite government centre on Beaux-Arts lines parallel to the Imperial Palace, on a new north–south axis of power further west.[29] Mao rejected this plan, and instead, following Soviet advice, he developed a counter-axis, from east to west, widening Chang'an Boulevard as a stretched armature, giant boulevard. Soviet planners developed an east–west linear industrial belt with workers' housing to the south of the imperial city (1953–4), in a first ring of a multiring model copied from Moscow (including an underground metro system). Further out, new towns and housing microdistricts in superblocks were planned beyond green belts. The microdistricts were built around factories, and work-unit brigades formed the basic social organisation of the new city, providing for all the workers' needs. At the optics- and electronics-producing Factory 798 at Dashanzi outside Beijing (1954), for instance, East German planners and engineers created a complete workers' microdistrict, with its own modern works, housing blocks, schools, hospital, police station and administrative offices, housing 10,000 to 12,000 people at its peak (it later became Beijing's arts district).[30] China exported its adaptation of the Moscow metropolitan model to Pyongyang, North Korea, where it became preserved in amber.

Mao's metropolitan example impressed many leaders of newly independent states in Asia who also sought Soviet help to industrialise rapidly. India's Nehru, who employed Le Corbusier at Chandigarh in 1947 (see chapter 4), also sought the help of Soviet technicians to plan a new steel town at Rourkela, Orissa to give India a modern industrial base.[31] Nasser, the Egyptian nationalist president, turned to the USSR for finance and technology to build the Aswan Dam on the Nile after the Suez Crisis of 1956. He built Nasr City as a modern new town outside Cairo in the1960s, an extension to the earlier Heliopolis.[32] Sukarno, who led Indonesia to independence from the Dutch colonial empire in 1949, also looked to Moscow, initiating a central symbolic Monas National Monument (1961) as well as planning a great state street armature Jalan Sudirman at the centre, with growth scattered in new towns across multiple islands around Jakarta.[33] Nkrumah, who led Ghana to independence in 1957, brought Soviet designers to build a huge hydroelectric dam on Lake Volta, as well as equipping Accra, the first independent capital in Africa, with an Independence Arch, Independence Avenue and Square, a state theatre and Pan-African Conference Centre.

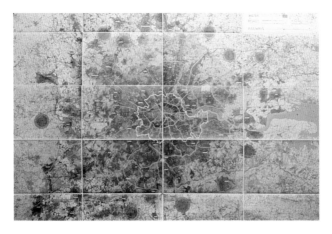

Patrick Abercrombie and John Henry Forshaw, Greater London Plan, UK, 1944
Prepared while bombs were still falling on London, this plan adapted Ebenezer Howard's *Garden Cities of To-morrow* (1902) ring-and-radial strategy with a 5-kilometre-deep (3-mile) Green Belt and 27 new towns. This proposal became law in 1947, leading to the construction of new towns like Harlow (1947) and new neighbourhood units like Lansbury (1949–53) in the heavily damaged East End. (Plan © courtesy of HMSO)

The city region: London and the European metropolis in 1945

At the end of the Second World War, large parts of London, Berlin and Moscow lay in ruins. These cities, along with Paris, Brussels, Copenhagen and Stockholm, had emerged by the end of the 19th century as centres of global empires. The facade of the old Imperial Hotel on Russell Square in London featured a map that showed how the sun never set on the British Empire. Ports connecting to empires – such as Portsmouth, Plymouth or Liverpool in Britain, Marseilles, Cherbourg or Le Havre in France, Hamburg in Germany, Antwerp in Belgium or Rotterdam in Holland – all suffered major damage in the war. Nazi U-boats restricted colonial trade, at one point reducing Britain to a six-week supply of food. In response, the British government promoted urban agriculture and allotment gardens. Meanwhile German bombers targeted the London Docks in the East End of London, at the heart of the British Empire.[34]

Against this background, Patrick Abercrombie and John Henry Forshaw began in 1943 to plan London as a modern, regional metropolis, leading to the Greater London Plan of 1944. Abercrombie had been Professor of Town Planning at the University of Liverpool in the 1930s and had prepared regional plans for smaller British cities. In London he applied the Garden City principles first advocated by Ebenezer Howard in his *To-morrow: A Peaceful Path to Real Reform* (1898; reprinted in 1902 as *Garden Cities of To-morrow*).[35] Howard argued that the new metropolis would consist of an old core city, the mother city, plus a ring of new satellite cities connected by ring-and-radial railway lines. This model had provided the inspiration for the Moscow Plan of 1936.

Howard never specified how the centre of the mother city would be reconstructed when people moved to the new towns. This became an urgent question in London after the war as London's population was 'decanted' from bombed areas, leaving the Nissen huts and prefabs temporarily built to house them. Abercombie proposed 27 new towns around London, beyond a three-mile-deep (five-kilometre) statutory Green Belt. His plan became law in 1947 as part of an experiment in social-democratic central planning by the Labour Government elected after the end of the Second World War. Like many European countries faced with the loss of empire, Britain introduced an extensive series of welfare programmes at home offering free health care, education, housing and unemployment benefits (mirroring the services offered in Soviet Russia).[36] All these services required new buildings, involving new hospitals, university campuses, schools and offices, as well as industrial estates. Urban designers and architects, like Frederick Gibberd, were involved in laying out these new town centres and their facilities.

London had a tradition of public authorities stretching back from the Royal Office of Public Works in the early 1800s to the creation of the London County Council (LCC) in 1888. This Council had long been controlled by the working-class Labour Party and seized the opportunity of the post-war reconstruction to advance its agenda. The LCC had never been able to extend the Aldwych–Kingsway, its 30-metre-wide (100-foot), Beaux-Arts, imperial axis begun in 1904, across central London from north to south.[37] Because of the First World War this was not completed until the 1930s with the construction of a series of imperial institutions – Canada House, India House and Bush House, the home of the BBC World Service. Abercombie's plan renounced such cross-centre grand boulevards, placing them in tunnels so as not to disturb the historic fabric of the capital.

The Nazi bombing of the south bank of the Thames presented the LCC with a great urban design opportunity for a new public enclave, opposite the Houses of Parliament in Westminster. The site was close to the continuation of the Aldwych–Kingsway armature south across Waterloo Bridge (completed 1945) to Waterloo Station. On this site the Labour Government and LCC presented the Festival of Britain Exhibition in 1951 in an austere time of food rationing, commemorating the first World's Fair held at the Crystal Palace, Hyde Park, London in 1851.[38]

The LCC prepared ambitious plans for urban designs on the South Bank site after the Festival of Britain closed. Their Architects' Department built the Hayward Gallery (1968) beside the Royal Festival Hall (1951) to one side of the Waterloo Bridge approach, and the Government built Denys Lasdun's National Theatre (1976–7) to the other side further east along the esplanade. The British oil company Royal Dutch Shell decided to construct its new headquarters beside Waterloo Station at the Shell Centre (Sir Howard Robertson, 1957–62).[39] Perhaps thinking of the Rockefeller Center, Shell insisted on a skyscraper tower with preserved open vista to the Thames through a plaza that has still not been constructed. In the late 1960s the LCC planned an opera house beside the Royal Festival Hall, but the Jubilee Gardens, the central plaza, has remained an open parking lot and undeveloped green space for 50 years.

This failure of urban design in the centre of the old imperial metropolis at the foot of a tower of one of the great global corporations is deeply symbolic of the changed role of European empires as global corporations came to the fore. This failure contrasts strongly with the success of the reorganisation of the hinterland planned by Abercrombie, where new neighbourhoods were built in the bombed East End and new towns built beyond the Green Belt.[40] The Labour government set up funds to enable the LCC to buy up bomb sites and plan large neighbourhood units as high-rise superblocks in the East End or enable New Town Authorities to build large Garden City cottage estates in the new towns.

Gibberd planned and designed Harlow New Town (1947, where he lived) and also the model Festival of Britain Lansbury Housing Estate (1949–51) in the East End (he also designed Heathrow Airport's new airline terminals in west London in 1955). Both Lansbury and Harlow centred on a focal square with an open-air market enclave and an approach street armature containing shops, linked to the town hall, civic centre and gardens in the case of Harlow.[41] Outside London, industrial cities like Coventry received successful new multilevel commercial centre implants linked to civic centres. Abercrombie himself redesigned the heart of the port city of Plymouth as a grid of shops and offices, with a grand armature on the cross axis leading down from the station and up to the town hall complex with views to the sea from Plymouth Hoe.[42] He provided for parking inside the commercial blocks, so that the grand armatures feel empty and most people now enter the city from the back parking lots.

Gibberd was unusual in that he wrote an important manual on urban design, *Town Design* (1953).[43] In this book he demonstrated a deep understanding of the imperial, Baroque and Beaux-Arts tradition of the metropolis, carving out space inside the city fabric for boulevards and squares, with distinct green belts and city boundaries from the countryside. Yet he also showed an appreciation of the art of positioning buildings in open space, of sizing and scaling buildings at intervals in the landscape. In particular he included early American examples of shopping malls as urban designs. He compared these simple armature-and-enclave designs directly to his own practices at Lansbury and Harlow. He also surveyed Europe, including behind the Iron Curtain (the rebuilding of Warsaw, for instance), with a particular admiration for the Scandinavian capitals, such as Stockholm, that will be examined in the next chapter.

The new European metropolis: revising the city section, Berlin, 1958

Caught between the clustered skyscrapers of New York and the scattered towers and social planning of Moscow with its superblock neighbourhood units, European designers faced the decline of their cities and of their empires' global role. By the end of the 1950s, modern architects argued that the old Beaux-Arts and imperial formula would not work in the age of the automobile. Le Corbusier's entry to the 1958 competition sponsored by the City of West Berlin shows his commitment to the symbolic display of state power, positioning state buildings on significant axes, with subsidiary residential units, commercial and industrial areas, all served by highways. Historic buildings stood as isolated monuments in the surrounding parkland. This design will be examined further in the next chapter in comparison to his built work at Chandigarh, India.

Frederick Gibberd, Harlow New Town, Harlow, UK, 1947
A central market square and main shopping street leads to the municipal civic centre and garden terraces, sloping down to a linear park along a streambed, surrounded by new self-contained neighbourhood units. In the 1970s the commercial centre shifted into a modern interior mall built behind the municipal building, and in the 1990s this building and the terraced civic gardens were rebuilt to accommodate underground parking garages for big-box retail developments. (Photo © David Grahame Shane)

The imperial, Beaux-Arts geometry and scale remained as memory traces in Le Corbusier's modern design. He did not win the 1958 Berlin competition as he expected, but another entry by the younger Smithsons team, future members of the breakaway Team X Group that would split off from the International Congress of Modern Architecture (CIAM) in 1959, received second prize.[44] The Smithson team also anticipated the arrival of the automobile in the centre of the historic city set in parkland. But their city did not emphasise the monumental, symbolic dimension of the state. They attempted to recombine urban functions in a new hybrid code that allowed for small-scale social and commercial interactions. At the same time they tried to remain true to the revolution in building construction that made modern space and services so appealing.

Like the New York RPA Plan of 1929, the Smithsons proposed to raise pedestrians up above the road system on a segregated deck system. Service and parking would be below this deck where commercial uses would animate street life in the 'fingers' stretching between small towers. Elevators in these towers would connect to a mixed-use section above, with offices and then housing. The Smithsons' Economist Building in London (1964) was a miniature, single-use, infill demonstration of this podium-and-tower idea.[45] In the Berlin scheme, most of the housing was in huge curving walls of apartments on the perimeter of the site overlooking the new city centre whose 'fingers' zigzagged over the old street grid and void of the parkland.

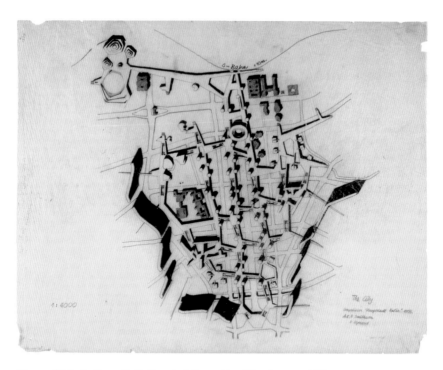

Alison and Peter Smithson, Berlin Haupstadt Competition, West Germany, 1958
The mixed-use section of this project placed the car at ground level in parkland, while the zigzagging 'finger buildings' connected the small tower clusters above, creating a network of communication between a multi-centric system of commercial nodes. This design suggested there might be multiple urban actors networked together in the city, creating a new dynamic metropolis without a single centre. (Drawing © Collection of the German Museum of Architecture, Frankfurt am Main, Germany)

The mixed-use section of the Smithsons' project broke one of the taboos of the CIAM code, while the zigzagging 'finger buildings' connecting the small tower clusters created a network of communication between a multi-centric system of commercial nodes. Instead of a single centre and Le Corbusier's concentration of enclaves along the spine leading to the 'head' administrative centre, this design suggested there might be multiple urban actors networked together in the city, creating a new dynamic. This low-rise mat of pedestrian decks, small towers and local roads would allow the car to penetrate into the city, while remaining flexible and adaptable on the upper levels. Students from the Smithsons' classes applied this lesson to the Mid-Levels in Hong Kong in the late 1980s, designing a wonderful upper-level escalator system, built in the early 1990s, that climbs the hill, intersecting with roads running across the contour and creating a dense urban grid filled with small towers and shop-house streets.

Conclusion: the metropolis in the late 20th century

Writing in 1978, Rem Koolhaas titled his first book *Delirious New York: A Retroactive Manifesto for Manhattan*.[46] By that date he thought metropolitan design and 'Manhattanism' was dead, killed by sprawling suburban growth, and he wanted to return to the big architecture of dense urban fragments, cities within cities, like the Rockefeller Center that featured prominently in his text. He named his own office the Office for Metropolitan Architecture (OMA, founded in 1975 with Elia and Zoe Zenghelis and Madelon Vriesendorp). The dream of the modern metropolis, without an empire, lived on as global commercial corporations took over in place of the European powers. In *Delirious New York* the skyline, marked and created by corporate skyscrapers, replaced the old imperial grand axes as demonstrations of an urban actor's power. Koolhaas was prescient in anticipating and spotting this shift, leading to his triumph at the CCTV Tower in Beijing (2002).[47] Here the Chinese national media giant built a symbolic tower to demonstrate its power in the new global network system, branding the skyline of Beijing with their distinct image. In the same period the rulers of China chose to place the new Olympic Park on axis with the old imperial north–south axis of the Forbidden City, ordering all the factories of the old Russian-designed east–west industrial belt to close during the Olympics to improve the air quality.[48] Ancient, modern and contemporary versions of the metropolis collided in these decisions, demonstrating the continued power of this ancient urban design concept in 2008.

Koolhaas's panegyric to the metropolis was 'retrospective' because cities in America went into precipitous decline as they were impacted by the growth of other urban systems favouring dispersal and fragmentation. The dropping of the atomic bomb in Japan had shown that the metropolis as a dense urban form was extremely vulnerable. In the USA, special subsidies favoured the switch to oil as a cheap energy source, supporting urban dispersal. The new energy source made the old freight railways, docks and coal mines redundant, favouring airports, trucks and highway developments. The old waterfront industrial cities became abandoned as new container ports and truck transfer stations moved to out-of-town locations, strategically located by highway connections. Factories and industries followed a similar logic, searching for cheap land to develop. New York almost went bankrupt in 1975.[49] Detroit became the classic example of the shrinking metropolis as documented by the Fabulous Ruins of Detroit website in the 1990s or photographer Camilo Vergara in his *American Ruins* (1999).[50]

Large areas of the metropolis became abandoned and local inhabitants had started small gardens on vacant lots, beginning the Green Thumb urban agriculture movement in New York.[51] In other parts of the city, drugs and prostitution ruined previously well-kept residential areas, while unemployed youth gangs patrolled the ruined streets. In America a long series of urban riots in large cities blighted the idea of the metropolis in the 1960s, as middle-class families moved to the suburbs in three great waves (40 million moved in 15 years).[52] New financial and business centres emerged in skyscraper districts, but other parts of the metropolis were unsafe. This created a dystopian image of the city highlighted in such films as *Blade Runner* (1982). While oil was cheap and land available on the periphery,

Morphosis, Phare Office Tower, La Défense business district, Paris, France, 2008 (photo 2008)
In order to protect the historic metropolitan skyline of Paris, dominated by the Eiffel Tower, the French government pioneered a special, mini-Manhattan, high-rise business district on the imperial axis to the west of the Arc de Triomphe in 1958. Recent efforts to spruce up this ageing commercial enclave have included the Grande Arche (Johann Otto von Spreckelsen, 1989) and the innovative Phare mixed-use skyscraper-mall, designed by Morphosis in 2008. (Photo © Unibail-Morphosis)

Americans moved to the outer suburbs, sapping the strength of the metropolis and resulting in a definition of a city that was primarily suburban and car based by the 1980s, as in the New Urbanism movement. The terrorist attacks of 11 September 2001 demonstrated yet again the vulnerability of the metropolis, but also showed its resilience as help flowed in from the megalopolis, the American hinterland.

Despite the decay of the metropolis in America, other countries around the word looked to New York rather than Moscow for their model of the metropolitan ideal. By the early 2000s, even the corporate moguls of Moscow sought to make their mark on the city skyline with their own mini-Manhattan area on the Third Moscow Ring, the Moscow International Business Centre.[53] This dense cluster of skyscraper towers sought to rival other business districts, replacing old factories. In the same period the Chinese Communist government established a similar metropolitan cluster of business towers at Pudong in Shanghai and on the Beijing 'Financial Street' designed by SOM as part of the International Financial Centre on the Second Ring west of the Forbidden City.[54] The French government pioneered this mini-Manhattan financial model in 1958 at La Défense, Paris, west of the Arc de Triomphe, on axis with the Louvre, in order to save the historic fabric of Paris. Fifty years later the area is still under development and in need of renovation.[55] The American firm Morphosis recently won a competition for a spectacular new 'Phare' (Lighthouse) skyscraper there, an innovative design that merges into a multistorey shopping mall leading to the car parks, Metro and regional railway lines below the base podium and rooftop plaza.[56] The metropolis still lives!

Notes

NB: See 'Author's Caution: Endnote Sources and Wikipedia', towards the end of this book.

1 On New York and Moscow, see: Tony Judt, *Postwar: A History of Europe Since 1945*, Penguin (New York), 2006, pp 112 and 218–25.

2 On the metropolis and its imperial hinterland, see: Spiro Kostof, *The City Shaped: Urban Patterns and Meanings Through History*, Bulfinch Press (Boston, MA), 1991, pp 31–4.

3 On early metropolitan centres, see: Kevin Lynch, *A Theory of Good City Form*, MIT Press (Cambridge, MA), 1981, p 73.

4 On the European peasant population in 1950, see: Judt, *Postwar*, p 327.

5 For New York City's influence on Europe, see: Jean-Louis Cohen, *Scenes of the World to Come: European Architecture and the American Challenge, 1893–1960*, Flammarion (Paris) and Montreal (Canadian Centre for Architecture), c 1995.

6 Sigfried Giedion, *Space, Time and Architecture*, Harvard University Press (Cambridge, MA), 1941, p 845 (available on Google Books).

7 For oil, see: Paul Roberts, *The End of Oil: On the Edge of A Perilous New World*, Houghton Mifflin (New York), 2004 and Judt, *Postwar*, p 455.

8 On John Graham, see: ML Clausen, 'Northgate Regional Shopping Center – paradigm from the provinces', *Journal of the Society of Architectural Historians* (*JSAH*), vol XLIII, May 1984, pp 144–61; also: Barry Maitland, *Shopping Mall Planning and Design*, Nichols Publishing (New York), 1985, pp 109–25.

9 On Faust and the metropolis, see: Marshall Berman, *All That Is Solid Melts Into Air: The Experience of Modernity*, Viking Penguin (New York), 1982.

10 For Superman and Gotham, see: http://en.wikipedia.org/wiki/Metropolis_(comics) (accessed 1 April 2010).

11 On the Rockefellers and New York, see: Robert Fitch, *The Assassination of New York*, Verso (London; New York), 1993, pp 56–9. For the Rockefeller Center, see: Rem Koolhaas, *Delirious New York: A Retroactive Manifesto for Manhattan*, Oxford University Press (New York), 1978, pp 150–200; also: Matthew Gandy, *Concrete and Clay: Reworking Nature in New York City*, MIT Press (Cambridge, MA), 2003. For the RPA, see: Jonathan Barnett, *Planning for a New Century: The Regional Agenda*, Island Press (Washington DC), 2001.

12 For setbacks, see: Hugh Ferris, *The Metropolis of Tomorrow*, Princeton Architectural Press (Princeton, NJ) and Avery Library, Columbia University (New York), c 1986.

13 For highways and parks, see: Robert A Caro, *The Power Broker: Robert Moses and the fall of New York*, Knopf (New York), 1974. For the 1929 RPA Plan, see: David A Johnson, *Planning the Great Metropolis: The 1929 Regional Plan of New York and its Environs*, E & FN Spon (London), 1996; for Moses' re-evaluation, see: Robert C Morgan, 'Conceptualism: reevaluation or revisionism?', in *Global Conceptualism: Points of Origin, 1950s–1980s*, exhibition catalogue, Queens Museum of Art (Flushing, NY), 1999.

14 For history of NYC zoning code see: Jonathan Barnett, *An Introduction to Urban Design*, Harper & Rowe (New York), 1982, p 122; also: Department of City Planning, New York City, *The Zoning Handbook*, New York, 1990.

15   For the Neighborhood Theory, see: Robert E Park and Ernest W Burgess, 'The Growth of the City: an introduction to a research project' (1925), reprinted in Richard T Gates and Frederick Stout (eds), *The City Reader*, Routledge (London), 1996, pp 95–6. For urban enclaves, see: Mark Abrahamson, *Urban Enclaves: Identity and Place in the World*, Worth Publishers (New York), 2005.

16 For Moses' parks and parkways, see: Caro, *The Power Broker*. For Riverdale and the Bronx, see: Matthew Gandy, *Concrete and Clay*.

17 For Co-op City, see: Robert AM Stern, *New York 1960: Architecture and Urbanism between the Second World War and the Bicentennial*, Monacelli Press (New York), c 1995, pp 969–70.

18 For Gorky Street, Moscow, see: Greg Castillo, 'Gorki Street and the Design of the Stalin Revolution', in Zeynep Çelik, Diane Favro and Richard Ingersoll (eds) *Streets: Critical*

Perspectives on Public Spaces, University of California Press (Berkeley, CA), 1994, pp 57–63; also: Anatolle Kopp, *Constructivist Architecture in the USSR*, St Martin's Press (New York), 1985; also: http://en.wikipedia.org/wiki/Tverskaya_Street (accessed 8 March 2010).

19   For Speer in Berlin, see: Lars Olof Larsson, *Albert Speer: Le Plan de Berlin, 1937–1943*, Archives d'Architecture Moderne (Brussels), 1983.

20   On the Yalta Pact, see: Judt, *Postwar*, pp 101–2,109; also: Edward Crankshaw, *Khruschev's Russia*, Penguin Books (Harmondsworth, Middlesex; Baltimore, MD), c 1962, p 59. For East Berlin urban design, see: Peter Müller, 'Counter-Architecture and Building Race: Cold War politics and the two Berlins', *GHI Bulletin Supplement* 2, 2005, pp 101–14; also Elke Sohn, 'Organicist Concepts of City Landscape in German Planning after the Second World War', *Planning Perspectives*, vol 18, issue 2, April 2003, pp 499–523.

21   On the Soviet central planning system, see: Tony Judt, op cit, pp 170–72.

22   On Khruschev panel blocks, see: http://en.wikipedia.org/wiki/Khrushchyovka.

23   On microraion, microrayon, or microdistricts, see: http://en.wikipedia.org/wiki/Microdistrict (accessed 8 March 2010).

24   On secret cities, see: Vladislav M Zubok, *A Failed Empire: The Soviet Union in the Cold War from Stalin to Gorbachev*, University of North Carolina Press (Chapel Hill, NC), 2007 (available on Google Books).

25   On Warsaw Market Square, see: Treasures of Warsaw Online, http://www.um.warszawa.pl/v_syrenka/perelki/index_en.php?mi_id=48&dz_id=2 (accessed 12 February 2010); also: Müller, 'Counter-Architecture and Building Race', op cit, pp 104-14.

26   On Nowa Huta, see: Judt, *Postwar*, p 170; also: http://en.wikipedia.org/wiki/Nowa_Huta (accessed 8 March 2010).

27   For Andrzej Wajda, *Man of Iron*, 1981, see: the Internet Movie Database, http://www.imdb.com/title/tt0082222/ (accessed 12 February 2010).

28   For Gulag labour camps, see: Aleksandr Isaevich Solzhenitsyn, *The Gulag Archipelago, 1918–1956: An Experiment in Literary Investigation*, Harper & Row (New York), 1978. On Soviet labour camps and rapid industrialisation, see: Judt, *Postwar*, pp 194, 215. For Soviet prewar factory towns, see: http://en.wikipedia.org/wiki/Magnitogorsk (accessed 8 March 2010); also: NA Miliutin, *Sotsgorod: The Problem of Building Socialist Cities*, MIT Press (Cambridge, MA), c 1974, pp 21–3, 116.

29   On Liang Sicheng, see: Cultural China website, http://history.cultural-china.com/en/50H7635H12631.html (accessed 8 March 2010).

30   On the history of the 798 Art District, see: Cultural Heritage of China website, http://www.ibiblio.org/chineseculture/contents/arts/p-arts-c04s01.html (accessed 14 February 2010).

31   On Indian new towns and steel city plans, see: http://en.wikipedia.org/wiki/Rourkela (accessed 14 February 2010). On SAIL, see: http://en.wikipedia.org/wiki/Steel_Authority_of_India_Limited (accessed 14 February 2010). On Bokaro, see: http://www.statemaster.com/encyclopedia/Bokaro-Steel-City (accessed 14 February 2010).

32   On Nasr new town plan, see: http://en.wikipedia.org/wiki/Nasr_City (accessed 14 February 2010); also: Andrew Beattie, *Cairo: A Cultural History*, Oxford University Press (New York), 2005, p 201.

33   On Sukarno, see: http://en.wikipedia.org/wiki/Sukarno (accessed 27 February 2010). On Sudirman (a street named after Sukarno), see: http://en.wikipedia.org/wiki/Sudirman (accessed 14 February 2010).

34   On the British Empire and war rationing, see: Judt, *Postwar*, p 163.

35   Ebenezer Howard, *To-morrow: A Peaceful Path to Real Reform* (1898), reprinted as *Garden Cities of To-morrow*, Swan Sonnenschein & Co (London), 1902 (available on Google Books).

36   On Europe and the welfare state, see: Judt, *Postwar*, p 77–8.

37   For the LCC and Aldwych–Kingsway, see: George Laurence Gomme and London City Council, *Opening of Kingsway and Aldwych by His Majesty the King: Accompanied by Her Majesty the Queen, on Wednesday, 18th October, 1905*, printed for the Council by Southwood, Smith (London), 1905.

38 For the Festival of Britain (FOB), see: Mary Banham and Bevis Hillier (eds), *A Tonic to the Nation: The Festival of Britain 1951*, Thames & Hudson (London), 1976 (available on Google Books).

39 For the Royal Dutch Shell Centre, see: http://en.wikipedia.org/wiki/Shell_Centre (accessed 15 February 2010).

40 For London's East End, see: Patrick Abercrombie, *Town and Country Planning*, Oxford University Press (London; New York), 1959.

41 For Lansbury and Harlow, see: Frederick Gibberd, *Town Design*, Architectural Press (London), 1953, revised 1959.

42 For Plymouth, see: Brian Mosley, Plymouth Data website, http://www.plymouthdata.info/Plan%20for%20Plymouth.htm (accessed 15 February 2010).

43 Frederick Gibberd, *Town Design*, 1953, pp 9–124.

44 For the Smithsons' entry for the Berlin Haupstadt competition, see: Alison Smithson (ed) 'Team 10 primer', Team 10, 1965; also: Team 10 website: ttp://www.team10online.org/team10/projects/hauptstadt.htm (accessed 8 March 2010); also: Nicolai Ouroussoff, 'New Ideals for Building in the Face of Modernism', *The New York Times*, 27 September 2006, http://www.nytimes.com/2006/09/27/arts/design/27ten.html (accessed 8 March 2010).

45 For the Economist Building, see: Alison Smithson and Peter Smithson, *The Charged Void: Architecture*, Monacelli Press (New York), 2001.

46 Rem Koolhaas, *Delirious New York: A Retroactive Manifesto for Manhattan*, Oxford University Press (New York), 1978.

47 For the CCTV Tower, Beijing, see: OMA website, http://www.oma.eu/index.php?option=com_projects&view=portal&id=55&Itemid=10 (accessed 15 February 2010).

48 For air quality, see: Shai Oster, 'Will Beijing's Air Cast Pall Over Olympics?', *Wall Street Journal*, 15 February 2007, http://online.wsj.com/article/SB117148719982908969.html (accessed 15 February 2010); also: Jim Yardley, 'Cities Near Beijing Close Factories to Improve Air for Olympics', *The New York Times*, 7 July 2008, http://www.nytimes.com/2008/07/07/sports/olympics/07china.html (accessed 15 February 2010).

49 On New York City near bankruptcy in 1975, see: Ralph Blumenthal, 'Recalling New York at the Brink of Bankruptcy', *The New York Times*, 5 December 2002, http://www.nytimes.com/2002/12/05/nyregion/recalling-new-york-at-the-brink-of-bankruptcy.html?pagewanted=1 (accessed 15 February 2010).

50 Fabulous Ruins of Detroit website, http://www.detroityes.com/home.htm (accessed 15 February 2010); Camilo J Vergara, *American Ruins*, Monacelli Press (New York), 1999; see also: Kenneth T Jackson, *Crabgrass Frontier: The Suburbanization of the United States*, Oxford University Press (New York), 1985

51 See: Green Thumb New York City website, http://www.greenthumbnyc.org/about.html (accessed 15 February 2010).

52 See: Jackson, *Crabgrass Frontier*, pp 283–305.

53 On Moscow International Business Centre, see: http://en.wikipedia.org/wiki/Moscow_International_Business_Center (accessed 15 February 2010).

54 For Pudong, Shanghai, see: http://en.wikipedia.org/wiki/Pudong (accessed 15 February 2010). For Beijing Financial Street, see: http://en.wikipedia.org/wiki/Beijing_Financial_Street (accessed 20 February 2010).

55 For La Défense, see: 'A new era: La Défense 2006–2015', http://en.wikipedia.org/wiki/La_Défense (accessed 15 February 2010).

56 For the Phare Tower, see: Morphopedia website, http://morphopedia.com/projects/phare-tower (accessed 15 February 2010).

CHAPTER 4

Illustrated Metropolis

The dream of the metropolis took many forms across the globe. It always depended for its realisation on urban actors who dreamt of creating a metropolis in a particular location at a particular time. The previous chapter presented the three main variants of the metropolis, supported by powerful groups of commercial urban actors in New York, Communists in the Soviet Union and the old imperial powers in Western Europe, where the old metropolitan model of the Beaux-Arts was questioned.

This chapter will highlight three sets of different conditions where local actors transformed the metropolis. The first part looks at the declining European powers, especially France, where Haussmann had established an exemplary model of urbanism and urban design that was exported around the globe. Within France there was a lively debate about the future of the metropolis as the country lost a series of colonial wars, from Algeria to Vietnam, and the government needed to expand Paris to house returning nationals. Designers like Le Corbusier believed they held the key to the future, while their students designed new capitals for emerging nations, like Oscar Niemeyer in Brasil. An older generation – architects such as Auguste Perret – still looked back to Haussmann. Less well-known French architects like Fernand Pouillon worked in the hybrid space between these two attitudes in Marseilles, Algeria and the new towns of Paris.

The second part of the chapter studies variations in the metropolis in special situations, specifically the Scandinavian countries where an elaborate welfare state was established after 1945. Stockholm, a metropolis scattered across an archipelago of a thousand islands, provided a powerful model of an imperial capital transformed by urban renewal at the centre. Sven Markelius's design for the Hötorgscity (1952–6) created an exemplary new arts and business district in a complex, three-dimensional matrix. He also planned the new town Vällingby beyond a green belt (see chapter 2). This part of the chapter also looks at the internal stresses on the metropolis as European powers abandoned their empires and shrank their military under the American nuclear umbrella.[1] Many European cities shrank and lost population as people moved to new towns and new suburbs. Squatters and students, sometimes with artists and musicians, often moved into these abandoned areas. The Christiania commune established in Copenhagen in 1973 is an example that has still survived in an old military base.[2]

The hippies in the Christiania enclave were privileged exiles from a rich, industrialised, urban society, seeking freedom in a progressive ex-colonial power that generously supported the United Nations. This chapter also examines the internal stresses of the metropolis, as the city transformed under pressure from people moving into the city from

Some of the 14 million refugees moved as a consequence of the 1947 British Partition of India (photo 1947)
This photo shows a camp outside New Delhi, many such camps became permanent settlements initiating the UN's involvement with the Asian refugee problem. (Photo © Margaret BourkeWhite/Time & Life Pictures/Getty Images)

the countryside or between cities. War and decolonisation put extraordinary stresses on the metropolis, resulting in refugees and new immigrants around the world building shantytowns in Tokyo, Berlin, Rome and many other imperial capitals after the war.[3]

Margaret Bourke-White was an American photographer who travelled widely for the American *Time–Life* magazine chain, documenting refugees in Europe, Russia and China behind the Iron Curtain, and the consequences of the British Partition of India.[4] At the end of the British colonial regime, 7 million refugees crossed the division between India and Pakistan in 1947 in both directions, resulting in huge refugee camps, self-built shantytowns that prompted the UN to intervene with aid. The UN also became involved in Hong Kong in 1954 after the Shek Kip Mei fire made 50,000 refugees from Mao's China homeless on Christmas Eve, jump-starting the new town programme proposed earlier by Patrick Abercrombie for the British colony.[5]

Meanwhile the Brussels World's Fair of 1958 provided an opportunity for a global survey of the metropolis, both the new and old forces, both state and corporate, as well as the switch to the new energy sources of oil and atoms.[6] At the foot of the Atomium in Brussels, Belgium created an African show village, a replica of villages in its Congo colony (where decolonisation and alleged CIA covert action would lead to poverty, civil war and disaster after independence in 1961).[7] On the other side of the Atomium, a replica of a typical Belgian village housed cafés and stores selling chocolates. Another pavilion showed the construction of motorways across the Belgian countryside, while an oil company showed a model of a refinery. The Brussels World's Fair also housed a replica of the Soviet Sputnik satellite in the Soviet Pavilion, heralding a communications revolution.

The final part of the chapter highlights New York as a demonstration of both the triumph and the limits of the metropolis, leading on to the emergence of the megalopolis as a new form of city based on the automobile.

Nehru, the leader of newly independent India, conceived of Chandigarh as a replacement capital for the state of Punjab, divided by the Partition of 1947 from its old capital Lahore, set inside Pakistan. The centre of Lahore was torn apart in race riots in 1947 and rebuilt as a modern street armature by the Pakistani Lahore Development Trust (1956–7). The new town was symbolic of the desire to house some of the 7 million refugees created by the Partition. Le Corbusier raised the density of the housing from an earlier plan by Albert Mayer, while accepting the basic layout of highways and creating superblock neighbourhood districts with segregated commercial, industrial and administrative enclaves distributed across the city territory.[8]

While his architecture marked the triumph of the modern state, Le Corbusier's ambition was to create a new metropolitan entity in monumental Indian terms to rival Edwin Lutyens' colonial New Delhi. In Chandigarh the public agora of his dreams never was able to function as a successful urban space, in part because of local politics but also because of urban design flaws in scale and conception that made it inhospitable to human inhabitation.[9]

In the 1980s the Chilean architect Rodrigo Pérez de Arce proposed to construct small city blocks of low-rise, courtyard housing across this sacred agora, but in the meantime the residents of the neighbouring village of Kansal have used it productively as a grazing ground for their cattle.[10] Le Corbusier scaled his agora to the Himalayas, not the local population, and now his design is seen as an important precursor to the Landscape Urbanism of the 1990s and layered design of 'event-cities' schemes like Bernard Tschumi's Parc de la Villette project, Paris (1982).[11]

Le Corbusier, Berlin Haupstadt competition plan, 1958
Le Corbusier's last urban design repeated themes from his Ville Radieuse (1934) design, some of which also recurred in Chandigarh. He envisioned a separate monumental state area, a commercial centre, museum district and industrial area in the south, all set in parkland with housing in blocks reminiscent of his Unité d'Habitation in Marseilles (1946–52). (Plan © FLC/ADAGP, Paris and DACS, London 2009)

Le Corbusier, Chandigarh commercial centre, Punjab, India, 1950s (photo 2008)
Here Le Corbusier's associates employed his 'Maison Domino' formula of open floor plans and simple grids of columns to create a flexible and successful commercial town centre. Even so, three informal markets grew up in other open spaces in the town, specialising in local fruit and vegetables, like temporary farmers' markets elsewhere. (Photo © David Grahame Shane)

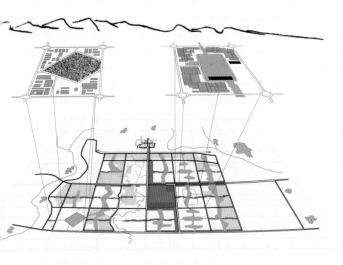

Le Corbusier's master plan for Chandigarh, Punjab, India, 1950s, redrawn to show pre-existing villages (redrawn by the author, 2010)
These villages are lodged inside the superblock neighbourhood units, each containing social facilities such as schools, shops and clinics. Le Corbusier did not participate in the design of the residential sectors, but the UN World Heritage Sites Committee has proposed the monumental agora and some housing sectors for historic preservation. (Redrawn plan © David Grahame Shane and Uri Wegman, 2010)

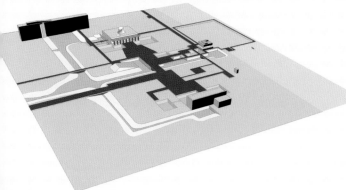

Le Corbusier, Chandigarh Capitol area, Punjab, India, 1950s (redrawn by the author, 2010)
Chandigarh was planned as the equivalent of Edwin Lutyens' New Delhi, with its axial Beaux-Arts arrangements symbolising the distribution of power between the various government agencies. Between these buildings, Le Corbusier planned a vertically segregated pedestrian and vehicular system crossing a great agora that was scaled to the distant Himalayas. (Redrawn drawing © David Grahame Shane and Uri Wegman, 2010)

Le Corbusier, Chandigarh Capitol area, Punjab, India, 1950s (photo 2008)
In Chandigarh the monumental administrative district was separated from the new town by a green belt. The neighbouring, pre-existing village of Kahal, never shown on Le Corbusier's plans, used the large agora between buildings as common land to graze cattle and play cricket. Ethnic divisions in the border state of Punjab also contributed to the construction of barbed wire security fences here, giving the planned agora an embattled face. (Photo © David Grahame Shane)

Lucio Costa's Pilot Plan for Brasilia, conceived in 1957, operated on a monumental scale.[12] The basic neighbourhood unit, the superquadra, was 300 metres by 300 metres (1,000 feet by 1,000 feet). Each neighbourhood unit contained 10 to 12 slab housing blocks raised on piloti columns to allow the landscape to flow beneath. The city was designed for automobiles and travelling at speed: although pedestrian paths were provided, the distances involved made car, bus or taxi a necessity.

Costa's bow-shaped curving highway brought the two residential wings together symmetrically about the monumental 'arrow' cross-axis of the Avenue of the Ministries. This avenue led from the radio tower at one end, by the national highway, to the twin towers and domes of the executive branch and two representative chambers, set against the shores of the artificial lake.

Brasilia has many obvious faults; its monumental scale is unrelenting, and its superquadras were deliberately made uniform, making it easy to get lost. Each superquadra has a complex address system, further adding to confusion, and the symmetrical north and south wings add a further element of confusion. A one-letter difference means the other side of town. In contrast to Rio de Janeiro, it is a calm oasis in the jungle and the life of the city is hidden in the informal *favelas* built by the construction workers in the surrounding region.

The government chose Costa's design because it wanted a monumental city to represent the nation. The public symbolism expressed the modernity of the state with an exemplary clarity and rigour. It drew on the Baroque and Beaux-Arts tradition of Europe for its power, but projected it on a tabula rasa, an empty jungle clearing. On a gigantic scale, the design re-created the metropolitan ideal of the structured and hierarchical approach to power. Although begun under a democratically elected and popular regime, it was completed under a military dictatorship and Oscar Niemeyer, the architect who designed the individual buildings of Brasilia, as a Communist, had to leave the country.[13]

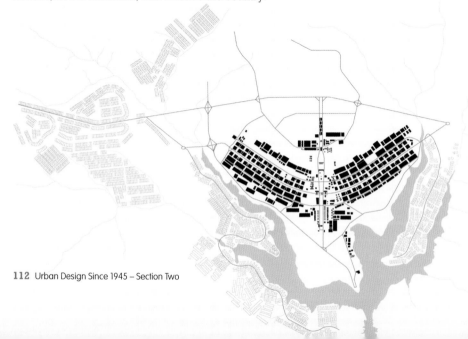

Lucio Costa, Avenue of the Ministries, Brasilia, Brazil, 1950s (photo 2004)
Lucio Costa and Oscar Niemeyer deliberately created a potent symbolic architecture and setting to express the power of the emerging modern nation in its new capital, the Latin American equivalent of Washington DC. The Avenue of the Ministries shown here was intended as Brazil's front lawn, like the Mall in Washington, a political space for the nation to gather in front of the symbols of power. (Photo © Paulo Fridman/Corbis)

Lucio Costa's master plan for Brasilia, Brazil, 1957,
redrawn to show workers' villages (redrawn by the author, 2010)
This dramatic 'bow and arrow' design contrasted the ceremonial axis of the Avenue of Ministries with the curving spine of the superquadra superblock residential neighbourhoods joined at the central intersection area (for banking, shopping, hotels and bus station). Each superquadra was an urban village with its own schools, parks, commercial centre and housing in eight-storey slab blocks (similar to those Le Corbusier had wanted in Chandigarh). (Redrawn plan © David Grahame Shane and Uri Wegman, 2009)

The French port city of Le Havre was heavily bombed in the Allies' invasion of Europe, making 40,000 people homeless. The reconstruction of Le Havre became an important symbolic act for the Allies, and the American Marshall Fund provided some of the finance for the project.[14] Perret, a modernist famous for his pioneering use of concrete, provided a conservative Beaux-Arts plan reminiscent of many Soviet designs, like the contemporary Karl Marx Allee in East Berlin. The scale was different from the Beaux-Arts original, but the public symbolism and organisational hierarchies were the same on both sides of the Iron Curtain.

Within this expanse of street grids, broad avenues and modernity, the decision to reconstruct the old port area on its old plan stands out as a strange anomaly. Here, as in Warsaw, the facades and plan of the old buildings were re-created between the two harbour basins, with modern construction behind. Another symbolic anomaly that distinguished Perret's design from contemporary Soviet work was that his concrete church spire higher up the hill towered over the City Hall skyscraper, an arrangement that would not have been tolerated in the USSR. From the sea this ecclesiastical dominance was especially marked.

Perret combined his enormous Beaux-Arts axes with modern housing blocks aligned with street and grid, creating a new hybrid metropolis. The result was reassuringly traditional in urban terms, while offering opportunities for mass production and standardisation of the buildings, a dream shared by Perret and Le Corbusier. The goal of this standardisation was to produce housing quickly and cheaply to shelter those made homeless by the war. Khrushchev in Moscow had similar goals but never achieved the refinement of proportion or detail of Perret, whose urban design is now listed as a UN World Heritage Site.[15]

Auguste Perret, Town Hall and Avenue Foch, Le Havre, France, 1947 onwards (photo 1959)
The monumental approach armature Avenue Foch leads from the cliffs overlooking the Channel to the square in front of the town hall. Perret, as a modernist, wanted an underground service level beneath the street, but he did succeed in creating an elegantly proportioned and detailed concrete panel housing block system, now listed as a UN World Heritage Site. (Photo © Roger Viollet/Getty Images)

Auguste Perret's plan for Le Havre, France, 1947 (redrawn by the author, 2010, to show urban villages)
Perret employed traditional Beaux-Arts urban design techniques at Avenue Foch leading to the city hall plaza. A subsidiary grid of housing blocks connected down to the old port behind a secondary avenue that followed the shoreline. The old port basins remained and a part of the old city was reconstructed using the old street patterns between the two port basins. (Redrawn plan © David Grahame Shane and Uri Wegman, 2010)

Sweden remained neutral in the Second World War and emerged unscathed and wealthy from the European carnage. The Swedish government supported the United Nations and provided peacekeepers in the world's trouble spots. At home, like many other northern European nations losing their empire, the government provided an extensive welfare programme. The City Council planned to rebuild the centre of Stockholm, demolishing a poor, medieval district that had once housed the hay market (Hötorget), replacing it with a new 'Hötorgscity' central business district.[16]

While the Hötorgscity is unmistakably modern, it also contains traces of the metropolitan tradition. It is located behind the old city core and Parliament Island, forming the commercial core of the city. It is beside the main shopping armature of the city and contains its own multi-level version of that armature within its design, connecting two important public squares. At its heart is Sergel's Square, where a traffic roundabout and underpass also links to the underground subway system and public meeting place in front of the city theatre.[17] Like the Rockefeller Center, it represents a miniaturisation of the larger city, a city within the city. Like that Center it contains mixed uses, a cinema and theatre, commercial uses and office towers. Unlike that Center its architecture is far more varied and by many hands.

Hötorgscity was an important urban design experiment for people who sought a way between the rigid Beaux-Arts designs of the Soviet Union and the formulaic urban designs of CIAM modernists, like Le Corbusier. Frederick Gibberd, the British architect and urban designer, included it as an important achievement in his book *Town Design* (1953).[18] Sven Markelius's design combined SOM's Lever House podium with traditional urban design concerns, to create a sophisticated, new, three-dimensional metropolis. Markelius was invited to America to advise on the planning of the United Nations complex (along with Le Corbusier and many others); he also joined the team planning the Lincoln Center, a Robert Moses performing arts centre project on the West Side of Manhattan (1969).[19] The recent restoration of the complex and its night lighting have renewed its appeal, adding a touch of modern glamour to downtown Stockholm.

Sven Markelius and others, Hötorgscity, Stockholm, Sweden (1952–6), with flower market (photo 2007)
The municipal theatre (left) and cinema building (right) frame the Hötorget (Haymarket) Square, leading to the Hötorgscity new shopping armature that connects through to the Sergelstorg traffic circle and Peter Celsing's municipal Culture Centre building (1968–73). The five towers are above the podium on the left. (Photo © David Grahame Shane)

Sven Markelius and others, Hötorgscity, Stockholm, Sweden (1952–6), night view (photo 2007)
Markelius's design was renovated in the 1990s and spectacular night lighting now differentiates the five 18-storey towers above the shopping podium on the left. The interior of the new municipal cinema from the 1990s is also brightly lit. (Photo © David Grahame Shane)

**Sven Markelius and others, Hötorgscity, Stockholm, Sweden (1952–6),
daytime view of Sergel's Square with a small political demonstration (photo 2007)**
Celsing's Cultural Centre opens directly onto the lower level of the square, also giving access to
the subway. The recessed nature of this public enclave protects it from the surrounding traffic,
which is subject to congestion charges in the city centre. (Photo © David Grahame Shane)

**Sven Markelius and others, Sergel's Square, Hötorgscity, Stockholm,
Sweden (1952–6), night-time view of lower pedestrian level (photo 2007)**
The illuminated subway entrance and entry to the Cultural Centre stand out at night. The fine
design of the floor surface distinguishes this public space. In the background the illuminated
Sergel's Square glass tower stands inside the traffic roundabout. (Photo © David Grahame Shane)

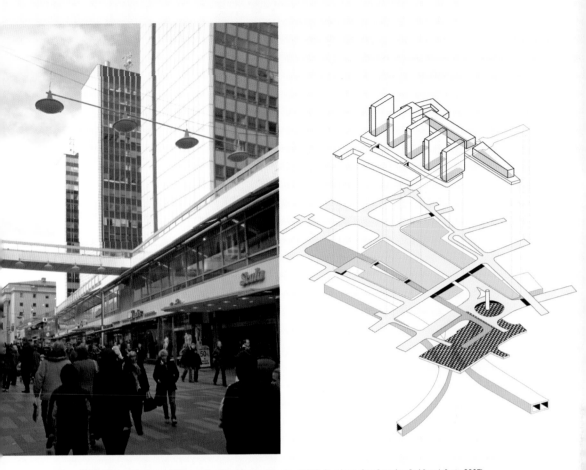

Sven Markelius and others, Hötorgscity, Stockholm, Sweden (1952–6), view of pedestrian bridge (photo 2007)
Markelius believed that the podium for the five towers could be a complicated three-dimensional commercial matrix. His inspiration was the Lever House podium in New York designed by Gordon Bunshaft of SOM (1951–2), but these upper levels proved hard to police and their vandalisation in the 1970s led to their closure. (Photo © David Grahame Shane)

Exploded axonometric of Hötorgscity complex, Stockholm, Sweden
Markelius planned the Hötorgscity project and built one of the five skyscrapers. The site sloped down to the water and so allowed him to develop a complex layered section, and connect into the Sergel's Square subway station. His upper-level pedestrian decks originally connected uphill back into the financial and insurance district, a link still preserved by the elevated roadway. (Drawing © David Grahame Shane and Uri Wegman)

Christiania represents the implosion of the metropolis, as the imperial city shrank and changed its role.[20] Denmark, like Sweden and Britain, had instituted a generous social welfare programme as it lost its imperial connections and concentrated its wealth at home. Like their counterparts in Britain and Sweden, Danish town planners constructed new towns, in this case following Steen Eiler Rasmussen's 'Finger Plan', constructing the towns along four railway routes leading out the city.[21] Between these fingers of development, the green belt stretched in as parks towards the city centre.

As people moved out to the new towns, the inner city became vacant, as in many European and American cities, leading to the abandonment of buildings and the decay of neighbourhoods. Squatters and artists moved into these areas, often students from the postwar baby boom entering university in the late 1960s without adequate university housing.[22] Many now desirable areas, like Camden Town in London or the East Village in New York, began their renaissance in this period of the 'alternative society' and 'flower power' hippies.[23] These urban pioneers began the adaptive reuse and conversion of buildings to serve new purposes. They created new urban villages within the shells of old institutional and industrial establishments. Their creativity was most often rewarded by eviction, but Christiania was unusual because of its survival through several generations.

Christiania is currently battling to survive. In an ironic twist of fate, this individualistic exception from the Danish welfare state will be closed down by a conservative government that wants to reignite Danish personal entrepreneurship and personal initiative. Difficult negotiations are taking place to form a cooperative to save Christiania, a manoeuvre complicated by the hippies' refusal of private property claims and complete inversion of normal property codes. The government wants to sell some of the previously abandoned property for luxury condominium development.

The Danish town planner Steen Eiler Rasmussen with lawyer Ole Krarup and writer Ebbe Kløvedal Reich with a suitcase containing 14,000 petitions against the government's policy in 1974 Rasmussen supported Christiania and wrote that if the government closed it down, Copenhagen would lose it soul. (Photo © Press Association Images)

Carl Madsen Square, Christiania, Copenhagen, Denmark, with bike shop (photo 2009)
Carl Madsen Square, at the end of the former Pusher Street, serves as the central square of Christiania, with a restaurant and bike shop beside it. Merchants have stands here selling crafts, but at one time it was marijuana being sold here and on Pusher Street to support the community, until the Copenhagen police removed the stands, one of which was taken to the National Art Museum for display. (Photo © David Grahame Shane)

Self-built housing, Christiania, Copenhagen, Denmark (photo 2007)
Besides occupying the abandoned military barracks and workshops, the hippy squatters of Christiania built themselves small collectively owned houses on the old ramparts of the city overlooking the water. Here they created an unusual public park, with facilities including a riding school. Also at intervals along the water's edge are communal and private family houses. (Photo © David Grahame Shane)

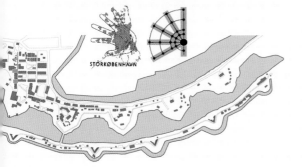

Grey Hall Community Centre, Christiania, Copenhagen, Denmark (photo 2009)
The Grey Hall, one of the abandoned military buildings, serves the Christiania community as its town hall, hosting community discussions and meetings, rock concerts for alternative music groups, cabaret and theatrical performances. Its exterior has been painted with graffiti representing Christiania's hippy origins. (Photo © David Grahame Shane)

Plan and location map of Christiania, Copenhagen, Denmark
The old Christiania military base was located on an island across from the city centre and adjacent to an area where squatters had already settled in abandoned buildings before 1972, when they moved into the base. In the 1990s the docks and naval yards in front of Christiania were converted into residential units and commercial offices, followed by the construction of the new national opera house, making the land very valuable. (Plan © David Grahame Shane and Uri Wegman; finger plan © David Grahame Shane, 2009)

Hong Kong was an important colonial outpost of the British Empire, linked to London as its colonial metropolis. In the Second World War the Japanese invasion showed just how fragile this link was, and Mao's Communist victory in the Civil War that followed the defeat of the Japanese brought many refugees to the city. The British Labour government commissioned Patrick Abercrombie to draw up a plan that, as in London, involved new towns and green belts. The plan was never implemented, but in any case Abercrombie planned low densities and did not envision the scale of the refugee problem.

On Christmas Eve 1954, a fire in the Shek Kip Mei refugee shantytown in Kowloon left 54,000 people homeless.[24] With the help of the United Nations, the colonial government housed people in tents and other temporary shelters. In the face of this disaster, the government began a housing programme that soon expanded into the framework that Abercrombie had envisioned for new towns, but at a far higher density than he ever imagined.

The Shek Kip Mei Mark 1 housing blocks were incredibly basic and crude, with concrete floors and columns like Le Corbusier's Maison Domino, but with tiny rooms for families. Khrushchev's mass-produced housing bocks were much more luxurious, with kitchens and bathrooms in each apartment (similar blocks were built in Beijing); Perret's blocks in Le Havre were far superior in every way; yet the Shek Kip Mei buildings were a great step forwards. They set a pattern of new town development and industrialised building production as the answer to housing problems in Asia.

A

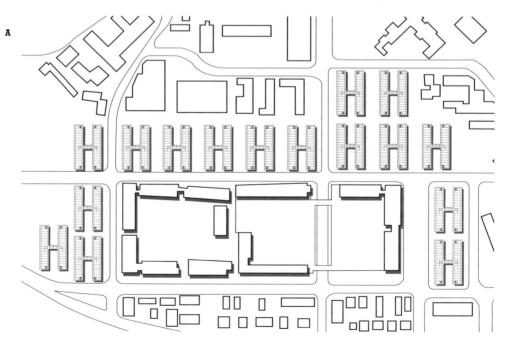

B

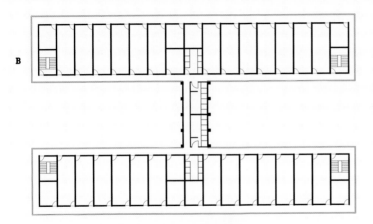

C

D

Shek Kip Mei Housing Estate, Kowloon, Hong Kong, 1964 (photos 2008)

(A) When it opened in 1964 with 44 Mark 1 slab blocks the estate housed 25,000 people. Many of the original estate blocks have already been demolished and replaced with high-rise slabs. A large superblock with a raised podium at the centre replaced many of the early Mark 1 blocks. (B) Families were housed in Mark 1 blocks with balcony access from a single loft-like room, with the bathrooms and toilets on a bridge between blocks with staircases at either end of the block. Cooking facilities were in the courtyard at ground level outside the building, washrooms and clothes lines were on the roof, with a small kindergarten (C) The open balcony access ways dominate the facade, and the laundry rooms and kindergarten buildings can be seem on the rooftop. The ground floor of these blocks contained stores when the block was aligned with the street as in this location; each block's identical end facade bore a large painted number to distinguish it from its neighbours. (D) Schoolboys walk through the fenced-off courtyard between two early Shek Kip Mei blocks that will be transformed into a housing museum. The communal cooking facilities can be seen at intervals along each side of the courtyard. Access balconies completely surround each floor of the block. (Photos and drawings © David Grahame Shane and Uri Wegman)

The Brussels World's Fair of 1958 was the first global exhibition since the end of the Second World War.[25] All the colonial and imperial powers of Europe were represented, along with the new superpowers, the USA and USSR.[26] The exhibition also had the usual colonial installations of African villages, precious jewels and diamonds from mining companies and exotic Asian displays. In addition, it housed a nostalgic re-creation of a typical Belgian village, complete with main square and sidewalk cafés.

Besides the Atomium – symbol of a new energy source – oil companies, Saudi Arabia and other Middle Eastern oil producers built pavilions, while Belgian construction companies built a sample highway cloverleaf intersection. One petroleum company pavilion showed roads being built across the Belgian countryside in an animated model. Automobile companies displayed new cars, and the Pan Am Airways pavilion featured a captured globe. Emerging global brands, like Coca-Cola and IBM, had pavilions, as did French information and publishing companies, like Hachette.

The three-dimensional structure of the Atomium formed a distinctive feature on the city skyline, providing a view over the city. It also offered a glimpse of the micro scale projected up to the mega scale, allowing the relationships between atoms to be frozen. Visitors were presented with a complex three-dimensional network model of a set of dynamic relationships. It was as if the city had exploded as a result of the atom bomb and a new network structure was emerging.

The Belgian Village at the Brussels World's Fair, Belgium, 1958
Belgium hosted the first World's Fair after the Second World War in 1958. At the foot of the Atomium, symbol of the new power source of the future, the Belgian government built a composite replica of a Belgian village. Shown here in a contemporary postcard photograph, it had a central square, gabled houses and sidewalk cafes.

The Belgian Congo Colonial Display at the Brussels World's Fair, Belgium, 1958
In line with a long tradition of World's Fairs, the Brussels Fair contained a replica of a colonial village, in this case imported from the Belgian Congo (now Democratic Republic of Congo) in central Africa (shown here in a contemporary postcard photograph). Nearby the reassuring pavilions of Belgian missionary societies and the mining companies completed the African picture for visitors.

Interior of the USSR Pavilion with *Sputnik*, Brussels World's Fair, Belgium, 1958

The pavilion had an advanced, suspended glass facade, but inside contained a symmetrical Stalinist display. Giant worker and peasant statues framed the entrance, while a giant statue of Lenin ended the vista. Behind Lenin a wall held the image of the skyline of Moscow the metropolis, while a replica of the recently launched *Sputnik* announced the arrival of the Space Age. (Photo © Michael Rougier/Time & Life Pictures/Getty Images)

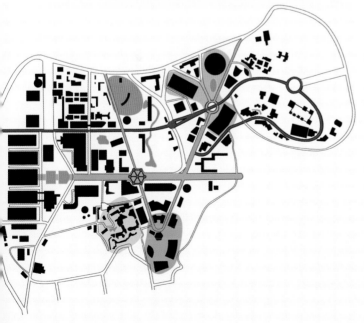

Plan of the Brussels World's Fair, Belgium, 1958

The layout of the Brussels World's Fair incorporated both Beaux-Arts axial arrangements and modern isolated pavilions spread across the landscape. The 'Big Three' – France, the USA and the USSR – faced each other around a circle, forming a triangle with the United Nations and the formal Brabant Gardens beside the Atomium. This stood at the intersection of the Beaux-Arts axial approach and one cross axis of the modern triangle, while a sample piece of elevated motorway formed a bypass bridge to the north across the gardens. (Plan © David Grahame Shane and Uri Wegman)

New York as the modern metropolis had been built on coal and steam power, fed by railways bringing produce from its hinterland and ships sailing into its docks and harbour. The city machine had been powered by coal and electricity, illuminated at night, a city that never slept. Skyscrapers and super-dense blocks made up its neighbourhoods, and its dynamic included socially and educationally upwardly mobile immigrants, who ultimately would join the middle class and move to the suburbs.

While New York did not have the grand axes and great squares of the imperial European capitals, its grid did allow for the flow of traffic until the advent of the automobile. Robert Moses spent his last years in office as Chairman of the Triborough Bridge and Tunnel Authority trying to figure out how to thread major highways across the dense metropolis.[27] He also recognised that the metropolis was hollowing out as people moved to the suburbs, proposing inner-city urban renewal schemes on the Corbusian model. He combined these two insights in designs for new housing along the edge of Manhattan in conjunction with his road schemes. Whenever he wanted to cross Manhattan with a highway, he faced many difficulties, and he never succeeded in building a cross-town expressway in Manhattan.

In contrast to Moses, the Rockefellers continued to support and build large urban complexes inside the city grid. The Rockefellers gave the land for the United Nations and built the first skyscraper in Downtown Manhattan since the Great Depression, their Chase Manhattan Bank, in 1961. These two institutions both had global implications, the UN in terms of politics and world peace, the Chase Bank in terms of world finance and global trade. The research of the New York Regional Plan Association (RPA), supported by the Rockefeller Brothers Fund, argued that New York should move away from manufacturing and trade towards finance, insurance and real estate (FIRE).[28] While Moses accommodated their investments in the automobile and basic portfolio in oil, as they shifted to automobiles instead of rail, the Rockefellers themselves looked even further forward towards a global financial system with New York as its hub.

Robert Moses in front of a map of Manhattan, New York, USA, 1950s
Moses epitomised the modern top-down approach to planning at an enormous scale without opposition until the 1960s. Without ever being elected, he used his public offices to modernise the metropolis with parks, parkways and new public infrastructure for the automobile age. (Photo © Bettmann/Corbis)

Plan of Lower Manhattan, New York, USA, with Robert Moses' 1950s road proposals

Moses planned to connect the Bridge and Tunnel Authority's infrastructure together with new elevated or buried highways cut across Lower Manhattan in the 1950s. He built roads along the waterfront, often with new housing as on the Lower East Side. He planned an unbuilt Midtown Manhattan Expressway between the Queens–Midtown Tunnel and the Lincoln Tunnel to cut through an extremely dense area, close to 34th Street and the Empire State Building. To reduce its impact in the city, Moses proposed to run the highway through specially reconstructed buildings, making new hybrid blocks with roads in the middle of the building section. Because of protests from local community groups in the 1960s, he never built the Lower Manhattan Expressway or the Brooklyn–Battery Bridge shown here. (Photo © Bettmann/Corbis; drawing © David Grahame Shane and Uri Wegman)

Skyscrapers

Skyscrapers posed an important problem for urban designers in the modern metropolis; indeed, the skyscrapers of New York were precisely the special new feature that distinguished the modern city from the old imperial, European metropolis. As early as the 1890s the American architect Louis Sullivan had proposed setting back skyscrapers along Chicago's streets and enforcing intervals to let the light down onto the sidewalks (following setback rules related to Haussman's Paris where the street width determined the height of building permitted).[29] In New York, the Zoning Code – introduced in 1916 as a result of the 90-metre (300-foot) Equitable Building overshadowing a 9-metre-wide (30-foot) street in the Dutch historic core – followed the Parisian example with setbacks related to street width, but allowed towers to go up much higher in the centre of the block, as exemplified by the Empire State Building of 1931.[30]

Modernist architects chaffed against the 1916 New York Zoning Codes and wanted to have towers in the park, as prescribed by Le Corbusier, or on plazas, as in Mies van der Rohe's Seagram Building (1958) on Park Avenue in Midtown New York.[31] SOM's Lever House (1952), also on Park Avenue, showed how the office tower could be combined with a low podium building and garden plaza or square under the existing regulations, as often advocated in Europe (such as in Stockholm's Hötorgscity scheme of 1952–6).[32] But in 1961, the New York City Planning Commission changed to the modernist's tower-in-plaza formulation, setting the scene for SOM's Chase Manhattan Plaza and Tower of 1961.[33] This was the first new tower downtown since the Great Depression of the 1930s and was built for David Rockefeller, the son of the builder of the Rockefeller Center and brother of Governor John Rockefeller of New York State, one of the sponsors of the World Trade Center (1968) in Downtown and the New State Government Mall in Albany, New York (1976) – all modernist tower-in-plaza schemes.[34]

Clusters of skyscrapers became the distinguishing characteristic of the modern metropolis as a centre of commercial activity and financial hub, distinguishing it from the earlier European imperial capitals with their grand axial armatures and great imperial enclaves of monumental buildings, arrayed in the landscape like at the Brussels World's Fair. For urban designers, the skyscraper became a pressing problem. How did you design a city that was made of towers, whose lobbies met the street? Mies proposed to make the towers as transparent as possible and appear to hover above the plaza as if on stilts, making a universal gridded space as the ground plane of the city (as in the creation of the level plaza on Park Avenue, which ignores the slope of the site down to Lexington Avenue). The same problem of a sloping site recurred at the Chase Manhattan Plaza, since Broadway ran on a ridge and Manhattan is not flat.

The 'Manhattan Timeformations' drawing by Brian McGrath shows the gradual build-up of the modern metropolis on Manhattan over a century, resulting in a city with hundreds of towers spread across the city grid in two great clusters, both Special Districts, that encouraged the concentration of towers with special bonuses.[35] The original Special District was to grandfather the Wall Street cluster downtown that had been built on solid bedrock.[36]

Entry to Chase Manhattan Plaza, New York, USA (photo 2009)
On the roof terrace of the podium is Jean Dubuffet's *Group of Four Trees* (1969). In the background is the City Services Building, an Art Deco tower now headquarters to AIG. The plaza walls are defined by the height of the surrounding tower blocks. (Photo © David Grahame Shane)

Skidmore, Owings & Merrill (SOM), Chase Manhattan Tower, New York, USA, 1961 (photo 2009)
The tower rises straight up out of Chase Manhattan Plaza, a paved roof terrace on a podium set against the slope of Manhattan down from Broadway to the East River. (Photo © David Grahame Shane)

Isamu Noguchi, sunken garden for Chase Manhattan Plaza, New York, USA, 1961–4 (photo 2009)
Noguchi's design exploits the section of the city as it slopes down from Broadway to the East River, opening up the banking hall below that gives access to William Street. (Photo © David Grahame Shane)

Panorama of Chase Manhattan Plaza, New York, USA (photo 2009)
This view shows the opening to the sculpture garden below. William Street, marked by a row of trees at the edge of the podium, is 9 metres (30 feet) wide, left over from the Dutch city plan. (Photo © David Grahame Shane)

South panorama from the Rockefeller Suite in Chase Manhattan Tower, New York, USA (photo 2008)

The Rockefeller office suite on the 60th floor looked directly down on the New York Stock Exchange and JP Morgan's headquarters on Wall Street. The Chase Manhattan Bank Tower was the first skyscraper to be built downtown after the 1929 crash and was surrounded by towers from that era. This photograph shows the view to the south over New York Harbor to the Statue of Liberty, Ellis Island, Staten Island and New Jersey shore beyond. (Photo © Peter Schultz Jørgensen)

North panorama from the Rockefeller Suite in Chase Manhattan Tower, New York, USA (photo 2009)

The view from the north of the Rockefeller office suite on the 60th floor of the Chase Manhattan Tower looked over City Hall and the Woolworth Building to the Empire State Building and Midtown cluster of skyscrapers around Grand Central Station. Executives on high floors of such corporate towers had the sense of owning the city, looking down from above, and simultaneously branding the city skyline with their corporate identity. The Chase Tower overlooked its neighbour to the north across Maiden Lane, the Federal Reserve Bank of New York, where one third of America's gold is stored in underground vaults. (Photo © Peter Schultz Jørgensen)

Axonometric of Chase Manhattan Plaza, New York, USA

At Chase Manhattan Plaza, entry from Broadway on the ridge of Manhattan is restricted, as the podium rises above the surrounding streets from all other sides. Stairs on two sides give access to the podium, which forms a roof terrace over the banking hall on William Street, while the subway threads its way below. (Drawing © David Grahame Shane and Uri Wegman, 2010)

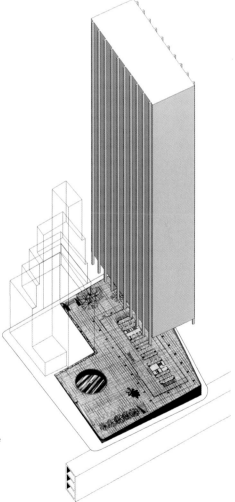

Brian McGrath, *Timeformations* drawing of New York, USA, 2000–2004
Brian McGrath's drawing from the New York Skyscraper Museum website shows New York as a layered
'Timeformation' of skyscrapers, each in its own time zone and correct spatial location in plan. This is one frame
taken from an animation that shows the city's accretion of skyscrapers until they form the contemporary skyline
(see: http://www.skyscraper.org/timeformations/intro.html). (Drawing © Brian McGrath)

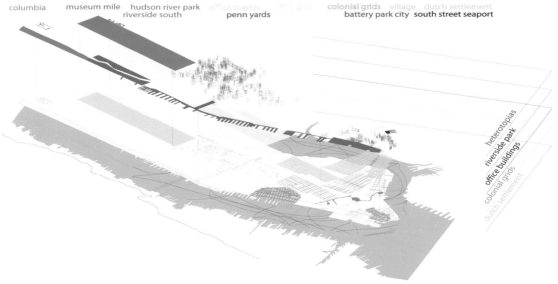

columbia   museum mile   hudson river park   office towers   1811 grid   colonial grids   village   dutch settlement
riverside south   penn yards   battery park city   south street seaport

heterotopias
riverside park
office buildings
colonial grids
dutch settlement

New York, USA as a layered metropolis
Dutch and British colonists established the fragmented pattern of Lower Manhattan, and after the Revolution
Americans set in place in 1811 the Manhattan Grid. This drawing maps these layers and the transformation of
the industrial port edge of Manhattan into parks, with large fragmentary developments inserted into the grid,
like the Rockefeller Center, Columbia University or the Time Warner Center complex at 59th Street. (Drawing
© David Grahame Shane and Rodrigo Guarda, 2005)

The Midtown cluster, around Penn Station, Grand Central Station and 42nd Street, was
originally based on easy access to rail transportation, the local subways, the East Coast
Corridor lines and then national systems linking to Chicago and Los Angeles. As New York
became a global hub, with the advent of the United Nations and global finance, connections
to airports also favoured the Midtown cluster that replaced Downtown as the international
financial hub, producing many new skyscrapers around 42nd Street, Grand Central, and
Madison and Park Avenues.

Conclusion
The Second World War and Hiroshima showed the vulnerability of the metropolis and
its associated systems of European empires, whose global reach supported the biggest
urban concentrations. As the Cold War commenced and European empires crumbled, to
be replaced by independent states and global corporations, the global oil economy also
emerged as a primary energy supply. The construction of this global economy involved
global financial hubs, like London, New York and Tokyo, that served as bases for the
deployment of the petrodollars generated by the new supply system which also enabled

Pudong, Shanghai, China, riverfront view (photo 2008)
Pudong on the riverfront, the new financial hub of Shanghai modelled on New York, is
often shrouded in fog in the winter, like New York in the early 20th century or London
in the 19th century. (Photo © David Grahame Shane)

millions to leave the metropolis for the megalopolis. Corporate headquarters could leave the
city centre along with metropolitan residents seeking new housing and leisure activities in the
suburbs. The decay of the metropolis followed just as new immigrants arrived seeking work
and finding only abandoned buildings, crime and drugs.

Metropolitan solutions imagined in Europe by Le Corbusier, for example, turned out not
to be the universal answer to urban design problems. These projections, though magnificent
in their own right, often turned out to be failures as places to live and difficult to maintain, as
at Chandigarh. These top-down solutions ignored many local factors, like urban villages,
and did not allow for the poverty and illiteracy left behind by the various European empires.
New towns and neighbourhood units made sense in the industrial north – in the welfare
states of Europe, for instance – but made little sense in the colonial south when poor people
had to built their own houses. While the USSR and Europe pioneered industrial production
of concrete panel housing construction, millions of Latin American and Asian peasants built
houses from scrap and the waste products of oil-rich, ex-colonial, newly independent cities.

Modernist architects and planners, preoccupied with the metropolis and its global reach,
failed to anticipate the development of the suburban megalopolis in its northern, industrial
form, or its southern-hemisphere *favela* format. The metropolis had been wedded to coal and
steam as its motive power, making railways its primary transportation system and the 'fried
egg' format (as defined by Cedric Price), its primary urban form, with fingers of development

following the streetcar and railway lines.[37] The oil infrastructure of refineries, pipelines, tank farms, petrol stations and garages appeared insignificant at first in comparison with the massive coal-fired electrical generation plants of the metropolis. Few were prepared to plan at a vast new scale of city territory that stretched hundreds of kilometres (or miles) and included tens of millions of people. Metropolitan concepts like new towns or neighbourhood units were ill fitted for the automobile and needed to be reformatted, So did all the urban elements of the city – enclaves like department stores, or armatures like streets, and hidden heterotopias like ghettos or red-light districts. The next chapter will examine the transformation of the metropolis into the megalopolis, the role of heterotopias, new energy sources and new urban actors in shifting from metropolitan downtown to the suburban mall of the megalopolis.

Notes

NB: See 'Author's Caution: Endnote Sources and Wikipedia', towards the end of this book.

1   On the western American nuclear umbrella, see: Tony Judt, *Postwar: A History of Europe Since 1945*, Penguin (New York), 2006, p 735.
2   On Christiania, see: The Phileas Fogg Project website, http://aroundtheworld.phileas-fogg.net/copenhagen/free-state.html (accessed 19 March 2010).
3   On postwar slums, see: Judt, *Postwar*, p 82. On Athens slums, see: Constantinos Doxiadis, *Architecture in Transition*, Oxford University Press (New York), 1963, p 35. On Tokyo slums, see: *Tokyo Metropolitan Government, A Hundred Years of Tokyo City Planning*, TMG Municipal Library No 28 (Tokyo), 1994, pp 46–7. On the slums of Dharavi, Mumbai, see: Mark Jacobson, 'Mumbai's Shadow City', *National Geographic*, May 2007, http://ngm.nationalgeographic.com/2007/05/dharavi-mumbai-slum/jacobson-text?fs=seabed.nationalgeographic.com (accessed 19 March 2010).
4   On the Partition of India, see: Barbara and Thomas Metcalf, *A Concise History of Modern India*, Cambridge University Press (Cambridge; New York), 2006, pp 203–27; also: http://en.wikipedia.org/wiki/Partition_of_India (accessed 19 March 2010).
5   On the Shek Kip Mei fire, see: United Nations Human Settlements Programme, 'Housing for All: The Challenges of Affordability, Accessibility, and Sustainability', UN-HABITAT (Nairobi), 2008, pp 33–4; also: http://en.wikipedia.org/wiki/Shek_Kip_Mei (accessed 19 March 2010).
6   Gonzague Pluvinage, *Expo 58: Between Utopia and Reality*, Lannoo Uitgeverij, 2008, pp 109–11.
7   On the Congo Crisis, see: Ch Didier Gondola, *The History of Congo*, Greenwood Press (Westport, CT), 2002; also: http://en.wikipedia.org/wiki/History_of_Democratic_Republic_of_the_Congo (accessed 25 March 2010).
8   Maxwell Fry and Jane Drew, 'Chandigarh and Planning Development in India', *Journal of the Royal Society of Arts*, vol CIII, no 4948, 1 April 1955, pp 315–33.
9   On Chandigargh and Lutyens' New Delhi, see: Kenneth Frampton, *Modern Architecture: A Critical History*, Oxford University Press (New York), 1981, pp 229–30; also: Kiran Joshi, *Documenting Chandigarh: the Indian architecture of Pierre Jeanneret, Edwin Maxwell Fry, Jane Beverly Drew*, Mapin Pub (Ahmedabad, India), c 1999.
10 On De Arce's review of Chandigarh, see: Geoffrey Broadbent, *Emerging Concepts in Urban Space Design*, Taylor & Francis (London), 1995, pp 202–4. For the village of Kansal in Chandigarh, see: Vikramaditya Prakash, *Chandigarh's Le Corbusier: The Struggle for Modernity in Postcolonial India*, University of Washington Press (Seattle; London), 2002, pp 65, 153–5.
11 On Landscape Urbanism, see: Charles Waldheim, *The Landscape Urbanism Reader*, Princeton Architectural Press (New York), c 2006. On Parc de la Villette, see: Bernard Tschumi, *Event-Cities 2*, MIT Press (Cambridge, MA), 2000, pp 44–225.

12   On Lucio Costa's pilot plan of 1957, see the reproduction of it on: http://www.infobrasilia.com. br/pilot_plan.htm (accessed 19 March 2010); also: Farès el-Dahdah (ed), *CASE 5: Lucio Costa, Brasilia's Superquadra*, Prestel (Munich; New York), 2005.

13   For Niemeyer, see: Paul Andreas and Ingeborg Flagge, *Oscar Niemeyer: A Legend of Modernism*, Deutsches Architekturmuseum (Frankfurt) and Birkhauser (Basel), 2003.

14   On Le Havre, see: Andrew Saint, 'In Le Havre', *London Review of Books*, vol 25, no 3, 6 February 2003, http://www.lrb.co.uk/v25/n03/andrew-saint/in-le-havre.

15   See: UNESCO World Heritage website, http://whc.unesco.org/en/list/1181 (accessed 21 March 2010).

16   On Hötorgscity, see: Susan Wiksten Desjardins, 'The City Centre and the Suburb: City Planning during the 1950s and 1960s in Stockholm and Helsinki', Masters Thesis, Åbo Akademi University, November 2003: http://www.wiksten.org/susan/ma_thesis_swd.pdf (accessed 21 March 2010); also: Olof Hultin, Bengt OH Johansson, Johan Mårtelius and Rasmus Wærn, *The Complete Guide to Architecture in Stockholm*, Arkitectur Forlag (Stockholm), 2004, p 90; also: http://en.wikipedia.org/wiki/Hötorget_buildings (accessed 21 March 2010).

17   On Sergel's Square, see: http://en.wikipedia.org/wiki/Sergels_torg (accessed 21 March 2010).

18   Frederick Gibberd, *Town Design*, Architectural Press (London), 1953, revised 1959.

19   On Markelius, see: Eva Rudberg, *Sven Markelius, Architect*, Arkitektur Förlag (Stockholm), 1989; also: http://en.wikipedia.org/wiki/Sven_Markelius (accessed 21 March 2010).

20   On Christiania, see: Kim Dirckinck-Holmfeld and Martin Keiding, *Learning from Christiania*, The Danish Architectural Press (Copenhagen), 2004; also: http://en.wikipedia.org/wiki/Freetown_Christiania (accessed 21 March 2010).

21   On Steen Eiler Rasmussen's 'Finger Plan', see: Thomas Hall, *Planning and Urban Growth in the Nordic Countries*, Taylor & Francis (London), 1991, pp 30–38.

22   On the postwar baby boom, see: Judt, *Postwar*, pp 330–36.

23   For Camden Town, see: http://en.wikipedia.org/wiki/Camden_Town (accessed 21 March 2010). For New York, see: Sharon Zukin, *Loft Living: Culture and Capital in Urban Change*, Johns Hopkins University Press (Baltimore), *c* 1982.

24   On Shek Kip Mei, see: http://en.wikipedia.org/wiki/Shek_Kip_Mei_Estate (accessed 21 March 2010); also: Hong Kong Housing Authority website, http://www.housingauthority.gov.hk/en/interactivemap/estate/0,,1-347-10_4926,00.html (accessed 25 March 2010); also: Public Housing in Hong Kong, The Hong Kong Housing Authority News, Promotion and Marketing Section (Hong Kong), September 1995, p 104.

25   Official Website on Expo '58: http://www.expo-1958.be/en/index.htm (accessed 21 March 2010). For the catalogue of Expo '58, see: Gonzague Pluvinage, *Expo 58: Between Utopia and Reality*, Brussels City Archives, State Archives in Belgium, Éditions Racine (Brussels), 2008 (available on Google Books).

26   On American influence, see: Victoria De Grazia, *Irresistible Empire: America's Advance Through Twentieth-Century Europe*, Belknap Press of Harvard University Press (Cambridge, MA), 2005.

27   On Moses' Lower Manhattan Expressway (LOMEX), see: Steve Anderson, NYC Roads website, http://www.nycroads.com/roads/lower-manhattan/ (accessed 21 March 2010); also: http://en.wikipedia.org/wiki/Lower_Manhattan_Expressway. On Moses' Mid Manhattan Expressway, see: Steve Anderson, NYC Roads website, http://www.nycroads.com/roads/mid-manhattan/ (accessed 21 March 2010); also: http://en.wikipedia.org/wiki/Mid-Manhattan_Expressway. See also: Robert A Caro, *The Power Broker: Robert Moses and the Fall of New York*, Knopf (New York), 1974.

28   On the Rockefeller Brothers Fund and 'FIRE', see: Robert Fitch, *The Assassination of New York*, Verso (London; New York), 1993, pp 145–56.

29   See: Donald Hoffman, 'The Setback Skyscraper City of 1891: an unknown essay by Louis H Sullivan', in *Journal of the Society of Architectural Historians* (*JSAH*), vol XXIX, no 2, May 1970, pp 180–87; also: Louis Henry Sullivan, 'The High Building Question', in Robert C Twombly (ed), *Louis Sullivan: The Public Papers*, University of Chicago Press (Chicago, IL), 1988, pp 76–9

30   See: *The Zoning Handbook*, Department of City Planning, New York City (New York), 1990.

31   On the Seagram Building, Jerold S Kayden, New York Department of City Planning and The Municipal Art Society of New York, *Privately Owned Public Space: The New York City Experience,* John Wiley & Sons (New York), 2000, pp 6–13, 53, 102.

32   On Lever House, ibid pp 9–13, 102, 144.

33   For the 1961 Zoning Resolution, see: New York City Department of City Planning website, http://www.nyc.gov/html/dcp/html/priv/priv.shtml (accessed 21 March 2010); also: Kayden, *Privately Owned Public Space*, On Chase Manhattan Plaza, ibid p 102.

34   On the World Trade Center, ibid pp 14, 99–100. For Albany, New York, see: Deyan Sudjic, *The Edifice Complex: How the Rich and Powerful – and Their Architects – Shape the World*, Penguin (New York), 2005, pp 229–32; also: http://en.wikipedia.org/wiki/Empire_State_Plaza (aka Governor Nelson A Rockefeller Empire State Plaza); also: Mary Ann Sullivan, 'Governor Nelson A Rockefeller Empire State Plaza', http://www.bluffton.edu/~sullivanm/empiresp/empiresp.html (accessed 21 March 2010).

35   On Brian McGrath's Manhattan Timeformations, see: Manhattan Timeformations website, http://www.skyscraper.org/timeformations/intro.html (accessed 21 March 2010). For Special Districts, see: Jonathan Barnett, *An Introduction to Urban Design*, Harper & Rowe (New York), 1982, pp 77–136; also: Jonathan Barnett, *Urban Design as Public Policy*, Architectural Record Books (New York), 1974.

36   For Lower Manhattan Special District, see: New York City Department of City Planning website, http://www.nyc.gov/html/dcp/html/zone/zh_special_purp_mn.shtml (accessed 21 March 2010); also: Richard F Babcock, *Special Districts: The Ultimate in Neighborhood Zoning*, Lincoln Institute of Land Policy (Cambridge, MA), *c* 1990.

37   Samantha Hardingham (ed), *Cedric Price: Opera*, John Wiley & Sons (London), 2003, pp 222–5.

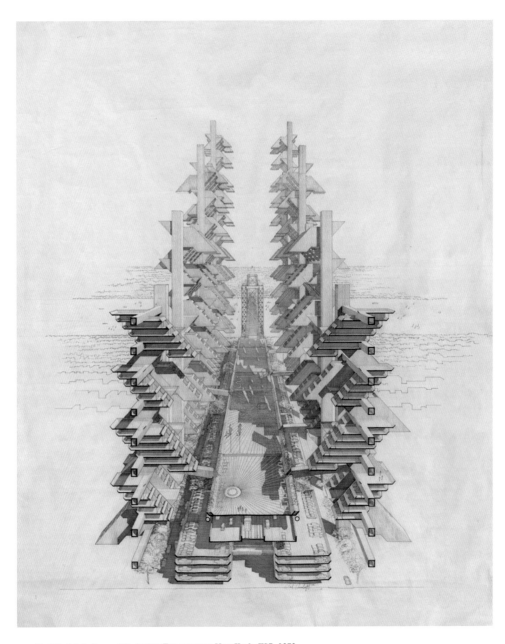

Paul Rudolph, Lower Manhattan Expressway, New York, USA, 1970
Drawing of multitiered proposal with Downtown Manhattan in the distance.
(Drawing © The Museum of Modern Art/Scala, Florence, 2009)

CHAPTER 5

The Megalopolis

The modern usage of the term 'megalopolis' or 'great city' (Greek) refers to an agglomeration of cities in a network that house many millions of people over an extended rural and urban area. The development of modern communications – telegraph, mail, telephone and radio – were crucial to the coordination of this new network urban form, as were modern transportation systems – ships and trains, later cars and planes. The continental scale of the USA allowed American corporations to grow and service a national population of 250 million without customs or other barriers. This provided a vast market for American corporations that developed national distribution systems, continental communication systems and computerised tracking systems and national advertising campaigns, creating a new 'mega' scale of operations that dwarfed national corporations in Europe (limited in Britain, for instance, to 50 million customers in the 1950s).[1]

The Second World War provided another big impetus for the development of the megalopolis at a new scale. In 1945 urban designers and military planners learnt much from the destruction of the historic city centre of Hiroshima in a one-second flash. Airpower and later long-range missiles made the targeting of centralised cities with atomic weapons a simple matter for the two superpowers with atomic weapons after the war. In addition the British mathematician Alan Turing, using early computer modelling techniques, had predicted in the early 1950s that planned rings of new towns around old central cities would transform into linear networks, based on the emergence of one dominant new town as an attractor on each side of the metropolis.[2] French geographer Jean Gottmann's analysis of the East Coast of the USA as a linear megalopolis in 1961 confirmed Turing's theory.[3]

A new mobility based on petroleum-powered internal combustion engines was another impetus for the redistribution of urban functions. The mobile tank battalions of the war (sheltered below an airpower umbrella) provided a lesson of how the city might dissolve into the countryside, a lesson reinforced by the evacuation of much of the civilian population of imperial capitals like London, Tokyo or Berlin. The war also demonstrated new patterns of urban mobility as in the construction of the temporary Mulberry Harbour on the beaches of Normandy in 1944, where over two million soldiers landed.[4] A temporary, underwater pipeline brought the tanks petroleum from storage tanks on the other side of the Channel. After the war the huge new refinery operations, pipelines and oil wells that had powered the mobile armies provided the power source for the redistribution of city functions across the American landscape.[5]

The postwar explosion of the American megalopolis forms the focus of the first part of this chapter, with a look at the simultaneous modernisation of the Middle East and other petroleum-rich states like Mexico, Venezuela, Nigeria and Indonesia. Here a hybrid megalopolis developed where the housing industry was not industrialised and self-built shantytowns proliferated as shadow cities. These low-income megacities broke down the universal goals of accessibility and service originally implicit in the dream of the American megalopolis. In wealthier states in Europe and Asia another variant of the megalopolis emerged, still dependent on railways and less dependent on oil and the automobile. Here architects and urban designers still dreamt of controlling the growth of the city through megastructures, scaled to the new dimensions of the highways as in Paul Rudolph's scheme for covering Robert Moses' Lower Manhattan Expressway (1970).[6]

As in the previous section, the next chapter will illustrate in more detail some of the urban designs, people, places and elements of change in the megalopolis, as well as looking at 'MegaTokyo' as an exemplary megalopolis with over 30 million inhabitants.

The emergence of the megalopolis: the American East Coast

European designers had a long history of looking at America to see the urban future. Le Corbusier, following Walter Gropius, looked at the grain elevators of Buffalo, New York, along with the storage silos, vertical elevator shafts and huge horizontal conveyor belts as future models of the metropolis in *Towards a New Architecture* (1927).[7] Such visitors ignored the rail network connections to the vast agrarian hinterland of the Great Plains that produced the grain and the wealth of Chicago, with its commodity market that set worldwide prices for agricultural products.[8] Jean Gottmann, in his *Megalopolis* of 1961, set this balance right, describing a highly distributed, multifunctional and multicentred, American city based on a national rail system, including the New York metropolis and the national capital Washington, a sprawling corridor that was 1,000 kilometres (600 miles) long, containing 32 million people. Today this same corridor houses over 56 million people.

Despite including hundreds of hectares (thousands of acres) of woodlands and farms, Gottmann's megalopolis as a whole had more people per square kilometre than the rest of America and most places on earth (except parts of Britain, Holland, India and China). Gottmann, an associate of Constantinos Doxiadis, pioneered a new scale of thinking about the city that anticipated the emerging mobility of automobile owners. These new drivers powered the conversion of East Coast farmland into large new suburban settlements, like Levittown, Long Island, New York (1947–51), quickly constructed using production-line systems on site. The Levitt Company built close to Republic Airport, home of the defence contractor Grumman with new factories from the Second World War. These huge housing estates created a new urban grain based on suburban setback regulations, house sizes and turning circles and street layouts created by the Federal Housing Authorities (FHA) after the Great Depression and in the New Deal of the 1930s. Other authors, like Kevin Lynch (1961, 1962), Christopher Tunnard (1963) and Iain McHarg (1969), recognised that this new megascale of housing operation and layouts based on automobiles and highways had implications for the American landscape, altering the sense of travel from a place orientation to a highway time-and-space duration.[9] Feminist architectural historians in the 1980s emphasised the shift in gender roles implicit in this new housing arrangement, isolating women as mothers in homes with few social networks.[10]

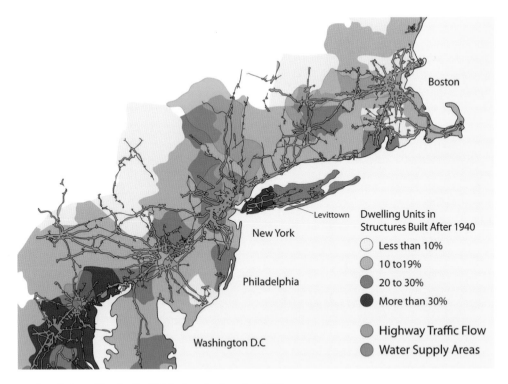

Jean Gottman, Megalopolis, 1961 (redrawn by the author, 2010)
This composite drawing shows highways, suburban expansion and water supply. (Drawing © David Grahame Shane and Uri Wegman, 2010; redrawn from Jean Gottmann, *Megalopolis: The Urbanized Northeastern Seaboard of the United States*, Twentieth Century Fund (New York), 1961, fig 63, p 223)

Based on a sense of this new network city, American urban planning theorists like Melvin Webber reversed the code of the metropolis and its 'central place theory' (as proposed by German geographer Walter Christaller in the 1930s), arguing that any place was as good as any other in the network as long as it had good transportation links.[11] Millions of people moved out of the American metropolis into suburban developments, resulting in the shrinking and abandonment of previously busy, industrial, commercial and residential areas. Meanwhile in Detroit, just across the city boundary at the '8-mile line', some of the wealthiest suburbs in America grew up around Grosse Point (the auto executive area) and new factories scattered across the suburban landscape were made possible by the new highway system. The hip-hop film *8 Mile* (2002) explored the differences around this division.[12] Federal regulations allowed considerable flexibility in house size, lot size and estate layouts, resulting in a highly differentiated housing market available for various income levels (but not African-Americans) within the overall housing sprawl.

Shoppers' World Mall, Framingham, MA, USA, 1951 (photo 1988)
(Photo © Richard Longstreth, 1988)

Detroit was not alone in this abandonment of the metropolitan centre, American highway engineers and architects created a new distribution system to service the dispersed cites, replacing city marketplaces with supermarket chain giant distribution hubs on the urban periphery. The Eisenhower Interstate and Defense Highway System, initiated in 1956, involved the construction of over 74,000 kilometres (46,000 miles) of highways, transforming America. The system followed a similar logic to that of the railways, seeking the low land in river valleys and waterfronts, but with a very different geometry of turning radiuses and segregated cloverleaf intersections that became the trademark of the megalopolis urban design (much celebrated by Reyner Banham in his BBC film *Reyner Banham Loves Los Angeles* (1972)).[13] Highways were often piggybacked above railway tracks in central city areas on elevated roadways, creating flyover highways that were much admired as a solution for the city centre in Asia.

Feeder roads led from residential cul-de-sacs in the housing estate layouts to commercial strips and then entrances to the highway at long intervals, setting in motion a new urban geometry based on the car. In the background an equally monumental system of petroleum processing and supply marked the megalopolis with huge depots, like that at Long Beach in Los Angeles, the Houston Ship Canal in Texas or the New Jersey shoreline south of New

York. Hundreds of kilometres of pipelines for oil and gas matched the national electrical grid to provide an equal service all across the country (similar networks supported the telephone system). The highway system eventually replaced the railway network, making old ports and industrial warehouse districts redundant, as peripheral airports and container ports handled the flows of trade in an increasingly global system.

All the elements of a city, from city hall, church, police station, courthouse and jail to museum, cinema, market, department store and restaurants, all moved to separate isolated, single-storey pavilions along the commercial boulevard on the periphery. Together they formed a new urban centre in a commercial strip, later to be concentrated by mall designers in what they considered new 'community centers' around a 200-metre-long (600-foot) exterior (and then interior) commercial armature modelled on the Rockefeller Center (as noted in chapter 3). In *Los Angeles: The Architecture of the Four Ecologies* (1971), Reyner Banham celebrated these new centres in his chapter on 'The Art of the Enclave', which included theme parks like Disneyland in Anaheim (1954), the historic Farmers' Market produce market from the 1930s (now part of The Grove mall, 2008) as well as Westwood, the student village built close to the Frederick Law Olmstead-designed UCLA Campus in the 1920s.[14]

The network city, symbolised by the all-pervasive grid of Los Angeles Boulevards and the Federal Highways, housed a myriad of enclaves. Some were village-like, some theme parks, some big commercial or office centres (like Century City (1963), planned by Welton Becket as a 'city-within-a-city' on an old studio lot). No one centre commanded the system, whose old city centre was a hollowed-out shell. Urban mobility gave the individual multiple choices within the system to satisfy their needs and fulfil their dreams (Los Angeles still housed the major American movie and TV studios). The oil wealth of Houston, Texas sponsored the first megamall in America, the Galleria complex, started by HOK in 1967 and built in increments over a decade with over 100,000 square metres of shops, thousands of parking places, attached hotels and office towers, cinemas and food courts, and a sports club on the roof (see chapter 6).

The emergence of the megalopolis: Middle East, Latin America and Australia

As American oil companies developed the oil fields of Saudi Arabia, it is not surprising that Saudi princes invested in Houston Galleria or that they imported the new urban system into their oil-rich kingdom, whose wealth and oil production skyrocketed after 1945 (see chapter 1) and especially after the OPEC Oil Embargo against the West (1973).[15] Nor is it surprising to find Gordon Bunshaft of SOM, the architects of the Rockefellers' Chase Manhattan Tower, ending his career in the 1980s designing the National Commercial Bank skyscraper in Jeddah (1977–83) and the 500,000-square-metre (5 million-square-foot), megastructural tent-covered Hajj airport terminal (1981, with engineer Fazlur Khan) at Jeddah's King Abdulaziz airport for pilgrims going to Mecca (see chapter 6).[16] SOM continues to play a leading role in Saudi Arabian urban design and planning, laying out King Abdullah Economic City near Jeddah to be completed by 2020.[17]

As a young man, Nelson Rockefeller Jnr, the future Governor of New York State (who built the Albany Mall (Harrison & Abramovitz, 1976)) and future Vice-President of the USA, supported modern planning in oil-rich Latin America, including Caracas, Venezuela, where Standard Oil still dominated production.[18] An early result of this policy was El Silencio housing complex (1942) by Venezuelan modernist architect Carlos Raúl Villanueva, and then Cipriano Dominguez's Centro Simón Bolivar government centre complex (1949) with its twin towers.[19] This enclave aligned with a grand Simón Bolivar Avenue approach armature planned in the Rotival Plan (1939), making a traditional armature-and-enclave assembly in modernist terms but at a vast scale.[20] The Parque Central megastructure terminated the other end of the axis in the 1980s.[21]

Villaneuva and others tried to house the influx of new immigrants attracted from the hinterland in large modernist town planning projects and modernist housing superblocks (like the 23 de Enero estate (1955–7)), now surrounded by informal development (see chapter 2).[22] Villaneuva's huge Central University Campus (1944–70) is a lasting modernist urban design masterpiece from this period of military dictatorship with its covered walkways, parks and covered public forum. Meanwhile the huge *ranchos* (self-built housing villages) built on the hillside of the planned green belt of the city are a testament to the oil-rich state's failure. Oil was cheaper than water, and the elevated highway infrastructure at the bottom of the river valley and that above the city at the 700-metre (2,000 feet) contour remain as permanent monuments to the oil boom of the 1960s and 1970s, while also setting limits to the self-built *ranchos*.

As in Los Angeles, the Caracas highways allowed those with automobiles to escape the city to villas perched on hills in the valley (like the spectacular Villa Planchart, designed by the Italian architect Gio Ponti in the 1950s for the local Chevrolet dealer).[23] The roads also gave access to self-built shacks in the hillside *ranchos*. Rio de Janeiro and São Paolo in Brazil, both with mountainous terrain close to the core, repeated this oil-powered, dual-city section, with *barrios* and *favelas* built above the city. Gas- and oil-rich Mexico City, Bogotá (Colombia), Quito (Equador) and Lima (Peru) all expanded horizontally with the poorer self-built *barrios* or *favelas* to one side of the city valley section. The same oil-economy pattern of rapid urban growth, government failure and self-built housing occurred in West Africa, in Lagos, Nigeria, after the end of the brutal war in the oil-rich area of Biafra (1967–9). In Venezuela in the 1960s the government planned a new steel town as an attractor in the south of the country at Ciudad Guayana, employing a joint Harvard and MIT team, including Kevin Lynch, to plan a vast highway network city between two pre-existing villages. Even now most people are too poor to have cars and the distances involved are enormous; many people live in shantytowns at an incredible, riverside site.

American designers also exported the megalopolis concept to other petroleum-exporting nations that belonged to OPEC after 1960. In the Middle East, Victor Gruen, the Los Angeles mall designer, drew up plans for a linear western extension of Tehran (1969, with local planners) for the Shah, based on a system of highways, green belts and new towns around malls.[24] Athens-based Doxiadis attempted to create a new urban form based on the traditional

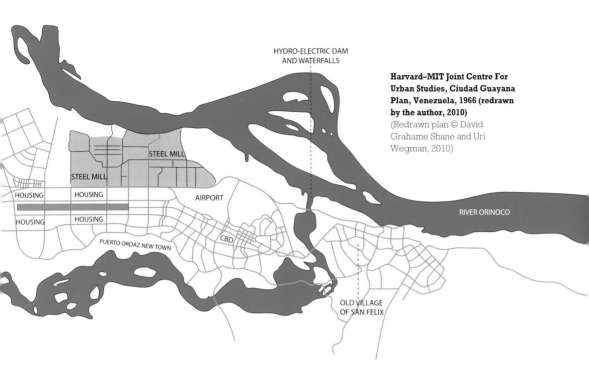

Harvard–MIT Joint Centre For Urban Studies, Ciudad Guayana Plan, Venezuela, 1966 (redrawn by the author, 2010)
(Redrawn plan © David Grahame Shane and Uri Wegman, 2010)

HYDRO-ELECTRIC DAM AND WATERFALLS

STEEL MILL

STEEL MILL

HOUSING

HOUSING

AIRPORT

HOUSING

HOUSING

PUERTO ORDAZ NEW TOWN

CBD

RIVER ORINOCO

OLD VILLAGE OF SAN FELIX

Harvard–MIT Joint Centre for Urban Studies, Cuidad Guayana Plan, Venezuela, 1966 (redrawn by the author, 2010)
Aerial view shows the scale of the central avenue oriented to the automobile, while most workers lived in shanty towns constructed around the old village of San Felipe, miles away without cars.
(Redrawn plan © David Grahame Shane and Uri Wegman, 2010)

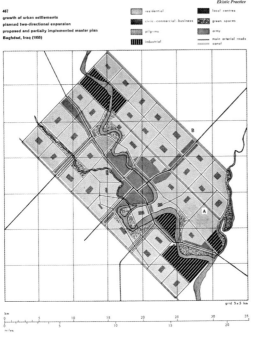

467
growth of urban settlements
planned two-directional expansion
proposed and partially implemented master plan
Baghdad, Iraq (1955)

Ekistic Practice

residential	local centres
civic · commercial · business	green spaces
pilgrims	army
industrial	main arterial roads
	canal

Constantinos A Doxiadis, master plan of Baghdad and photograph of model of the Western Baghdad Sector 10, Iraq, 1955–8
(Plan and photograph © Constantinos A Doxiadis Archives, courtesy of the Constantinos and Emma Doxiadis Foundation)

Kim Swoo-Geun, Sewoon Sangga Market, Seoul, South Korea, 1966 (photo 2007)
This large megastructure was invaded by small-scale traders from an informal electronics market in the parking lot and is scheduled for demolition (see concluding text of this chapter). (Photo © David Grahame Shane)

Islamic courtyard house and alleyway access, but adapted to the car and highways of the megalopolis.[25] He filled the highway grid with a neighbourhood unit on a smaller-scale grid. He planned a mall-like pedestrian, commercial and civic armature as a spine at the centre of each neighbourhood. This sponsored a linear direction of growth for future extensions. Sadly the Doxiadis-designed back lanes of Sadr City became a place of terrible bloodshed during the American invasion of Iraq in the early 2000s (and now an investment opportunity). While Doxiadis worked in Baghdad and Beirut and designed Islamabad, the new capital of Pakistan, British firms in the 1960s re-planned oil-rich Kuwait. Here, the designers employed a large a highway grid, ring road and new town centre similar in scale to Harlow, UK, with small office towers (see chapter 3), close to Abadan, Iran, the site of one of the world's largest oil refineries (destroyed in the Iran–Iraq War, 1980–8) with its earlier British-designed new town (1920s–1930s).[26]

Urban designers and architects in Australia also welcomed the American megalopolis, based on oil from the Middle East, Indonesia and Brunei. These designers developed an extremely luxurious version of the Los Angeles model with about one third of the population density in Melbourne, Sydney, Brisbane or Perth suburbs. Here the American model could spread out as a logical system with very few people, forming a clear example for Asian visitors from the crowded Pacific Rim. House sizes expanded, glass walls opened to the landscape, which could be integrated as in Los Angeles, and relaxed zoning codes allowed the American system to sprawl into the interior desert lands, as it would do later in Las Vegas or Dubai. The contrast between the planned low-density expansion of Melbourne, for instance, and the rapid high-density, self-built *desa-kota* (town-village) expansion of Jakarta, Indonesia in the 1970s, one source of Australian energy supplies, highlights the dark shadow that always lay behind the global expansion of the American megalopolis.

The contrast between the megalopolis and its self-built, shadow shantytown was especially stark in the Middle East, the main beneficiary of the enormous wealth created by the new, global oil energy economy. Here the European powers and American government were happy to solve their post-war refugee problem by offering 350,000 survivors of Hitler and Stalin's ethnic cleansing policies a choice of moving from UN refugee camps to Israel. The result was that Israel, beginning with a communal kibbutz system of small urban-rural settlement villages set in the landscape, quickly developed into a super-modern megalopolis city-state, planned from the top down, surrounded by jealous neighbours kept in poverty in self-built camps in the Lebanon, West Bank and Gaza. The oil-rich states of the Middle East and Israel modernised themselves and provided all the services of the American megalopolis – airports, highways, universities, hospitals, sewage treatment, electricity and water supplies. Meanwhile in Gaza and the Lebanon camps continued to fester as symbols of inequality and injustice, whose volatility only increased the price of oil on the global market after the formation of OPEC.

The emergence of the global megalopolis: European variations

The modernity of Israeli state planning reflected advanced European theories from the 1930s and war years, when Anglo-Saxon planners had expanded their scope beyond the metropolis to take in enormous areas of the city hinterland, still within the top-down colonial framework (as in Abercrombie's city-regional Greater London Plan (1944) in chapters 3 and 4). The British version of these Town and Country Planning schemes still relied on railways as the basic framework of transportation, whereas German versions from the 1930s onwards added in autobahns, initially, like Robert Moses' parkways, restricted to recreational driving of automobiles. Later these parkways expanded to modern highways, with heavy trucks and buses, especially under the American occupation after the end of the Second World War. The émigré German urban designer, Ludwig Hilberseimer, friend of Mies van der Rohe and author of the hyper-rationalist *Grosstadt Architektur* (Metropolitan Architecture, 1927), incorporated this 'organic' merger of machine and landscape in his low-density, sprawling plans for rationalising Chicago suburbs shown in his *The Nature of Cities* (1955).[27]

The big difference between the American megalopolis and the European 'city landscape' variants was that in most northern European nations, national zoning codes protected agricultural land and forests as scarce resources. These regulations prevented the unplanned sprawl of cities, through top-down planning restrictions in the interest of a romantically defined conception of 'nature'. Railways still played a major role in European transport planning, creating a different, pedestrian-oriented grain inside the megalopolis. In Britain, the Modern Architecture Research Group (MARS Group) plan for London of 1939 (later eclipsed by Abercrombie's ring-and-radial Greater London Plan of 1944) anticipated many features of the new open dynamic of the megalopolis, but without highways.[28] The plan involved restructuring London as a series of north–south linear cities running at right angles to the River Thames inside a huge loop road and railway. With its logic of neighbourhood units, districts and civic centres set in linear corridors and surrounded by parkland, it was a European *Stadtlandschaft* plan, linked to the German education of the MARS Group's chairman, Arthur Korn. A similar logic influenced the planners of the Dutch Randstad (Ring City with a green centre, 1940s, developed further in the 1960s) that depended on railway and tram (streetcar) systems linking a myriad of compact small towns, shaping another version of the megalopolis.[29] The special Belgian version involved railway stations and then highway exits at every small town, since these powerful towns had formed part of a vast European marketing and trading exchange system in the Middle Ages and 19th century and were represented in the Belgian parliament. Their central market halls and peripheral trade fair buildings only slowly gave way to America's modern marketing techniques of advertising, national brands, supermarkets and new distribution patterns of megamalls and outlet stores, serviced by truck warehouses, airports and container ports.

Gottmann's book about America reflects the European realisation that a new network city, the megalopolis, was emerging in the 'economic miracle' of the 1960s. Italian CIAM (International Congress of Modern Architecture) member Ernesto Rogers thought that urban design was an autonomous discipline with its own traditions and rules that could be modernised, while attacking Banham as a 'lover of refrigerators'.[30] Italian urban designers dreamt about urban design controls and regional plans as they suffered from chaotic, speculative development, sometimes by gangsters as shown in Francesco Rosi's film *Hands Over the City* (1963).[31] Italians were very aware of the switch to Vespas and Fiats, offering new choices and personal mobility but threatening the old historic centres and urban traditions (sponsoring a strong conservation movement). Each city had its own history and regional pattern that shaped local codes and zoning. The result was a peculiar Italian, microscaled megalopolis, a sprawl that included agriculture, industry, housing and offices in unplanned corridors of development. Giuseppe Samonà, a professor at Venice in 1962, first identified this as a hybrid 'urbanised countryside' mixture, later called the 'Diffuse City' (*Città Diffusa*) by his successor Bernardo Secchi in 1990.[32]

In contrast to their Italian contemporaries, British town planners and urban designers with their national Town and Country controls and new town regulations could easily switch from railway-based 'conurbations' (Howard (1896) and Geddes (1915)) to the highway-based megalopolis.[33] Colin Buchanan's report, entitled *Traffic in Towns* (1963), advocated creating low-scaled, pedestrianised enclaves surrounded by high-intensity roads forming a system of superblock neighbourhoods not unlike Rudolf Schwarz's earlier plan for Cologne (see chapter 6).[34] Buchanan added high-density raised pedestrian decks along the streets on the block periphery. A sample of this system was built in the third-generation British New Town at Cumbernauld (designated 1955) outside Glasgow, Scotland. The Town Centre block consisted of a huge heterotopic megastructure, part housing block, part civic centre, part first UK interior shopping mall, part car park and bus station, all raised above a highway (1963–7). At Milton Keynes (designated a New Town in 1967, with Llewelyn-Davis, Weeks & Partners appointed as planners, and built in several phases) the influence of Melvin Webber and Banham is clear, as the city dissolved into the landscape as a network of residential housing estates, as in Levittown or Los Angeles, connected by highways, but including old village centres and landscape features as protected conservation zones.[35] Here a huge, single-storey, single-function, American-style interior mall served as a giant civic centre (as proposed by Gruen in his 1969 Tehran Plan).[36]

Derek Walker and Helmut Jacoby, helicopter view of Milton Keynes Town Centre, UK, 1972
(Drawing © Derek Walker; rendering by Helmut Jacoby)

Derek Walker, plan of Milton Keynes, UK, 1972 (redrawn by the author, 2010)
The plan is redrawn to show existing villages subject to Historic Preservation plans. (Redrawn plan © David Grahame Shane and Uri Wegman 2010)

Gruen was also involved in the early planning for two corridors of new towns with mall centres set in the landscape of the Seine Valley, north and south of Paris. Here President Charles de Gaulle re-housed the returning colonists after the French loss of Algeria (1962). Based on malls, each of these new towns had its own Gruen-style shopping centre, later changed to civic centres that were versions of the Dutch new-town 'forums'. This hybrid, interior public space involved the location of social services, schools, a healthcare centre and a youth centre in the mall (as at Cumbernauld). The historic French emphasis on Paris as the national capital never allowed these centres to develop, leading to later problems. French state power and finance also enabled megaforms in provincial new towns such as Toulouse-Le Mirail, associated with the French aviation industry, designed by French Team 10 members Georges Candilis and Shadrach Woods in 1968.[37]

Banham in his *Megastructures: Urban Futures of the Recent Past* (1976) highlighted many European projects but gave pride of place to Japanese designers who in 1960 first published gigantic megastructural schemes. Europeans followed this booming Asian economy as architects attempted to take control of sprawling low-density cities, proposing instead megastructures, big architectural ensembles, a new big architecture. Banham included work from Italy (Florence School), Holland and Belgium (the Situationist International Group and Constant Nieuwenhuys's *New Babylon* project 1957–74), from France (Yona Freidman and his megastructure that floats over Paris, *Paris Spatial* 1960), as well as the Archigram group in London. Their projects for *Walking City* (Ron Herron, 1964) or *Plug-In City* (Peter Cook, 1964) inspired his analysis of Los Angeles and its megastructural enclaves. Banham's 1976 book cover featured Paul Rudolf's project over Robert Moses' Lower Manhattan Expressway with a linear, A-frame megastructure (1970).

The emergence of the global megalopolis: Japan and 'MegaTokyo'

Banham ascribed the terms 'megastructure' and 'megaform' to the young Harvard-educated Japanese architect Fumihiko Maki, who had studied with CIAM member and student of Le Corbusier JL Sert, Walter Gropius's successor as chairman at Harvard.Sert had created the first American Urban Design course there in 1956 and was a close friend of Ernesto Rogers in late CIAM. Sert saw urban design as an emerging discipline to design large fragments in the city, as well as a surrounding matrix of low-rise development. He held onto the metropolis as the key to design and large fragments like the Rockefeller Center as the domain of the architect and urban designer. His *Can Our Cities Survive?* (1942) was highly critical of suburban sprawl and development. [38]

After their success in the Berlin Haupstadt competition in 1958, the Smithsons and the Team 10 group broke away from CIAM over the issue of community associations and multi-use clustering, while accepting the megascale network of the megalopolis, especially its highways and their landscape scale. At their 1959 Otterlo Conference, American Team 10 member Louis Kahn showed a set of circular, megastructural parking garages surrounding low-rise central

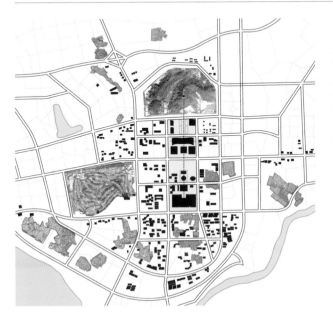

Shenzhen Planning Commission and Llewelyn-Davies, Weeks & Partners, master plan for Shenzhen, China, 1980–84 (redrawn by the author, 2010)
The plan is here redrawn to show urban villages. The designers of Milton Keynes also consulted on planning Shenzhen (see chapter 8). (Redrawn plan © David Grahame Shane and Uri Wegman, 2010)

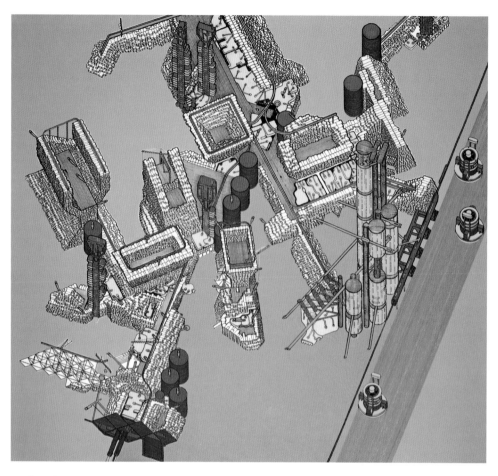

Peter Cook / Archigram, Plug-In City, 1964
(Drawing © Peter Cook)

Fumihiko Maki, Investigation in Collective Form diagram, 1960
The image shows three diagrams of collective forms: (from left to right)
modern architecture, megastructure and group. (Diagram © Fumihiko Maki)

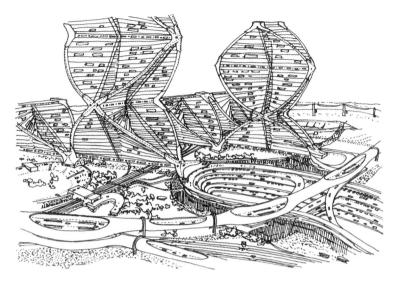

Mikio and Kisho Kurokawa, Helix City, 1961
(Drawing © Mikio Kurokawa, Kisho Kurokawa architect & associates)

Philadelphia from 1952 and elaborated a theory of 'urban rooms' as new public spaces in the city.[39] Each circular tower from the 1952 project was a different colour along the inner ring highway, with parking below and a central circular garden on the garage roof, surrounded by a thin curving slab of offices and housing above, open to views of the city centre.

At the 1960 World Design Conference in Tokyo, where the Smithsons, Kahn and Kenzo Tange were also participants, Maki presented his megastructure theory.[40] He described three modes of urban design. First there was the old style of 'composition', whether Beaux-Arts or Modern, that placed buildings as objects in space and the landscape. Then there was the system of 'megastructures', giant building systems that contained all the life of a city within them, like Cumbernauld town centre. Finally there was the system of 'group form', a horizontal urban network or 'organic' mesh of small-scale buildings across the landscape as in the German *Stadtlandschaft* tradition, with rules that governed their relationship to each other and the landscape. In his article published in 1965, Maki illustrated three diagrams of each design system, ending with a design for the long-planned Shinjuku Tokyo subcentre as a fragmented 'group form' system (his later small-scale work at Hillside Terrace (1969 onwards), also in Tokyo, was a better example). While this analysis linked directly to the global urban design discourse, it also resonated strongly in Japan in the 1960s boom years.

Maki belonged to a group of Tange's students in Tokyo University Laboratory who became the Metabolist group, seeking more organic forms, while retaining the enormous scale of the megalopolis and rejecting the low-rise 1945 Tokyo War Damage

Rehabilitation Plan by Eiyo Ishikawa.[41] Banham gives this group pride of place, anticipating the European interest of Archigram, Superstudio and other groups in his *Megastructures* (1976). In searching for a more organic clustering form, the Metabolists could turn to the Japanese version of the German *Stadtlandschaft* tradition incorporated in Ishikawa's plan. The neighbourhood units of this plan had an unusual, organic time dimension, so that pedestrian-scaled neighbourhood units (with traditional temple cores in addition to nursery schools, communal bath houses and markets) were no more than five minutes' walk from a commercial centre that in turn was no more than 20 minutes by mechanised transport from a major commercial and cultural centre, ascending through a network to the old city centre. Kisho Kurokawa's Helix City project (1961) projected the basic spiral of Tokyo's design, around the Imperial Palace, up into three dimensions in the Ginza commercial district, at the centre of Ishikawa's system. The double-helix spirals of housing hovered above commercial zones and highways, with an Olympic stadium and further highways set in the surrounding parkland. Arata Isozaki's Space City project (1960), also from Tange's Laboratory, takes Kahn's separation of servant and served spaces and makes a giant erector kit of neoclassical columns (servant spaces) supporting occupied bridge structures (served spaces), high above the city ground plane.[42]

As in the modern metropolis of 1950s New York, comic-book designers captured the huge dimensions of this emerging Japanese megalopolis in manga graphic novels and animated films, focusing on 'MegaTokyo'.[43] While some teenagers concentrated on racing fast motorbikes and customised cars on the elevated highways above the city (the subject of countless video games), 'MegaTokyo' as a mythic urban construct seemed to grow and extend forever like a giant machine. Robots and megastructures dominate the urban landscape, overshadowing old small-scale neighbourhoods and villages. Computers and media interact with citizens everywhere, making a veritable cyber-city available to all, but at the same time both potentially controlled by evil forces or running out of control (with a robotic mind of its own). Nature plays little part in this city, except in a ruined, post-apocalyptic landscape relating to atom bombs or earthquakes. Villains constantly threaten megacity Tokyo, but, like in New York, incorruptible superheroes save the day – a lonely *noire* detective, an ex-policeman, a teenage ninja orphan or a cyborg-half-human princess.

Tokyo emerged as the exemplary megalopolis, recognised by Gottmann as 'Tokaido', the linear city stretching down the bullet train line to Osaka.[44] In his *Megalopolis Revisited: 25 Years Later* (1987), Gottmann saw MegaTokyo as a 'city-system' housing 39 million people, the largest in the world. Initially conceived as a shrinking city of 4 million, with a single core and ring of satellites beyond a green belt in the 1958 plan, after the Korean War Tokyo grew into a corridor incorporating the huge industrial complex around Yokohama, Nagoya, the old capital of Kyoto, and ending in the commercial port of Osaka. In the plains near Tokyo the parallel Yamanote line included the new town of Tama (planned by Ishikawa beyond a green belt, it grew to 4 million by 2000). Tange's Tokyo Bay scheme proved prophetic in its linear, megastructural scale and grid format, but underestimated the power of the Japanese National Railway Company with its own subcentre logic.[45] Tokyo's rapid transformation into a global

**Design Partnership, William Lim and Tay Kheng
Soon, early drawings of Woh Hup (Golden Mile)
Megastructure, Kallang, Singapore, 1973**
(Drawings © Tay Kheng Soon and William Lim)

**Design Partnership, William Lim and Tay Kheng
Soon, Woh Hup (Golden Mile) Megastructure,
Kallang, Singapore (photos 2009)**
(Photos © Jonathan Lin)

Kim Swoo-Geun, Sewoon Sangga Market, Seoul, South Korea, 1966 (photo 2007)
A modern, mixed-use megastructure invaded by an informal electronic street market,
currently scheduled to be demolished. (Photo © David Grahame Shane)

megalopolis inspired much admiration within its old imperial territories, Korea, Taiwan and Singapore, now under the American nuclear umbrella on the Pacific Rim. These countries also adapted the combination of state planning, giant corporations, high-speed rail nets, real-estate-driven hubs and raised highways crossing old city cores, to form a characteristic Asian megalopolis, with characteristic Asian megastructures like the Singapore Golden Mile Complex (initiated 1967, completed 1972–3).[46]

Conclusion: critiques of the global megalopolis

Gottmann's euphoric description of the largely unplanned megalopolis on the American East Coast seaboard created a new model as an inspiration for planners working on a huge new scale and also for state planning bureaucracies, from Latin America, Western Europe and Asia. State planners dreamt of manipulating the state highway grid, planning new towns, factories and offices, shopping centres, etc to give the maximum of choice to residential estates, all coordinated by highways to serve citizens with automobiles. Meanwhile a vast shadow megalopolis developed in cities without industrialised housing construction sectors, as people built their own houses, and the city grew house by house (creating what Maki called an informal 'group form'). The scale and scope of urban design changed under these circumstances, some architects dreaming of megastructures, huge building systems with all the functions of the city within giant fragments, others seeking to correct the faults of the bottom-up, self-built urban form of the *barrios* and *favelas* with either traditional closed plazas or open modern service spaces (see chapter 6). In Asia the Sewoon Sangga Market megastructure in Seoul, South Korea, represented a 'failed', modernist megastructure that was invaded by an informal market.

The megalopolis took its place alongside the metropolis as a way of making modern cities in the 1950s and 1960s, marking the efforts of America to distinguish itself from the USSR and its more traditional central planning. By the 1990s the megalopolis had become the dominant form of city expansion even in Moscow and Beijing. It was a relatively simple system made up of enclaves and armatures and infinitely expandable as long as there were energy, infrastructure and cheap land. Kevin Lynch in *Good City Form* (1981) accurately described the structure of the American megalopolis as a 'city as a machine' in a diagram of rectangular white enclaves arranged in a rough grid with two types of armatures, continuous or intermittent, connecting them together into a system.[47] In addition Lynch inserted two nonconforming black enclaves, my heterotopias, a circle and a triangle, exceptions to the general system, spaces of difference or places of change, helping stabilise the overall system (they might be the city dump, an illicit market, hidden workers' housing or a red-light district). Contemporary plans for Dubai show this enclave-and-armature system in its starkest form as global oil production perhaps reaches its peak. Here each enclave is closed and controlled, air-conditioned and policed, connected by the highway along the coast to spectacular attractors, malls with ski slopes, artificial islands and luxury hotels. The 'ideal' fully functional city-machine in the harsh desert environment draws visitors from around the globe to this mirage, a fragment of the expiring, modern, oil-powered megalopolis.

Notes

NB: See 'Author's Caution: Endnote Sources and Wikipedia', towards the end of this book.

1   For populations, see: US Census International Data Base (IDB), http://www.census.gov/ipc/www/idb/country.php (accessed 18 February 2010).

2   See: Paul R Krugman, *The Self-Organizing Economy*, Blackwell Publishers (Cambridge, MA), 1996, pp 22–9, 48–9.

3   For the megalopolis, see: Jean Gottmann, *Megalopolis: The Urbanized Northeastern Seaboard of the United States,* Twentieth Century Fund (New York), 1961.

4   For Mulberry Harbour, see: Encyclopaedia Britannica, http://www.britannica.com/dday/article-9344572; also: http://en.wikipedia.org/wiki/Mulberry_harbour (accessed 11 July 2010).

5   For oil consumption, see: Paul Roberts, *The End of Oil: On the Edge of a Perilous New World*, Houghton Mifflin (Boston, MA), 2004.

6   On Paul Rudolph's Lower Manhattan Expressway, see: *Paul Rudolph & His Architecture*, University of Massachusetts Dartmouth Library, website, http://prudolph.lib.umassd.edu/node/14453 (accessed 18 February 2010).

7   Le Corbusier, *Towards a New Architecture*, Payson & Clarke (New York), (1927).

8   For Chicago wealth, see: William Cronon, *Nature's Metropolis: Chicago and the Great West*, WW Norton (New York), c 1991.

9   For the impact of highways on landscape, see: Kevin Lynch, *The Image of the City*, MIT Press (Cambridge, MA), 1961; also: Donald Appleyard, Kevin Lynch and John R Myer (eds), *The View from the Road*, MIT Press (Cambridge, MA), 1964; also: Kevin Lynch, *Site Planning*, MIT Press (Cambridge, MA), 1962. For city expansion and landscape, see: Christopher Tunnard, *Man-made America: Chaos or Control? An Inquiry into Selected Problems of Design in the Urbanized Landscape*, Yale University Press (New Haven, CT), 1963. For landscape and urbanism, see: Ian McHarg, *Design with Nature*, published for the American Museum of Natural History (Garden City, NY), 1969.

10 For a feminist critique of suburbia, see: Gwendolyn Wright, *Building the Dream: A Social History of Housing in America*, Pantheon (New York), 1981.

11 Melvin M Webber, 'The Urban Place and the Nonplace Urban Realm', *Explorations into Urban Structure*, University of Pennsylvania Press (Philadelphia, PA), 1964; see also: Melvin M Webber, 'Tenacious Cities' online resource, http://www.ncgia.ucsb.edu/conf/BALTIMORE/authors/webber/paper.html (accessed 20 February 2010). Walter Christaller, *Central Places in Southern Germany*, Prentice Hall (Englewood Cliffs, NJ), 1966.

12 For *8 Mile*, see: the Internet Movie Database, http://www.imdb.com/title/tt0298203/ (accessed 20 February 2010).

13 *Reyner Banham Loves Los Angeles*, BBC television documentary by Julian Cooper, 1972, 52 minutes, http://video.google.com/videoplay?docid=1524953392810656786 (accessed 20 February 2010).

14 Reyner Banham, *Los Angeles: The Architecture of Four Ecologies*, Harper & Row (New York), 1971, pp 119–20.

15 For OPEC oil embargoes, see: Roberts, *The End of Oil*, pp 100–103; also: Peter Odell, *Oil and World Power*, Penguin (Harmondsworth, Middlesex; New York), 1983.

16 For SOM's Hajj terminal, Jeddah, see: Zach Mortice, 'SOM's Saudi Arabia Hajj Terminal is Honored with 2010 Twenty-five Year Award', American Institute of Architects (AIA) website, http://www.aia.org/practicing/awards/aiab082164 (accessed 21 February 2010).

17 For King Abdullah Economic City, see: Crispin Thorold, 'New Cities Rise from Saudi Desert', 11 June 2008, BBC News website, http://news.bbc.co.uk/2/hi/middle_east/7446923.stm (accessed 8 March 2010); also: *SOM City Design Practice*, SOM website, http://www.som.com/video/citydesign/index.html, pp 16–17.

18 On Caracas, see: Leslie Klein, 'Metaphors of Form: weaving the *barrio*', Columbia University website, http://www.columbia.edu/~sf2220/TT2007/web-content/Pages/leslie2.html (accessed 11 March 2010).

19   On El Silencio, see: Villanueva Foundation website, http://www.fundacionvillanueva.org/ (accessed 25 March 2010).

20   On the Rotival Plan, see: Valerie Fraser, *Building the New World: Studies in the Modern Architecture of Latin America, 1930–1960*, Verso (New York; London), 2000, p 203.

21   On the Parque Central complex, see: http://en.wikipedia.org/wiki/Parque_Central_Complex (accessed 11 March 2010).

22   For architect Carlos Villaneuva, see: Paulina Villaneuva and Maciá Pintó, *Carlos Raúl Villanueva, 1900–1975*, Alfadil Ediciones (Caracas; Madrid), 2000. For the fate of the 23 de Enero neighbourhood, see: Joshua Bauchner, 'The City That Built Itself', http://canopycanopycanopy.com/6/the_city_that_built_itself (accessed 10 July 2010).

23   For Villa Planchart, see: Antonella Greco (ed), *Gio Ponti: La Villa Planchart a Caracas*, Edizioni Kappa (Rome), 2008.

24   For malls, see: Victor Gruen, *The Heart of our Cities: The Urban Crisis – Diagnosis and Cure*, Simon & Schuster (New York), 1964. For Tehran, see: Wouter Vanstiphout, 'The Saddest City in the World: Tehran and the legacy of an American dream of modern city planning', available at http://www.bezalel-architecture.com/wp-content/uploads/2009/09/The-Saddest-City-in-the-World.pdf and on Crimson Architectural Historians' 'The New Town' website, http://www.thenewtown.nl/article.php?id_article=71 (accessed 11 July 2010).

25   On Doxiadis, see: Constantinos A Doxiadis website, http://www.doxiadis.org/ (accessed 20 February 2010). For Doxiadis's Baghdad master plan, see: Panayiota Pyla, 'Back to the Future: Doxiadis' plans for Baghdad', *Journal of Planning History*, vol 7, no 1, pp 3–19; also: Constantinos A Doxiadis, *Architecture In Transition*, Oxford University Press (New York), 1963, pp 109–16.

26   On Abadan Refinery, see: http://en.wikipedia.org/wiki/Abadan_Refinery (accessed 21 February 2010); also: US Energy Information Administration website, http://www.eia.doe.gov/emeu/cabs/Iran/Profile.html (accessed 11 July 2010). For new town growth, see: International New Town Institute website, http://www.newtowninstitute.org/ (accessed 20 February 2010).

27   Ludwig Hilberseimer, *Grossstadt Architektur*, Julius Hoffmann (Stuttgart), 1927; Ludwig Hilberseimer, *The Nature of Cities: Origin, Growth and Decline; Pattern and Form; Planning Problems*, Paul Theobald (Chicago), 1955.

28   For the MARS plan for London, see: A Korn and FJ Samuely, 'A Master Plan for London', *Architectural Review*, no 91, January 1942, pp 143–50; also: Design Museum website, http://designmuseum.org/design/the-mars-group (accessed 11 July 2010); also: P Johnson-Marshall, 'Arthur Korn: Planner', in Dennis Sharp (ed), *Planning and Architecture: Essays Presented to Arthur Korn by the Architectural Association*, Barrie & Rockliff (London), 1967. See also: E Marmaras and A Sutcliffe, 'Planning for Postwar London: the three independent plans, 1942–3', *Planning Perspectives*, no 9, 1994, pp 431–53.

29   For Randstad, see: http://en.wikipedia.org/wiki/Randstad; also: E Brandes, 'The Randstad: face and form', International Forum on Urbanism conference 2006, Beijing, http://www.evelienbrandes.nl/Randstad%20Form%20and%20Face.pdf (accessed 4 April 2010).

30   For CIAM and the city, see: J Tyrwhitt, JL Sert and EN Rogers (eds), *International Congress of Modern Architecture, The Heart of the City: Towards the Humanisation of Urban Life*, Lund Humphries (London), 1952, p 69; also: José Luis Sert, *Can Our Cities Survive? An ABC of Urban Problems, Their Analysis, Their Solutions; Based on the Proposals Formulated by the CIAM, International Congresses for Modern Architecture*, Harvard University Press (Cambridge, MA) and H Milford / Oxford University Press (London), 1942.

31   For *Hands Over the City*, see: the Internet Movie Database, http://www.imdb.com/title/tt0057286/ (accessed 8 March 2010).

32   On the diffuse city, see: Paola Viganò, 'Urban Design and the City Territory', in Greig Crysler, Stephen Cairns and Hilde Heynen (eds), *The SAGE Handbook of Architectural Theory*, SAGE Publications (London), 2011, Part 8. For urban elements, see: Paola Viganò, *La Città Elementare*, Skira (Milan; Geneva), 1999. For the dispersed city, see: Bernard Secchi and Paola Viganò, 'Water and Asphalt: the projection of isotropy in the metropolitan region of Venice',

in Rafi Segal and Els Verbakel (eds) *Cities of Dispersal, Architectural Design*, vol 78, issue 1, January/February 2008, pp 34–9.

33   Ebenezer Howard, *To-morrow: A Peaceful Path to Real Reform* (1898), republished as *Garden Cities of To-morrow*, Swan Sonnenschein & Co (London), 1902 (available on Google Books). Sir Patrick Geddes, *Cities in Evolution: An Introduction to the Town Planning Movement and to the Study of Cities*, Williams & Norgate (London), 1915.

34   For the Buchanan Report, see: British Ministry of Transport, *Traffic in Towns*, Penguin Books (Harmondworth, Middlesex; Baltimore, MD), 1963.

35   For Reyner Banham on Los Angeles, see: Banham, *Los Angeles,* pp 28-9 and pp 95-111. For Milton Keynes, see: Derek Walker, *The Architecture and Planning of Milton Keynes*, Architectural Press (London) and Nichols Pub (New York), 1982; also: http://en.wikipedia.org/wiki/Milton_Keynes_Development_Corporation and http://en.wikipedia.org/wiki/Central_Milton_Keynes_Shopping_Centre (accessed 20 February 2010).

36   For Victor Gruen's plan of Tehran, see: Wouter Vanstiphout, 'The Saddest City in the World: Tehran and the legacy of an American dream of modern town planning', 2 March 2006, The New Town research project website, http://www.thenewtown.nl/article.php?id_article=71 (accessed 20 February 2010).

37   For French new towns, see: Clement Orillard, 'Between Shopping Malls and Agoras: a French history of protected public space', in Michiel Dehaene and Lieven De Cauter (eds), *Heterotopia and the City: Public Space in a Postcivil Society*, Routledge (London; New York), 1998, pp 117–36. On Toulouse-Le Mirail, see: Team 10 website, http://www.team10online.org/team10/meetings/1971-toulouse.htm.

38   On Maki megastructure/megaform, see: Reyner Banham, *Megastructure: Urban Futures of the Recent Past*, Thames & Hudson (London), 1976, pp 217–18; also: Fumihiko Maki, 'Some Thoughts on Collective Form', Gyorgy Kepes (ed), *Structure in Art and Science*, George Braziller (New York), 1965, pp 116–27; also: Sert, *Can our Cities Survive*, 1942.

39   On the 1959 CIAM conference in Otterlo, see: Team 10 website, www.team10online.org/team10/meetings/1959-otterlo.htm (accessed 21 February 2010). On the Louis Kahn proposals, see: Robert C Twombly (ed), *Louis Kahn: Essential Texts*, WW Norton & Company (New York), pp 36–61.

40   For the Tokyo World Design Conference of 1960, see: Raffaele Pernice, 'The Transformation of Tokyo During the 1950s and Early 1960s', *Journal of Asian Architecture and Building Engineering*, vol 5, no 2, pp 253–60, available at http://www.jstage.jst.go.jp/article/jaabe/5/2/253/_pdf (accessed 23 June 2010). For Maki's megastructure theory, see: Maki, 'Some Thoughts on Collective Form', Kepes (ed), *Structure in Art and Science*, pp 116–27.

41   On Metabolism, see: Kisho Kurokawa, *Metabolism in Architecture*, Studio Vista (London), 1977. On Kenzo Tange, see: Udo Kultermann (ed), *Kenzo Tange, 1946–1969: Architecture and Urban Design*, Praeger Publishers (New York), 1970. On Ishikawa's plan, see: Carola Hein, 'Machi: Neighborhood and Small Town – the foundation for urban transformation in Japan', *Journal of Urban History*, vol 35, no 1, 2008, pp 75–107.

42   On Isozaki's *Space City Project*, see: Banham, *Megastructure*, pp 54–7.

43   For MegaTokyo in comics, see: *MegaTokyo* website, http://www.megatokyo.com/strip/1; also: MegaTokyo Reader's Guide website, http://rg.megatokyo.info/ (accessed 21 February 2010).

44   Jean Gottmann, *Megalopolis Revisited: 25 Years Later*, University of Maryland Institute for Urban Studies (College Park, MD), 1987, pp 20–24.

45   On Kenzo Tange, see: list of books on Kenzo Tange, http://architect.architecture.sk/kenzo-tange-architect/kenzo-tange-architect.php (accessed 15 March 2010). On Kenzo Tange Tokyo Bay Project, see: Banham, *Megastructure*, pp 49–53.

46   On the Golden Mile complex today, see: http://en.wikipedia.org/wiki/Golden_Mile_Complex (accessed 16 March 2010); also: Norman Edwards, *Singapore: A Guide to Buildings, Streets, Places*, Times Books International (Singapore), *c* 1988.

47   Kevin Lynch, *Good City Form*, MIT Press (Cambridge, MA), 1981, p 81.

Aerial photograph of Dubai, United Arab Emirates (photo 2008)
(Photo © G Bowater/Corbis)

CHAPTER 6

Illustrated Megalopolis

Few designers in the 1950s would have predicted that the urban experiments of the oil-powered American megalopolis would emerge as the dominant global urban form of the second half of the 20th century. By the late 1950s, British Team 10 members like Alison and Peter Smithson had identified the American highway system as a megastructural element at a new scale in the city and tried to incorporate this infrastructure in their work, like the Berlin Haupstadt scheme (1958). Jean Gottmann, the French geographer whose book *Megalopolis* (1961) first described networked cities of 32 million on the American East Coast, did not share the architects' enthusiasm for automobiles and highways, which were in their infancy in 1961.[1]

Gottmann documented the growth of new suburbs like Levittown on Long Island, but railways still dominated commuter patterns in his work. He continued his analysis identifying an Asian megalopolis in the Tokyo–Osaka corridor he called 'Tokaido', and also in the Rhine–Ruhr Valley stretching into Holland. This German version of the megalopolis drew on a long tradition of romantic state planning, idealising the forest and field and delicately trying to place the city in the landscape (a reaction against the earlier, rapid, heavy industrialisation of the Ruhr Valley). The nearby Saar Valley provided coal for industry and, during the German occupation, planners in the Second World War made ideal *Stadtlandschaft* (city-landscape) plans for cities there.[2]

Gottmann's geographical vision of the megalopolis encompassed a huge city territory and included several variants based on different levels of energy consumption, wealth and position in the global trading system. While postwar North America provided his original inspiration, not everywhere was as wealthy, organised, industrialised or as wasteful as this global superpower that spanned a continent of over 180 million inhabitants (250 million by the 1990s).[3] Oil-rich countries that had petro-dollars might aspire to this form of the megalopolis for their elite in select suburbs but, as in Caracas, Venezuela or Jakarta, Indonesia, the lack of an industrialised housing sector might result in the development of a *favela* megalopolis of self-built housing for the new immigrants. Professional planners and the UN were quick to condemn these new city extensions as slums, not up to proper professional, modern standards.

Other countries might aspire to the North American model or its European variant with railways through state planning from the top down, carefully controlling development like Hong Kong in the New Territories or Seoul with its high-density new towns that fit inside the highway superblock grid. This chapter will explore these global variants of the megalopolis before ending with a look at 'MegaTokyo'. This Asian megalopolis is based on rail, includes green belts and agriculture, and has grown to be one of the largest megacities with 50 million inhabitants, transforming the American model.

Kevin Lynch in *The Image of the City* (1961) and *The View From the Road* (1964, with John R Myer and Donald Appleyard) documented the impact of the megalopolis on the metropolis as Boston's Central Artery cut across downtown (see chapter 7).[4] This elevated and buried highway cut downtown in half and opened up new territories for suburban development on the periphery. Lynch showed the brutal impact of the highway in cutting the city apart, destroying people's habitual routes and mental maps of the dense urban core with its urban village-like neighbourhood structures.

In Europe the British Buchanan Report (1963) also stressed the potentially devastating impact of highways in historic European city cores, showing the difference in scale between a cloverleaf interchange and the squares of Bloomsbury, London.[5] With Myer and Appleyard, Lynch described how driving on raised highways and through cuts in hillsides in the suburban landscape gave a new sense of scale, time, distance and movement that could be designed as well as any boulevard in the traditional city. Reyner Banham learnt a lot from Lynch when writing *Los Angeles; The Architecture of Four Ecologies* (1971), describing the role of the highways and boulevards in relationship to the landscape of the bowl of the city, caught between the mountains, the desert and the sea.[6] He celebrated the death of Downtown, turned into a parking lot. Lynch invented a new conceptual and visual notation system to describe the new city territory occupied by automobiles and pedestrians, sponsored by dynamic, new, oil-powered, economic forces (featuring malls and truck stops) set against a sense of ecological and landscape limits.

Both Lynch and Banham were influenced by Ian McHarg's *Design With Nature* (1969) that focused on how to make decisions about where to develop city territory in an ecologically responsible manner, trying to protect farm land and forest, sites of natural beauty and estuaries.[7] McHarg's great innovation, in the landscape tradition of Patrick Geddes' *Cities in Evolution* (1915), was to computerise his analysis of the city territory.[8] The result was a system of graphic layers mapping different actors and forces, making a complex analysis possible by comparing different layers of territory from different perspectives. Banham developed this systematic analysis into his four-layered ecologies of coast, mountains, plains and infrastructures (with new nodes or enclaves). He emphasised the importance of transport infrastructures in his analysis of Los Angeles, praising the freedom given to individuals in automobiles within the superblocks of the highway system that he celebrated in the BBC film *Reyner Banham Loves Los Angeles* (1972) as monuments of space-time travel in the modern age.[9]

Banham's fourth ecology included enclaves, attractors or places to visit, attached to the stretched armatures of the highways, places like the UCLA campus designed by Frederick Law Olmsted or malls designed by Victor Gruen or Welton Becket. These enclaves almost invariably contained village-like, pedestrian-scaled armatures that organised an approach to a nested centre. Banham devoted a chapter to the 'Art of the Enclave' in his book, including all sorts of formal and informal shopping centres, urban villages and theme parks. Banham was upbeat on the ability of the infrastructure of stretched armatures to host a large variety of enclaves from villages to megaprojects, a scheme that was applied in the Mark 3 British new town of Milton Keynes (1972).[10] There, the chief designer Derek Walker followed the 'nonplan' argument advanced by Banham and his friends (planner Peter Hall, Archigram member Peter Cook, British architect and pioneer of cybernetic architecture Cedric Price, and Paul Barker, the editor of *New Society*) in 1969. Banham, Hall and Price all were influenced by Melvin Webber's argument for freedom and mobility in an open system, where place and nonplace were equally desirable within a well-developed transport and communication grid.[11]

The harsh reality of the unplanned American megalopolis was reflected in the strange heterotopia of illusion built by American gangsters in the Mojave Desert at Las Vegas, close to the Hoover Dam that provided both water and electricity for the nearby atomic bomb testing range. Michel Foucault considered casinos to be one of the prime heterotopias of illusion, where rules changed quickly with a roll of the dice or turn of the roulette wheel.[12] The city also featured legal prostitution, effectively becoming America's national red-light district for a period. Foucault also listed bordellos as another of his heterotopias of illusion, although the city was allegedly owned through long-term ground leases by the Mormon Church (Foucault also included missionary settlements as heterotopias).[13]

The team of Robert Venturi, Denise Scott Brown and Steven Izenour revelled in the vast spaces and signs of the Las Vegas Strip that mirrored and enlarged the 'miracle mile' of McDonalds, department stores and shopping malls growing outside every American city in the early-1950s period of suburban expansion. Venturi, Scott Brown and Izenour accurately gave a sense of the scale and new dynamics of the automobile-based urbanism that formed the basic communal structure of the emerging American megalopolis. The team stressed its popular and democratic, Pop art characteristics as a new monumental, mass communication system of giant signs (though not mentioning the media and advertising that supported such Pop icons, as did Andy Warhol). Their 'directional space diagram' (1972) captures the super-scaled spatial logic of the pavilion in the parking lot on the Strip as mass car ownership developed and parking required ever more space.[14] It also encapsulates a beautiful lesson in urban design ecologies, as the street morphs from medieval pedestrian alley, to American Main Street, to commercial strip outside of town, to Las Vegas Strip and then interior, regional mall (not studied in detail by the Venturi, Scott Brown and Izenour team).

Although the American megalopolis appeared to be unplanned, it depended on many Federal policies. New Deal legislation from the 1930s, for instance, provided loans for mass housing built on cheap land outside of cities made accessible by cheap oil and cheap mass-produced cars. These cheap, federally insured loans were segregated until a 1964 Supreme Court decision removing restrictive covenants placed on land by racial segregationists.[15] The new Federal urban design ecology supported the American middle class that could move in the 1950s from the dense metropolis to the new single-family homes in the megalopolis. Developers like the Levitt Brothers, designers and builders of Levittown, quickly learnt to make on-site-assembly production-line houses, with foundations and drains built by one crew, another doing the carpentry framing and roof, another the plumbing and electrical systems, another the interior and exterior finishes, moving through the estate.[16]

DIRECTIONAL SPACE

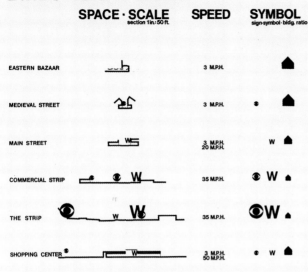

SPACE · SCALE · SPEED · SYMBOL

Robert Venturi, Denise Scott Brown and Steven Izenour, directional space diagram of Las Vegas, Nevada, USA, 1972
An illustration of directional space and speed on the Las Vegas Strip, from *Learning from Las Vegas*, MIT Press (Cambridge, MA), 1972, p 11. (Diagram © courtesy Venturi Scott Brown & Associates)

Every house would have high-energy consumer durables – washing machine, dryer, dishwasher, refrigerator, electric hot water heaters and televisions. The developers learnt to advertise their houses like products, and to entice lucky winners to their building sites by offers of free televisions. In the background of their adverts, in the midst of a former potato field, the new automobiles are lined up on the cul-de-sac street that is intended to make it safe for children's play. Advertisers precisely defined gender roles in the early postwar years of the 'American Dream' in these suburbs, as men commuted to work and did handyman, build-it-yourself chores at the weekend. Women stayed home with the family, watching television in the advertiser's dream, with their only official release being a shopping trip to the mall, quickly inspiring feminist outrage in the 1960s.[17]

As the megalopolis developed in scale, it engulfed earlier settlements, agricultural villages, small industrial towns, even the metropolis itself. Each outward expansion necessitated a re-centring on the outer periphery as well as setting in motion changes at the central core of the metropolis: decay and abandonment. Efforts at urban renewal were rarely successful for a variety of reasons, as global corporations emerged as the new financial actors on the urban stage, seeking suburban headquarters or new towers in new central business districts (CBDs). Victor Gruen, the early mall-designer architect, in his *The Heart of Our Cities; the Urban Crisis Diagnosis and Cure* (1964) described this suburban and core-re-centring process.[18] He, like Venturi, Scott Brown and Izenour later, observed the re-centring

Suburban house and equipment, *c* 1947
Potential homebuyers admire the winners of a free
television in a show house floor layout, demonstrating all
the electrical home appliances of the new suburban living
experience, with the necessary automobiles parked on
the unbuilt street in the background. (Photo © Thomas D
McAvoy/Time & Life Pictures/Getty Images)

**Aerial view of suburban development at
Levittown, New Jersey, USA, *c* 1947**
(Photo © Hulton Archive/Stringer/Getty Images)

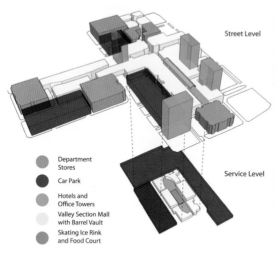

Street Level

Department
Stores

Car Park

Hotels and
Office Towers

Valley Section Mall
with Barrel Vault

Skating Ice Rink
and Food Court

Service Level

**Hellmuth, Obata & Kassabaum (HOK), Houston Galleria I,
Houston, Texas, USA, 1967 (redrawn by the author, 2010)**
Layered axonometric sketch of Houston Galleria. The
Galleria I mall featured a running track on the mall roof,
attached hotel and office towers, and an Olympic-sized
ice rink in the base. (Diagram © David Grahame Shane
and Uri Wegman, 2010)

**Hellmuth, Obata & Kassabaum (HOK), skating rink,
Galleria I, Houston, Texas, USA, 1967 (photo 1999)**
Photograph of interior ice skating rink at the Galleria Mall in
Houston, Texas. (Photo © David Grahame Shane)

process of suburbia from strip to mall, marking stages in the evolution of the mall towards ever more complexity as a pseudo-urban centre diagram. Where the Venturi, Scott Brown and Izenour team celebrated the evolution of the Las Vegas Strip, Gruen was disappointed that malls never achieved their full potential because developers focused on shopping and rents, not mixed uses, social life or cultural amenities.

The logic of the regional mall had a great simplicity. Each mall needed 16 hectares (40 acres) for parking, two department stores and a 200-metre (600-foot) armature to build the basic dumbbell mall that could be financed and paid for with generous tax deductions in 5 years.[19] Gruen documented that such a mall needed 500,000 people to be within 20 minutes' driving distance to be successful, according to the formulas of the 1950s.[20] The original open-air malls could later be enclosed and made split level through manipulations of the parking lot ground plane, giving access to both levels directly from parking lots. This simple, successful formula prompted developers to think of super-regional megamalls that had several department stores and several armatures, attracting people from a larger region, even nationally or internationally in the case of the Mall of America (1992) designed by Jon Jerde outside Minneapolis, beside the airport, which attracted 40 million visitors at its peak in 2006.[21]

Gerald Hines, the developer of the first megamall – the Houston Galleria at Houston, Texas, begun in 1967 (designed by Gyo Obata of HOK) – intended the mall to replace downtown Houston, which it did in 15 years.[22] The original regional mall featured an Olympic-sized ice skating rink and a three-storey arcade of shops, transforming the model of Milan's Galleria into a high-end armature with balconies accessible directly from a multistorey car park. The upper balcony featured expensive jewellery stores for visiting oil men and their families, while on the roof there was a running track and sports club with attached hotel and office towers. At one end of the armature a high-end Neiman Marcus department store served as anchor, with a valet parking service for the visitors' Rolls-Royces. The store often featured luxury yachts and expensive Ferraris in its three-storey atrium. Hines originally secured financing from the Saudi royal family and TIAA-CREF, the giant American teachers' pension fund set up by the Carnegie Foundation.[23]

It was impossible to buy everyday needs or a refrigerator in the air-conditioned Galleria I complex, which Banham included in his *Megastructures* book of 1976, before its further expansion to over 186,000 square metres (2 million square feet) in four stages (Galleria II–IV).[24] The original regional Galleria I mall had 5,000 parking spaces, landscaped in two-storey gardens on one side and in a multistorey structure on the other. Philip Johnson and John Burgee later added a replica of the Empire State Building (Transco Tower, 1983, now known as Williams Tower) to the east end of the complex, creating a super-scaled beacon on the western skyline of Houston. The complex set a model for future megamall developments worldwide with its dense, three-dimensional matrix of malls and multistorey car parks at the base of several different towers containing mixed uses. Where the Houston Galleria version had no public transportation, Asian and European versions would add connections to these networks.

THE EUROPEAN MEGALOPOLIS: THE *STADTLANDSCHAFT* (CITY-LANDSCAPE) TRADITION IN GERMANY, THE MIDDLE EAST AND ASIA

Gottmann's geographic concept of the megalopolis was deeply influenced by European landscape traditions, even though it found its best expression in the East Coast of America undamaged by the Second World War. European and imperial city and regional planning shared a long history of large-scale thinking. Patrick Geddes' work *Cities in Evolution* (1915) had influenced German city-landscape (*Stadtlandschaft*) planning as well as their Japanese wartime allies in the Second World War. After the war the German architect Hans Scharoun participated in plans to shrink Berlin to 4 million people, and give it an agricultural and park belt.[25] The Japanese planner Ishikawa made similar plans for Tokyo (see p 178). Scharoun imagined parks running from east to west across central Berlin following the River Spree valley, seizing on the Allied bombing as an opportunity to make a green, low-rise city. His plan for the Berlin *Haupstadt* competition of 1958 showed his intention to make a green metropolis in detail, creating vast urban fragments on an east–west axis. This megastructure would be accessed by a highway grid and subways, floating in a sea of parkland and parking. These fragments, not unlike the Houston Galleria, were intended to be mixed-use and multifunctional replacements for the old, dense downtown, but set in landscape.

While Scharoun had withdrawn from public life during the Nazi regime, many of Europe's most distinguished German urban planning professionals had served the regime, making plans for occupied Poland or parts of France (as many collaborative Frenchmen did in Vichy, including Le Corbusier). The German *Stadtlandschaft* tradition with its emphasis on landscape and hygiene had fitted well with Nazi propaganda about race, soil and purity.[26] In both East and West Germany, professionals had to excise some of their history to participate in the much-needed rebuilding of the cities, often along city-landscape lines, involving large city territories, aerial surveys and a respect for forest and waterways. Rudolf Schwarz, a fervent religious man and ex-Nazi, provided the classic statement of city-landscape theory, as well as re-planning downtown Cologne and its surrounding countryside with new industry in valleys and housing on the surrounding rural hillsides, linked by rail and autobahn (1946–52, summarised in *The New Cologne* (1950)).[27] His theoretical *Milky Way* diagram showed the dream of a central communal 'city crown', described in his *Von der Bebauung der Erde* (Of the Construction/Cultivation of the Earth (1949)), encompassing mainly state facilities, beside a lake, with swimming and other healthy recreational activities around its rim.[28] For Schwarz the cathedral held a special central place in this approach as an almost mystical expression of a shared communal aspiration. While Schwarz protected downtown Cologne from automobiles, pedestrianising the rebuilt main street, he also widened other streets as boulevards leading to the autobahn ring and radials. These plans fit well with the ideas of the Allied occupation forces, especially the Americans with their emphasis on the automobile and trains.

Cologne lay at the heart of the West German autobahn system connecting the Rhine and Ruhr valleys, forming a vast city-landscape territory that also connected to the contemporary Dutch Randstad (Ring City) to the north on the Rhine estuary (linking Amsterdam, The Hague

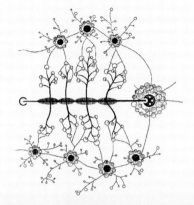

Rudolf Schwarz, *Stadtlandshaft*
'Milky Way Diagram', 1948
Diagram of a city and
landscape as a 'Milky Way'
constellation. (Diagram ©
Maria Schwarz)

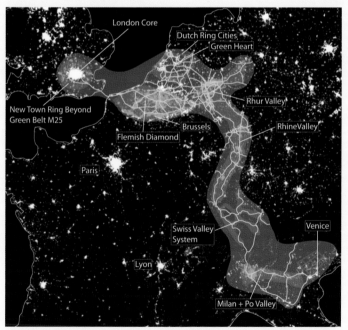

London Core

Dutch Ring Cities
Green Heart

Rhur Valley

New Town Ring Beyond
Green Belt M25

RhineValley

Brussels

Flemish Diamond

Paris

Swiss Valley
System

Venice

Lyon

Milan + Po Valley

Sketch of the 'Blue Banana' based on NASA night photo of Europe, 2009
The sketch shows the European Union's main urban concentrations across the
NASA night photo, forming the 'Blue Banana' of European cities stretching from
London to Milan. (Sketch © David Grahame Shane and Uri Wegman, 2010)

Aryeh Sharon, diagram of Israeli master plan of population dispersion into new towns, 1968 (redrawn by the author, 2010)
Based on Sharon's collages in *Kibbutz + Bauhaus: An Architect's Way in a New Land*, Kramer Verlag (Stuttgart), 1976. (Diagram © David Grahame Shane and Uri Wegman, 2010)

Skidmore, Owings & Merrill (SOM), Hajj Terminal, Jeddah, Saudi Arabia, 1981
This photograph of a 747 jet at the Hajj Terminal gives a sense of the scale of this megastructure built for pilgrims. (Photo © Skidmore, Owings & Merrill LLP)

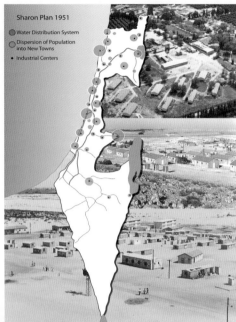

Sharon Plan 1951

Water Distribution System
Dispersion of Population into New Towns
Industrial Centers

Skidmore, Owings & Merrill (SOM), Hajj Terminal, Jeddah, Saudi Arabia, 1981
The Hajj Terminal's roof 'tents'. (Photo © Skidmore, Owings & Merrill LLP)

and Rotterdam in a city network around a green core). Together these two rail and highway networks linked from Holland to Belgium and the Flemish network of cities in the Rhine delta, including Brussels, Bruges, Ghent and Antwerp. The high-speed railway station at Lille in northern France, within OMA's Euralille (1991–4), forms the link to Paris and the Channel Tunnel, leading to the southern rail and highway networks around London. Together these networks create the northwest European megalopolis, recognised by Gottmann in *Since Megalopolis* (1990).[29] This megalopolis connects through the Rhine Valley to Switzerland and then down to northern Italy, Milan, the Po Valley and the Veneto, forming the 'Blue Banana' city-landscape megacity that is the core of the European Union (EU).[30] High-speed rail and meganodes like Euralille play a major role in this conurbation, unlike in the American version of the megalopolis with its megamalls and automobiles.

In the Middle East, Israeli planning followed this German city-landscape tradition because so many Israeli professionals had been active in Germany, especially at the Bauhaus. Aryeh Sharon, for instance, studied with Walter Gropius and Hannes Meyer, before becoming one of the chief planners of modern Israel, planning several new towns as well as a kibbutz. The new state was planned as an ecological unit, including its water supply and agricultural and industrial resources.[31] Sharon went on to plan modern hospitals and schools for the subsequent Israeli welfare state, starting a global practice that extended into Africa and Asia.

Oil-rich Saudi Arabia also employed modern planners and American architectural firms, like SOM, to construct the new state buildings, bank towers, housing developments and mosques. SOM built a magnificent modern megastructure under a many-domed tent roof for the Hajj Terminal at Jeddah (1981), serving the millions of pilgrims flying in each year to Mecca.[32] Mecca itself expanded out into the desert along new highways with suburban estates, served by malls and established new camping grounds for the pilgrims. Riyadh, the Saudi capital, also invested some of its oil wealth in state-of-the-art hospitals and schools for their welfare state, as well as offices, malls, towers and suburbs, serving both the local population and the many expats in service industries.

Saudi Aramco, the Saudi oil company originally set up with Standard Oil in the 1940s, always sought modern design for its facilities, including the now disused Trans-Arabian Pipeline (Tapline) from the Gulf to the Mediterranean in Lebanon.[33] Begun in 1947, the Tapline, set up by Aramco, Standard Oil and other American companies, was designed to replace the Suez Canal if it should close in wartime. The company built small, American-style, air-conditioned, suburban towns at intervals along the Tapline to house its workers in the desert, served by private schools, a private airline and a television broadcasting service (see Middle East diagram in chapter 1). Water was pumped up from deep aquifers below the desert, as refugee camps were established in Israel, Gaza and the Lebanon.

The modernisation of the Middle East depended heavily on oil profits and the American form of the megalopolis, with automobiles and highways. Railways remained key to the Japanese version of the megalopolis and to many Asian states that retained powerful, national central governments wanting to speed up industrial development without a total dependence on imported oil. Tokyo built elevated highways set at 20 metres (60 feet) above the city in time for the 1964 Olympics, setting an example copied all over Asia. But railways remained the core of Tokyo's transport system, stretching out to form a particular Asian megalopolis. Japanese railway companies remained important developers, shaping commercial hubs with malls and towers around their railway stations as at the Shinjuku subcentre in Tokyo (see pp 178, 180, 183).

Seoul, the capital of South Korea, expanded rapidly as a planned megalopolis, learning many lessons from Tokyo in developing its expansion plans, again emphasising rail as well as road. Seoul also learnt from Hong Kong where developers and large construction companies had built high-rise new towns around subway stations following government blueprints, housing large numbers very quickly in industrially produced neighbourhood units with high-rise towers. Seoul followed in this hybrid urban design ecology as the Korea Land Corporation built Bundang New Town (1989–96) in six years to house 1 million people.[34] Bundang has a very clear organisational structure based on high-rise neighbourhood units and superblocks, with dense, mid-rise commercial blocks in each neighbourhood around a street axis. It has a central park and is surrounded by mountainside parks, creating a green city setting for its linear central core that runs beside the river.

Model of Bundang New Town apartment, Seongnam, South Korea (photo 2008)
The central living room of the apartment echoes the traditional courtyard layout of Korean houses. (Photo © David Grahame Shane)

Korea Land Development Corporation, master plan of Bundang New Town, South Korea, 1989
(Plan © courtesy of Korean Land Development Corporation)

Aerial view of Bundang New Town central park, Seongnam, South Korea (photo 2008)
Bundang's central park with lake and memorial temple, surrounded by high-rise tower developments. (Photo © David Grahame Shane)

Aerial view of Bundang New Town neighbourhood unit, Seongnam, South Korea (photo 2008)
A Bundang high-rise residential neighbourhood unit around a multistorey commercial centre with neon signs on the exterior. (Photo © David Grahame Shane)

New town construction required a degree of governmental organisation and planning that was often lacking in developing nations, even oil-rich ones that could hire local or international professionals. The result was that many oil-rich nations expanded without a master plan or, in the case of Caracas, Venezuela, without the means to enforce the green belt of the master plan in the face of a massive movement of population from the countryside. Planners and professionals argued that industrially produced new towns were the answer to the megalopolis as exemplified by Bundang, but many oil-rich nations did not have the industrial capacity to create such complex, planned communities, resulting in the creation of self-built city extensions. These informal, unmapped and often illegal *favela* settlements mirrored the suburban and new town extensions of the megalopolis. They were often contained within the superblocks or megablocks of the highway system, forming sprawling, low-rise urban village constellations across the landscape.[35]

The *favela* built form could not be confused with the isolated forms of the modernist slab block or the garden city villas of American suburbia. The *favela* houses shared walls with each other; property perimeter walls were often the first sign of occupation with a shanty inside. Over time the shanty would expand into a row house, courtyard house or some hybrid, with extra rooms and floors added later as needed. Although such houses may have been built on public or private land without permission, after a time people could buy and sell their houses through an informal system. Schools and other community facilities might be organised. Various gangs might provide some semblance of security in the absence of state authorities. In some cases these gangs might link with the landowners of the property, who could not develop the land legally, but with the gangs could collect illicit rents. In other cases gangs might become violent drug and

Caracas *ranchos* street junction (photo 2008)
The self-built *ranchos* townships take on the quality of Italian hilltop villages over time, without adequate services or construction. (Photo © David Gouverneur)

arms dealers at war with the police, as in Rio de Janeiro, sending cocaine from Colombia out to the world once the US government sealed the Mexican border.[36]

The informal *ranchos* of Caracas built on the planned green-belt moutainside look down on the rest of the city, including the wealthy suburbs with their golf course communities and malls.[37] Access to these steep slopes is difficult, often involving steep staircases and winding mountain tracks only accessible by four-wheel-drive vehicles. The areas are subject to mudslides in extreme weather conditions. While many houses have cesspits for sewage, others use the streams running down into the wealthy city neighbourhoods. All water has to be carried by hand up into the houses, to be poured into the rooftop tanks that service them. On the roof a satellite dish might link to global systems, using electricity 'borrowed' from nearby national grid pylons.

Millions of small-scale urban actors desperate for homes built the *favela* megalopolis from the bottom up in stages, using scraps from legitimate buildings in the central city. The first floor might be finished in tiles, with gates and a steel grille protecting the entrance and owner's apartment. A steel staircase acquired from a downtown office might lead to the first-floor rental apartment, less well finished, and then a wooden staircase leads up to the concrete shell of the second floor, still under construction, with a ladder to the roof. Here magnificent views across the valley show Caracas in all its splendour, while a goat grazing on the rooftop reminds the visitor of the rural origins of the inhabitants, recently emigrated from Honduras to inhabit this rental property. The mandatory water tank and satellite dish handle local and global needs. In Caracas such housing could invade even the most modern and orderly estates built by the government of the military dictatorship, occupying the parkland planned between slab blocks, creating a new hybrid urban form as at Carlos Villanueva's 23 de Enero estate (1955–7, see chapter 5).[38]

Caracas *ranchos* panorama (photo 2008)
In Caracas the self-built *ranchos* townships fill the hillsides above the valley floor of the city. (Photo © Thireshen Govender)

In the 1970s and 1980s the World Bank attempted to remedy the lack of basic services in these communities by proposing a 'sites and services' approach, where the state or municipality provided the basic infrastructure before people built their shanties. The American economic scholar Michael Cohen, who in the 1970s worked on many of these projects in Africa, argued in 2004 that without larger economic provisions such as jobs, slum upgrading and good intentions were not enough.[39] Part of the problem was that only the middle class had the skills and bureaucratic knowledge to take advantage of this system, resulting in gentrification rather than upgrades in the *favela* megalopolis.[40]

The prominent Indian architect BV Doshi, who had worked with Le Corbusier and Louis Kahn, participated in a World Bank 'sites and service' scheme for the Indore Development Company at the expanding industrial town of Aranya in 1982–7, anticipating a population of 65,000.[41] Doshi provided street armatures with small gathering grounds where temple structures could be built on platforms, to be shaded by sacred banyan trees. The central community facilities have still not been built, but some houses have become stores and lively traders with mobile stalls move through the streets, along with the sacred cows.

Doshi provided some simple sample houses, and a small bathroom structure at the back of the plot, connected into a cesspit system. Each plot owner developed their own house in stages as and when they could afford a room or a floor while, as Cohen observed in Africa, others parts of the estate gentrified quickly. The houses themselves represent a strange hybrid of state and private endeavour, both ancient and modern, with shrines and satellite dishes for TVs and computers.[42] While there are still empty plots in Aranya, and some houses are still served by water taps in the street (which run only occasionally, as in other poor Indian settlements), the nearby concrete works supplied jobs essential to the overall success of the project as a hybrid city expansion. Now a mall and a multiplex cinema have appeared close by on the road leading to the plant. Doshi is currently developing plans for a new town of 1 million, Cyberabad, begun in 2000, outside the Indian IT capital of Hyderabad, employing some of the lessons learnt at Aranya to incorporate poorer inhabitants.[43]

Balkrishna Doshi, Aranya Township, Indore, India, 1982 (photo 2005)
Exterior stairs of a self-build street house on Aranya 'Sites and Services' development. (Photo © Krystina Kaza)

Banham envisioned a microscale freedom for individuals within the macroscale infrastructures of the highways that gave mobility and choice, presuming everyone had a car. The *favela* metropolis provides the freedom to construct your own housing, but without the same mobility as envisioned by Banham. The highways also represent barriers to growth in some cases, defended by planning institutions. Instead informal bus systems, motorbikes and scooters provide chaotic, low-cost transportation networks for individuals inside the *favela* megalopolis. Planners turned a blind eye to the *favela* megalopolis; in Chandigarh, Le Corbusier did not show the existing villages in his grid plan of highways and neighbourhood units in megablocks (see chapter 4). Derek Walker recognised the existing villages within the 1972 Milton Keynes megablocks as historic conservation areas, but preserved them in aspic. Milton Keynes employed the same megablock approach that was also used in Shenzhen, the first Chinese Special Economic Zone (SEZ), and subsequent mainland megacity plans. In Shenzhen existing farming communes, created by Mao, had no limitations and were owned by the peasant cooperatives.[44] They developed into high-rise, informal housing and entertainment districts within the planned superblocks and their high-rise towers, making the peasants into millionaires (see chapter 8). In Hong Kong the city government demolished the Walled City of Kowloon; but elsewhere shantytowns, like Dharavi in Mumbai, India, have survived over 60 years and become recognised as settlements in their own right (see chapter 10).[45]

Balkrishna Doshi, Aranya Township, Indore, India, 1982 (photo 2005)
Interior photograph of Arunya self-build home steps. (Photo © Krystina Kaza)

Balkrishna Doshi, Aranya Township, Indore, India, 1982 (photo 2005)
A public square, showing the *maidan* (common ground) platform with sacred tree, temple and cow. (Photo © Krystina Kaza)

In his later work *Since Megalopolis* (1990), Gottmann proposed Tokyo as an exemplary Asian version of the megalopolis. The terrible impact of the Second World War in terms of firebombing and destruction allowed Tokyo to transform rapidly from a large metropolis of 7 million at the heart of an East Asian empire into a key megalopolis of 32 million within a global network of communications by 1961. Tokyo maintained many traces of the old, mono-centric urban pattern that focused on the Imperial Palace at the centre of city. Traces of the merchants' canal system remain in Ginza, and the old imperial gates have become stations on the inner circle railway line.[46] The wide boulevards which, as in Paris, hid the medieval city fabric, still symbolise the modern, Meiji-era city with its tramway system expanding the city like in Los Angeles. But the war damage allowed Ginza to be rebuilt as a commercial hub, while the government took over the old aristocratic palaces on the surrounding hills to set up new ministerial and corporate headquarters. The railway companies kept expanding outwards, making more land available for housing.

Eiyo Ishikawa's 1945 plan for the dispersal and shrinking of Tokyo into the landscape, like Scharoun's contemporary plan for Berlin, depended on a widespread network of railways and a strict hierarchy of neighbourhood units inherited from the German *Stadtlandschaft* planning tradition.[47] The railway company planners seized on this strategy to develop powerful hubs that created large urban fragments in a sea of small-scale housing, governed by earthquake regulations. Ishikawa's plan became ineffectual except in the creation of some parks and highway belts, as the railway companies continued their tradition of developing land along their railway lines, even though they were state-owned corporations.

This huge city of 32 million did not run on automobiles. Railways still provided the backbone of transportation, and the early development of the bullet train meant that much agricultural land was within easy reach in the Asian megacity, continuing a long tradition. Indeed the Japanese railway companies, in developing nodes like Shinjuku and high-speed railway hubs like at Kyoto, pioneered the combination of the railway, mall and parking, with or without office tower clusters.

In 1968 the Tokyo government published a plan that followed the ring-and-radial model employed by Patrick Abercrombie in London in 1943 and recognised the reality of the sprawl and clusters at key nodes, but still clung to green belts, proposing a big new town at Tama on the main commuter line west of Tokyo in the agricultural plains beyond the green belt.[48] Tama eventually grew to house 2 million people, creating a garden city enclave, with later high-rise towers around a strong street armature that led to the railway station. This was an exceptional development: most of Tokyo, like Los Angeles, consisted of small houses on small plots. Each house had to remain separate in case of earthquakes, but the plots were so small, and the land so valuable, that houses often filled their entire plot, leaving only a tiny parking spot for motorbikes or a mini car. Atelier Bow-Wow in its various publications, like *Made in Tokyo* (2001) or *Pet Architecture* (2002), captures the hybrid microcoding of such low-rise, compressed, dense urban spaces precisely.[49] In this ocean of small houses stretching across the plain, the infrastructure of the megalopolis played a key role in the

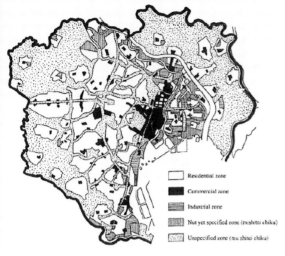

Residential zone

Commercial zone

Industrial zone

Not yet specified zone (mishitei chiku)

Unspecified zone (mu shitei chiku)

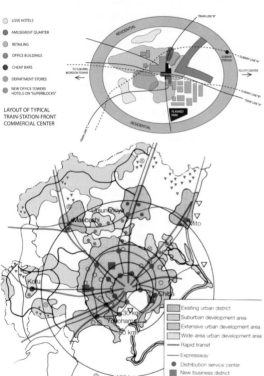

○ LOVE HOTELS

● AMUSEMENT QUARTER

○ RETAILING

○ OFFICE BUILDINGS

● CHEAP BARS

● DEPARTMENT STORES

● NEW OFFICE TOWERS
HOTELS ON "SUPERBLOCKS"

LAYOUT OF TYPICAL
TRAIN-STATION-FRONT
COMMERCIAL CENTER

Existing urban district

Suburban development area

Extensive urban development area

Wide-area urban development area

— Rapid transit

— Expressway

● Distribution service center

■ New business district

⊗ City with colleges or research centers

○ Large-scale residential district

● Industrial city

▨ Recreational area

▽ Port

▼ Large-scale livestock farming

132. Second Basic Plan for the Greater Metropolitan Region (1968).
This plan, which was drawn up in the same year as the new City Planning Law, was a wholesale revision of the first basic plan.

Eiyo Ishikawa, Reconstruction Plan for Tokyo, Japan, 1946
Ishikawa was influenced by German *Stadlandschaft* theories and planned for Tokyo to shrink, allowing green belts between rebuilt settlements.

Tokyo City Planning Department, master plan for Tokyo, Japan, 1968
Diagram of local transport hub arrangements, showing multiple rail hubs, new towns and a green belt. Adapted from Roman Cybriwsky's analysis in *Tokyo: The Shogun's City at the Twenty-First Century*, John Wiley & Sons (New York), 1998. (Plan © David Grahame Shane and Uri Wegman, 2010)

Suburban street with Bolles + Wilson's Suzuki House (1995), Tokyo, Japan (photo 2010)
Because of earthquake regulations and fire concerns, after the Second World War, Tokyo suburban houses were limited in height and forbidden to touch each other. Residents put trees in containers on the narrow sidewalks and value every inch of their space (note the roof gardens). (Photo © Benika Morokuma, 2010)

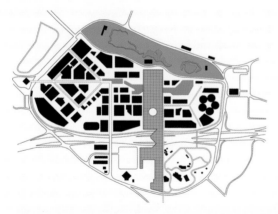

Kenzo Tange, site plan for Expo '70, Osaka, Japan, 1970 (redrawn by the author, 2010)
Tange planned both the layout of the World's Fair site and the megastructure running at right angles across it, sheltering giant robots and forming a new, electronic agora. (Redrawn plan © David Grahame Shane and Uri Wegman, 2010)

Kenzo Tange, megastructure for Expo '70, Osaka, Japan, 1970
Photographs by Archigram's Dennis Crompton showing the view of the exterior of the Tange megastructure from the Archigram capsule under the roof, overlooking the public space, and the view from the plaza of robots in the public space designed by Arata Isozaki in Tange's office. (Photos © Dennis Crompton)

expansion and extension of the city, not just in terms of highways and new housing estates, but also in terms of new public space and high-density nodes.

Just as the Tokyo Olympics of 1964 provided the impetus for the construction of highway megastructures, the Osaka World's Fair of 1970 provided a giant experimental example of this new public space in the enormous, covered Festival Plaza.[50] Here Kenzo Tange, with Arata Isozaki as assistant, constructed an experimental megastructure to house planned spectacles and media events in a mechanised forum. Giant robots in the forum could take various configurations for different events, providing seating, screens, kiosks, control points and smaller enclosures. This vast exhibition space, a high-tech heterotopia of illusion, tied into global media feeds. Small capsules in the roof provided exhibition spaces, one occupied by Archigram of London.[51] These modules could also be seen as residential units tucked into the vast space frame spanning the forum. Later versions of this festival space became standard at meganodes in the Tokaido corridor, such as at Hiroshi Hara's Umeda Sky Building project in Osaka (1993), and the same architect's Kyoto Station (1997).[52]

Small urban villages survived even in the centre of the dense Shinjuku meganode, inside the megalopolis stretching from Tokyo to Osaka. Many of these urban villages were remnants from the period when Tokyo had been reduced to ruins and people lived in small shanties, re-creating the life of the ruined city from scratch. Often these villages owed their continued existence to their use as red-light districts and entertainment areas, under the patronage of powerful crime syndicates or gang organisations; at other times they were hidden behind new developments and forgotten.[53] Their dangerous reputation kept away most citizens, allowing the survival of a 1.2-metre-(4-foot) wide street like Golden Gai in the midst of the skyscrapers of Shinjuku. Throughout Tokyo and beside many of the new high-rise nodes, such traditional, small-scale streets, sometimes of ill repute, provide a foil to the gleaming towers of the commercial meganode. Some of these streets are attracting the sharp-eyed attention of Japanese historic preservationists, concerned that the last traces of the postwar shantytowns will disappear from the Tokaido corridor.[54]

Hiroshi Hara, Kyoto Station, Japan, 1997
Aerial view, showing the historic centre by the river in the background. (Photo © Ichiso Saiki/ Getty Images)

Hiroshi Hara, Kyoto Station, Japan, 1997 (photo 1999)
Interior view showing the monumental arrival hall with
intermediate-scale café structures and escalators to the roof,
designed to break the scale. (Photo © David Grahame Shane)

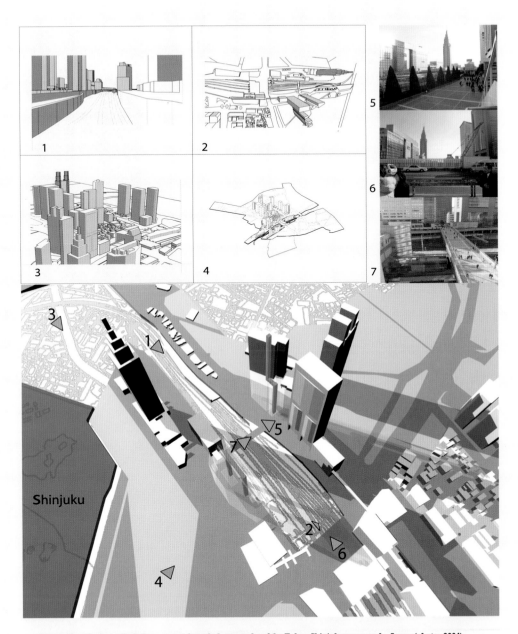

Layered analysis, exploded axonametric and photographs of the Tokyo Shinjuku meganode, Japan (photos 2004)
The Tokyo Shinjuku subcentre grew up in large increments around a railway station with especially good links to the expanding western suburbs and traditional central business district in Ginza. (Diagrams © David Grahame Shane and Rodrigo Guarda; photos © David Grahame Shane and Tatsuya Utsumi)

Kenzo Tange, Tokyo Metropolitan Government Building, Japan, 1991
The central plaza and twin towers of the new city hall, with nearby hotel, also by Tange,
in the background. Note double layered traffic system. (Photo © Osamu Murai)

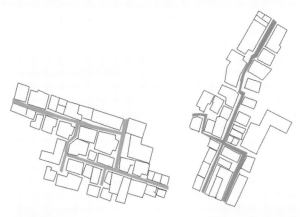

Golden Gai historic district, Shinjuku, Tokyo, Japan (photos 2010)
Lower photos and plans are of neighbouring rojis of the Kagurazaka district. Golden Gai is the remnants of an earlier village street in the midst of the high-rise Shinjuku megahub. (Photos © Benika Morokuma)

Conclusion

Gottmann recognised many potential variations in the megalopolis that he saw as an extended city territory, stretching many miles. His first observations concerned the northeast coast of America which, when he was writing in 1961, was still based on railways but by 1971 provided an alternative automobile-based form of urbanism celebrated by Reyner Banham in his Los Angeles studies and movie. Lynch provided key concepts and mapping tools to describe this city that ran for miles in the landscape, connecting it to earlier European landscape traditions like those of Patrick Geddes in Britain or the *Stadtlandschaft* tradition in Germany.

Here the automobile did not rule the city as in Banham's vision, but a hybrid of train and highway formed a fuel-efficient hybrid version of the American high-energy original. The American original predominated wherever oil was cheap and plentiful, especially in the Middle East with its oil-based income. Patches of American urbanism, like the small towns along the Tapline, appeared across the region and the world from Nigeria to Venezuela, wherever oil wealth drew immigrants and workers. Sometimes the result might be neat new towns where there were few people, as in Saudi Arabia; at other times the result could be vast self-built shantytowns where there were larger populations who did not share in the wealth.

Tokyo as a megalopolis contains all this history. At the end of the Second World War it stood in ruins and many people built shanties and lived in hovels amongst the ruins. Today some of these shanties survive in the centre as entertainment districts, close to meganodes, but most such urban villages have been demolished. Yet the Tokyo suburbs in their sprawling, small-scale extent represent a vast kind of mega-*favela* constellation, with all modern services provided. Sanitation systems are still being upgraded, but water goes to every house, poles carry in overhead electricity and telecommunications wires with big transformers hum above the street. Cellphone towers provide constant and universal coverage. Tiny lanes allow cycling and walking, but are hard for cars, especially large ones. Sidewalks are full of plants in pots, as few houses have gardens. Wealth, educational services, health care and elaborate policing make these sprawling suburbs of micromansions desirable places to live, even though their physical form is not so far from that of a *favela*.

MegaTokyo comprises all these sprawling neighbourhoods, as well as the traces of the old metropolis and its ring-and-radial structure, with green belts and Tama New Town. Tokyo has a ring of American-style automobile-based suburbs and highways that are based on automobiles and loop around the city to the new airport in the northeast. Here planned new universities and research centres replicate California and Los Angeles in their large-scale enclave layouts, forming megablocks and business campuses. These roads cross downtown Tokyo with difficulty, high above the city. The average speed in the daytime is scarcely above walking, but people still pay to enter the raised highway. At night motorcycle enthusiasts and gangs ride through the serpentine curves at high speed. Above and below the raised highway infrastructure, all sorts of strange uses collect in this section of the city, creating small heterotopic pockets.

Besides the *favela*-megalopolis and the classic American automobile-based megalopolis, Tokyo also contains a specifically Asian version of the megalopolis based on high technology,

Layered analysis of MegaTokyo
Tokyo stretches to the north towards the new airport and to the south, along the high-speed rail line, towards Osaka, via Yokohama and Kyoto. A parallel inland rail line in the coastal plain connects from Shinjuku towards Tama, a new town with 4 million inhabitants. (Diagram © David Grahame Shane and Yuka Teruda, 2009)

mass communications and high-density nodes. This Asian version depends on extensive railway systems and bullet trains, like the European megalopolis of the 1990s, but also encompasses large agricultural areas within its city territory. Japanese agricultural policy protected rice paddies and sought some semblance of national food security in times of war (Britain had similar policies after the Second World War). This meant that many peri-urban parcels were protected from development and were valuable because of the crops they could produce. The result was the extension of the city territory, seen from the high-speed train, in a long corridor between sea and mountain, from Tokyo to Osaka, with a mixture of green belt and agricultural patches woven in.

Travelling at high speed in a bullet train or on a highway, it seemed that the triumph of the megalopolis was complete. From the USA, to the EU or Saudi Arabia, to the USSR or China, the highway system seemed triumphant. Dubai in 2007 represented the hubris of the oil-powered megalopolis at its peak. Oil provided the energy to enable humans to ignore all natural limits, whether the heat of the desert, the rage of the sea or the absence of oxygen at high altitudes when flying.

At the same time there were many signs in the northern hemisphere that cities were shrinking and the age of the automobile might be coming to an end. Scientists told of human-induced climate change and blamed tailpipe emissions from automobiles, along with heavy industry, for a large part of the environmental damage. Much of the urban expansion in the USA, as in Dubai, was taking place in very hostile environments requiring high-energy inputs that further impacted the climate situation. The GNP of the USA was tied to new construction and expansion of the suburbs; when this slowed, a recession followed. Against this background, a series of OPEC oil embargoes in the 1970s and 1980s caused urban designers to question the megalopolis as an urban design ecology, anticipating the great recession of 2008.

Tokyo, with its railways and monorail, provided an alternative megalopolis to the American model, whose advantages became clearer in the 1990s. Then the EU began to fund the high-speed rail system in Europe and develop the Japanese culture of meganodes and transportation hubs. The next chapter will examine the resultant meganodes and hubs as large urban fragments set inside networks that stretch across the city territory and the globe. The collision of the metropolis and megalopolis produced a fragmented system of urban design, a new urban design ecology that focused on the control of the fragment to the exclusion of all else. Each new fragment contained a clear order within its boundaries, but increased the disorder or entropy outside itself, with many unintended consequences for the city and the planet.

Notes

NB: See 'Author's Caution: Endnote Sources and Wikipedia', towards the end of this book.

1. Jean Gottmann, *Megalopolis: The Urbanized Northeastern Seaboard of the United States*, Twentieth Century Fund (New York), 1961.

2. For Saar planning, see: Elke Sohn, 'Organicist Concepts of City Landscape in German Planning after the Second World War', *Planning Perspectives*, vol 18, issue 2, April 2003 , pp 119–46. For the German *Stadtlandschaft* tradition, see: Panos Mantziaras, '' Rudolf Schwarz and the concept of *Stadtlandschaft*', *Planning Perspectives*, vol 18, issue 2, April 2003, pp 146–76.

3. For US population estimates, see: Population Estimates Program, Population Division, US Census Bureau website, http://www.census.gov/popest/archives/1990s/popclockest.txt (accessed 10 July 2010).

4. Kevin Lynch, *The Image of the City*, MIT Press (Cambridge, MA), 1961, pp 16-32; Donald Appleyard, Kevin Lynch and John R Myer (eds), *The View from the Road,* MIT Press (Cambridge, MA), 1964.

5. For the Buchanan Report, see: British Ministry of Transport, *Traffic in Towns*, Penguin Books (Harmondworth, Middlesex; Baltimore, MD), 1963.

6. Reyner Banham, *Los Angeles: The Architecture of Four Ecologies*, Harper & Row (New York), 1971, pp 23, 35-6, 87-93.

7. Ian McHarg, *Design with Nature*, published for the American Museum of Natural History (Garden City, NY), 1969.

8. Sir Patrick Geddes, *Cities in Evolution: An Introduction to the Town Planning Movement and to the Study of Cities*, Williams & Norgate (London), 1915.

9. *Reyner Banham Loves Los Angeles*, BBC television documentary by Julian Cooper, 1972, 52 minutes, http://video.google.com/videoplay?docid=1524953392810656786 (accessed 20 February 2010).

10. On Mark 3 new towns including Milton Keynes, see: John Udy, *Man Makes the City: Urban Development and Planning*, Trafford Publishing (Victoria, BC), 2004, pp 164–6.

11. On the nonplace urban realm, see: Melvin M Webber, *Explorations into Urban Structure*, University of Pennsylvania Press (Philadelphia), 1964, p 79.

12. Michel Foucault, 'Of Other Spaces: utopias and heterotopias', in Joan Ockman (ed), *Architecture Culture, 1943–1968: A Documentary Anthology*, Columbia University Graduate School of Architecture, Planning, and Preservation, Rizzoli (New York), 1993, p 425; see also: Michel Foucault, 'Of Other Spaces', Catherine David and Jean Francois Chevrier (eds), *Documenta X: The Book,* Cantz-Verlag, Kassel, Germany, 1997 (originally published in *Diacritics* 16-1, Spring 1986).

13. Reyner Banham, *Scenes in America Deserta*, Gibbs M Smith (Salt Lake City), 1982.

14. For the directional space diagram, see: Robert Venturi, Denise Scott Brown and Steven Izenour, *Learning from Las Vegas*, MIT Press (Cambridge, MA), 1972, p 11.

15. On 1964 banned restrictive covenants, see: Kenneth T Jackson, *Crabgrass Frontier: The Suburbanization of the United States*, Oxford University Press (New York), 1985, p 178.

16. On the racial mix at Levitttown, see: Barbara M Kelly, *Expanding the American Dream: Building and Rebuilding Levittown*, State University of New York Press (Albany, NY), c 1993.

17. See: Kenneth T Jackson, 'Race Ethnicity, and Real Estate Appraisal: the Home Owners' Loan Corporation and the Federal Housing Administration', *Journal of Urban History*, 6 (4), 1980, pp 419–52; also: Becky M Nicolaides and Andrew Wiese (eds), *The Suburb Reader*, Routledge (New York), c 2006 – on restrictive covenants, pp 324–8 and on FHA loans, pp 251–8. For feminist critique of suburbia, see: Gwendolyn Wright, *Building the Dream: A Social History of Housing in America*, Pantheon (New York), 1981.

18. For Gruen on malls, see: Victor Gruen, *The Heart of Our Cities: The Urban Crisis – Diagnosis and Cure*, Simon & Schuster (New York), 1964; also: Jeffrey M Hardwick, *Mall Maker: Victor Gruen, Architect of an American Dream*, University of Pennsylvania (Philadelphia, PA), c 2004.

19. Margaret Crawford, 'The World in a Shopping Mall', in Michael Sorkin (ed), *Variations on a Theme Park: The New American City and the End of Public Space*, Hill & Wang (New York), 1992, pp 3–30.

20   See: Gruen, *The Heart of Our Cities*, pp 189–94.

21   See: Frederique Krupa, 'The Mall of America: The New Town Center', 1993, http://www.translucency.com/frede/moa.html (accessed 10 March 2010)

22   For the development of the Houston Galleria, see: Stephen Fox and Nancy Hadley, *Houston Architectural Guide*, American Institute of Architects, Herring Press (Austin, TX), 1990. For HOK's first designs for Galleria I, see: *Architectural Record*, March 1967, and again on completion of project in 1969. For critique, see: *Architectural Design*, November 1973, p 695. See also: http://en.wikipedia.org/wiki/The_Galleria_(Houston,_Texas) (accessed 10 March 2010).

23   On the financing of the Houston Galleria, see: 'Shopping mall set for Houston', *The New York Times*, 21 May 1967, Real Estate section, p R18.

24   For critique, see: *Architectural Design*, November 1973, p 695.

25   On Hans Scharoun's Berlin Plan, see: Elke Sohn, 'Organicist Concepts of City Landscape in German Planning after the Second World War', *Planning Perspectives*, vol 18, issue 2, April 2003, pp 119–46. On Scharoun's Philharmonic Hall and Prussian State Library, see: James Corner, *Recovering Landscape: Essays in Contemporary Landscape Architecture*, Princeton Architectural Press (New York), 1999, pp 94–9.

26   For *Stadtlandschaft* tradition see Panos Mantziaras, 'Rudolf Schwarz and the concept of *Stadtlandschaft*', *Planning Perspectives*, vol 18, issue 2, April 2003, pp 146–76.

27   Rudolf Schwarz, 'Das Neue Köln, ein Vorentwurf', in Stadt Koln (ed), *Das neue Köln*, Verlag JP Bachem (Cologne), 1950.

28   R Schwarz, *Von der Bebauung der Erde*, Verlag Lambert Schneider (Heidelberg), 1949.

29   Jean Gottmann and Robert Harper, *Since Megalopolis: The Urban Writings of Jean Gottmann*, Johns Hopkins University Press (Baltimore, MD), 1990.

30   For the 'Blue Banana', see: http://en.wikipedia.org/wiki/Blue_Banana (accessed 10 March 2010).

31   For Israel's modern plan, see: Aryeh Sharon, *Kibbutz + Bauhaus: An Architect's Way in a New Land*, Kramer Verlag (Stuttgart), 1976.

32   On SOM's Hajj Terminal, see: SOM website, http://www.som.com/content.cfm/king_abdul_aziz_international_airport_hajj_terminal (accessed 11 March 2010).

33   For the Tapline, see: *Aramco World*, New York Arabian American Oil Company, vols 1–18, 1949–1967 (continued by Aramco world magazine); see also: 'Al Mashriq: The Levant – cultural riches from the countries of the Eastern Mediterranean' website, run by Østfold College, Halden, Norway, http://almashriq.hiof.no/lebanon/300/380/388/tapline/ (accessed 11 March 2010). On Aramco, see: 'Aramco: an Arabian–American partnership develops desert oil and places US influence and power in middle east', *LIFE*, vol 26, no 13, 28 March 1949, pp 62–77.

34   For the Korea Land Corporation (KLC) and Korea National Housing Corporation, see: Korea Land & Housing Corporation website, http://world.lh.or.kr/englh_html/englh_about/about_1.asp (accessed 11 March 2010). For Bundang, see: HS Geyer, *International Handbook of Urban Systems: Studies of Urbanization and Migration in Advanced and Developing Countries*, Edward Elgar Publishing (Northampton, MA), 2002; for Bundang as an 'industrially produced new town', see: http://en.wikipedia.org/wiki/Bundang (accessed 11 March 2010).

35   See: Frederic J Osborn and Arnold Whittick, *The New Towns: The Answer to Megalopolis*, MIT Press (Cambridge, MA), 1969.

36   See: Janice E Perlman, *The Myth of Marginality: Urban Poverty and Politics in Rio de Janeiro*, University of California Press (Berkeley, CA), 1976, pp 135–61.

37   On Caracas, see: Leslie Klein, 'Metaphors of Form: weaving the *barrio*', Columbia University website, http://www.columbia.edu/~sf2220/TT2007/web-content/Pages/leslie2.html (accessed 11 March 2010).

38   For architect Carlos Villaneuva, see: Paulina Villaneuva and Maciá Pintó, *Carlos Raúl Villanueva, 1900–1975*, Alfadil Ediciones (Caracas; Madrid), 2000. For the fate of the 23 de Enero neighbourhood, see: Joshua Bauchner, 'The City That Built Itself', http://canopycanopycanopy.com/6/the_city_that_built_itself (accessed 10 July 2010).

39   Michael Cohen, *Learning by Doing: World Bank Lending for Urban Development, 1972–1982*, The World Bank (Washington DC), 1983.

40   On urban upgrading, see the bibliography at: http://web.mit.edu/urbanupgrading/upgrading/resources/bibliography/Implementation-issues.html (accessed 11 March 2010).

41   For Aranya, see: James Steele, *Rethinking Modernism for the Developing World: The Complete Architecture of Balkrishna Doshi*, Whitney Library of Design (New York), 1998; see also: BV Doshi website, http://www.sangath.org/project/1982aranya.html (accessed 11 March 2010); also: Vastu-Shilpa Foundation website, http://www.vastushilpa.org/activities/research/poe.htm (accessed 11 March 2010).

42   On Aranya community housing, Indore, India, see: ArchNet website, http://www.archnet.org/library/sites/one-site.jsp?site_id=1124 (accessed 11 March 2010). On Aranya community and satellites, see: Krystina Kaza, 'Shrines & Satellites: Doshi's Aranya District, Indore', in David Graham Shane and Brian McGrath (eds), *Sensing the 21st Century City: Close-up and Remote, Architectural Design*, John Wiley & Sons (London), 2005, pp 70–72.

43   On Cyberabad, see: BV Doshi website, http://www.sangath.org/project/2000cyberbad2.html (accessed 11 March 2010).

44   On Shenzhen, the first Chinese SEZ, see: http://en.wikipedia.org/wiki/Shenzhen (accessed 11 March 2010).

45   On Dharavi in Mumbai, see: http://en.wikipedia.org/wiki/Dharavi (accessed 11 March 2010).

46   On Ginza, see: http://en.wikipedia.org/wiki/Ginza (accessed 11 March 2010).

47   On the Ishikawa Plan, see: Carola Hein, 'Machi – Neighborhood and Small Town – the foundation for urban transformation in Japan', *Journal of Urban History*, vol 35, no 1, 2008, pp 75–107.

48   See: Tokyo Metropolitan Government, *A Hundred Years of Tokyo City Planning*, Municipal Library no 28 (Tokyo), 1994, pp 56, 74.

49   Atelier Bow-Wow (Junzo Kuroda and Momoyo Kaijima), *Made in Tokyo*, Kajima Insitute Publishing (Tokyo), 2001 and *Pet Architecture*, World Photo Press (Tokyo), 2002.

50   On Expo '70, see: Pieter van Wesemael, *Architecture of Instruction and Delight: A Socio-Historical Analysis of World Exhibitions as a Didactic Phenomenon (1798-1851-1970)*, 010 Publishers (Rotterdam), 2001, pp 563–645; also: website of the Commemorative Organization for the Japan World Exposition '70, http://www.expo70.or.jp/e/ (accessed 11 March 2010); also: http://en.wikipedia.org/wiki/Expo_'70 (accessed 11 March 2010); also: http://www.bsattler.com/blog/?p=2232 (accessed 11 March 2010).

51   For Archigram, see: Peter Cook, *Archigram*, Studio Vista (London), 1972.

52   On Hiroshi Hara buildings, see: archINFORM website, http://eng.archinform.net/arch/608.htm; for plans of Kyoto Station, see: DB Stewart and Kukio Fuagawa, *Hiroshi Hara, GA Architect*, no 13, ADA Edita (Tokyo), 1993, pp 229–33. On Tange's Tokyo buildings, see: Tokyo Architecture Info website, http://www.tokyoarchitecture.info/Architecture/6/4040/KB2CKZ/Architect.php (accessed 11 March 2010); for a map of Shinjuku with Tokyo Metropolitan Government and Shinjuku Station, see: Tokyo Metropolitan Government website, http://www.metro.tokyo.jp/ENGLISH/TMG/map.htm (accessed 11 March 2010).

53   On railway hubs and Kabukicho love hotels, see: Roman Cybriwsky, *Tokyo: The Shogun's Cityat the Twenty-Frst Century* John Wiley & Sons (New York), 1998, p 760.

54   See: Benika Morokuma, 'The preservation of the urban cultural landscape: a case study of the Rojis in Kagurazaka', Columbia University Historic Preservation Thesis, Tokyo, 2007. On Tokaido corridor, see: http://en.wikipedia.org/wiki/Tokaido_Corridor (accessed 11 March 2010).

CHAPTER 7

The Fragmented Metropolis

The success of the American model of the megalopolis and its peripheral growth, joining cities into linear networks around the world, seriously impacted the metropolis as the European powers lost their empires. Many people and activities moved from the metropolis to the suburbs of the megalopolis. Urban designers, who had wholeheartedly embraced and advanced the cause of megalopolis and the automobile, like Victor Gruen who helped invent the shopping mall, recognised that there were limits to the megalopolis. As global oil supplies were disrupted, sometimes by embargoes, sometimes by technical difficulties, states and cities had problems with their finances. The inner city became a place of poverty and urban riots as commercial interests faltered, the tax base shrank and drug gangs seized territories abandoned by the police, creating dystopian urban scenarios. Under these circumstances urban actors scaled back their grandiose plans for the metropolis. Designers also had to recognise that their giant megastructures imported from the megalopolis had to be scaled down and broken up into fragments in order to enable their development and finance in phases. Designers found that one way to achieve this in older cities was to use the traditional street and block as increments of urban development, also facilitating a more flexible link into the context of old cities. Modernist attempts to renovate old cities had inevitably involved the large-scale demolition of historic structures to accommodate automobiles, highways and parking. So much demolition gave rise to local opposition. UNESCO recognised the Historic Preservation movement with its World Heritage Convention (1972), an award system to protect special areas of cultural importance.

This chapter presents the breakdown of the megalopolis as it interacted with the metropolis, creating a new hybrid: the fragmented metropolis. As it collapsed, the metropolis opened to reveal a Pandora's box of urban actors, who not only resisted the megalopolis but demanded to be heard, wanting protection for their urban villages in the megalopolis. The first part of the chapter focuses on the impact of urban activist Jane Jacobs, and on other examples of American and European community action in the 1960s and 1970s. Yet the basic theme of the destruction of the old in order to make the new is felt in fast growing Asian cities today with equal force. Indeed the theme of urban villages, first met in connection with Le Corbusier and Chandigarh (see chapter 4) and later in Shenzhen (see chapter 5), here re-emerges as a contemporary urban design issue. The servicing and incorporation of immigrants' informal, self-built settlements located close to the centre of globalising cities is a problem worldwide. American urban designers in the 1960s had to scramble to meet Jane Jacobs' challenges, inventing new rules for urban villages as special patches within the city, where different codes applied. This system of urban enclave design enabled urban actors to

Jane Jacobs in the White Horse Tavern, Greenwich Village, New York City, USA (photo 1961)
(Photo © Cervin Robinson, 2009)

control a small fragment of the city, while not dictating rules for everyone else. The chapter studies the evolution of this fragmentary design ecology and how it became the new norm for global capitalist development as well as community activism. The chapter also begins to trace how this fragmentary mode of design worked for both shrinking European and American cities, and fast-expanding Asian cities after 1990.

New urban actors: urban villages and Jane Jacobs

In the year before her death, Jane Jacobs returned to New York to promote her last book *Dark Age Ahead* (2004).[1] The book accurately predicted an imminent financial breakdown of the American system of making cities, because it linked economic success to a mass suburbanisation that was becoming unsustainable not only economically, but also socially and ecologically. Jacobs' first book, *The Death and Life of Great American Cities* (1961), has become the bible of community groups and activists worldwide because of its advocacy of local street life inside mixed-use, socially complex, small-scale, historic neighbourhoods.[2] These same neighbourhoods often appeared as derelict slums to modern architects like Le Corbusier or planners like Robert Moses. Moses wanted to run a cross-island highway through Lower Manhattan to serve the suburbs. Jacobs became the articulate representative of all the repressed minorities who had no voice in the modernist project, the Village 'peasants': the WASP, Italian, Jewish and African-American bohemian intellectuals and their blue-collar neighbours, the gays and lesbians of Greenwich Village, the mothers with families, the old people and children who all lived there together. Jacobs helped organise the Friends of Cast Iron Architecture historic preservation society to protect the neighbouring

19th-century SoHo warehouse district, illicitly colonised by artists' lofts. Jacobs also warded off attacks from the prominent American architectural critic Lewis Mumford, who believed in moving people out of the slums of New York to rural retreats, expanding existing villages in the New York city-region.[3]

Jacobs was well aware of what was at stake in terms of the decay of the metropolis as the megalopolis replaced public transportation and public space with private automobiles and malls in the suburbs. Many writers, like Reyner Banham in his *Los Angeles: The Architecture of Four Ecologies* (1971), revelled in the abandonment of the old city and demolition of Downtown (see chapter 6).[4] The Village folk singer Joni Mitchell wrote a wistful and sad folk song about demolition and how 'they paved paradise and put up a parking lot' (*Big Yellow Taxi*, 1970). Ridley Scott captured the dystopic image of the future fragmented metropolis of Los Angeles in his film *Blade Runner* (1986), based on Philip K Dick's science-fiction novella *Do Androids Dream of Electric Sheep?* (1968).[5] Countless noir comic books, like Frank Miller's *Sin City: The Hard Goodbye* (1991), updated Raymond Chandler detective stories in graphic novel format.[6]

Banham's Los Angeles had been described earlier by Robert M Fogelson as a *Fragmented Metropolis* (1967).[7] Edward Soja echoed this historical theme in his *Postmodern Geographies* (1989) and his *Postmetropolis: Critical Studies of Cities and Regions* (2000).[8] The urban geographer David Harvey in *The Condition of Post-Modernity* (1989) linked the urban fragmentation to the collapse of the modern Bretton Woods financial system based on nation states, and its replacement by a new system of global corporations that relentlessly sought profits but then had the problem of investing that profit in safe, urban enclaves to preserve its value.[9] In Mrs Thatcher's Britain and Ronald Reagan's America, huge urban fragments became feasible. The pioneer atrium and mall developer-architect John Portman's Renaissance Center (1977) in downtown Detroit perfectly represented this system of isolated fragments. This walled city within an abandoned city stood by the waterfront and highway, connected to its surroundings by a driverless monorail that was seldom used. The shock of the stark contrast between weed-strewn, still abandoned city blocks and this megastructural urban fragment or enclave still reverberates in the work of documentary photographers, like Camilo Vergara in *American Ruins* (1999).[10]

Jacobs argued that dense cities, not spread-out suburbs, were the engines of world economic growth and important places of innovation. She loved the 'ballet' of her street in the Village, which different people used at different times in different ways over the course of 24 hours, a week, a month, the seasons and years.[11] She praised the complexity of the interactions on the city's sidewalks in terms of cybernetics and feedback, as individuals randomly interacted with each other. She understood the role of urban actors at the micro scale and their role in creating the city, wanting to give the small people of the city a democratic voice in the top-down planning process of the metropolis as it fell apart (in the mid-1970s New York City barely escaped bankruptcy).[12]

Jacobs' early journalism and advocacy of cities brought invitations to conferences on Urban Design at Harvard, where the Dean José Luis Sert (Le Corbusier's student, a

View of empty lots, abandoned houses and the downtown skyline of Detroit, USA (photo 2005)
(Photo © Jeff Haynes/Getty Images)

member of the International Congress of Modern Architecture (CIAM) and Walter Gropius's successor) sought to establish the first course on Urban Design in the mid-1950s.[13] Sert wanted to eclipse rival Team 10 member Louis Kahn's course on Civic Design at the University of Pennsylvania, begun in 1951. Sert hoped to give the modernist vocabulary a new, more sensitive, small-scale lease of life through Jacobs' vision, but his own work in Latin America in that period remained tied to large plazas and broad pedestrian promenades.[14] His later work, such as the Harvard University Holyoke Center (1965), successfully and skillfully married a modernist slab building into a dense, small historic block close to Harvard Square. Jacobs' work connected with many urban designers' aspirations for a small-scale and active life on the street. The pioneer American mall designer Victor Gruen also lived in New York's Greenwich Village and befriended Jacobs, who endorsed his plan to pedestrianise the centre of Fort Worth (1955), surrounding it with a series of vast, multilevel car parks on a ring road and an underground service road for trucks (like many contemporary malls).[15]

Sert, like Le Corbusier at St-Die-des-Vosges and at Chandigarh (see chapters 2 and 4), segregated pedestrians and automobiles in his designs for fragmentary new civic-centre malls, as in his scheme with Le Corbusier for Bogotá or his work with Paul Lester Wiener in Latin America. His student IM Pei took this idea and designed pedestrian malls in the suburbs, like the vast, single-storey Green Acres Mall in Long Island, New York (1956). Ernesto Rogers, the modern architect from BBPR in Milan and CIAM member, shared Sert's hope for a revival of modernism while respecting the old scale and traditions of the central city.[16] Rogers designed a heterotopic, mixed-use, pre-cast and pre-tensioned, advanced concrete design skyscraper, the Torre Velasca in Milan (1958), housing a small shopping arcade, offices and luxurious apartments (a mixture that broke the modernist taboo of segregating out all functions into separate buildings). Banham attacked the tower because it looked like the Gothic Campanile of Milan Cathedral, with its many fins.[17] Banham accused Rogers of 'betraying modernism', while Rogers dismissed Banham as a 'lover of refrigerators' (a reference to his love of Pop icons and Los Angeles).[18]

Reinventing urban design: Special Districts, enclaves and urban design guidelines

These early European skirmishes between generations mark the collapsing of the old order of the imperial metropolis and different responses to the emerging megalopolis and American commercial dominance in the Cold War. Ernesto Rogers, as a professor at the Milan Polytechnic in the 1950s and editor of the magazine *Casabella*, described urban design as an emerging discipline with a long European tradition.[19] As a discipline, Rogers argued the emerging field had its own rules, standards and codes, a specialised body of knowledge that formed the basis of decisions. Italian urban designers, because of the strength of the Italian Communist Party, were unusual in Western Europe in knowing about Soviet urban design. They were familiar with the super-scaled monumentality and grand plans for Moscow, while rejecting their monumentality as a reminder of Mussolini's Totalitarian era. Rogers' conception of urban design as a continuous tradition was influenced by the typological and morphological studies of the University of Venice since the 1930s under the leadership of Giuseppe Samonà (see chapter 5). In the 1950s Rogers and his firm Banfi, Belgiojoso, Peressutti & Rogers (BBPR), worked in the centre of Milan and sought to contextualise their still-modern buildings. They added elaborate podiums with mixed uses, arcades scaled to surrounding 19th-century structures and short cuts through courtyards that honoured old lanes and paths. The firm tried to renew the architecture of the street and building facade within a small-scale modernist vocabulary. Rogers saw architecture and the city as languages that had structural elements which defined their relationship and discourse within an urban context. Rogers' vision, like that of Le Corbusier, expanded in scale to include huge suburban superblocks, scaled like the industrial mills, factories and monuments of the industrial age that would inspire his student Aldo Rossi in the 1960s (see chapter 8).[20]

Rogers found a natural ally in his search for a new European urban architecture that could relate to the small scale of the historic city in the *Architectural Review*, a privately owned architectural magazine in London, for which Gordon Cullen wrote and illustrated a monthly column called 'Townscape' (later published as a book, *The Concise Townscape* (1961)).[21] The magazine's owner H de Cronin Hastings worked closely with the geographer Thomas Sharp and, like Cullen, loved the intimate, personal design scale of villages.[22] These favoured places might be picturesque English villages like Blandford Forum, or Italian hill towns like Bergamo. Cullen saw Italian hill towns as the epitome of good urban design. Cullen created a new language and system of elements for designing small-scale urban settings, describing 'urban rooms', 'enclaves', 'precincts', 'outdoor rooms' and 'passages' that allowed pedestrians to move elegantly and comfortably about the village through a series of urban enclosures. (Louis Kahn, in the breakaway Team 10 conference that ended CIAM at Otterlo, also spoke of urban 'rooms' and enclosures.[23]) In his book and magazine articles, Cullen attacked the open plan and vast open spaces of modern urban design, occupied by no one and loved by few, especially in the British new towns.

Cullen created one brilliant drawing summarising his 'serial vision' of how a person moved through an ideal Italian village or hilltop environment.[24] In this drawing, like a cinematic storyboard, sketches showed how, after entering the city walls through a city gate,

Gordon Cullen, 'Casebook: Serial Vision', from
The Concise Townscape, **1971**
(Source: Gordon Cullen, *The Concise Townscape*,
The Architectural Press (London), first paperback
edition, 1971, p 17)

Banfi, Belgiojoso, Peressutti & Rogers (BBPR),
Torre Velasca, Milan, Italy, 1958 (photo 2009)
(Photo © David Grahame Shane)

a series of bounded squares led to the cathedral square and beyond to a Mussolini-style semicircular plaza that opened out to views of the distant horizon and hills. Other sketches in *Concise Townscape* showed that Cullen did not oppose mixing new buildings amongst the old, or limited access for automobiles, as long as bollards and cobblestones limited their speed and territory within a system of closed, urban fragments. In late drawings for Covent Garden, London (1971), Cullen included an underground highway and parking, although not opposing a nearby (LCC) proposal for a megastructure over the Strand, covering a proposed highway beside the Thames.[25]

Kevin Lynch, in his *The Image of the City* (1961), sought to provide a pragmatic base for Cullen's aesthetic preferences, which he knew from publications and shared students like David Gosling at MIT.[26] Lynch interviewed over 1,000 inhabitants of central Boston just as a new elevated Central Artery cut off the business core from the waterfront and North End Italian community on its small hilltop site (at the same time Gruen was busy demolishing another part of the West End of Boston for high-rise slab blocks set in a park in 1962). Lynch

**Ben Thompson, perspective drawing of Faneuil Hall,
Boston, Massachusetts, 1971–6**

(Grateful acknowledgement is given to the family of
Carlos Diniz for permission to reproduce his work)

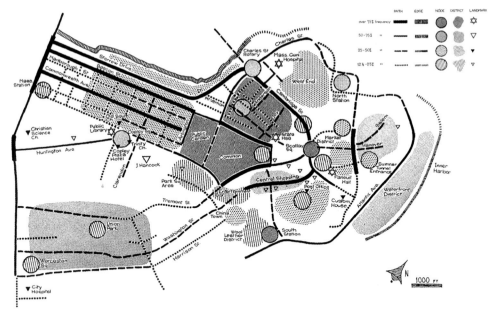

Kevin Lynch, map of Boston, Massachusetts, USA, from *The Image of the City*, 1961
(Map and key ©1960 Massachusetts Institute of Technology, by permission of the MIT Press;
source: Kevin Lynch, *The Image of the City*, MIT Press (Cambridge, MA), fig 35, p 146)

showed that the Boston inhabitants shared a fragmentary mental map of the central city that
had distinct neighbourhoods or 'districts', enclaves that were bounded fragments with distinct
visual and social characteristics. These were connected by, and organised around, main
streets or 'paths'. In addition, people on foot used particular buildings as navigational devices
or 'markers', especially church towers or tall buildings, and certain key street interchanges
acted as 'nodes', interchanges within this system of 'paths'. In 1959, based on this research,
Lynch and his associates from MIT advised a new urban development agency created to
remodel the inner city, the Boston Redevelopment Authority (BRA), on how to remodel around
the elevated Central Artery, proposing a new public square and City Hall to the west and
historic preservation of Quincy Market, the old waterfront, to the east.[27] Sert's Harvard Urban
Design graduate IM Pei won the subsequent urban design competition (1961) and Kallman,
McKinnell & Knowles won the competition for the new City Hall (1962). Ben Thompson (of
Harvard) restored Quincy Market as a 'Festival Market' (1971–6) and finally the Central
Artery was buried underground in the 'Big Dig' in the early 2000s.

Lynch demonstrated the power of fragmentary urban design when coupled with the
BRA. While Lynch advocated the historic preservation of Quincy Market, he also argued for
the destruction of Foley Square, a historic sailors' red-light district, but sought to preserve

the nearby historic urban village of North Boston. This fragmentary patchwork combination of selective historic preservation and piecemeal modern intervention set a pattern for the redevelopment of many historic downtowns across America in the 1960s. In 1961 the New York City Planning Commission revised New York's basic Zoning Code (established in 1916, with the setback regulations that created the metropolitan image (see chapter 4)) to allow new towers on plazas, based on Mies van der Rohe's Seagram Building (1958) on Park Avenue. A rash of modern towers built on plazas to gain extra height ensued, resulting in the code being amended in the early 1970s. The later code revisions reverted to the street and the theory of Special Districts or patches in a city, instead of an overall master plan. The first American, municipal Urban Design Department created by Mayor John Lindsay in 1967 wrote these new regulations. The department developed the Boston idea of urban fragments as a micro-zoning tool, creating exceptional Special Districts. Legally these were based on the original 1916 Special District of Wall Street where pre-existing skyscrapers broke the new setback codes and were 'grandfathered', or not penalised, because they predated the new regulations. Based on these Special Districts, the urban designers introduced Contextual Zoning Codes designed to protect the street armatures of Downtown and then Midtown and Fifth Avenue.[28]

Jonathan Barnett explained in *An Introduction to Urban Design* (1982) how Special Districts were originally intended to protect urban villages, like Chinatown and Little Italy, or the Theater District, but expanded with incentives to promote urban design goals, like the maintenance of the street wall on Fifth Avenue in Midtown or historic preservation in Greenwich Village.[29] The system allowed for community input within a defined urban boundary from the bottom up. Barnett showed that the system was expanded to cover Battery Park City in the mid-1970s as a way of spurring development, creating a Special District that was controlled by an independent authority, financed by New York State. Here new regulations created by Alexander Cooper (an Urban Design team member) and Stanton Eckstut in 1978 set urban design guidelines to create new streets and squares. The plan re-created a historic New York district or urban village, modelled on the Upper West Side neighbourhood, but at a new modern density under the influence of the Cornell Contextualists (see p 202) and European Rationalists (see chapter 8). After the success of Battery Park City in the 1980s, Special Districts and urban design guidelines became the new norm of global development, along with independent state authorities that could aid development and finance (used, for instance, at Canary Wharf, London, Potsdamer Platz, Berlin or Pudong, Shanghai in the 1990s, not to mention Dubai or Saudi Arabia in the 2000s). Barnett went on to write *The Fractured Metropolis* (1995), in which he extended the fragmentary analysis to the design of the city territory, studying the development of large urban fragments, malls, office towers, large housing estates, industrial parks and recreational areas scattered within the American landscape.[30] Not all the later large urban fragments in Asia or the Middle East maintained the contextual design guidelines of Battery Park City. Pudong and Dubai, for instance, developed huge skyscraper towers on mall podiums in isolated megablocks beside wide boulevards set in parkland or desert.

Cathedral Square, Lucca, Italy (photo 2004)
The Contextualist author Camillo Sitte in the 1890s praised Lucca's urban design because
the monumental buildings, such as churches, were buried in the city and did not stand in
the middle of the square or plaza like modern buildings. (Photo © David Grahame Shane)

The fragmented metropolis: collage city and the city archipelago

Before writing the *The Image of the City* (1961), Lynch spent time in the late 1950s as a Rome Scholar drawing the sequence of squares, passages and lanes of Lucca, a medieval Italian town much studied by Camillo Sitte, the late-19th-century Austrian urban theorist of Contextualism.[31] In his *City Planning According to Artistic Principles* (1889), Sitte extolled the beauty of the irregular sequence of small-scale market squares at the city centre that led from one to another, terminating in the cathedral square (also an inspiration for Cullen's picturesque 'serial vision').[32] He pointed out that all the public buildings of the sequence were buried in the street walls of the squares: none stood as isolated objects in a plaza. He argued that it was the small-scale enclosures and community's involvement that formed these intimate environments. Sitte had grown up and attended school in central Vienna; in his view, the new Imperial Ring Strasse (Ring Road from the 1860s) with its vast open parks, squares, boulevards, palaces, museums, parliament houses, universities and operas was a soulless metropolitan space that should be subdivided and made more community friendly (he provided schemes for this in his book).

The Urban Design programme at Cornell University, founded by Colin Rowe in the early 1960s, followed up on this critique of the open landscapes of the modern city, but still adhered to large-scale superblocks of the Corbusian formula. Thomas Schumacher's *Casabella* article 'Contextualism: urban ideals plus deformations' (1971) very clearly elaborated the Cornell School argument that urban designers had to deform ideal utopias and geometric building morphologies to work in particular urban contexts.[33] Schumacher documented how many designers recognised the small-scale micro-environment, providing historical precedents from many periods (including modernism). In 1978 the designers of Battery Park City created Urban Design Guidelines that took these micro-codes seriously, controlling the facade proportions, setback regulations, sidewalk widths, even landscape elements, as well as laying out small block plans and development subdivisions. This sophisticated design advance took control away from the individual landowner, whose bottom-up input had to be within the overall regulatory framework. Within the Special District fragment, Cooper and Eckstut invented new micro-codes and micro zoning techniques (related to cybernetic theory and participatory feedback systems, according to Barnett).[34]

In the same year the American architect Michael Graves organised the *Roma Interrotta* competition to investigate what a city of fragments might look like if designed by different urban designers and architects.[35] Graves took as his basis Giambattista Nolli's 1748 figure-ground map of Rome that showed open spaces as white plazas against the black 'figure' of the building footprint, a favourite device of the Contextualists (designed to show urban space in high contrast). Rowe, together with his Cornell ex-students Barbara Littenberg, Steven Peterson, Judith DiMaio and Peter Carl designed one segment; the Venturi–Scott Brown team designed another, based on their Las Vegas theories; the Rationalist Krier brothers (see next chapter) designed two segments; the British architect James Stirling ironically created one segment made up entirely of his large-scale projects set as isolated fragments in the landscape; while other designers conceived modernist fragments of housing set in long,

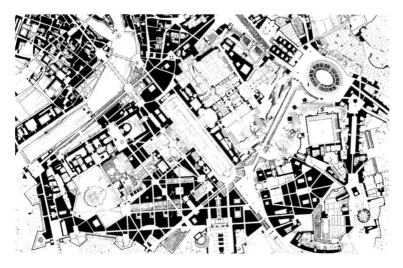

Colin Rowe, Barbara Littenberg, Steven Peterson, Judith DiMaio and Peter Carl, *Roma Interrotta* sector, 1978
(Drawing © Barbara Littenberg)

thin slab blocks. Few of the fragments, whatever their individual quality, connected to their neighbours. Rowe created a fantasy history for his team and together they designed three urban neighbourhood enclaves on three of the Roman hills, with armatures running along the valley from the Tiber to the Forum. It is perhaps not so surprising that Rem Koolhaas's *Delirious New York*, with its subtitle 'A Retroactive Manifesto for the Metropolis', appeared the same year with its nostalgic dream of control and a metropolitan order established within a single grid, setting up the skyline of the city (see next chapter).[36]

Like *Roma Interrotta, Collage City*, published in 1978 by Rowe and his Cornell colleague Fred Koetter, advocated an 'open city' where multiple urban actors were free to build their fragmentary, utopian designs.[37] Like Battery Park City, this marked a fundamental shift away from the coordinated master plans of modernist architects like Le Corbusier towards the apparent freedom of a fragmentary patchwork city. For Rowe and Koetter, this fragmentary ideal also included the recognition and accumulation of historical precedents for design and different urban fragments from past eras. The Cornell Contextualists' ability to recognise different life worlds in design patterns embodied in different urban fragments took a radical step forward, becoming a layered design methodology, as historic district laminated upon historic district to form the fragmented metropolis. In practical terms, these fragments could align with Special District designations. The same method of analysis could also be applied to the periphery of the megalopolis, where extensive big-box retail establishments, megamalls, Levittown housing estates, office parks and industrial estates formed large single-storey fragments across the landscape, connected by highways.

For Koetter and Rowe, like Lynch, the key to the reintegration of the various fragments was a mental map carried in the heads of urban actors and designers. In *Collage City*, this map involved an intimate knowledge of the city and its history that gave it its particular character (Rowe wrote a fictitious historical script for his *Roma Interrotta* team). At the end of *Collage City*, Koetter and Rowe outlined five key urban elements that helped activate a sense of the city as a whole, despite its fragmentation. These elements, like the elements espoused by Ernesto Rogers, pointed towards an emerging discipline, including:

1 'great streets' (armatures)
2 'stabilizers' (enclaves with a single centre)
3 'fields' (large, nested enclaves with shared fabric patterns and multiple centres, like the Forbidden City in Beijing)
4 'scenic overlooks' where the whole city could be seen from above (to aid conceptual reintegration in a mental map)
5 'ambiguous and composite buildings' that combine different urban fields working at multiple scales over time (heterotopias).[38]

Koetter, together with his partner Susie Kim, went on in the early 1990s to design the urban design guidelines for Canary Wharf, London with SOM for the same Canadian developers that built the World Trade Center in Battery Park City.[39]

Rowe and Koetter's colleague, the often critical Dean OM Ungers at Cornell (Koolhaas's teacher), proposed the 'city archipelago' as an alternative model to 'collage city' in his Berlin Summer Schools of 1976–7 (co-taught with Koolhaas).[40] The key difference was that Ungers stressed the spaces between the fragments (he called the fragments 'cities within cities', where urban actors designed their environments, usually within orderly grids). These green spaces came to have an ecological and landscape value to later urban designers. In the Berlin Summer Schools, Ungers stressed the 'green spaces', parklands, garden villa districts and derelict areas of West Berlin that had originally been a suburban district of the German capital stretching between urban fragments. His inspiration was perhaps Guy Debord's psycho-geographic 'atmospheres' in his fragmentary map of 'The Naked City' (1956–7).[41] Here Paul Klee-like red arrows of desire connected across the blank void of the white paper to urban fragments cut from a standard Paris map. Ungers highlighted these blank, in-between spaces as well as the fragments, seeing them as green spaces in the tradition of Hans Scharoun and the German *Stadtlandschaft* tradition (see chapter 6). In the 1980s Rowe in his retirement was hired by West Berlin's IBA (*Internationale Bauausstellung/ International Building Show*) to consult on the reunification of the capital, learnt from Ungers, proposing green corridors through the city that both separated and integrated urban fragments into a larger conceptual model.

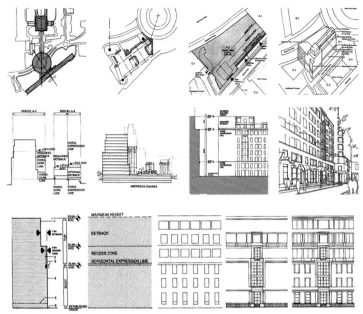

**Koetter Kim & Associates
with SOM, urban design
guidelines for Canary Wharf,
London, c 1992**
(Diagram © Fred Koetter)

**Guy Debord, 'The Naked
City', 1957**
A Situationist diagram of Paris
with 'atmosphere' fragments
connected by red arrows.
(Diagram © Collection FRAC
Centre, Orléans, France.
Photographe François
Lauginie)

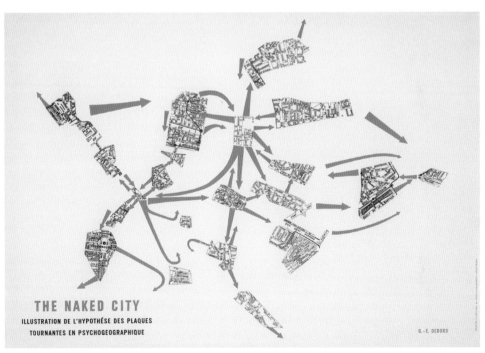

THE NAKED CITY
ILLUSTRATION DE L'HYPOTHÉSE DES PLAQUES
TOURNANTES EN PSYCHOGEOGRAPHIQUE

G.-E. DEBORD

Fragmenting the metropolis: fractal design and informality – the city section

The big problem with 'collage city' as an urban design operating system for the shrinking European metropolis was how to connect and relate the urban fragments created by urban actors, as shown in the *Roma Interrotta* urban fantasy. Rowe and Koetter favoured Munich in the 1840s as an ideal model, where a benevolent prince of a small kingdom facilitated urban actors' dreams, whether Gothic or neoclassical, industrial Crystal Palaces or Romantic 'English garden' landscape parks.[42] Critics pointed to the relative simplicity of this system of top-down organisation and the contrast with contemporary cities with their many stakeholders, creating complex post-modern urban politics. The multiple actors and many conflicting voices made resolving these contrasting visions difficult (as demonstrated by the delays in rebuilding the New York World Trade Center after 9/11).

The isolation of the Special District system and fragmentary urban design also posed problems for urban actors. Fragments could be very isolated, like Canary Wharf in the London docks, which was disconnected from subways and highways during the 1990s, causing the bankruptcy of its developers. For many years after 1945 the racist South African regime pushed this logic of isolation and fragmentation to an extreme in its apartheid policies, with its segregated camps and townships (see chapter 8). Eyal Weizman and others in *A Civilian Occupation* (2003) have shown that a similar, but in some ways as brutal, logic has informed the vertical segregation of Jewish and Arab settlements in the Palestinian West Bank.[43] Saskia Sassen, in *The Global City: New York, London, Tokyo* (1991), argued that every major global city, besides containing global financial service centres, like Canary Wharf, also contained its ghettos and immigrant enclaves that were essential as sources of cheap labour.[44]

In other situations the isolation of the fragmented metropolis could be turned into an advantage by developers of gated communities or theme parks, where only paying guests, registered inhabitants or their servants could gain access to a specific urban fragment. Walt Disney demonstrated in his Disneyland theme park in Anaheim, California (1954, see chapter 5) how a planned urban fragment could serve to psychologically reassure anxious citizens in a fast-changing world. Thanks to television advertising, the fantasy Main Street of Disneyland attracted 12 million people in its first year of operation, and it continues to do so. Walt Disney World in Florida has attracted over 30 million people a year even in bad times. Nostalgic urban village vistas play a key part in marketing these theme parks to people who mainly live in suburbs or in fast-expanding cities in Asia, Latin America or Africa.[45] These frozen urban vistas provide enclave developers, designers and occupants with a prefabricated urban image, as a stable and fixed stage set. This scenographic element served many marketing purposes for the developer. A similar picturesque strategy can be seen at work in the marketing of Dubai with its theme parks and malls throughout the oil-rich Middle East and Islamic world. In Britain, Prince Charles's re-creation of a small urban village on his private Poundbury Estate outside Dorchester (begun 1993) echoes the same theme of psychological reassurance through microcodes, like Battery Park City, but this time allied to the British tradition of picturesque urban villages, great estates and their powerful landowners.[46]

Main Street, Disneyland, Anaheim, California, USA, 2005
(Photo © David Grahame Shane)

Another advantage of the fragmentary system of urban design was that a known urban formula could be repeated in a different location, with further improvements built into the new fragment, creating an iterative fractal or evolving fragment. In the case of Battery Park City and the World Financial Center, for instance, the success of the initial fragment was replicated around the world, in Hong Kong, Tokyo and Mumbai to name but a few cities. These enclaves came along with Special District designations, involving special tax regimes, legal exemptions, special authorities, special design codes and special housing enclaves. From Johannesburg in South Africa to Moscow, shopping mall podiums combined with skyscraper towers made new business districts in the centre and on the edge of existing cities. Housing towers could also be plugged into these commercial podiums, creating a new urban design type that was first pioneered in the Hong Kong new towns of the 1980s (see chapter 7). This new hybrid urban fragment became a pattern that was endlessly repeated and altered by designers and urban actors for each site and time period, resulting in a repetitive fractal pattern that was never the same twice. A similar fractal pattern existed in the residential development of the 'Great Estates' of London in the 18th and 19th centuries (see chapter 2, pp 48-9 and chapter 8) and in the work of New Urbanist pioneers Andrés Duany and Elizabeth Plater-Zyberk at Seaside, Florida (started 1979). Brian McGrath's 'Manhattan Timeformations' at New York's Skyscraper Museum website shows that the evolution of skyscrapers as urban elements can also be seen as a genealogical, fractal pattern of repetition and constant innovation.[47]

The fragmentation of the metropolis opened the way for many urban actors to take control of their own, local urban environment, patch or enclave, emerging from their ghettos. The result was a mosaic of self-organising systems and urban patterns in place of one single dominant centre. The fragmentation of the metropolis also affected its former colonies (both Gandhi and Mao had stressed peasant villages as the basis of their nation's regeneration). Two years before *Collage City*, the United Nations first recognised the vast array of self-built shantytowns at the UN-HABITAT I meeting in Vancouver (1976). Here the British architect John Turner, Canadian economist Barbara Ward and her assistant David Satterthwaite organised a separate conference for the uninvited NGO representatives in a disused seaplane hangar.[48] By the time of HABITAT III in Vancouver in 2006, the NGOs occupied most of the exhibition space in the conference centre. By this time self-built housing vernaculars had become recognised as what Fumihiko Maki called 'group forms' in his 1960 Tokyo Manifesto (see chapter 5). These could be arranged around contours, like the Italian hill towns beloved by Cullen, as in the hilltop *favelas* of Rio de Janeiro, Brazil or the *ranchos* of Caracas, Venezuela (see chapter 6). Or on the plains of Mexico City or Bogotá where *barrios* (neighbourhoods) could be laid out within government-provided superblock armatures that became the main commercial streets and access ways. Within the apparent chaos of the myriad of self-built houses simple rules applied, creating house types and conditions of access that Christopher Alexander, John Turner and many others saw as small-scale fractal systems generating complex, large-scale urban structures.[49] BV Doshi tried to learn from this tradition in his Aranya, India, scheme of 1981, applying Turner's self-build ideas within the World Bank 'Sites and Services' setting (see chapter 6).

Decaying modernist megastructures, like the Sewoon Sangga Market (architect Kim Swoo-Geun, mid-1960s) in Seoul, South Korea, could form unexpected, hybrid and heterotopic urban elements in the fast-shifting dynamic of the fragmentary metropolis.[50] Like Villaneuva's 23 de Enero estate in Caracas, Venezuela (see chapter 2, p 77), small-scale shanties invaded the open spaces around the modernist megastructure of the Sewoon Sangga Market, stretching two city superblocks. Built as a modern armature with an upper pedestrian deck over traffic to house a market by an old city gate, the upper levels of the block provided mass housing in a long, modern, panel-built structure. The market quickly expanded into the surrounding parking lots and became an informal shantytown of lanes and huts. Meanwhile various shops in the market expanded vertically up into the housing block to become small department stores. The large-scale clarity of the initial design soon became subverted by a million tiny moves that had their own fractal logic. Small urban actors created a new kind of hybrid structure that broke all the city's zoning rules, mixing housing, commerce, offices and industry and creating a complex vertical urban village and megablock hybrid section (soon to be demolished for a new Koetter Kim & Associates project, also with a hybrid section).

The Sewoon Sangga Market hybrid, like the now-demolished Walled City of Kowloon, Hong Kong, demonstrates the importance of the city section in fragmentary urban design ecologies.[51] Alvin Boyarsky, in his article 'Chicago A La Carte' (1970) and as director of the Architectural Association School (AA) in London, encouraged sectional experimentation in

Kim Swoo-Geun, Sewoon Sangga Market, Office and Housing Megastructure, Seoul, Korea, mid-1960s (photo 2008)
Photograph showing the surrounding informal, self-built market that has invaded the 1960s buildings, which are scheduled for demolition (see chapter 5, p 176). (Photo © David Grahame Shane)

complex urban projects in the 1970s.[52] There Zaha Hadid, while teaching with Koolhaas and Elia Zenghelis of OMA, won the Peak Competition in 1982 for a new facility at the top of the funicular on a spectacular site overlooking Hong Kong (AA graduate Terry Farrell eventually built a different facility on the site).[53] Hadid's design opened up the centre of the modernist megastructure, placing the hotel rooms in long thin bars above and below a new public space that looked down on the skyscrapers of Hong Kong. Within the sandwich of hotel accommodation, Hadid created a curved, drive-in entranceway on stilts that led to a reception foyer, with a bar and swimming pool floating above, looking down the mountainside onto the city. The spectacular three-dimensional ramp experience, while undeniably picturesque, was far removed from Cullen's concept of 'serial vision' in an historic urban village. Here the city section was activated in a novel way, creating a new, hybrid public space that could accommodate small-scale, potentially bottom-up innovations, as well as top-down codes.

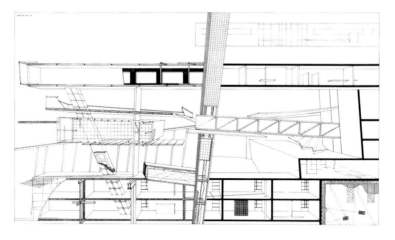

Zaha Hadid Architects, two drawings for The Peak, Hong Kong, 1981
(Drawings © courtesy Zaha Hadid Architects)

Conclusion

The collapse and reformulation of the metropolitan urban design ecology under pressure from the megalopolis reflected a loss of state power and the rise of commercial forces in the marketplace as competing urban actors. The 1980s era of President Ronald Reagan and British Prime Minister Margaret Thatcher represented a shift away from the Bretton Woods agreements and American Marshall Plan that had supported the rebuilding of Europe, Japan and the 'Asian Tigers' after the Second World War. In the new era of neo-Liberal economics, the gigantic oil profits of global American oil companies and OPEC oil-rich nations powered the rise of international and global financial institutions that could recycle these profits in safe urban developments and enclaves.

American corporations had long enjoyed the economy of scale that came from a national market of approximately 150 million, where Britain, for instance, only had a population of approximately 50 million in 1945.[54] American national corporations had the skills and brands to pioneer the global market, as the EU formed into a second trading block of a similar size. These large international markets required much energy and coordination, involving computational power and global communication systems on a new scale beyond even the US market. The scale of these global corporations was vast, perhaps serving 500 million worldwide, but they palled beside the size of the Asian markets. Both India and China had populations of around a billion people by the year 2000, with only one third living in cities.[55]

The emergence of India and China has challenged global energy, financial, industrial and electronics corporations to scale up their organisations by a factor of 2 if they want to be successful in just one market, say China, and by a factor of 4 if they enter both. By 2010 China is expected to have 7 out of 10 of the world's largest megamalls, all of them larger than the

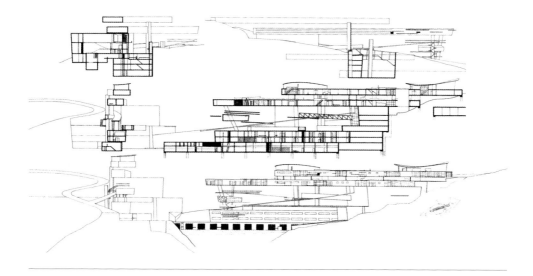

original American megamall, the Mall of America near Minneapolis (1992).[56] In the face of this challenge and the rise of India and China as global commercial powers, a massive transfer of organisational and information technologies is underway to set up the urbanisation of Asia in the 21st century. Large urban fragments – whether in South Delhi along Cyber Alley, in Beijing along the central business district (CBD) strip on the Second Ring Road, or in Pudong's Special Skyscraper District, capping Shanghai's high-rise towers – represent the global urban portals of this massive exchange. The Euro-American tradition of the fragmentary metropolis is being transformed here by the emerging outlines of the Asian megacity.

Koolhaas's dramatic China Central Television (CCTV) headquarters in Beijing stands as a monumental, corporate symbol of the Asian future of the city and as a supersized XXL piece of fragmentary urbanism. It is scaled as a spectacular public symbol for the 1 billion potential customers of the ambitious state media giant. It is a vast urban fragment, a 'city-within-the-city', with shops, hotels and offices, unflatteringly referred to by Beijing taxi-drivers as the 'Trouser Building' (because of the constant view up into its crotch from the highway). This giant corporate urban icon, a megastructure worthy of a megalopolis, has its own irrational logic separated from its surrounding city within its enclave and plaza. Despite its connection to media systems and mass communications, the CCTV building stands as a monument isolated from the city. It is a monster of energy consumption and absurd structural display. Its complex interior arrangements are hidden in the singular megaform. This signature shape of dancing trousers soon gets lost on the city horizon amongst a forest of competing towers in this vast city. This apparently all-powerful, triumphant symbol of the informational city of the future disappears with a slither into the traffic flows of the CBD on the outer ring road of an emerging Asian megacity.[57]

Notes

NB: See 'Author's Caution: Endnote Sources and Wikipedia', towards the end of this book.

1   Jane Jacobs, *Dark Age Ahead*, Random House (New York), 2004.

2   Jane Jacobs, *The Death and Life of Great American Cities*, Vintage Books (New York), 1961.

3   On Lewis Mumford and Jane Jacobs, see: Alice Sparberg Alexiou, *Jane Jacobs: Urban Visionary*, Rutgers University Press (Pitscataway, NJ), 2006.

4   Reyner Banham, *Los Angeles: The Architecture of Four Ecologies*, Harper & Row (New York), 1971.

5   Philip K Dick, *Do Androids Dream of Electric Sheep?*, Random House (New York), 1996 (originally published by Doubleday (Toronto), 1968).

6   Frank Miller, *Sin City: The Hard Goodbye*, Dark Horse Press (Milwaukie, OR), 1991.

7   Robert M Fogelson, *Fragmented Metropolis: Los Angeles, 1850–1930*, Harvard University Press (Cambridge, MA), 1967.

8   Edward Soja, *Postmodern Geographies: The Reassertion of Space in Critical Social Theory*, Verso (London; New York), c 1989; Edward Soja, *Postmetropolis: Critical Studies of Cities and Regions*, Blackwell Publishers (Malden, MA), 2000.

9   David Harvey, *The Condition of Post-Modernity: An Enquiry into the Origins of Cultural Change*, Blackwell (Oxford, UK; Cambridge, MA), 1989.

10 Camilo J Vergara, *American Ruins*, Monacelli Press (New York), 1999.

11 On the 'ballet' of the Village street, see: Jacobs, *The Death and Life of Great American Cities*, pp 60–61.

12 On New York City near bankruptcy in 1975, see: Ralph Blumenthal, 'Recalling New York at the Brink of Bankruptcy', *The New York Times*, 5 December 2002, http://www.nytimes.com/2002/12/05/nyregion/recalling-new-york-at-the-brink-of-bankruptcy.html?pagewanted=1 (accessed 15 February 2010).

13 For Sert and the development of Urban Design at Harvard, see: Eric Paul Mumford, 'From the Heart of the City to Holyoke Center: CIAM ideas in Sert's definition of Urban Design', in *Josep Luis Sert: The Architect of Urban Design, 1953–1969*, Yale University Press (New Haven, CT), 2008.

14 For modernism and suburbia, see: JL Sert, *Can Our Cities Survive?*, Harvard University Press (Cambridge, MA), and H Milford, Oxford University Press (London), 1942.

15 For mall development and suburbs, see: Victor Gruen, *The Heart of Our Cities*, Simon & Schuster (New York), 1964, pp 214–19.

16 On Rogers and BBPR see: 'Torre Velasquez, Milan, Italy, 1958', *A+U: extra edition*, December 1991, pp 197–206. On Team 10 and Torre Velasca, see: Team 10 website, http://team10online.org/team10/meetings/1959-otterlo.htm (accessed 2 March 2010).

17 For Banham on Torre Velasca, see: 'Neoliberty: the Italian retreat from modern architecture', *Architectural Review*, no 747, April 1959; also: Luca Molinari 'Giancarlo De Carlo and the Postwar Modernist Italian Architectural Culture: role, originality and networking', Team 10 website, http://www.team10online.org/research/papers/delft2/molinari.pdf.

18 Ernesto Rogers, 'The Evolution of Architecture: reply to the Custodian of Frigidaires', *Casabella Continuita*, June 1959 (republished in: *Editoriali di architettura*, Einaudi (Turin), 1968, pp 127–36).

19 For Rogers on Urban Design as a discipline, see: EN Rogers, *Gli elementi del fenomeno architettonico*, Laterza (Bari), 1961, also: Paola Viganò, La Città Elementare, Skira (Milan; Geneva), 1999, p 9.

20 For Rossi and Rogers/Casabella, see: Alberto Ferlenga (ed), *Aldo Rossi: The Life and Works of an Architect*, Konemann (Cologne), 2001, p 14.

21 See: Gordon Cullen, *The Concise Townscape*, Architectural Press (London), 1961; also: David Gosling, *Gordon Cullen: Visions of Urban Design*, Academy Editions (London), 1996.

22 See: Erdem Erten, 'Thomas Sharp's collaboration with H de C Hastings: the formulation of townscape as urban design pedagogy', *Planning Perspectives*, vol 24, issue 1 (January 2009), pp 29–49.

23 For the Team 10 conference at Otterlo, 1959, see: Team 10 website, http://team10online.

org/team10/meetings/1959-otterlo.htm (accessed 12 July 2010). For Kahn's 'urban room' references, see: DG Shane, 'Louis Kahn', in Michael Kelly (ed), *The Encyclopaedia of Aesthetics*, Oxford University Press (Oxford), 1998, vol 3, pp 19–23.

24   On Cullen's 'serial vision', see: Gosling, *Gordon Cullen*, p 9.

25   On Covent Garden, see: Kenneth Browne, 'A Latin Quarter for London', *Architectural Review*, vol cxxxv, no 805, March 1971, pp 193–201.

26   Kevin Lynch, *The Image of the City*, MIT Press (Cambridge, MA), 1961, p 109.

27   For Lynch and urban design in Boston, see: David Gosling and Maria-Cristina Gosling, *The Evolution of American Urban Design: A Chronological Anthology*, Wiley-Academy (Chichester, UK; Hoboken, NJ), 2003, pp 55 and 124–5; also: Kenneth Halpern, *Downtown USA: Urban Design in Nine American Cities*, Whitney Library of Design (New York), 1978, pp 183–99. For Lynch on the Boston downtown plan, see: Kevin Lynch, *City Sense and City Design*, MIT Press (Cambridge, MA), 1962, pp 665–74.

28   For Special Districts and Contextual Zoning Codes, see: Department of City Planning, New York City, *The Zoning Handbook*, New York, 1990; also: Richard Babcock and Wendy Larsen, *Special Districts: The Ultimate in Neighborhood Zoning*, Lincoln Institute of Land Policy (Cambridge, MA), 1990; also: DG Shane, *City of Fragments*, Bauwelt (Berlin), 1992.

29   Jonathan Barnett, *Introduction to Urban Design*, Harper & Rowe (New York), 1982, pp 77–136.

30   Jonathan Barnett, *The Fractured Metropolis: Improving The New City, Restoring The Old City, Reshaping The Region*, HarperCollins (New York), 1995.

31   For Lynch in Italy, see: Lynch, *City Sense and Design*, 1962, p 287. For Contextualism and Lucca, see: Camillo Sitte, *The Birth of Modern City Planning*, annotated and translated by George R Collins and Christiane Crasemann Collins, Rizzoli (New York), 1986.

32   Camillo Sitte, *City Planning According to Artistic Principles* (1889), translated from the German by George R Collins and Christiane Crasemann Collins, Random House (New York), 1965.

33   For Contextualism, see: Thomas Schumacher, 'Contextualism: urban ideals plus deformations', *Casabella*, no 104, 1971, pp 359–66.

34   On Battery Park City Urban Design Guidelines, see: Barnett, *Introduction to Urban Design*, 1982, pp 121–4.

35   For the Rowe team design, see: Colin Rowe et al, 'Nolli Sector 8', in *Roma Interrotta*, Officina Editione (Rome), 1979, pp 136–58; also: Colin Rowe, *As I Was Saying: Recollections and Miscellaneous Essays* (edited by Alexander Caragonne), MIT Press (Cambridge, MA), 1996, pp 127–53.

36   Rem Koolhaas, *Delirious New York: A Retroactive Manifesto for Manhattan*, Oxford University Press (New York), 1978.

37   Colin Rowe and Fred Koetter, *Collage City*, MIT Press (Cambridge, MA), 1978.

38   Ibid pp 152–81.

39   For Canary Wharf, see: Alan J Plattus (ed), *Koetter Kim & Associates: place/time*, Rizzoli (New York), 1997; also: SOM website, http://www.som.com/content.cfm/canary_wharf_master_plan (accessed 3 March 2010).

40   For 'city archipelago', see: 'Learning from OM Ungers' programme information, 9 May 2007, Eindhoven University of Technology website, http://www.citytv.nl/page/Tue/TUe.html (accessed 1 April 2010); also: Oswald Mathias Ungers, Rem Koolhaas, Peter Riemann, Hans Kollhof, Peter Ovaska, 'Cities within the City: proposal by the sommer akademie for Berlin', *Lotus International*, 1977, p 19. For Ungers projects, see: OM Ungers, *OM Ungers: The Dialectic City*, Skira (Milan), 1999.

41   Guy Debord, *The Situationist City*, MIT Press (Cambridge, MA), 1999, pp 20-1.

42   For Munich, see: Rowe and Koetter, *Collage City*, pp 126–36.

43   Rafi Segal and Eyal Weizman (eds), *A Civilian Occupation: The Politics of Israeli Architecture*, Babel (Tel Aviv) and Verso (New York), 2003.

44   Saskia Sassen, *The Global City: New York, London, Tokyo*, Princeton University Press (Princeton, NJ), 1991.

45   For Disney, see: Karal Ann Marling (ed), *Designing Disney's Theme Parks: The Architecture of Reassurance*, Canadian Centre for Architecture (Montreal) and Flammarion (Paris; New York), 1997.

46   On Poundbury, see: Leon Krier, *The Architecture of Community*, Island Press, 2009 (Washington, DC), p 435.

47   For Seaside, see: David Mohney and Keller Easterling, *Seaside: Making a Town in America*, Princeton Architectural Press (Princeton, NJ), 1991. On Brian McGrath's Manhattan Timeformations, see: Manhattan Timeformations website, http://www.skyscraper.org/timeformations/intro.html (accessed 3 March 2010). For fractal and iterative patterns, see: Michael Batty and Paul Longley, *Fractal Cities: A Geometry of Form and Function*, Academic Press (San Diego, CA), 1996.

48   On Barbara Ward and the 1976 conference, see: Barbara Ward, *The Home of Man*, WW Norton & Company (New York), 1976.

49   For self-built housing, see: John Turner, *Housing by People: Towards Autonomy in Building Environments*, Pantheon Books (New York), 1977. On the history and current status of self-built housing, see: David Satterthwaite, *The Transition to a Predominantly Urban World and its Underpinnings*, IIED (London), 2007.

50   For Sewoon Sangga Market, see: Heui-Jeong Kwak, *A Turning Point in Korea's Urban Modernization: The Case of the Sewoon Sangga Development*, Harvard University, 2002 and *Archive 22* at http://condencity.blogspot.com/; for Kim Swoo Geun, see: http://en.wikipedia.org/wiki/Kim_Swoo_Geun.

51   On the Walled City of Kowloon, see: Greg Girard and Ian Lambot, *City of Darkness: Life in Kowloon Walled City*, Watermark Publications (Haslemere, Surrey), 1993.

52   Alvin Boyarsky, 'Chicago A La Carte', in Robin Middleton (ed), *The Idea of the City: Architectural Associations*, Architectural Association (London), 1996 (article first printed in *Architectural Design*, no 11, December 1970, pp 595–640.

53   On the Peak Project, see: Zaha Hadid, 'Two Recent Projects for Berlin and Hong Kong', *Architectural Design*, vol 58, 4 March 1988, pp 40–45.

54   For US population estimates, see: Population Estimates Program, Population Division, US Census Bureau website, http://www.census.gov/popest/archives/1990s/popclockest.txt (accessed 10 July 2010). For the British figure, see: British Population Animation, British History section, BBC website, http://www.bbc.co.uk/history/interactive/animations/population/index_embed.shtml (accessed 12 July 2010).

55   See: Population Division of the Department of Economic and Social Affairs of the UN Secretariat estimates 2008, Revisions of estimates for China at http://esa.un.org/unpp/p2k0data.asp and India at http://esa.un.org/unpp/p2k0data.asp   (accessed 12 July 2010).

56   On Chinese megamalls, see: David Barboza, 'For China, new malls jaw-dropping in size', *The New York Times*, 25 May 2005 http://www.nytimes.com/2005/05/24/world/asia/24iht-mall.html (accessed 28 June 2010).

57   On tall buildings, see: Guy Nordenson and Terence Riley, *Tall Buildings*, The Museum of Modern Art (New York), 2003, pp 102–9; also: http://en.wikipedia.org/wiki/China_Central_Television_Headquarters_building (accessed 3 March 2010). For popular commentary on the CCTV tower, see: http://www.danwei.org/newspapers/cctv_underpants_and_hemorrhoid.php (accessed 1 April 2010).

**Rem Koolhaas and OMA, China Central Television Headquarters,
Beijing, China, 2009 (photo 2009)**
(Photo © David Grahame Shane)

Aldo Rossi, *Città analoga (The Analogous City)*, **1976**
(Drawing © Eredi Aldo Rossi, courtesy Fondazione Aldo Rossi)

CHAPTER 8

Illustrated Fragmented Metropolis

Urban design emerged as a distinct discipline between architecture and town planning, as predicted by Patrick Abercrombie in his 1943 report, with the collision of the metropolis and megalopolis.[1] Both faced problems by the 1970s. The metropolis, as the centre of an imperial system, suffered with the collapse of the European empires in the Cold War when the USA and USSR emerged as global superpowers. Metropolitan centres shrank and ports, docks and industrial areas declined in the European capitals; communities in urban villages became stressed and stranded. At the same time the American system of the megalopolis expanding into the suburbs faced its first challenges as oil-producing nations formed a cartel and asked for a larger share of the enormous, global revenue stream that circulated beyond the control of nation states. The price of oil trebled.[2] A series of oil price spikes occasioned major economic disruptions and recessions within the oil-based, global economy controlled from London, New York and Tokyo, the emerging global financial centres of the late 20th century.

In this period of difficulty, urban designers invented a system of fragmentary urbanism that provided the possibility of control within a small patch of real estate. As Kevin Lynch pointed out, this basic strategy was similar to suburban mall design where designers were in complete control of an environment, but in this case design extended to a larger fragment including outside spaces, streets and squares. The character of the fragments could vary enormously within the system and there was no need, in theory at least, for any overall control or master plan (reflecting neo-liberal economic theories of the emerging global corporations). Shantytowns, urban villages, planned communities like Levittown, shopping malls, office parks or industrial parks could all function as fragments within the superblocks of the modern city framed by a network of highways (as exemplified by Reyner Banham's study of Los Angeles; see chapter 5). The fragmentary metropolis as an urban design ecology allowed for many new urban voices to surface and participate as actors in the debate about the city. These voices varied from feminists angry about suburban isolation, to ethnic minorities and gay pride groups seeking justice and equality. The fragmented metropolis suited both community activists who sought social justice and developers who sought secure fragments, safe enclaves for their investments.

This chapter examines the evolution of urban fragments as devices in the hands of various global urban actors with different agendas. The new urban design ecology of fragments emerged early in the 1970s, but it was best reflected in Disney's heterotopia of illusion at EPCOT, Florida (opened 1982) that captured the role of communications and transport in linking the global system of fragmented urban villages together. Olympic games also provided another heterotopic display of the fragmentary system in Barcelona in 1992 and again in London in 2012. Indeed London designers, as the city shrank as an imperial capital, were able to adapt their piecemeal and pragmatic urban tradition to a new global role as the city emerged as an corporate finance and cultural node, making it the exemplary fragmented metropolis at the end of the 20th century.

Aldo Rossi's drawing of the *Analogous City* (1976) represented this situation of fragmentation.[3] A sad figure in the top left-hand corner points to the old city with its single centre that is fractured and broken. Rossi mischievously uses Andrea Palladio's illustration of Daniele Barbaro's 1556 translation of Vitruvius, which shows an ideal Renaissance circular-plan city as the historic, single-centre, *archi-città* model but inserts his own projects and the Spanish Steps in Rome leading to the Pantheon within the classical ring-and-radial pattern. In the left-hand upper quadrant of the drawing, the shadowy figure of Rossi in his room looks out of his window onto the plan of the medieval fabric of the historic centre of an Italian town and dreams of scientific grids and a modern city order of the *cine-città* (again Rossi uses one of his own projects for student housing at Trieste as the example). Finally, in the lower half of the drawing, the old platonic controlling geometry is falling out of the image frame. A wild Alpine landscape from a 19th-century engraving is breaking inside the city walls, creating a new hybrid city territory, the *tele-città* perhaps, extending to an open flat field that stretches out towards the viewer.

The flexible patches of the fragmented metropolis enabled urban designers to handle the many transitions impacting the city in the second half of the 20th century. Whenever the major systems of the era, the metropolis or megalopolis, entered into a stress period, heterotopic fragments provided a way of handling the situation. From these new fragments, over time a new form of urbanism gradually emerged as the centre of global urban population shifted from Europe to Asia. By the end of the century, Europe was importing urban ideas from Asia – like the dense, mixed-use, skyscraper-cum-railway-station Shard Building in London – as new developments in Asia set the pace for the next urban century.

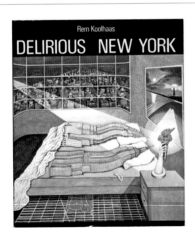

Madelon Vriesendorp, cover painting for Rem Koolhaas's Delirious New York, 1978 (Image © OMA/Madelon Vriesendorp)

The young Dutch architect Rem Koolhaas published *Delirious New York: A Retroactive Manifesto for Manhattan* in 1978 shortly after the near bankruptcy of the modern metropolis in 1975.[4] In 1978 Colin Rowe and Fred Koetter's *Collage City* appeared and Cooper & Eckstut won the Battery Park City competition in New York (see chapter 7).[5] Koolhaas saw Manhattan as a dynamic collection of large urban fragments, like the Rockefeller Center, which made it a modern, commercial metropolis distinct from the imperial capitals of Europe (and from the megalopolis, as in the automobile-based American gambling capital of Las Vegas described by the Venturi, Scott Brown, Izenour team in 1972).[6]

Koolhaas's vision of New York included a role for the heterotopia of illusion, like Coney Island and Luna Park at the end of peripheral subway lines. These fairgrounds helped shape the skyscraper image of the modern metropolis lit at night in the popular imagination. Madelon Vriesendorp's cover illustration playfully captures the idea of a city of giant, competing, urban fragments resting in bed, while other skyscrapers look on through the window. A picture on the wall shows a lone car speeding out through the suburban landscape in a leafy world surrounding the metropolitan node.

Twelve years earlier, in *The Architecture of the City* (1966), Aldo Rossi had proposed seeing the life of the city in terms of its monumental buildings as expressions of civic pride, collective memory and a tradition of public institutions that enabled people to live together (another theme of Team 10 member Louis Kahn's 'urban room' speech at Otterlo in 1959).[7] Rossi's book highlighted the Rationalist tradition of making cities that descended from the Greeks and Romans and, via the Renaissance, led to the technical improvements in urban design in the 19th century, in metropolitan cities like Ildefons Cerdá's Barcelona (1859) or Haussmann's Paris (1852–70).

Skipping Le Corbusier's modernism, Rossi attempted to link back to this earlier Rationalist tradition of making cities with streets, blocks, squares and gardens, much like the contemporary Contextualist group at Cornell University, led by Rowe. Rossi discovered Joseph Stübben's *Der Städtebau* ('City Building') handbooks (1876–1924) that encapsulated this approach, and sought out the German architect OM Ungers who also valued this tradition.[8] Together they influenced Ungers' student and assistant Rob Krier who, with his brother Leon – who worked for the British architect James Stirling in London – organised the exhibition 'Rationalist Architecture: The Reconstruction of the European City' in 1978.[9]

This exhibition followed on Rob Krier's *Stadtraum in Theorie und Praxis* (1975) that developed Ungers' idea of an urban fragment as a formula for the creation of gridded city extensions in the Rationalist tradition of Cerdá.[10] Krier saw the city as a recombinant system made up of rules that created city blocks with height limits and defined street widths that provided clear organisation, much like the New York grid. Ungers' competition entry for the Roosevelt Island housing competition of the same year replicated a small-scale version of the New York City grid, complete with a miniature central park. Rob Krier encapsulated this systemic view in one drawing that showed all the different formal manipulations that might transform such a grid in the urban design process.

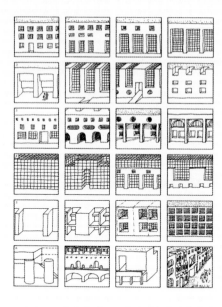

**Rob Krier, matrix
drawings of urban
facades, 1976**
(Drawings © Rob Krier)

This drawing when applied in combination with the Special Districts invented in New York by the Urban Design Group in the late 1960s defined the standard operating system for urban designers for a generation. Where the American group stopped at the overall massing of the block and city, Krier continued to define the building lot, plan, section and elevation as recombinatory building systems that operated within a gridded matrix. His brother Leon drew simple cartoons of small cities and urban villages constructed from such basic building elements, deeply influencing the following generation of urban designers.

Rob Krier's work stressed the formal dimension of the large urban fragment and its internal codes, always presuming some form of community input. The American firm Urban Design Associates (UDA) in Cincinnati, Ohio, pioneered an approach of community consultations based on Jane Jacobs' work, led by David Lewis, a student of Kevin Lynch's at MIT in the 1960s. Lewis helped write the American Institute of Architects' (AIA) proposal for a national Uniform Land Use Review Procedure (ULURP) that allowed for community input into large urban design projects and was adopted by many cities (including New York).[11] This legal structure balanced developers and community activists, giving them a forum for negotiation.

UDA went on to develop this process, creating very clear graphics so that community members could understand the process, adapting the Krier brothers' work to their needs and the American marketplace, like other members of the American New Urbanism movement. UDA made it possible for local community groups to participate actively and intelligently in urban design and code-making decisions, often in a long-drawn-out and exhausting series of meetings to find consensus, Their poster for an 'Assembly Kit' explains how the community might 'assemble' a design through consultations, often on sensitive infill sites with existing city networks.[12]

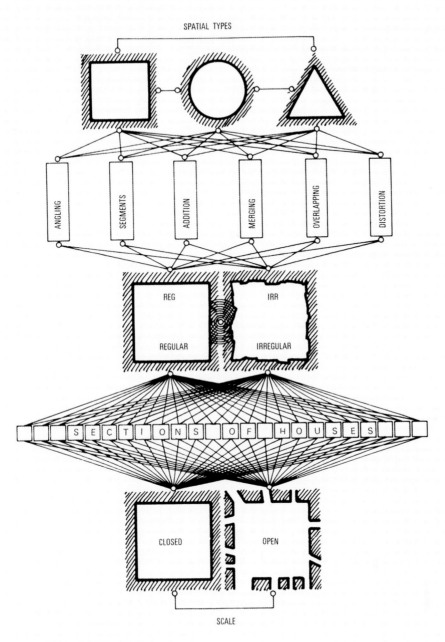

Rob Krier, urban space matrix, 1976

(Diagram © Rob Krier)

OM Ungers, city archipelago drawing of Berlin with 'green lagoons', 1977 (redrawn by the author, 2010)
(Redrawn drawing © David Grahame Shane and Uri Wegman, 2010)

The same drawing of the 'Assembly Kit' could also be used to make new suburbs on greenfield sites, creating vast new city territories entirely based on the automobile and oil, as in the work of members of the New Urbanism movement groups like Duany Plater-Zyberk, starting at the isolated resort village of Seaside, Florida in the 1980s.[13] Other New Urbanism movement founders stressed alternatives to the automobile, as in Peter Calthorpe and Doug Kelbaugh's *Pedestrian Pocket Book: A New Suburban Design Strategy* (1989), which planned a hypothetical string of small pedestrian-oriented villages along a streetcar, light-rail line south of San Francisco.[14] In Vriesendorp's cover for *Delirious New York* (1978), suburban automobiles cruised on empty Robert Moses highways with only two lanes, unlike the crowded multilane two-hour commutes that began to be the staple of the extended, multicentred megalopolis of the 1980s and 1990s.

Koolhaas worked with OM Ungers as a student at Cornell and then as a colleague in the Berlin Summer Schools of 1976–7, developing a reply to Rowe and Koetter's impending *Collage City* (1978). Ungers asked students to identify large urban fragments within the green expanse that had once been the luxurious bourgeois western suburbs and garden city area of imperial Berlin. These islands of urbanity formed a 'city archipelago' set within green 'oceans' and 'pools'.[15] After identifying the urban fragments, the students working with Ungers proceeded to reinforce existing grids and develop new ones with large, regular, cubic masses. Those working with Koolhaas developed enormous commercial centres around key intersections, attempting to replicate mini-Rockefeller Centers and mini-Manhattans. Both shared the vision of these large urban fragments floating in a green forest. Unlike Rowe and Koetter, Ungers and Koolhaas like Stirling in *Roma Interrotta* (1978, see chapter 7), saw a positive value in the green spaces in between the large urban clusters.[16]

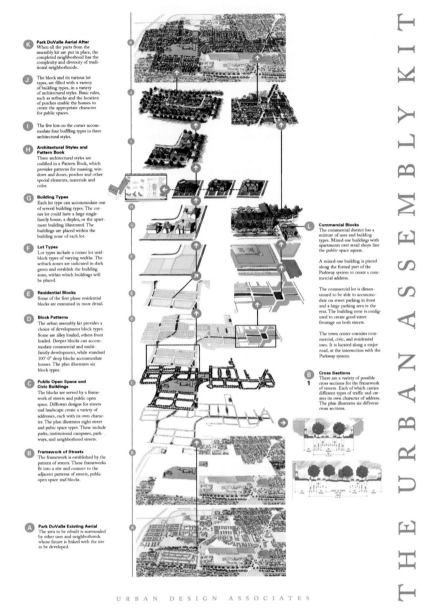

K Park DuValle Aerial After
When all the parts from the assembly kit are put in place, the completed neighborhood has the complexity and diversity of traditional neighborhoods.

J The block and its various lot types, are filled with a variety of building types, in a variety of architectural styles. Basic rules, such as setbacks and the location of porches enable the houses to create the appropriate character for public spaces.

I The five lots on the corner accommodate four building types in three architectural styles.

H Architectural Styles and Pattern Book
Three architectural styles are codified in a Pattern Book, which provides patterns for massing, windows and doors, porches and other special elements, materials and color.

G Building Types
Each lot type can accommodate one of several building types. The corner lot could have a large single-family house, a duplex, or the apartment building illustrated. The buildings are placed within the building zone of each lot.

F Lot Types
Lot types include a corner lot mid-block types of varying widths. The setback zones are indicated in dark green and establish the building zone, within which buildings will be placed.

E Residential Blocks
Some of the first phase residential blocks are examined in more detail.

D Block Patterns
The urban assembly kit provides a choice of development block types. Some are alley loaded, others front loaded. Deeper blocks can accommodate commercial and multi-family development, while standard 100'-0" deep blocks accommodate houses. The plan illustrates six block types.

C Public Open Space and Civic Buildings
The blocks are served by a framework of streets and public open space. Different designs for streets and landscape create a variety of addresses, each with its own character. The plan illustrates eight street and public types. These include parks, institutional campuses, parkways, and neighborhood streets.

B Framework of Streets
The framework is established by the pattern of streets. These frameworks fit into a site and connect to the adjacent patterns of streets, public open space and blocks.

A Park DuValle Existing Aerial
The area to be rebuilt is surrounded by other uses and neighborhoods whose future is linked with the site to be developed.

L Commercial Blocks
The commercial district has a mixture of uses and building types. Mixed-use buildings with apartments over retail shops line the public space square.

A mixed-use building is placed along the formal part of the Parkway system to create s commercial address.

The commercial lot is dimensioned to be able to accommodate on street parking in front and a large parking area in the rear. The building zone is configured to create good street frontage on both streets.

The town center contains commercial, civic, and residential uses. It is located along a major road, at the intersection with the Parkway system.

B 1 Cross Sections
There are a variety of possible cross sections for the framework of streets. Each of which carries different types of traffic and creates its own character of address. The plan illustrates six different cross sections.

URBAN DESIGN ASSOCIATES

Urban Design Associates (UDA), The Urban Assembly Kit, *c* **2003**
UDA pioneered community participation and advocacy in the USA in the 1970s and then, like Krier, developed an elaborate manual to help groups plan urban designs. UDA later linked to the New Urbanism movement. (Poster © courtesy of Urban Design Associates)

Collage city and the city archipelago provided alternative methods for dealing with the fragmentation of the metropolis and the sense of losing central control as European empires fell apart and a new global system based on the megalopolis emerged. Within the Soviet Bloc, satellite countries continued to orbit Moscow, even as China broke away after Stalin's death. Walt Disney, who had first built Disneyland in California in 1954, long dreamt of opening a multi-enclave theme park at Orlando in Florida that would be like a World's Fair showing the organisation of the *Pax Americana* (the American global alliance).[17] Disney also hoped that this heterotopia of illusion would be a futuristic world city, a science-fiction-based demonstration of the power of American corporate technology. Beginning with a replica of the original Disneyland in 1971, the Disney corporation opened his heritage project, the scaled-down Experimental Prototype Community of Tomorrow (EPCOT), in 1982 after his death.[18]

In EPCOT, a Buckminster Fuller dome representing the planet Earth dominated the entrance approach from a vast car park (Mickey Mouse ears are sometimes attached to stress the global brand). The American moon shot had produced classic images of the green planet Earth floating in space. Inside the dome, the American Telephone & Telegraph Company (AT&T) sponsored a promotional ride through a history of communications from the Stone Age to today's cellphones. Originally, a cluster of American corporate pavilions surrounded the Buckminster Fuller dome at the entry, including General Motors, General Electric and Kodak. Beyond the dome, Disney promoted a mini-World's Fair, his 'World Showcase', consisting of representative national pavilions at intervals around the lake's periphery. The message was clear: American technology and telecommunications tied all the urban national fragments together, while ferries across the lake connected the miniature cities and countries. Each fragment represented a city and a nation. Walt Disney World now houses five other theme parks besides EPCOT and 24 hotels; it employs 66,000 people and is the largest single-site employment centre in the United States (in 2007 the Magic Kingdom was visited by 17 million people, making it the number one theme park worldwide, with EPCOT visited by 10.9 million).[19]

EPCOT provides an insight into the global structure of the fragmented metropolis, also portrayed in collage city and the city archipelago. As the European empires collapsed and Asian and African countries gained their independence, the old European metropolis became, in Disney's view, a picturesque urban image sheltered below the American nuclear umbrella. The company's 'Imagineers' designed each image space to represent each ex-imperial metropolis on the perimeter of the lake, set amongst the surrounding shrubbery. A miniature Eiffel Tower marks Paris from afar, while a small alley represents a Parisian boulevard with a pavement café. London has Big Ben and a pub, Tokyo an elaborate wooden temple and shrine, and China a circular temple modelled on the Temple of the Sun, Beijing. Italy is represented by Venice, accessible from a ferry stop, with a miniature Campanile of the Piazza San Marco marking the skyline. The position of the Campanile and Doge's Palace are combined and reversed so that no one would confuse this simulacra with the original in Venice. In addition, across the piazza, a rural peasant inn with vine-draped trellises completes this strange transformation of the heart of the Venetian empire into a Kodak moment (Venice, Italy, is visited by 12 million people a year, the same number as the original Disneyland).[20]

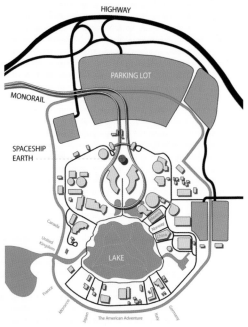

Disney Imagineers, 'Venice' in Disney's EPCOT theme park, Walt Disney World, Orlando, Florida, USA, 1982 (photo 2005)
Venice is represented at the EPCOT by a 'Doge's Palace' and 'Campanile' beside the central lagoon. (Photo © David Grahame Shane)

Disney Imagineers, plan of Disney's EPCOT at Walt Disney World, Orlando, Florida, USA, 1982 (redrawn by the author, 2010)
The theme park plan presents a coherent vision of the new global corporate system emerging in the 1980s, as cities became linked in global electronic networks. (Redrawn drawing © David Grahame Shane and Uri Wegman, 2010)

This heterotopia of illusion, like the Brussels World's Fair before it, accurately mirrored the larger global system in its miniature model, showing the segregation and separation of all the urban actors within the corporate system that replaced the global imperial system. The Brussels World's Fair had contrasted the Belgian village with its plaza, cafés and chocolates with the African village and its live-in chieftains imported from the Belgian Congo, enshrining the imperial mission of bringing European 'civilisation' and modernity to fictive 'savages' (see chapter 4). In Walt Disney World's EPCOT it was the imperial capitals that became picturesque villages, small nodes in the global communication and transportation network benevolently engineered by corporate America. The Brussels World's Fair still dreamt that power remained in the metropolitan control centres of the European global system, while Disney reflected the fragmentation of the *Pax Americana* and global corporate power in 1982.

For a period in the 1970s and 1980s, the imperial and American systems coexisted as the American global corporate system emerged, replacing the earlier imperial systems in the

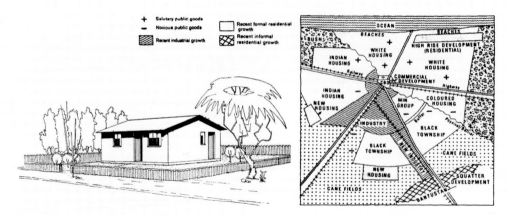

Western Bloc. The historic Anglo-Dutch commercial empire that supported British imperial power in 1945, for instance, was falling apart. Both India and Pakistan gained independence in 1947, Dutch Indonesia soon followed, and Ghana became the first newly independent nation in Africa in 1957. Each of these nations embarked on rebuilding their country, whose boundaries were an imperial fiction, but now turned to a new, self-improving purpose (quickly attracting the attention of the two superpowers, the USA and USSR, as in the Congo).

In South Africa, remnants of the Anglo-Dutch imperial system persisted in a desperate and extremely violent urban design attempt by the Boer settlers to continue imperial rule. The Nationalist Party's apartheid segregation codes from 1948 deprived Africans of their right to live in their homes of choice, taking their property, and then in 1958 deprived them of their citizenship rights. Pushing the colonial sorting process to a hard-edged extreme, millions of Africans were moved and others returned to their supposed 'homelands' (racist enclaves imposed by the government, often in scrublands and impoverished deserts). During the Second World War German *Stadtlandschaft* planners under the Nazi regime had created ghettos as supposedly self-governing enclaves, like the South African *Bantustans*, while the land and property of the segregated citizens was taken by the state to sell to others, supposedly for the good of the nation. In South Africa the state built minimal single-family housing units (like Mandela's house in Soweto), in segregated areas, to resettle some of the dispossessed. Others were forced to move to the *Bantustans*, only to return illegally into segregated shantytowns close to industrial and domestic employment.[21]

Elsewhere in the decaying Anglo-Dutch colonial empire, a softer segregation persisted after the departure of the imperial regime. In Indonesia, for instance, President Sukarno, like Gandhi and Mao, sought to reformulate the agricultural village as a basis for the new, dignified culture of the independent nation. This perpetuated but hopefully improved on the old colonial regime that had kept labourers on the land and away from the cities, illiterate and impoverished. In this improvement process (involving schools and new housing), the Dutch city-landscape pattern that had formed part of the heritage of colonial Batavia, now Jakarta, became transformed into the agricultural, distributed city system of the *desa-kota* or city-

Images of South African apartheid planning, 1950s
A view from the road of the standardised township house type, 1953; a City Planning Racial Segregation diagram; and an aerial view of a planned township settlement outside Johannesburg. (Photo of house type reproduced from: DM Calderwood, 'Native Housing in South Africa', unpublished PhD thesis, University of the Witwatersrand (Johannesburg), 1953, p 31, fig 4; map reproduced from: JJ McCarthy, 'Problems of Planning for Urbanization and Development in South Africa: The Case of Natal's Coastal Margins', *Geoforum* 17, 1986, pp 276–88; aerial photo © Hulton-Deutsch Collection/CORBIS)

village.[22] The Dutch had organised Batavia in an estuary with many islands, an archipelago city on an island with a castle and warehouses around a canal and with spice-growing plantations around its perimeter.[23] This linear north–south organisation meant that the city and countryside were never far from one another and informal settlement villages, or *kampungs*, formed along this spine amongst the rich rice paddies and fishponds, and later factories, to provide labour.[24] Later additions developed the urban spine inland, allowing the agricultural areas to be close to the dense, central corridor of development.

The Canadian geographer Terry McGee, in *The Urbanization Process in the Third World* (1971), highlighted this strange mixture as a new form of typically Asian *desa-kota* (city-village) urbanism.[25] Urban elements became mixed in and distributed through the countryside as a result of the newly independent nations' government polices. Rural agriculture and industrial uses stood right beside the capital with its monumental independence boulevard and office towers, producing a new hybrid urbanism. Other variants of the *desa-kota* urbanism could also be found in India and China, as well as in the 'Asian Tigers' and in Japan along the Tokyo–Osaka megalopolis corridor. Later researchers, like Steven Cairns of Edinburgh University, used the mental mapping techniques, interviews and notation systems of Kevin Lynch to uncover in detail the strange microcodes underpinning the mixtures of the new distributed urbanism of the *desa-kota* city territory.[26]

This new urban invention transformed the urban development pattern of the Anglo-Dutch empire towards an Asian tradition of urban agriculture based on canal irrigation systems that extended back millennia in India and China. Even in metropolitan Holland the same strange mixture could be found around Amsterdam, where greenhouses and intense agricultural uses intermingled with the cities in the Randstad (Ring City, 1940s onwards). With the end of the Anglo-Dutch empire, in Amsterdam the Borneo and Java wharfs and warehouses that once served the Indonesian trade became empty and redundant. The British Prime Minister Margaret Thatcher spearheaded the conversion of London's imperial West and East India Docks into the Canary Wharf global office park (1988–91, see p 242), setting a pattern for post-industrial development.

In Amsterdam, the Dutch firm West 8 and its founder Adriaan Geuze won the competition for the rehabilitation of the Borneo, Sporenburg and Java island dockland area in 1993 as a large urban fragment in the archipelago city (Amsterdam, like Venice, spans many islands).[27] West 8's scheme consisted of a large urban fragment layered in a three-dimensional matrix at two scales. The first scale was a carpet of low-rise, high-density townhouses, sometimes beside canals. Here, West 8 created a three-dimensional matrix that cleverly transformed the original Amsterdam townhouse morphology of the historic core, with its gable fronts, long cascade staircases up one side giving access to front and back rooms on every floor, and crane to hoist goods up into the attic.

The West 8 urban design created a dense urban village in a matrix that allowed courtyards inside the typical deep house lots, replacing the traditional back gardens. The ground floor could house garages, offices and small gardens; above, the living and sleeping areas worked around the internal courtyard, while the garden was transferred to the roof. Within this carefully coded matrix, many Amsterdam architects built variants depending on the wealth and market sector of their clients, producing a great diversity of solutions to create a dense urban village. At strategic intervals in this low-rise texture, West 8 positioned high-rise apartment structures that operated like the churches in the old city, making markers on the skyline and also relating by sightlines and park strips back to the old city core.

As in Battery Park City (1978) and Walt Disney World (1982), the image of the historic city core returned like a ghost to haunt, transform and inform the new urban fragment, creating urban village settings. Even within planned urban expansions and Special Economic Zones in China, urban villages survived as elements inside the new towns, as they had done at Chandigarh in India (early 1950s, see chapter 4), Brasilia in Brazil (1957, see chapter 4) and

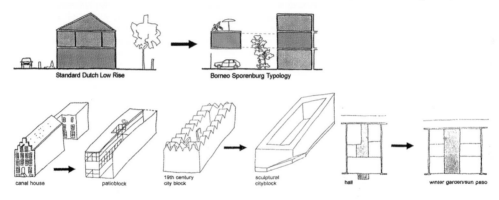

Self-built housing structures and shanties, Johannesburg Townships, South Africa (photo 2005)
(Photo © Emmanuel Pratt of Makeshift Media)

Milton Keynes in the UK (1967 onwards, see chapter 5). Where Le Corbusier had turned a blind eye to the existence of the villages, in Brasilia they originally housed the construction workers and in Milton Keynes pre-existing villages were preserved as untouchable historic relics. This pattern was continued in Shenzhen, the first Special Economic Zone (SEZ) developed under Deng's reforms in 1979 (with the support of Mrs Thatcher, who also began the negotiations for the handover of the British Hong Kong colony to China).

Chinese planners improved on the Milton Keynes new town that had been planned by their British partners, Llewelyn-Davies, Weeks & Partners 12 years before.[28] As at Milton Keynes, the existing agricultural villages were left in small green belts, but not subjected to historic preservation (they had been rebuilt by Mao as part of his collectivisation drive). Instead of a central shopping mall as at Milton Keynes, Shenzhen boasted a large central park, overlooked by the new civic centre and town hall, aligned with a small hill behind which Deng's statue stood commanding the central axis. A huge exhibition centre terminated the axis at the other end, with underground connections to subways below the wide boulevards that formed the megablocks of the new town. Around this formal core, high-rise office and residential towers represented the official, planned city, alongside a proliferation of golf courses for executives of global corporations. Shenzhen became a great success and basis for China's entry into the global manufacturing system (all the world's iPods are manufactured here).[29]

In Shenzhen the urban villages took on an unexpected role as the city became one of the major manufacturing centres of the world, feeding on Hong Kong's global connections and a vast labour force that moved from the agricultural hinterland to the coast. From rural enclaves the Shenzhen urban villages developed into dense, vertical urban fragments, like Kowloon's

West 8, competition entry for the rehabilitation of Borneo-Sporenburg and Java Island docks, Amsterdam, The Netherlands, 1993
The West 8 entry included schematic diagrams to reformat the traditional Amsterdam townhouse and block for the 21st century. (Diagrams and photo © West 8 urban design & landscape architecture)

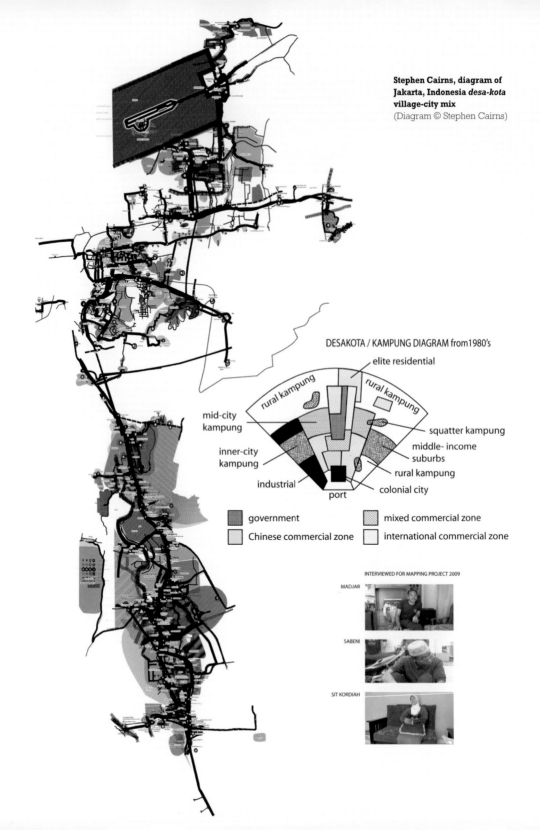

Stephen Cairns, diagram of Jakarta, Indonesia *desa-kota* village-city mix
(Diagram © Stephen Cairns)

DESAKOTA / KAMPUNG DIAGRAM from 1980's

elite residential

rural kampung

rural kampung

mid-city kampung

squatter kampung

inner-city kampung

middle-income suburbs

rural kampung

industrial

colonial city

port

government

mixed commercial zone

Chinese commercial zone

international commercial zone

INTERVIEWED FOR MAPPING PROJECT 2009

MADJAR

SABENI

SIT KORDIAH

earlier Walled City, housing a large percentage of the unregistered workers drawn to work in the factories.[30] Within the central area there were over 40 villages in 11 major clusters subject to special study by the authorities in 2005.[31] The official plan called for the elimination of most of the villages and their replacement by high-rise development as the government considered the living standards were very bad (narrow alleyways, poor sanitation and water supply, no light or green spaces). A lively public debate ensued as so few villages were to be conserved and yet so much of the life of Shenzhen was concentrated there, often on very valuable land. The report found that there were 320 villages within the greater Shenzhen area, housing up to an estimated five million people.

The Shenzhen-based architectural group Urbanus has proposed that rather than pull the urban villages down, they could be reconditioned by permitting the development of a new layer of urban facilities above them on their rooftops.[32] Besides many speculative large-scale projects, Urbanus was unusual in building many small-scale infill schemes in urban villages in the early 2000s, like their project for the Drum Tower Area Renewal, Tianjin Old Town (2000), or the Dafen Art Museum (2005–7) in the urban village of Dafen in Shenzhen. This village specialises in cheap reproduction paintings of great masterworks, supplying a global and national demand. Urbanus added a carefully placed museum to the village that was full of artists and their shops. The contemporary museum, one of Michel Foucault's heterotopias of illusion (see chapter 2), provided another outlet for the many young artists involved in the commercial activity of copying, long revered in China.

As a result of these infill experiences, Urbanus proposed that the city demolish only three plots in Gangxia urban village that lay close to the Shenzhen town hall and central civic park. Three new towers would rise from these sites to carry a new snaking upper-deck building that contained community facilities, housing and other needed amenities in a mixed-use sandwich that opened out onto the many low-rise, high-density building roofs of the village. Urbanus imagined new public spaces, commercial uses and green houses combining to create a new, three-dimensional matrix improving on the long-demolished Kowloon Walled City enclave but with a system of green roofs. This upgrade proposal provided many of the same amenities built by Indian architect BV Doshi at Aranya in the early 1980s, but at a much higher density and cost, projected up into a new, super-dense, three-dimensional matrix like a mini-megastructure.

Stephen Cairns, aerial photograph of Jakarta, Indonesia, showing *desa-kota*, 2008
(Photo © Stephen Cairns)

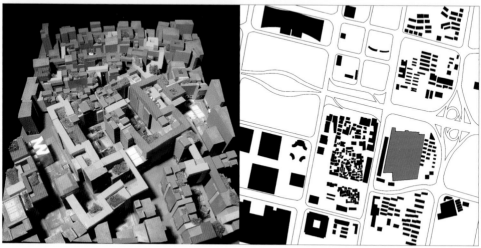

**Urbanus, village research programme for
Gangxia urban village, Shenzhen, China, 2005**
(Plans, drawings and photos © Urbanus)

Master plan for Yokohama, Japan, 1983 (redrawn by the author, 2010)
Mirato Mirai 21 is light grey area at top left, original foreigners' settlement is light grey area lower right. (Redrawn plan © David Grahame Shane and Uri Wegman, 2010)

Until the 1820s, when the European nations overtook them with their industrial revolution and established the colonial system, China and India had long been the largest global economies.[33] In Asia, China and Japan had long excluded foreign merchants from trade. Japan, under the threat of American warships, allowed foreigners to trade at the small fishing village of Yokohama after 1859. Yokohama, like contemporary Hong Kong or Shenzhen, was a special extra-territorial zone, a gateway port city.[34] This heterotopia contained multiple foreign nationalities within one enclave that was separated from the traditional culture of 19th-century Japan.

Yokohama village added a small grid where foreign merchants could live and trade at the docks, with a small Chinatown off the grid that eventually became the largest in Japan. There were separate French and American quarters, with British villas up on the hills along curving picturesque lanes overlooking the town. Many foreign inventions first appeared here and the first railway in Japan connected to Tokyo. Even now the expanded Yokohama port area is one of the most efficient container ports serving Tokyo, comparable to Rotterdam in scale and modernity. Close to the old village, the industrial giant Mitsubishi shuttered its great 19th-century shipbuilding yards in the late 1970s and converted them into Tokyo's Battery Park City-like planned community, the large Minato Mirai 21 urban fragment, begun in 1983.[35]

Mitsubishi's urban designers planned this large urban fragment long before Canary Wharf in London, replacing the docks with a grid of generous streets and waterside promenades. The American architect Hugh Stubbins designed the tallest skyscraper in Japan, the Landmark Tower (1990–93).[36] This mixed-use tower contains offices below a hotel with complex, anti-earthquake dampening systems in its upper stories. At the base of the tower the large Queens Square shopping mall and Yokohama Convention Centre connect into the old Mitsubishi dry dock that is used as a recreation space and courtyard by surrounding bars and restaurants.

In the heterotopic tradition of Yokohama, the Minato Mirai 21 enclave and special district benefited from the nearby location of Tokyo's equivalent of New York's Coney Island, the giant Cosmo Clock Ferris wheel and fairground built for the Yokohama Exotic Showcase (YES) of 1989. Other attractions, also heterotopias of illusion, included the skyscraper viewing deck, shopping mall, convention centre, historic centre, maritime museum, art museum, and park with seaside beaches. Japanese railway companies had a long tradition of locating fairgrounds and Ferris wheels as attractions in the open land at the end of the line, learning from Coney Island. Because of its isolation, the development has moved ahead slowly, especially the planned residential district, but a new direct subway connection to Tokyo is under construction.

The lesson of Yokohama for urban designers worldwide was that even a great global corporation like Mitsubishi had to connect its urban fragment into the surrounding network of transportation and communications (the same lesson was brought home by the financial difficulties of Canary Wharf in London in the early 1990s). The deliberate isolation of the original foreigners' port was no longer sustainable. The switch from imperial shipyard or dockyard to global corporate hub required different connections. Even the added attraction of a local heterotopia of illusion, like the Ferris wheel, the historic district or the fairground, was not enough to tip the balance.

The addition of a global attraction, like the Olympic games or a Disney theme park, could alter the equation, as the skilful urban designers of the 1992 Barcelona Olympics proved.[37] There the construction of a new ring road tied all the peripheral suburbs developed in the valleys behind the city to the renewed, post-industrial seafront. The road slid under the new parkland connection of the Ramblas to the port, but surfaced to connect to the Poblenou Olympic village with its small skyscraper tower and marina. Skilful terracing and landscaping scattered new Olympic facilities like the Enric Miralles-designed archery range along the route of the ring road in Vall d'Hebron valley, as well as amongst the remains of the 1929 International Exposition on Montjuic mountaintop, with the dramatic Santiago Calatrava-designed Montjuic Communications Tower (1992).

The Barcelona Olympics demonstrated how the heterotopic pulse of the Olympic games as an international media and sporting event, with its huge global audience and advertising revenues, could be used to make strategic interventions in the host city. Shortly afterwards the EU began its annual City of Culture competition proposing a local, cultural equivalent (Antwerp was the eighth EU City of Culture, in 1993).[38] The Barcelona city council and architects' association had a deep understanding of the urbanism established by Cerdá in the 19th century and wanted to continue and elaborate on this Rationalist tradition. As part of their Olympic bid, the city renovated many public squares in the centre of the city and then later pedestrianised the entire, historic Gothic Quarter, the medieval city-village core. Following up on the modern plaza opened up by Richard Rogers and Renzo Piano in Paris in front of the Pompidou Centre (1971–7), Barcelona designers, like their Danish counterparts in Copenhagen, developed a new sense of the modern, pedestrianised streetscape during the 1990s with new street furniture, lighting, benches and landscaping techniques. Spain again provided a key example of using a strategic investment in a heterotopia of illusion to push an ongoing urban renaissance in an old city centre, in the opening of the Frank Gehry-designed Guggenheim Museum, Bilbao in 1997.[39]

Berlin provides another European example of fragmented and strategic investment in an old, shrinking city core at the end of the Cold War. The city and the German state were unprepared for the demolition of the Berlin Wall in 1989, despite all the postwar planning – from the Scharoun Plan (1947), to the Haupstadt Competition with Le Corbusier's and the Smithsons' entries (1958), to the OM Ungers and Rem Koolhaas Summer School (1976–7). The disappearance of the Cold War barrier transformed West Berlin from a peripheral heterotopia of illusion, promoting capitalism inside the Eastern Bloc, into a national capital. This transformation raised many questions for urban designers as the new national government, mayor and city council formulated briefs for international urban design competitions for a series of large urban fragments, following the city archipelago model.

One major 1993 urban design competition focused on creating a large urban fragment for the reunified German federal government on a site close to the Reichstag building

**Yokohama, Japan: the waterfront, including skyscrapers and
amusement park (photo *c* 2000)**

(Photo © Steven Vidler/Eurasia Press/Corbis)

Master plan for Barcelona Olympics, Spain, 1992 (redrawn by the author, 2010)

(Redrawn plan © David Grahame Shane and Uri Wegman, 2010)

Barceloneta Waterfront Park, Spain (photo 2005)

(Photo © David Grahame Shane)

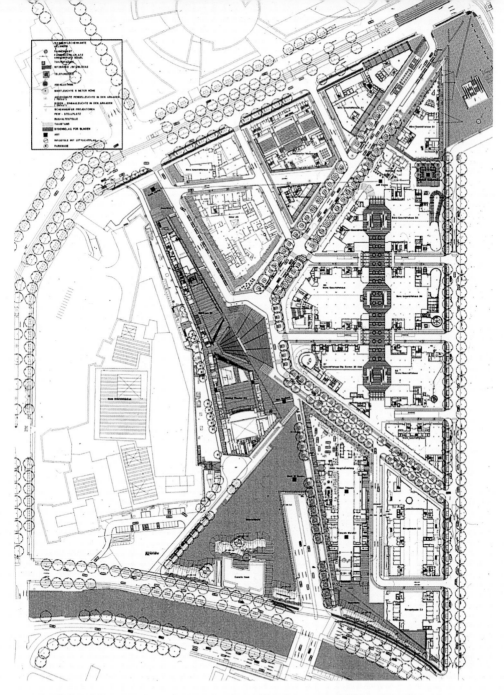

Renzo Piano Building Workshop, master plan for Potsdamerplatz Project, Berlin, Germany, 1993
(Photo © Michel Denancé)

(reconstructed by Norman Foster in 1999). Axel Schultes, Charlotte Frank and Christoph Witt won this competition with their long, thin, east–west-oriented buildings, a 'ribbon of government' beside the Spree river with an associated new presidential palace in the Tiergarten Park.[40] In the same year, another competition proposed an unrealised new skyscraper cluster around the Alexanderplatz area in former East Berlin (1993) beside a major railway station. In 1995, a competition for the redesign of the Berlin Hauptbahnhof (Central Station, completed 2005) across the Spree river from the Reichstag included an underground highway and four railway tunnels for future high-speed and local railway links connecting the Potsdamerplatz site to the south. Here the federal government sponsored the first international competition for the rebuilding of a new commercial centre as a large urban fragment in 1991, on the site of the Berlin Wall. Further international competitions developed the winning Hilmer & Sattler master plan in four parts.

At Potsdamerplatz, Renzo Piano's intervention for DaimlerChrysler Corporation provided crucial leadership in transforming the master plan. Piano was not afraid to connect a new theatre, cinema and casino (all heterotopias of illusion) onto Hans Scharoun's masterpieces, the neighbouring Concert Hall and Library on the Culture Forum that turned their back to the site of the Wall. In addition, Piano provided a clever fan-shaped street layout that led to these new heterotopic facilities with a branching interior pedestrian street that ended in a highly successful arcade shopping mall. Within this fan-shaped layout and urban design guidelines, other architects like Richard Rogers, Arata Isozaki and Hans Kollhoff, provided individual buildings.[41]

Across the street, the American architect Helmut Jahn designed another segment of Potsdamerplatz as a giant urban fragment, a single building made of many pieces. The Sony Centre (completed 2000) consists of a traditional Berlin perimeter block turned inside out to make a new public atrium. Offices, apartments and a hotel surround a central atrium covered by a stretched, circus-tent-like tensile structure (with an office tower above). Cinemas, theatres and restaurants cluster below the tent-like structure on a variety of levels, around a large interior public square with free Wi-Fi and giant JumboTron screens as found in Shinjuku public spaces in Tokyo (see chapter 6). This privately owned, corporate public space has hosted many commercial spectacles and promotions, like those associated with World Cup soccer matches, that could be broadcast and webcast live. Like New York's Times Square, but interior and private, this became a new place of televised public spectacle and mass meeting.[42]

Sony built other lifestyle promotion centres around the world, in San Francisco and New York for instance, in order to buttress its global brand and sales of high-end electronics. Here Sony sold hand-held devices, cellphones, televisions, sound systems, computers and cameras – all the equipment necessary for a digital citizen. These miniaturised devices replaced the theatre and cinemas, Foucault's traditional heterotopias of illusion, enabling people to record and represent their own lives in their own living room or share across the globe on the Internet.

If Berlin after reunification in 1990 represented the city archipelago of large urban fragments set in a sea of green, London continued a long-established tradition of urban collage, using big, planned urban fragments belonging to large landowners. This tradition stretched back to the Renaissance, when royal permission was required to develop large tracts of land outside the limits of the medieval City of London. The Earl of Bedford asked King Charles I for permission to develop his Covent Garden estate in 1632, and the autocratic king required the puritanical landowner to employ the Italian-trained court architect Inigo Jones.[43] Jones laid out a grand square with Dutch-style side streets and supporting mews for stables. This large planned urban unit set the pattern of central square supporting side streets and servants' mews for the next 200 years of development in West London, as the wealth of the empire grew and the residential estates became more palatial with multiple gardens and squares.

Like Shenzhen or Chandigarh, the westward expansion of new town fragments in London often incorporated earlier agricultural villages, like Marylebone High Street, St Giles High Street or St Martin's Lane. In *Georgian London* (1946), Sir John Summerson described the proliferation and elaboration of these 'Great Estates', whose landowners could be richer than the royal family and held the land for many generations through a system of ground leases that is only now being eroded.[44] Each estate owner had their own administrative office and set of controls and codes, seeking to preserve the value of their residential developments, often opposing innovations such as electricity, telephones, trams or railways. Hidden mews served these islands of order and decorum, while their boundaries often remained earlier agricultural farm boundaries, marked by now-hidden streams and rivers linked to the engulfed villages and surfacing in the royal parks (the Westbourne stream in the Serpentine, for instance).

In London a succession of royal offices and then the Metropolitan Board of Works, the predecessor of the elected London County Council (LCC, created 1888 after a massive dock strike), attempted to coordinate the fragmentation of the city, creating a system of armatures to bypass or cut through the enclaves blocking the centre. In central London, around Covent Garden, the result was the formation of a megablock with curving perimeter boulevards that carefully avoided the large landholders' estates, exploiting the old streambeds and their shantytown slums.[45] New Oxford Street (1840s), the Victoria Embankment (1860s), Charing Cross Road and Shaftesbury Avenue (both 1870s) and then the Aldwych–Kingsway (1905) all surrounded Covent Garden, whose market in the original square had become the centre for the distribution of fruit and vegetables in the metropolis.[46] The Circle Line railway (1866) and then the deep-level tube lines of the 1890s and 1910s avoided the great landowners by burrowing beneath their properties to tie the city together.

A similar system of large urban fragments controlled by big landowners also shaped the development of East London where the commercial docks serving the empire were guarded with 12-metre-(40-foot) high walls to prevent theft. As in West London, each dock formed a separate enclave and the dock workers lived in village shantytowns on their periphery, seeking day labour in seasonal spurts connected with the trade winds until the introduction of steamships. In the Second World War, German bombers concentrated on destroying the

London Docks as the heart of the British Empire, bombing much of the surrounding housing in the process. The postwar Labour government planned many large public housing estates here under the Abercrombie Plan of 1943 (see chapter 3).

After the war the imperial trade to the docks revived briefly, only to collapse again with the loss of empire and containerisation of global corporate trade. The local authorities had neither the capital nor the skills to plan the redevelopment of such a vast area that stood stagnant and unused for a generation, beside the Lea Valley, planned as a park by Abercrombie. The Conservative Thatcher government removed all planning regulations in the late 1970s, creating a special district or economic zone following the Battery Park City model, leading to the construction of Canary Wharf, with the tallest skyscraper in Britain (begun in 1988).[47] Here Rowe's co-author Fred Koetter of Koetter Kim & Associates worked with SOM on the Urban Design Guidelines for the new enclave for the same Canadian developers of the World Financial Center at Battery Park City in New York.[48]

The isolation of the London Docks enclave, like that in Yokohama earlier, led to an emphasis on connective armatures and links to surrounding urban flows later in the 1990s, as the EU financed the extension of the London underground Jubilee Line to Canary Wharf and beyond. It took time for the British planning profession to recover from the chaos induced by the Thatcherite abolition of the elected Greater London Council (GLC) and redistribution of responsibilities to the local municipalities and various new corporations.[49] These responsibilities were then recentralised with the creation of the Greater London Authority (GLA) under Labour, with the appointing of a Mayor of London who could influence overall planning. Richard Rogers and Terry Farrell emerged as key urban designers advising the central government and mayor. Both advocated an expansion of London to the east, into the Thames estuary, in a new Thames Gateway scheme (beginning 2003) protected from flooding by the Thames Barrier (1982).[50]

Beyond the Barrier, the Gateway Plan showed a huge regional recreational park spanning many islands, marshlands and mudflats with large urban fragments scattered at intervals in a vast variant of the city archipelago scheme of Berlin. Here the Gateway proposed the conversion of the 700-hectare (1,800-acre) Anglo-Dutch Shell Haven oil refinery and tank farm, which had served London since the 1930s, into a new container port and staging area owned by the Peninsular & Oriental Steam Navigation Company (P&O), the old British imperial steamship company that had served Africa, India and China and become a major container line and port operator (bought by the Dubai World sovereign wealth fund in 2006).[51] At one point the same sovereign wealth fund backed plans for a new London airport in the estuary on an artificial island that was overruled by ecological objections (the estuary is a major bird sanctuary on a major European bird flight path).

The Gateway Plan concentrated new, large, dense urban fragments at hubs connected to rail and highway links, like Stratford East (master planned by architects Fletcher Priest, 2005), where the high-speed rail link to the Channel Tunnel first entered North London.[52] Here, on the edge of the Lea Valley, Westfield, the American owner of the mall in Battery Park City, New York, proposed a huge megamall development (140,000 square metres (1.5 million square feet)) that

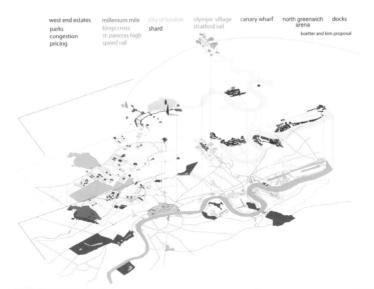

west end estates   millenium mile   city of london   olympic village   canary wharf   north greenwich   docks
parks   kings cross   shard   stratford rail   arena
congestion   st. pancras high   koetter and kim proposal
pricing   speed rail

Layered drawing of London, UK, with London 2012 Olympic and Paralympic fragments
(Drawing © David Grahame Shane and Uri Wegman, 2010)

Koetter, Kim & Associates, Canary Wharf, London, UK, 1988–2000
(Photo © Fred Koetter)

London, UK as a fragmented metropolis
(Plan © David Grahame Shane, 1971)

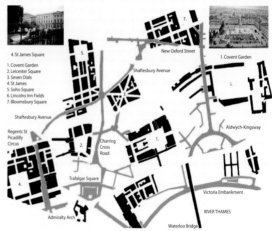

London squares and Covent Garden enclave, London, UK, with later armatures
(Plan © David Grahame Shane, 1971)

Fletcher Priest Associates, three-dimensional rendering of the master plan for Stratford East, London, UK, 2005
(Rendering © Lend Lease)

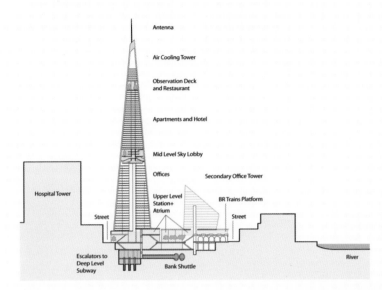

Antenna

Air Cooling Tower

Observation Deck
and Restaurant

Apartments and Hotel

Mid Level Sky Lobby

Offices

Secondary Office Tower

Hospital Tower

Upper Level
Station+
Atrium

BR Trains Platform

Street

Street

Escalators to
Deep Level
Subway

Bank Shuttle

River

**Renzo Piano Building
Workshop, sectional
drawing of the Shard,
London, UK, 2009 (redrawn
by the author, 2010)**
(Redrawn drawing © David
Grahame Shane and Uri
Wegman, 2010)

Sellar Property Group, panoramic perspective of the Shard, London Bridge and City of London, UK, 2009
(Perspective © courtesy of the Sellar Property Group)

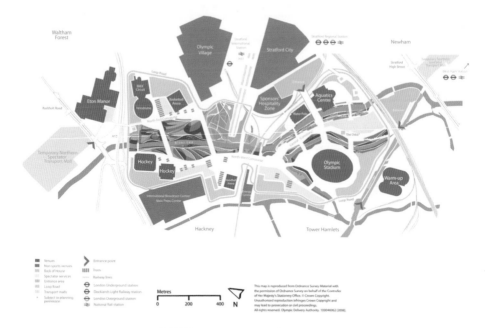

Greater London Council, Thames Barrier, London, UK, 1982 (photo 1991)
(Photo © Skyscan/Corbis)

Plans and perspectives for London 2012 Olympic and Paralympic Games, UK
The Lea Valley Park, part of Abercrombie's Plan from 1943, will become Queen Elizabeth Olympic Park and will remain as a legacy of the 2012 Olympics, while the main stadium will be reduced in size. The aerial perspective shows neighbouring residential communities, with Canary Wharf and the City of London towers in the distance. (Plans and drawings © Olympic Delivery Authority)

curved to connect to the regional and international rail hub, with two very high office towers (50 and 30 storeys) above, and a network of medium-rise residential apartment blocks on a new surrounding grid of streets to the north, as in Battery Park City, New York or Yokohama, Japan. Fletcher Priest recognised that no one person would design the entire complex and from the start involved other firms, including young Dutch practices such as Mecanoo, to design variants of parts of the scheme, breaking the urban fragment into manageable pieces.

The same 'collage city', fragmented metropolis system of urban design ecology extended to the London 2012 Games Bid that incorporated Stratford East and the Lea Valley as the key urban regeneration sites for East London. The northern housing area became part of the planned Athletes' Village, while the new stadium and the Aquatics Centre in the Lea Valley Park gained temporary access ways and security clearing areas on the approach from the new mall and station. The Olympic Stadium by Populous is designed to be dismountable so that the stadium capacity can be reduced to ensure it is appropriate for legacy use, while around the edge of the park many other sports venues will remain and the International Broadcast Centre/Main Press Centre (IBC/MPC) and support buildings will be converted to new industrial or commercial uses. Besides Stratford East, other London 2012 Games venues were scattered all across London, as in Barcelona in 1992, even including beach volleyball on Horse Guards Parade close to Buckingham Palace.[53]

London, like New York, had no master plan approved by a central governing authority during the 1980s, 1990s or early 2000s. Instead, special areas of development received special district status and local municipalities had much leeway in approving schemes, which could be appealed to the central government. Protected-view corridors or cones of vision from privileged viewpoints on surrounding hills were one of the few overall controls to survive from the era of GLC planning in the 1980s. These view corridors meant that London followed the Moscow 'scatter pattern' favoured by the early LCC planners after the Second World War, which prevented the clustering of skyscrapers except on the east hill of the City of London around the Stock Exchange. Canary Wharf, like La Défense in Paris, drew many of the new skyscrapers away from the centre of the City of London; the City responded by lifting its regulations and allowing higher density on smaller plots, especially around railway stations. Here, new high-rise urban fragments, like the Shard at London Bridge Station – designed by Renzo Piano in 2000, with a dense three-dimensional matrix at the base of the skyscraper connecting into the local railway systems and subways – became possible.[54]

The Shard introduced a new mixed-use type of skyscraper into London where previous high-rise buildings had been either office or residential, rarely a combination. The main tower of the Shard development contained apartments, a hotel and offices stacked one above another, with a mid-level sky-lobby and top-floor public viewing platform. The base of the tower became a complex three-dimensional, layered matrix. The viaduct of the existing London Bridge Station remained, with a new roof and shopping mall integrated into its mezzanine leading down to street level, and the subway entrance to the deep-level tube. Besides becoming the tallest building in London, as high as New York's Empire State Building, the tower features an eco-fin system on its peak that helps with heating and cooling.

Conclusion

The breakdown of the metropolis and its associated, global imperial system opened the way for the emergence of the USA and USSR as the two global superpowers in the Cold War. After 1945 the oil-based megalopolis grew, with American oil companies and global corporate power setting up a parallel system of banking, administration and manufacturing beyond national boundaries. The impossibility of controlling the sprawling megalopolis that stretched over many cities and municipalities was both a problem and an advantage. The advent of the automobile and mass mobility provided ample scope for local interests and local participation within the megablock grid system of the highways, allowing both urban villages and 'great estates' space (as envisioned by Reyner Banham in Los Angeles). At the same time, the fragmentation enabled by mass mobility and communication systems also allowed large corporate enclaves and new urban fragments, which quickly became meganodes like the Houston Galleria and its offspring.

The new urban designers of the fragmented metropolis created customised urban enclaves for the new urban actors, with special districts with urban design guidelines and strict zoning codes. The large urban fragments stood out against the surrounding urban fabric or field, as described by Ungers and Koolhaas, forming a city archipelago of urban islands in a sea of low-rise housing set in a green landscape. These urban patches might be office blocks, malls or residential towers, connected by highways forming megablocks. At the intersection of these highways, meganodes formed the communal public space, often owned and operated by corporate interests around shopping malls.

While the city archipelago housed the needs of the global corporations and its employees, it did not address the psychological needs and sense of loss (but liberation) of the inhabitants of these new districts set apart in a sea of modernity, without roots and memory. Koetter and Rowe's *Collage City* attempted to do this without resorting to the kitsch or nostalgia of Walt Disney World, but recognising the irrational, phenomenological and psychological needs of people that went beyond common sense and saving a dime. Rowe and Koetter recognised that building the city in incremental fragments might seem rational, but the overall collage took on an irrational conceit of its own, whatever the good intentions of the individual designer. Koolhaas also recognised the impossibility of overall control, but tried to hold the irrational impulses of the city within his large fragments, setting them within a grid. The irrational life of the city became sublimated in the imaginary life of the corporate skyscrapers and their romances (shown in *Delirious New York*) or exiled to theme parks and heterotopias of illusion like Coney Island or Radio City Music Hall at the Rockefeller Center.

The fragmented metropolis, unlike the coal-fired metropolis, depended on oil for its energy supply, heating and cooling, electricity and mobility. The practitioners of this urban design ecology were deeply enmeshed with the megalopolis and automobile culture, even if, like the New Urbanism movement, they proposed to cluster the new single-family houses a little closer. The 1990s provided much cheap oil after the oil shocks of the 1970s and 1980s, easing the expansion of the megalopolis and fuelling the development of leisure meganodes like Dubai or Las Vegas. In 2008 this system of megablocks, meganodes and seas of single-family houses ground to a halt under the impact of a massive oil price spike that caused the American housing system and its associated banking system to collapse.

The designers of the fragmented metropolis, like the American megalopolis itself and automobile industry (also destroyed by the price spike), needed to reconsider how to continue in the future. Suddenly attention shifted to the explosion of the Asian megacities and how their urban design ecologies required 1/30th of the energy per capita used in Europe and North America. The distributed urbanism of the Indonesia *desa-kota* took on a new meaning for the future of the city.

Notes

NB: See 'Author's Caution: Endnote Sources and Wikipedia', towards the end of this book.

1   Patrick Abercrombie and John Henry Forshaw, *County of London Plan*, Macmillan & Co (London), 1943.

2   For the price of oil, see: Paul Roberts, *The End of Oil*, Houghton Mifflin (Boston; New York), 2004, pp 100–101; also: Peter R Odell, *Oil and World Power: A Geographical Interpretation*, Penguin (Harmondsworth), 1970, p 163.

3   On Rossi's *Analogous City* (1976), see: Alberto Ferlenga (ed), *Aldo Rossi: The Life and Works of an Architect*, Konemann (Cologne), 2001, p 72.

4   Rem Koolhaas, *Delirious New York: A Retroactive Manifesto for Manhattan*, Oxford University Press (New York), 1978. On New York City near bankruptcy in 1975, see: Ralph Blumenthal, 'Recalling New York at the Brink of Bankruptcy', *The New York Times*, 5 December 2002, http://www.nytimes.com/2002/12/05/nyregion/recalling-new-york-at-the-brink-of-bankruptcy.html?pagewanted=1 (accessed 15 February 2010).

5   Colin Rowe and Fred Koetter's *Collage City*, MIT Press (Cambridge, MA), 1978.

6   See: Robert Venturi, Denise Scott Brown and Steven Izenour, *Learning from Las Vegas: The Forgotten Symbolism of Architectural Form*, MIT Press (Cambridge, MA), 1972.

7   For Aldo Rossi, see: Aldo Rossi, *Architettura della Città* (The Architecture of the City), Marsilio (Padova. Italy), 1966, introduction by Peter Eisenman, trans Diane Ghirardo and Joan Ockman, revised for the American edition by Aldo Rossi and Peter Eisenman, MIT Press (Cambridge, MA), c 1982. For Kahn's 'urban room' references, see: DG Shane, 'Louis Kahn', in Michael Kelly (ed), *The Encyclopaedia of Aesthetics*, Oxford University Press (Oxford), 1998, vol 3, pp 19–23.

8   For Rationalist architecture, see: Joseph Stübben, *Der Städtebau*, Vieweg (Braunschweig; Wiesbaden), 1980 (reprint from 1890).

9   For the Rationalist exhibition in 1978, see: *Rational Architecture: The Reconstruction of the European City / Architecture Rationnelle: La Reconstruction de la Ville Européenne*, Éditions des Archives d'architecture moderne (Brussels), 1978.

10   For Rob Krier, see: Rob Krier, *Stadtraum in Theorie und Praxis*, Krämer (Stuttgart), 1975, trans Christine Czechowski and George Black, as: Rob Krier, *Urban Space*, Academy Editions (London), 1979.

11   On Lewis and the Uniform Land Use Review Procedure (ULURP), see: David Gosling and Maria-Cristina Gosling, *The Evolution of American Urban Design: A Chronological Anthology*, Wiley-Academy (Chichester, UK; Hoboken, NJ), 2003, p 71.

12   On the UDA 'Assembly Kit', see: Ray Gindroz, Karen Levine, Urban Design Associates, *The Urban Design Handbook: Techniques and Working Methods*, WW Norton & Company (New York; London), 2002, pp 33–4.

13   For New Urbanism, see: Andres Duany, *Towns and Town-Making Principles*, Harvard University Graduate School of Design (Cambridge, MA) and Rizzoli (New York), 1991. For Seaside, see: David Mohney, Keller Easterling, *Seaside: Making a Town in America*, Princeton Architectural Press (New York), 1991.

14   For urban villages, see: Peter Calthorpe and Doug Kelbaugh, *Pedestrian Pocket Book: A New Suburban Design Strategy*, Princeton Architectural Press (New York) in association with the University of Washington, 1989.

15   For the Berlin Summer School, see: Oswald Mathias Ungers, Rem Koolhaas, Peter Riemann, Hans Kollhof, Peter Ovaska, 'Cities within the City: proposal by the sommer akademie for Berlin', *Lotus International*, 1977, p 19. For Ungers projects, see: OM Ungers, *OM Ungers: The Dialectic City*, Skira (Milan), 1999.

16   For Stirling and *Roma Interrotta*, see: 'Roma Interrotta', in Michael Graves (ed), *Architectural Design*, vol 49, no 3–4, 1979.

17   For Disney see: Karal Ann Marling (ed), *Designing Disney's Theme Parks: The Architecture of Reassurance*, Canadian Centre for Architecture (Montreal) and Flammarion (Paris; New York), 1997.

18   For EPCOT, see: http://en.wikipedia.org/wiki/Epcot (accessed 17 March 2010).

19   For Disney World and EPCOT figures (2007), see: Themed Entertainment Association / Economics Research Associates, Attraction Attendance Report, 2008, http://www.connectingindustry.com/downloads/pwteaerasupp.pdf (accessed 12 July 2010).

20   For Venice tourism statistics, see: Elizabetta Povoledo, 'Venetian transport leaves tourists high and dry', *The New York Times*, 1 February 2008, http://www.nytimes.com/2008/01/21/world/europe/21iht-venice.4.9383559.html?_r=1 (accessed 12 July 2010).

21   On apartheid, see: AJ Christopher, *The Atlas of Apartheid*, Routledge (London), 1994 (available on Google Books). For standard house type, see: Mandela House website, http://www.mandelahouse.com/ (accessed 17 March 2010). On *Bantustans*, see: http://en.wikipedia.org/wiki/Bantustan (accessed 17 March 2010).

22   On the *desa-kota* hypothesis, see: Terry G McGee, *The Urbanization Process in the Third World: Explorations in Search of a Theory*, Bell (London), 1971; also: Terry McGee, 'The Emergence of Desakota Regions in Asia: expanding a hypothesis', in Norton Ginsburg, Bruce Koppel and TG McGee (eds), *The Extended Metropolis: Settlement Transition in Asia*, University of Hawaii Press, (Honolulu), 1991, pp 3–26.

23   On the history of the Dutch East India Company, see: Els M Jacobs, *In Pursuit of Pepper and Tea: The Story of the Dutch East India Company*, Netherlands Maritime Museum (Amsterdam), 1991; also: http://en.wikipedia.org/wiki/Dutch_East_India_Company (accessed 17 March 2010).

24   On Batavia *kampungs*, see: Christopher Silver, *Planning the Megacity: Jakarta in the Twentieth Century*, Routledge (Abingdon, UK), 2008.

25   TG McGee, *The Urbanization Process in the Third World*, G Bell (London), 1971.

26   For contemporary Jakarta, see: 'Reciprocity. Transactions for a City in Flux', workshop and exhibition curated by Stephen Cairns and Daliana Suryawinata, 4th International Architecture Biennale, Rotterdam, 2009, http://www.iabr.nl/EN/open_city/_news/workshop_jakarta.php (accessed 17 March 2010); also: Stephen Cairns, 'Cognitive Mapping the Dispersed City', in Christophe Lindner (ed), *Urban Space and Cityscapes: Perspectives from Modern and Contemporary Culture*, Routledge (London), 2006, pp 192–205; also: Stephen Cairns, 'Jakarta and the Limits of Urban Legibility', in Will Straw and Douglas Tallack (eds), *Global Cities/Local Sites*, Melbourne University Publishing (Melbourne), 2009, http://www.u21onlinebooks.com/index.php/component/option,com_u21/task,essay/book_id,1/id,29/ (accessed 29 June 2010).

27   On the Borneo-Sporenburg project, see: West 8 website, http://www.west8.nl/projects/all/borneo_sporenburg/ (accessed 17 March 2010).

28   For Llewelyn-Davies & Weeks and Shenzhen Institute of Urban Design and Research Plan, see: Charlie QL Xue, *Building a Revolution: Chinese Architecture since 1980*, Hong Kong University Press (Hong Kong), 2005, pp 75–6 (available on Google Books). On Shenzhen SEZ, see: http://en.wikipedia.org/wiki/Special_Economic_Zones_of_the_People's_Republic_of_China (accessed 17 March 2010).

29   On China's urbanisation, see: John Friedmann, *China's Urban Transition*, University of Minnesota Press (Minneapolis, MN), c 2005.

30   On the mapping of urban villages in China, see: Zhengdong Huang, School of Urban
      Design, Wuhan University, 'Mapping of Urban Villages in China', undated presentation,
      Center for International Earth Science Information Network, Columbia University, New
      York, http://www.ciesin.columbia.edu/confluence/download/attachments/34308102/
      Huang+China+UrbanVillageMapping.pdf?version=1 (accessed 17 March 2010). On peasant
      citizens, see: Jonathan Bach, 'Peasants into Citizens: urban villages in the Shenzhen Special
      Economic Zone', presentation, 28 April 2009, Watson Institute for International Studies,
      Brown University, Providence, Rhode Island, http://www.watsoninstitute.org/events_detail.
      cfm?id=1360 (accessed 1 April 2010). On housing and migrants, see: Ya Ping Wang and
      Yanglin Wang, 'Housing and Migrants in Cities', in Rachel Murphy (ed), *Labour Migration and
      Social Development in Contemporary China*, Taylor & Francis (London), 2008, pp 137–53.
      On urban villages, see: Ma Hang, 'Villages in Shenzhen: typical economic phenomena of
      rural urbanization in China', Villages in Shenzhen 44th ISOCARP Congress 2008, ISOCARP
      website, http://www.isocarp.net/Data/case_studies/1145.pdf (accessed 17 March 2010).
      For photographs of urban villages, see: Desmond Bliek, 'Urban Village, Shenzhen Style', 28
      June 2007, Urbanphoto website, http://www.urbanphoto.net/blog/2007/06/28/urban-village-
      shenzhen-style/ (accessed 17 March 2010).
31   On Shenzhen urban villages, see: Him Chung, 'The Planning of "Villages-in-the-City" in
      Shenzhen, China: the significance of the new state-led approach', in *International Planning
      Studies*, vol 14, issue 3, August 2009, pp 253–73.
32   On Urbanus, see: *Urbanus Selected Projects 1999–2007*, China Architecture and Building Press
      (Shenzhen), 2007, pp 212–21, http://www.urbanus.com.cn/books.html (accessed 1 April 2010).
33   On China, India and world trade, see: Janet Abu-Lughod, *Before European Hegemony: The
      World System AD 1250–1350*, Oxford University Press (New York), 1989, p 464.
34   On the history of Yokohama, see: Plan for Yokohama, Yokohama City Planning Department,
      published by Match & Co, 1991, pp 19–33; also: http://en.wikipedia.org/wiki/Yokohama
      (accessed 17 March 2010).
35   On the Minato Mirai 21 development, see: Susan D Halsey and Robert B Abel, *Coastal Ocean
      Space Utilization*, Elsevier Science Publishing Co (New York), 1990, pp 191–206; also: http://
      en.wikipedia.org/wiki/Minato_Mirai_21 (accessed 17 March 2010).
36   On the Landmark Tower, see: http://en.wikipedia.org/wiki/Yokohama_Landmark_Tower
      (accessed 17 March 2010).
37   On the Barcelona Olympics, see: Oriol Nel-lo, 'The Olympic Games as a Tool for Urban
      Renewal: the experience of Barcelona '92 Olympic Village', in Miquel de Moragas, Montserrat
      Llinés and Bruce Kidd (eds), *Olympic Villages: A Hundred Years of Urban Planning and Shared
      Experiences – International Symposium on Olympic Villages*, International Olympic Committee
      (Lausanne), 1996, pp 91–6.
38   On European Cities/Capitals of Culture, see: European Commission Culture website, http://
      ec.europa.eu/culture/our-programmes-and-actions/doc413_en.htm (accessed 17 March 2010);
      also: http://en.wikipedia.org/wiki/European_Capital_of_Culture (accessed 17 March 2010).
39   For the Pompidou Centre and the Bilbao Guggenheim, see: David Grahame Shane,
      'Heterotopias of Illusion From Beaubourg to Bilbao and Beyond', in Michiel Dehaene and
      Lieven De Cauter, (eds), *Heterotopia and the City: Public Space in a Postcivil Society*, Routledge
      (Abingdon), 2008, pp 259–74.
40   On the 1993 competition, see: Annegret Burg, 'The Spreebogen: site, history, and the
      competition's objectives', *Parliament District at the Spreebogen*, *Capital Berlin*, International
      Competition for Urban Design Ideas 1993, pp 21–44. For the winner, see: Axel Schultes and
      Charlotte Frank, ibid pp 47–9.
41   For Potsdamerplatz 1992–2000, see: Renzo Piano Building Workshop website, http://rpbw.r.ui-
      pro.com/ (accessed 17 March 2010); also: Wolfgang Sonne, 'Building a New City Center:
      Berlin, Potsdamer Platz, Renzo Piano and others, 1991–98', Polis Urban Consulting website,
      http://www.polis-city.de/polis/media/downloads/pdf/10berlin.pdf (accessed 12 July 2010).

42   For global media companies and cities, see: Saskia Sassen and Frank Roost, 'The City: strategic site for the global entertainment industry', in Dennis R Judd and Susan S Fainstein (eds), *The Tourist City*, Yale University Press (New Haven), 1999, pp 143–55 (available on Google Books); also: Frank Roost, 'Re-creating the City as Entertainment Center: the media industry's role in transforming Potsdamer Platz and Times Square', *Journal of Urban Technology*, vol 5, issue 3, December 1998, pp 1–21.

43   For the Covent Garden Estate, see: John Summerson, *Inigo Jones*, Penguin, (Harmondsworth, UK), 1966, pp 83–96; also: FWH Sheppard (ed), *Survey of London XXXVI: Parish of St Paul, Covent Garden*, Athlone Press (London), 1970.

44   For the 'Great Estates' of London, see: John Summerson, *Georgian London*, C Scribner's Sons (New York), 1946, pp 163–76.

45   For the streambeds in central London, see: Nicholas Barton, *The Lost Rivers of London: A Study of their Effects upon London and Londoners*, Phoenix House (London), 1962.

46   For London street improvements, see: PJ Edwards, *A History of London Street Improvements, 1855–97*, London County Council (London), 1898. For the Aldwych–Kingsway, see: George Laurence Gomme and London City Council, *Opening of Kingsway and Aldwych by His Majesty the King: Accompanied by Her Majesty the Queen, on Wednesday, 18th October, 1905*, printed for the Council by Southwood, Smith (London), 1905.

47   For Canary Wharf, see: Alan J Plattus (ed), *Koetter Kim & Associates: place/time*, Rizzoli (New York), 1997; also: Paul Goldberger, 'Architecture View: a Yankee upstart sprouts in Thatcher''s London', *The New York Times*, 26 November 1989, http://www.nytimes.com/1989/11/26/arts/architecture-view-a-yankee-upstart-sprouts-in-thatcher-s-london.html?pagewanted=all (accessed 17 March 2010).

48   On the history of London Docklands development, see: London Docklands Development Corporation (LDDC) website, http://www.lddc-history.org.uk/beforelddc/index.html (accessed 17 March 2010).

49   For the GLC, see: http://en.wikipedia.org/wiki/Greater_London_Council (accessed 17 March 2010).

50   On the Thames Gateway plan, see: UK Communities and Local Government website, http://www.communities.gov.uk/thamesgateway/ (accessed 17 March 2010).

51   For Shell Haven, see: http://en.wikipedia.org/wiki/Shell_Haven (accessed 17 March 2010).

52   For the Thames Estuary airport, see: Tim Donovan, 'Mayor keen on island airport plan', 16 October 2009, BBC News website, http://news.bbc.co.uk/2/hi/uk_news/england/london/8311442.stm (accessed 17 March 2010).

52   For Stratford East, Arup Associates, Fletcher Priest Architects and West 8, see: Stratford City Design Strategy Booklet, Chelsfield Stanhope LCR (London), July 2003; also: Fletcher Priest website, http://www.fletcherpriest.com/ (accessed 17 March 2010).

53   For the 2012 London Olympics scatter plan, see: BBC Sports News website, http://news.bbc.co.uk/sport2/hi/olympic_games/4608029.stm (accessed 17 March 2010). For Lea Valley concentration, see: Environmental Systems Research Institute (ESRI) website, http://www.esri.com/mapmuseum/mapbook_gallery/volume21/planning9.html.

54   On the Shard, see: The Shard website, http://www.shardlondonbridge.com/ (accessed 17 March 2010).

CHAPTER 9

The Megacity/Metacity

The young American urban planner Janice Perlman coined the term 'megacity' to describe the self-built *favelas* of Rio de Janeiro, Brazil in her PhD studies, published in 1976, which highlighted the rapid growth of a vast city built from scrap materials that was invisible on the official plans and uncounted in the official census. These new urban expansions had a physical reality on the ground – you could visit them – but, like the shantytowns of India and Pakistan after the 1947 Partition, they were not visible on maps, nor did they appear like traditional urbanism. They were widely spread out, with facilities distributed across enormous areas, with and without modern infrastructures. Over the last 60 years self-built cities have proliferated throughout Latin America, Asia and Africa. They are still growing and their network formation is often best seen in night-time views from satellites (see chapter 1, NASA-NOAA image p 33).

This chapter traces the emergence of the megacity both as a physical presence on the ground and as a metacity, a statistical construct in the UN debates about urbanisation and globalisation. The emergence of the megacity as a global phenomenon in the 1990s marks the shift of the urban centre of gravity, in terms of global urban population, away from Europe and towards Asia and Africa. The megacity takes form in two distinct narratives that later intertwine. The first is the story of the massive growth of both formal and informal new towns in Latin America, Asia and Africa. The other side of this growth phenomenon is the shrinking European and North American cities, with a side issue in their attempts to reduce their fossil fuel dependency.

Urban designers working in megacities acknowledged that they needed to reorganise their profession to recognise the vast urban territories built by their inhabitants without professional advice or an overall plan. Designers needed to develop new tools and techniques to operate in this altered situation, where there might be no top-down authority and very small changes might yield big results, as in emergent systems where new patterns start small and spread like a virus. At the same time, urban designers had to recognise that their favourite fragmented metropolitan model, where they might control every detail, had its limitations in bypassing and ignoring its surroundings, so there was a new concern for context.

This new concern for context focused on connections to surroundings, as well as making good links to other big urban fragments, especially through high-speed rail lines instead of roads and highways. Designers learnt techniques from landscape architects to make these connections, focusing on long sections or 'transepts' across the city territory. Besides transport, this landscape orientation opened up layered aspects of the city not seen by urban designers before, like agriculture, food and water supplies, drainage and sewage systems that were very important for the maintenance of the city in either its northern shrinking or its southern fast-expanding condition.

Besides concentrating on the connections and spaces between large urban fragments, in landscape or informal settlements, urban designers also worked on the interior organisation of urban fragments. Here some designers used a similar layered approach to reconnect urban functions and actors that had previously been segregated into separate functional zones. This sectional development began with conventional modernist codes, but Deconstructivist architects challenged and questioned these codes in their attempts to create a new three-dimensional public space within their buildings (a move quickly picked up by mall developers). The heterotopic space between functional zones and fragments became the Deconstructivist palette, a space greatly enriched with the introduction of media first on large screens, and then on hand-held personal communication devices like cellphones.

The first part of the chapter concentrates on the variety of forms that the extended megacity can take as a city territory, a widely distributed system of urbanism spread across a more or less well serviced network space in a seemingly random formation organised from the bottom up. Megacities vary from the first impoverished Latin American appearances to the Asian variants with their inclusion of agriculture, as well as the wealthy, emerging European and American versions. Latin American megacities that began as squatter settlements are often 50 years old now and have their own distinctive patterns generated by their builders on difficult hill or valley terrain. Asian megacities also have their own characteristics, related to water control systems, agriculture and village craft traditions that survived inside the city, often also in difficult waterlogged terrain. European and American shrinking cities and eco-cities have their characteristics shaped by post-industrial attempts to lessen the eco-footprint of high-energy, fossil-fuel-dependent urban ecologies. The shift to the megacities promises some hope for a reduction in human induced climate change, as people move closer together, but also recognises that fossil-fuel-based global climate change will impact coastal and desert Asian megacities especially hard.

The second part of the chapter traces the emergence of the informational 'metacity', a term first used by the Dutch group MVRDV (Winy Maas, Jacob van Rijs and Nathalie de Vries) in their book and exhibition entitled 'Metacity/Datatown' (1999/2000).[1] The crucial insight here is that the megacity could not exist without an invisible communications revolution made possible by computers and new personal communications systems, whose only trace might be a cell tower or invisible satellite in orbit. The space across a city territory and between urban fragments no longer represented a barrier but now has become a means of connection, making possible new urban forms. MVRDV's project acknowledged the cybernetic revolution and the massive data-handling capacity of modern computers, making the concept of the megacity possible. In some ways these cities were invisible bundles of statistics and information, massive census counts and assemblies of data collected by governments for their own purposes, more or less accurate with various definitions of what is urban or what constitutes a city. At the same time the MVRDV project offered a critique of the idea that data crunching might lead to any particular urban metacity form. The UN accepted the term, transforming it to describe cities of 20 million in 2008, turning away from the concentration on the vast megacities to study widely distributed urban networks involving sets of cities containing 1 to 2 million that analysts predicted would contain 92 per cent of the world's urban population, especially in Asia and Africa, where the UN predicts most of the future urban growth in the next 50 years.[2]

This shift towards city territory as space between fragments containing flows of energy and information between urban actors in a mixed ecology of uses, recognised that many Asian and African urban conglomerations do not necessarily conform to European-American technocratic definitions of what constitutes urbanism. In particular the relationship with agricultural production, water supply and sanitation, as well as energy standards, deviates from the assumed norms of modern development. Nonetheless these cities can support huge populations and develop intense nodes within their extended networks that include modern communications systems and media. Vast city territories are neither metropolis (with a single centre), nor megalopolis (a sprawl within a modern infrastructure network), nor fragmented metropolitan formations, despite containing a multitude of enormous urban fragments. Designers in the city territory concentrate on the space between city fragments, but at the same time the megacities have their characteristic urban forms. These forms – the meganode, megablock and megamall, all urban forms made possible by the widespread use of communication technologies and multiple transport infrastructure connections – are examined at the end of the chapter. These super-dense, global nodes and hybrid mega-developments symbolically register the shift of the majority of the world's population into cities, with still many more yet to come in Asia and Africa.

Megacities

In creating the term 'megacity' in 1976, Perlman pointed not only to the scale jump but also to the shifting morphology of the new city form.[3] Up to 60 per cent of some Latin American megacities of the period were self-built *favelas*.[4] These urban settlements were not counted as part of the official city. New self-built city extensions often included agricultural elements, small fields or chicken coops long expelled from the imperial capitals. These small agricultural patches, reminiscent of the villages immigrants came from, might later be infilled, but lay alongside small industrial workshops, informal offices and businesses in a complex web of associations not permitted by modern planning laws (hence these areas were often condemned as 'slums' by officials). Such city extensions possessed multiple centres and were built by multiple actors, many of whom built their houses with their own labour. The Latin American megacities of the 1970s were the product of the failure of the state or local businesses to house the enormous numbers of people attracted to cities during the oil boom years of the 1950s and 1960s (Lagos followed the same pattern in Africa).

Perlman went on to found the Mega-Cities Project to study megacities of 8 million and then 10 million people, with oil-rich Mexico City being the fastest-growing giant of that period.[5] The UN adopted the term 'megacities' in 1986 as applying to cities that were

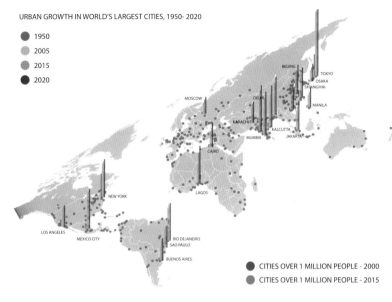

URBAN GROWTH IN WORLD'S LARGEST CITIES, 1950- 2020

● 1950
● 2005
● 2015
● 2020

● CITIES OVER 1 MILLION PEOPLE - 2000
● CITIES OVER 1 MILLION PEOPLE - 2015

Global megacities growth map, 2009
Global megacities house only 8% of the global urban population (shown in red), while 92% live in smaller cities of 1 to 2 million (shown in blue). Diagrams sourced from UN Reports of 2003, 2005 and 2007 formed the base for mapping the past 15 years and 2010 and 2015 projections. (Map © David Grahame Shane and Uri Wegman. Statistics from the UN State of the World's Cities Report, UN-HABITAT, 2006, p 8, data from the 2005 revision)

expected to have a 'population of at least 8 million by 2000', and followed with an upward definition above 10 million inhabitants in 1992. By 2006, when 50 per cent of the world's population was expected to live in cities, the UN at HABITAT III in Vancouver defined the megacity as a city of 20 million. This definition grabbed the news headlines as a potential urban disaster. The UN pointed to the social imbalance in megacities, where up to a third of the population might be housed in desperate conditions. One third of the 3 billion global urban population added up to 1 billion people in slums, ringing UN-HABITAT's alarm bells, but obviously not all 1 billion were in megacities.[6]

The UN tracked the emergence of the megacity, recognising a new class of urban actors in the NGOs and a new bottom-up city model in a space outside the official definition of a city. Perlman described the complex lives of *favela* dwellers in her 1976 PhD, and then at HABITAT III in 2006 movingly told of trying to revisit the same people 25 years later (many were already dead).[7] John Turner placed a similar emphasis on urban designers and planners working with the informal builders and inhabitants of the *favelas* at the HABITAT I in 1976. There David Satterthwaite, as an assistant to the influential British economist Barbara Ward, organised the first meeting of NGOs recognised by the UN body.[8] Turner's teacher Otto Koenigsberger, the planning professor at the AA and later UCL in London, had worked with the UN in India to try to house the 7 million refugees in temporary shanties and camps as a result of the Partition settlement (1947). Koenigsberger had endorsed various bottom-up, self-help strategies as emergency measures and planned five new towns for Nehru (for the steel industry).

Turner's *Housing by People* (1977), like the Brazilian Bernard Rudofsky's earlier *Architecture Without Architects* (1964), understood that the shanty settlements could come

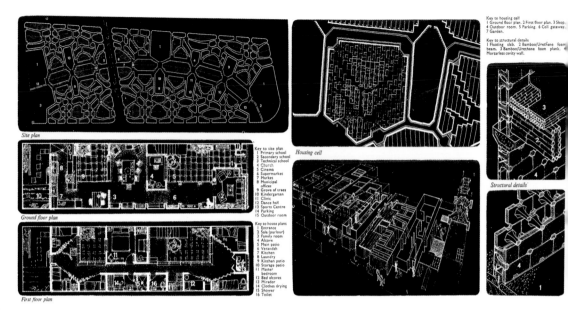

Key to housing cell
1 Ground floor plan. 2 First floor plan. 3 Shop.
4 Outdoor room. 5 Parking. 6 Cell gateway.
7 Garden.

Key to structural details
1 Floating slab. 2 Bamboo/Urethane foam
beam. 3 Bamboo/Urethane foam plank. 4
Mortarless cavity wall.

Site plan

Ground floor plan

First floor plan

Housing cell

Structural details

Key to site plan
1 Primary school
2 Secondary school
3 Technical school
4 Church
5 Cinema
6 Supermarket
7 Market
8 Municipal
offices
9 Grove of trees
10 Kindergarten
11 Clinic
12 Dance hall
13 Sports Centre
14 Parking
15 Outdoor room

Key to house plans
1 Entrance
2 Sala (parlour)
3 Family room
4 Alcove
5 Main patio
6 Verandah
7 Kitchen
8 Laundry
9 Kitchen patio
10 Storage patio
11 Master
bedroom
12 Bed alcoves
13 Mirador
14 Clothes drying
15 Shower
16 Toilet

Christopher Alexander and team, self-build project for Lima, Peru, 1981
Alexander's team attempted to improve the self-build methods of Lima shantytown inhabitants, proposing
a long, thin, repetitive house type with courtyards that could be extended with a second floor. Inside the
megablock, a central armature stretched from community stores to communal facilities (gym, school,
playground and bus access). (Designs © Center for Environmental Structure)

in from the outside and become a permanent part of the city.[9] They had their own internal
sets of rules and bottom-up organisation. Like Rudofsky, Gordon Cullen, the British author of
Townscape (1961), had a similar preoccupation with microcodes and vernacular design of
European urban villages.[10] Fumihiko Maki's 1960 article coining the term 'megastructure', had
also recognised 'group forms' – small-scale, village-like groupings – as a viable alternative
(see chapter 5).[11] The French architectural historian and theorist Françoise Choay described
the microcodes that governed local relationships between neighbours within village structures
as a 'syntagmatic' system or local language in 'urban semiology', contrasting these bottom-
up local codes with large, top-down, timeless geometric layouts.[12] Christopher Alexander
also saw the *favelas* as small-scale, self-organising systems with local codes that could be
manipulated by architects. Along with other competitors in the 1981 Lima, Peru housing
competition (organised by Turner), Alexander and his team tried to harness the skills of the
local *favela* builders and update their building techniques, introducing new materials, low-
tech prefabrication and standardised plans.[13] The World Bank adopted Turner's ideas in the
1980s, resulting in 'Sites and Services' projects in Africa and Latin America, providing basic
infrastructure and simple building codes as in Doshi's Aranya Estate (described in chapter 6).

Perlman and Turner were not alone in their megacity research in the 1970s. In 1971 the Canadian sociologist Terence G McGee first noted the Indonesian *desa-kota* (town-village) term to describe the hybrid city territory he observed in Jakarta (see chapter 8).[14] McGee emphasised the mixture of modern urban functions in close proximity to ancient agricultural traditions, fish farms and rice paddies. He also noted how the immigrants to the city spread across surrounding villages, creating a mixed-use, dispersed city territory, laced with canals and ancient waterways, railways and highways. This pattern had a long history before European colonisation: the ancient Asian Hindu civilisation of Angkor Wat in Cambodia had depended on extensive canal and irrigation systems to support its estimated peak population of 1 million,[15] China also had a long tradition of irrigation, rice paddies, fish ponds and canals in its two great river basins. Thailand also had a long tradition of cultivation of the rich alluvial delta of the Chao Phraya river with its many islands and meanders, just as the Vietnamese cultivated the Mekong delta. Nonetheless the Thai king sent an expedition to Batavia (Jakarta) to observe the modern Dutch canal system and plantations based on the latest developments in the late 1800s.

The Dutch East India Company had founded Jakarta in the 16th century as their colonial trading base midway between India and China, from where, via Capetown, South Africa, they could sail back to Amsterdam.[16] The city had a canal at its core, with a fort, governor's palace, merchants' warehouses and surrounding plantations that grew spices using slave labour. The great colonial empires of the 19th century, like the Chinese and Indian trading empires before them, had held the majority of the population in serfdom to work the land. Indonesian nationalists saw the colonial city and serf villages as evidence of their failure. The newly independent, nationalist governments of Mao, Gandhi or Sukarno all concentrated on the space between cities, seeing the modernised, agricultural village as a distinctive feature of a new national identity, de-emphasising the colonial cities.[17] They sought to create a new post-colonial culture in the villages, influenced by Stalin's Soviet collective farms of the 1930s (similar experiments were made in Africa, in Ghana and Tanganyika in the 1960s).[18] Later global agribusiness corporations and the 'Green Revolution' of fossil-fuel-based fertilisers and tractors subverted this nationalist modernisation process, consolidating farmland and sending peasants off the land to the cities in the 1970s and 1980s.[19]

In oil-rich Jakarta, Sukarno, Indonesia's leader after independence, created the characteristic Indonesian city territory hybrid with his agricultural and modernisation policies, distributing urban facilities over a wide area. Imperial metropolis and colonial foundation both shared a culture of canals and distributed urban functions mixed with agriculture in a delta city. Amsterdam, Holland, the colonial Dutch company's European headquarters, even today retains one half of its city territory in agriculture on the opposite river bank from the city.[20] This is a common megacity model for the fast-growing Asian megacity: Shanghai, for instance, reserves half of its urban area (like Amsterdam) for food production and Beijing has a vast green belt including its mountain watershed.[21] Shanghai also planned to build the first Asian eco-city at Dongtan, a satellite new-town design based on a hybrid of Asian practices and north European shrinking-city models with traditional Asian canals and ponds, originally linked to Expo 2010 (see chapter 10).

When Perlman founded the Mega-Cities Project in 1988 there were five megacities: two in the developed world (Tokyo and New York) and three in developing countries (including Mexico City). In 1945 there had been just two, London and New York, with 8 million each in a metropolis format. Today there are 20 with 20 million, including a great variety of cities with different roles and urban forms in the global network, ranging from capitals like Beijing, Delhi, Jakarta, Mexico City and Seoul to commercial cities like Calcutta, Mumbai or Shanghai. Tokyo–Osaka and New York–Newark survive as megacities but the UN listed none in Europe (the Anglo-Dutch, northern 'Blue Banana' megaplex might qualify by some definitions, but crosses national boundaries). By 2015, the UN expects there to be 26 megacities, all but four of them in the less developed world. These cities vary enormously depending on the codes that regulate the spaces in between urban fragments across their territory. The next sections examine some of these city territory variations, highlighting the codes that govern the spaces in between fragments and connect the city into a network formation. Different codes govern global financial centres, national capitals, commercial entrepôts or industrial centres in the global system of cities, while still others mix all these functions in the space in between fragments, creating the vast city territories of rich or poor megacities alike.[22]

Shrinking cities and eco-cities

As the urban population of Asian megacities expands, from a global perspective the population of European and American cities is stabilising, and often even shrinking as people have fewer children, are more educated, and move to the suburbs or extended city territories that include agricultural belts and abandoned farmhouses, second homes and country houses. As in Asia, a new urban morphology of widely distributed urban functions emerged in the 1990s era of cheap oil, with the city set inside the landscape. Richard Register in *Ecocity Berkeley* (1987) welcomed the shrinking of American cities as an opportunity to introduce new parks and urban agriculture into the city, freeing long-hidden streambeds, uncovering natural features and contours and restoring lost ecologies (themes repeated in *Ecocities: Rebuilding Cities in Balance with Nature*, 2001).[23] In 1987 John Seymour and Herbert Girardet's *Blueprint for a Green Planet* also provided a beautifully illustrated 'practical guide' for restoring the urban environment, incorporating many Californian ideas (like recycling, organic farming, low-energy homes, solar generation of power, etc) in Europe.[24]

Register organised the Ecocity Builders institute, advocating urban shrinkage and the construction of eco-villages.[25] The institute held a long series of conferences in leading-edge eco-cities, starting with Berkeley, California (1990), and subsequently in Curitiba (2000), with its innovative bus system and dynamic mayor, Jaime Lerner, retrofitting Latin American *favelas* with public transport and services.[26] Doug Kelbaugh's *Pedestrian Pocket Book* (1989) summarised the urban design implications of this 'small is beautiful' counterculture ideal, proposing small, dense, pedestrian-centred new towns around tram stops in agricultural green belts.[27] In the 1990s, smaller American cities in Pacific North West America, like Eugene, Oregon or Seattle, Washington, as well as neighbouring Vancouver, Canada (host

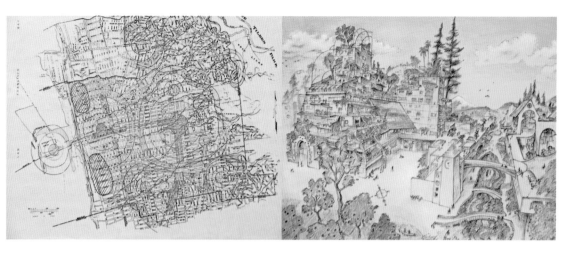

Richard Register, map and view of village centre of Eco-City Berkeley, California, USA, 1987
Register imagined a shrinking city where natural features like streams and valleys would re-emerge as places of leisure, pleasure and urban agriculture, linking urban village centes that would make private cars redundant. (Drawings © Richard Register)

of UN-HABITAT I and III), developed distinctive ecological zoning patterns, green belts, public transportation systems and bike paths. In Vancouver, William Rees and associates first published the concept of measuring urban energy consumption to calculate the 'ecological footprint' of cities in 1992.[28]

Europe and America provide many small-scale examples of both urban agriculture and the "greening" of the inner city, converting old industrial buildings to new uses. In Germany's Rhine–Ruhr industrial belt, some cities have instituted plans for large-scale brownfield remediation and created parks in old industrial plants, like the Duisburg-Nord Landscape Park by Peter Latz (1991–2002, see chapter 10).[29] Will Allen's Growing Power Farm in Milwaukee's North Westside, for instance, included an abandoned factory building converted into a fish farm and greenhouses in the early 2000s.[30] Detroit city council is considering legislation to allow large-scale urban agriculture in the centre of the city (2009), changing the zoning code from residential or commercial to farming. Elsewhere in the US, as in upstate New York's Hudson Valley, new, small-scale farmers are beginning to grow organic crops for delivery to neighbouring cites' 'grow local' farmers' markets, as in Italy's contemporary Slow Food movement.[31]

In the 1990s Thomas Sieverts, the city planner who framed the strategy for Duisburg-Nord Landscape Park, updated the German *Stadtlandschaft* (city-landscape) tradition in his *Cities Without Cities* (1997), recognising a new kind of distributed urbanism where people were mobile and facilities could be widely spread out and shared within a network of smaller cities (see chapters 1 and 6).[32] Paola Viganò in *La Città Elementare* (1999) advanced a similar

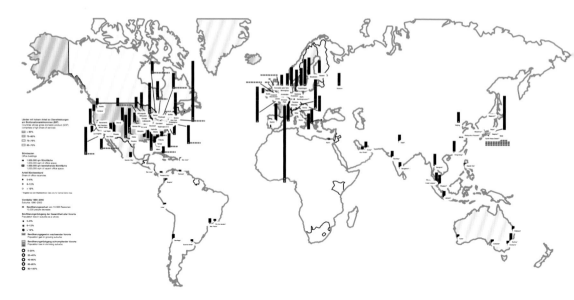

Philipp Oswalt, cities in danger of desertification, from *The Atlas of Shrinking Cities*, Hatje Cantz (Ostfildern), 2006
The *Atlas* illustrated that, as deserts expand and fresh water supplies dry up, shrinking cities could occur in the global south, in North Africa and the Southern Sahara belt. In addition parts of India, Japan and Australia will be affected, as well as many countries in the Middle East and around the Gobi Desert in Asia. (Diagram © Philipp Oswalt)

networked urban vision of the 'reverse city', a city of voids, spacing and intervals widely dispersed across a network and landscape, citing the canal-laced agri-urbanism of the Italian Veneto region behind Venice as a prime example (see below).[33] Today exemplary German eco-cities like the university town of Freiburg have rigorous energy-saving building codes, cooperative housing organisations, solar panels and insulation manufactured by local green industries, an efficient tram system, limited car ownership and pedestrianised city centre. In Vauban, Freiburg's German eco-rival, only 5 per cent of the population owns a car, using trams, trains, taxis or car-sharing for their travel, with many biking or walking to work.[34]

Philipp Oswalt and his team in *The Atlas of Shrinking Cities* (2006) projected the Northern European and American model of shrinking cites and a distributed urbanism onto the emerging patterns of the global megacities highlighted by the UN in 2003.[35] While Oswalt's research began in the shrinking industrial belt of Germany, the team quickly realised that other European and American industrial centres were also shrinking behind immigration barriers. In addition the team grasped that global climate change would lead to shrinking cities in many other locations, not only from the flooding of the megacities of the global river deltas (see p 263), but also from the rise in extreme temperatures around the equator. This meant expanding deserts around the Sahara in Africa, in southern Spain, across the Middle East and Turkey, in Central Asia and in the southwest of the United States (making cities like Las Vegas, Phoenix or Los Angeles uninhabitable).

Al Gore's film *An Inconvenient Truth* (2006) summarised the ecological argument while UN and other statistical models mapped out the urban implications, depending a lot of the rate of the ice melt at the poles (impacting sea levels and storm strength). With half the world's population of 6 billion thought to be living in cities in 2005, the traditional one third of urban dwellers in slums became a billion people. The urban future seemed grim from this perspective, encapsulated in the UN Report *The Challenge of the Slums* (2003) which borrowed the term 'slum' from the European industrialisation process of the 19th century, although many very large megacities in the year 2000 lacked a formal industrial base.[36] In 2007 the UN published a graphic showing that Cuba was the most sustainable country and impoverished Havana the most sustainable city in the world, with a high quality-of-life index, growing its own food in an urban agricultural belt with restricted private car ownership.

After the 2003 UN report sounded the alarm, the Marxist critic Mike Davis in *A Planet of Slums* (2007) amplified the UN's analysis.[37] Davis condemned global capitalism and past colonial empires for the slums, but he saw a revolutionary potential in the misery of the disenfranchised masses. By 2007 the UN-HABITAT report had moved on to the dangers of climate change, while still maintaining earlier megaslum themes such as the crime levels in megacities and the lack of secure tenure, but stressing their liability to flooding or desertification under global warming scenarios.[38] Columbia University's Center for International Earth Science Information Network (CIESIN) laboratory, using satellite imagery, also showed in 2007 that an extreme 10-metre (30-foot) rise in sea level would put many of the world's great delta cities underwater, making Beijing almost a coastal port (with Shanghai and Tianjin under water).[39] The flooding of the Ganges delta would severely impact Bangladesh and India (Kolkata and Dhaka). Bangkok, Buenos Aires, parts of Hong Kong, London and New York as well as most of Holland would be underwater, not to mention the disappearance of Egypt's Alexandria in the Nile estuary and Lagos flooding on the west African coast.[40]

The megacity and metacity: the city as information

The UN-HABITAT reports, the *Shrinking Cities* maps, the CIESIN disaster projections and *An Inconvenient Truth* all used computers to manage enormous amounts of data to construct pictures of global urban patterns emerging in city territories in the future. According to these projections, enormous numbers of people will be moving and cities shrinking and expanding around the globe, creating new city territories by self-built expansions or planned new towns, part of vast megacities with a new urban form. In 2006 the UN-HABITAT organisation revised its definition of a megacity upwards to 20 million, renaming the city territory expansion a 'metacity'. This major urban design move recognised the different form of the Asian megacity, the further evolution of the Latin American megacities and the changing morphology of the Euro-American shrinking cities. The term also recognised the role of information technologies and communication systems in forming extended city territories. The new term recognised that urban designers could not design from the top down for 20 million, they could instead break megacities down into their component parts and systems, making them more manageable, more responsive to citizens' needs and allowing designs to emerge from the bottom up.

In 2006 at HABITAT III in Vancouver, David Satterthwaite argued that a far greater proportion of the world's urban population would live in the over 400 cities with populations of 1 to 2 million than in the megacities.[41] Satterthwaite also showed that the great majority of these cities lay inside urban networks and constituted city constellations where self-help, self-organisation, municipal-level local government interventions as well as micro-financial institutions and media networks could have a big impact. These cities extended over agricultural territories and included areas of expanding self-built, mixed-use, shanty settlements. Satterthwaite identified four top-down responses to self-built shantytowns by authorities. The first was to ignore them, the second was to try to demolish them, the third to re-house and relocate their populations in new towns and the fourth to 'upgrade' them.[42]

None of these top-down responses recognised the self-organisational capacity, knowledge base and constructional skills of the inhabitants. Satterthwaite highlighted Shack/Slum Dwellers International (SDI), as an exemplary organisation that began in India as a self-help association of NGOs and then spread, via the World Wide Web, to Africa and South America. The SDI became an international knowledge-sharing network of best practices for neighbourhood improvement techniques, organisational and financial support, as well as public relations management on a global and state scale. The integration of the global dimension of information technology, as well as the recognition of the widespread local use of hand-held personal communication devices, like cellphones, marked the metacity. The World Social Forum (WSF), an organisation of NGOs that first met at the Brazilian town of Porto Alegre in 2001, represented the same kind of bottom-up global network. In the 7th World Social Forum in 2007 in Nairobi, Kenya, there were 66,000 registered attendees and 1,400 participating NGOs.[43]

The term 'metacity' originated in an exhibition organised in the year 2000 by the Dutch architectural group MVRDV, who were fascinated by the elaborate sectional organisation of the Hong Kong shantytown, the Walled City of Kowloon.[44] The multilayered, super-dense, close-packed Walled City (also known as 'The City of Darkness') represented an extreme example of Satterthwaite's shantytown settlements, an illegal city-within-a-city. From the British colonial perspective, the slum was a disgrace and a public relations disaster, showing poverty in the midst of wealth. The temporary housing complex built by squatters on an old fort park, belonging to China, but trapped inside the British colony of Hong Kong, provides a perfect example of a time-based, bottom-up design process at an incredibly high density. The vast self-built complex once housed thousands of immigrants from mainland China in terrible conditions with no running water or proper sanitation. The short, dramatic history of Kowloon's Walled City illustrates the first two points of Satterthwaite's four official responses to self-built housing: first to turn a blind eye, and second to demolish it, as was done in 1992 prior to handing the colony back to China. For years the heterotopic enclave was not shown on Hong Kong maps because legally it was part of China. The mixed-use Walled City had shops, factories, offices, social meeting places and services scattered throughout its section on different floors, with no apparent overall logic, all packed within the high-density meganode highlighted in MVRDV's *FARMAX: Excursions on Density* (1998).[45]

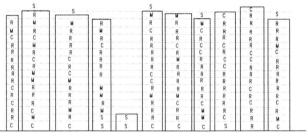

VERTICAL DISCONTINUITY OF PROGRAMS PRODUCES EVEN DISTRIBUTION OF DIVERSITY
SOCIAL INTERCOURSE OCCURS BOTH HORIZONTALLY AND VERTICALLY AT DIFFERENT LEVELS

R = RESIDENTIAL
M = MIXED
C = COMMERCIAL
S = SOCIAL

The Walled City, Kowloon, Hong Kong, in the 1990s
This self-built, vertical, skyscraper shantytown housed thousands from the 1950s until its demolition in the early 1990s. Its compact cubic form, complex layering and interior self-organising community made it an inspiration for groups studying density, like the Dutch architects MVRDV. (Images © Laurence Liauw & Suenn Ho)

MVDVR went on in 1999 to propose a three-dimensional construct in which all the information about human settlements on earth was packed into a tight data cube, a virtual version of the Walled City, their *Metacity/Datatown*.[46] The then recently demolished Kowloon complex had earlier been featured as a giant cube of data, an illicit data haven in the virtual-reality world of William Gibson's cyberpunk science-fiction novel *Neuromancer* (1984).[47] Using the metaphor of this cube of data, MVRDV created a three-dimensional city made of data based on quantifying the segregated, global, urban functions as strata within the cube forming the architecture of their exhibition and book *Metacity/Datatown*, co-authored with Richard Koek. MVRDV's layered approach used techniques outlined earlier in Colin Rowe and Fred Koetter's *Collage City* (1978) and by the Deconstructivist architects of the 1980s (like Zaha Hadid for The Peak – see chapter 7).[48]

During the 1990s, a digital revolution transformed how urban designers represented and designed space. This was a result of the introduction of powerful personal computers that could model three-dimensional space on a desktop. Whereas a huge, air-conditioned laboratory had been necessary for University of California Berkeley's pioneering Sim Lab headed by Peter Bosselmann in the 1980s, or for the later New York University Sim Lab headed by Michael Kwartler in the 1990s – both of which contained cameras on gantries to move over huge models, photographing views of proposed zoning changes – by the early 1990s a laptop with form.Z could create realistic virtual models on the computer screen.[49] Shortly afterwards, many young designers spent time in virtual city spaces, driving cars and fighting in video games like *Grand Theft Auto* (starting 1997). These visualisation tools augmented traditional perspective and allowed for accelerated movement and flight through the simulated city, radically altering the previously static, fixed-viewpoint conception of the image of the city, and allowing anyone to imagine the city in three dimensions, as if flying. The image of the city became detached from its place in geography, as in the Las Vegas casinos (see p 273), and could be manipulated for advertising or place-promotion purposes.

Faced with this explosion of data and apparent freedom of imagination, MVRDV's design for *Metacity/Datatown* conceived of all the data contained within the restraints of a giant cube, creating a symbolic megaform that was tightly constrained, but had many interior strata (echoing a giant fragment from Koolhaas's 'city archipelago' – see chapter 8 and p 272). This was a closed form, in contrast to the Deconstructivist Swiss architect Bernard Tschumi's design for the Parc de la Villette, Paris (1982), which demonstrated the application of a systematic layered network design approach to make narratives for different urban actors in a new three-dimensional public space across a large, horizontal ground plane, borrowing from dance and landscape notation systems to create an open ended matrix.[50] His previous *Manhattan Transcripts* (1994) had told the story of a murderer's escape through the three-dimensional matrix of a decaying New York around Times Square and 42nd Street, presenting a very different picture from Koolhaas's *Delirious New York*.[51]

In Tschumi's La Villette scheme, the red cube pavilions at grid intersections acted as node points within the controlling meshwork that coordinated two other layers in the urban design. Koolhaas's entry to the same competition had a serial arrangement of linear plantings framing

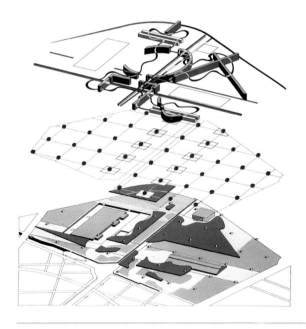

Bernard Tschumi, layers diagram of Park de la Villette, Paris, France, 1982
Tschumi's design has only three layers: one archaeological, one timeless Platonic geometry and one cinematic and more personal. The red cube pavilions on the grid intersections hold the three layers together, creating a new, complex, three-dimensional, public space of interaction. (Diagram © Bernard Tschumi Architects)

events and structures, working with five different layers, while Tschumi's had only three. Tschumi created an open system and distributed network model with his red cubes and grid. Tschumi assigned the bottom layer to the archaeology of the existing buildings on the site and the fields or areas around and in between them. The middle layer was a formal, connective grid of points or red pavilions that held the design together and structured the public space. The top layer held a curving 'cinematic' path or irrational, montage narrative that led through the ghostly memories, outlines of a series of Platonic forms, a square, a circle and a triangle. President Mitterrand promised that the French government would complete the park in 40 years, building a pavilion a year, giving the project a long time duration.

The Deconstructivist emphasis on information and flows between urban actors in different strata of the network city meant that architects and urban designers had the possibility of making new kinds of three-dimensional public spaces in the metacity. Ever since the Scottish biologist Patrick Geddes' *Cities in Evolution* (1915), urban designers have understood that great cities very often sit at the mouth of a great river and their hinterland is shaped by the Geddes 'valley section', the space of the watershed behind the delta estuary and its islands.[52] Ian McHarg, the landscape architect professor and James Corner's predecessor at the University of Pennsylvania in the 1960s, extended the Geddes 'valley section' approach into the computer age. His *Design With Nature* (1969) proposed a layered approach to urban ecologies in which each urban actor's territory was mapped on a transparent sheet within the valley and watershed, and then compared through the overlays to find the best sites for various urban functions in the city territory.[53]

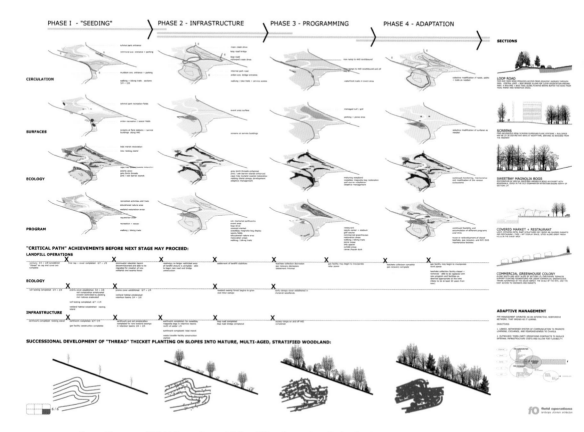

PHASE 1 - "SEEDING"   PHASE 2 - INFRASTRUCTURE   PHASE 3 - PROGRAMMING   PHASE 4 - ADAPTATION

James Corner and Field Operations with Stan Allen, layered analysis of park programme for Freshkills Park competition, Staten Island, New York, 2006
Robert Moses created the gigantic Freshkills rubbish dump on Staten Island in the 1950s. Corner's design had 10 interactive strata and created a complex, three-dimensional, interactive field between the environmental remediation programme and human activities over time. (Diagram © James Corner Field Operations)

Corner extended McHarg's vision to allow multiple actors to participate in a complex interweaving process to create the city over time. He understood how urban actors could work in a layered, three-dimensional spatial matrix space in between fragments, relating to data flows, Geographic Information Systems (GIS) and urban imagery, as well as opening up to ecological flows in the valley section. He proposed that local urban actors created differentiated 'commons' or shared public spaces, Indian maidans, which could be compared to ecological patches that changed over time, resulting in a complex, interactive field of dynamic relationships.[54] Corner was well aware of the environmental damage that the metropolis and megalopolis inflicted on the planet, flying across the country with aerial photographer Alex MacLean to document opencast mining removing mountains, agribusiness farming practices and sprawling suburbs in *Taking Measures Across the American Landscape* (1996).[55] Corner co-edited *Recovering Landscape: Essays in Contemporary Landscape Architecture* (1999), outlining an approach identified as 'landscape urbanism' by Charles Waldheim in an important travelling exhibition of that name in Chicago, New York and Philadelphia in 1997 (restaged for the Urban Design conference at the University of Pennsylvania in 1999).[56] Waldheim himself co-edited *Stalking Detroit* (2001), proposing solutions to the shrinking-city symptoms using urban landscape strategies derived from Corner's time-based, 'performative' urbanism teachings and practices described further in his *Landscape Urbanism Reader* (2006).[57]

Corner and Field Operations concern with the interactions between complex urban actors over a long time duration within a layered three-dimensional matrix is clear in the project for Freshkills Park on Staten Island, New York (construction begun 2006) planned in association with architect Stan Allen.[58] The team worked with 10 interactive strata, each with its own time dimension, for the remediation of the old city landfill opened by Robert Moses. The lowest level was a pre-existing methane gas extraction network that powers a generating plant. Above that is an impermeable barrier to prevent toxins leaching out of the waste below, while above that Corner mapped the existing bodies of surface water and roads, shown in relation to the contour, with vegetation cover and soil types mapped above. The top three layers show the Field Operations team's interventions, firstly in creating new ecological habitats and patches along the hedgerows, secondly with new pathways around the contours, and finally the multiple new programs to be installed in these new environments, represented by simple icons. Field Operations made the heterotopic transformation from rubbish dump to park appear simple and easy by their layered, informational approach, just as they provided a miniature demonstration of this technique with Diller, Scofidio + Renfro at the High Line Park, New York, 2009 (see chapter 2).

Bernardo Secchi and Paola Viganò employed a similar layered, three-dimensional approach in their Antwerp Structure Plan (2003–6) described in their *Antwerp: Territory of a New Modernity* (2009).[59] Following in a rural urbanisation study tradition initiated by Giuseppe Samonà at the University of Venice in the upper Adige Valley in the 1960s, Secchi and Viganò had engaged the city territory of Venice in the Po River delta in their previous work. They studied the Veneto territory, which Secchi christened the '*Città Diffusa*' in 1992, looking at the spacing between building complexes with many different functions often mixed across the urbanised countryside, made accessible by roads, canals and ditches (some built in Roman times), the railway and then the car.[60] Secchi and Viganò compared this area with its 50-kilometre (30-mile) extent to Los Angeles and Holland, both dispersed city territories with far higher populations and very different urban patterns of development. They updated this work in their recent Venice Biennale work 'Water and Asphalt' (2008) and *Landscapes of Water* (2009), which included notes on changes in the hydraulic system over time and its landscape impact on hedgerows and tree planting, as well as proposing a new park and retention pond in an abandoned quarry.[61]

**Bernardo Secchi and Paola
Viganò, Antwerp Fabric
Porosity Diagram and
remodelled Theaterplein
Square project, Antwerp,
Belgium, c 2008**
The Porosity Diagram shows
how Antwerp neighbourhoods
could open up to each other
and the previously isolated city
core linked to the surrounding
inner suburbs. (Diagram and
photo © Studio 09_Bernardo
Secchi, Paola Viganò)

Antwerp, as the great port serving the Belgian empire in the Congo, suffered from the European loss of empire and lost population to the surrounding network of Belgian cities that emerged as the 'Flemish Diamond' in the European North West Metropolitan Area (NWMA), an important segment of the EU's 'Blue Banana' megalopolis stretching from London to Milan (see chapter 6).[62] The EU had designated Antwerp as the City of Culture in 1993, hoping to turn the shrinking city's image around in conjunction with the grassroots NGO *Stad aan de Stroom* (City and River) group. Ten years later, Secchi and Viganò worked for a new mayor who sought to coordinate many different levels of government planning in one document to guide future shrinkage and renovation, as the high-speed Eurostar arrived in an underground mall at the Central Station (2009). This high-speed link sponsored the redevelopment of Kievitplein square in front of the station with a controversial MVRDV-designed skyscraper node. The Secchi–Viganò Structure Plan coordinated this project with a 'hard spine' that paralleled the old quayside of the city, with a tram line extending north and south beyond traditional city boundaries, connecting to the abandoned petrochemical works in Hoboken in the south and the newly renovated Eilandje dock area in the north. The Structure Plan also advocated a 'soft spine' of new parks along the old quayside in the central area and in wetlands and abandoned industrial brownfield sites, which would ring the city as a series of green fragments, reinforcing the drainage and dyke system that made the entire delta city territory habitable.[63]

The Secchi–Viganò Antwerp Structure Plan was a strategic plan, an advisory document not a master plan, that made suggestions for coordination between pre-existing plans and a few, small strategic interventions. The plan contained 'microstories' from various planning agencies, including people who were moving back to renovate buildings in the city, as well as a series of 'scenarios' including the densification of garden city and modern blocks in the uncertain future. The goal was to have a uniform higher density across the city. Secchi and Viganò designed two small parks on the northern edge of the city, where the high-speed train emerged and abandoned dockyards began. They also won the international competition for the renovation of the old municipal theatre facade by not proposing to change the facade. Instead they designed the renovation of the entire theatre square (Theaterplein, 2004–8) as 'commons' beneath a light, high roof on multiple, thin columns, creating an extraordinary cubic void space that redefined the ground plane of the city as a performance space for temporary events. The neighbouring Oude Vaartplaats street market, for instance, expands under the cube roof on Saturdays, while theatre groups and festivals can also use the lighting at night. The water from the roof descends to a recessed garden on one side of the cube, creating a retention pond that also preserves the pre-existing trees, while another side of the square serves as a service road, accessing the underground parking and service bays of the theatre and containing dramatic new escape stairs under the roof. The cubic form of this extraordinary, layered, new public space, constructed on a very limited budget, beautifully symbolised the modestly scaled proposed renovation of the city and its extended territorial network in one elegant strategic gesture.[64]

Metacities and meganodes

Secchi and Viganò's Antwerp Structure Plan transformed and re-scaled a long tradition of network city urban planning strategies stretching back to 1947 that had linked their small delta cities, like Amsterdam, Delft, the Hague and Rotterdam, into the Randstad or Ring City network surrounding a large, protected wetlands park at the centre. In the metacity, widely distributed informational and communication networks enabled the city to spread across the landscape territory while also powering the construction of new dense, layered nodes where mobile individuals could meet in person on a new mass scale (as in Antwerp Central Station mall and MVRDV's high-rise towers). Koolhaas, in his collaboration with OM Ungers (1976–7), had seen Berlin as a similar kind of 'city archipelago', a city made up of large urban fragments that floated in a sea of green spaces (see chapter 8).[65] Koolhaas had applied a similar layered network and node analysis to the suburban sprawl of Atlanta, Georgia, USA in *S,M,L,XL* (1995), concentrating on the shopping centres and suburban office towers as urban nodes.[66]

In his attempts to scale up the city archipelago model to the megacity, Koolhaas in *Mutations* (2001) proposed that the disorganised impoverishment of Lagos be seen as a system of urban islands and patches spread across the lagoon and delta city, where traffic congestion and raw sewage were part of the city's charms.[67] The British geographer and social critic Matthew Gandy in his article 'Learning from Lagos' (2005) argued that there was no reason for this spectacle of mass poverty, infrastructural collapse and urban chaos, while a 'cleptocratic' elite profited from the nation's massive oil reserves.[68] In *The Great Leap Forward* (2002), Koolhaas scaled his analysis up again to the vast city territory of the Pearl River Delta, China, including Hong Kong.[69] The Pearl Delta became an archipelago city on a megascale, occupying many islands with many urban fragments, like the Dutch Randstad, but taking many hours to get from island to island, from city to city, from meganode to meganode.

The multilayered, close-packed cube of Kowloon's Walled City that inspired MVRDV's 'Metacity/Datatown' exhibition represents an extreme heterotopic and informal example of an urban meganode, a city-within-a-city in Koolhaas's city archipelago. As noted earlier, the fate of the Walled City represents Satterthwaite's first and second official options, first turning a blind eye and then demolition. Hong Kong also provides many examples of Satterthwaite's third option, the replacement of shantytowns by industrially produced megablock housing estates or new towns. As MVRDV highlighted in *FARMAX* (1998), these Hong Kong estates and new towns are themselves hyper-dense, multilayered megablock complexes unlike anything in Europe or the USA (developing from the Shek Kip Mei housing of the 1950s – see chapter 4).[70]

Soviet and Chinese housing estates and new towns followed the same industrial model, forming a parallel top-down response to rapid growth but initially at a lower density. In China, megablocks and their associated factories and work-brigade housing estates form the modernist background in many Asian megacities, including Beijing and Shanghai (replacing the older *hutong* and *lilong* urban village structures inside the city grid of highways). This

Tsing Yi New Town Station Podium and Tierra Verde Blocks with Cheung On Estate blocks and Tsing Yi North Bridge, Hong Kong, 1997–8 (photo 2009)
The Hong Kong public transportation authority collaborated to create a system of complex, layered, three-dimensional new town cores in a network around the old city centre in the 1980s. The subway opened up into a multilevel mall that forms the public podium base for megablock public and private housing developments in towers above. (Photo © David Grahame Shane)

top-down response to housing shortages is still an option for other Asian states as the rapid construction of super-dense Bundang New Town, south of Seoul, South Korea demonstrated where 1 million people were housed in slab and tower blocks in five years (see chapter 6).[71] Where Bundang and Chinese examples often have separate commercial buildings and malls, the Hong Kong model incorporates the mall and subway in the base podium of the towers, making a three-dimensional layered matrix (like Hötorgscity in Stockholm – see chapter 4). The base podium links to the network of the other new towns via the subway system, as well as roads. Above the subway and mall podium a roof garden forms the base for the housing towers, while the podiums can be linked from mall to mall by skybridges to make an extensive, three-dimensional, interior, air-conditioned new city fabric.

The transformation of the Las Vegas Strip in the 1990s shows another version of the podium base and tower megablock in the metacity, where the urban image as information replaces the roadside signs and neon celebrated by the Venturi, Scott Brown and Izenour team in 1972 (see chapter 6).[72] Here, in the desert heat, the armature could take on a new pedestrian-oriented form, creating a new kind of three-dimensional urban space and image. All this spectacle is ideally seen at night, when the street armature is cooler, and the night-time illuminations of the fountains at the Bellagio Casino, on the former car park site, transform memories of Lake Como in Italy into a rainbow of coloured plumes of water that can dance in time with music (supplied by speakers hidden in the antique street lights). Across the street, the Venetian offers the spectacle of the Piazza San Marco as a forecourt on the street

Wimberly Allison Tong & Goo (WATG), plan and section of The Venetian, Las Vegas, Nevada, USA, 1999 (redrawn by the author, 2010)

In the 1990s, casino owners replaced the parking lots along the Las Vegas Strip with three-dimensional urban simulacra. In a complex sectional move the Venetian features the Grand Canal shopping mall above a town square of slot machines, with a hill town of villas in gardens on the tower rooftop. (Redrawn diagrams © Uri Wegman and David Grahame Shane)

Wimberly Allison Tong & Goo (WATG), forecourt of the Venetian Casino, Las Vegas, Nevada, USA, 1999 (photos 2009)

The Campanile from Piazza San Marco, the Rialto Bridge, the Grand Canal and the Doge's Palace make a three-dimensional urban collage. Across the street, the sign for the Treasure Island Casino fronts another spectacular water feature. (Photos © David Grahame Shane)

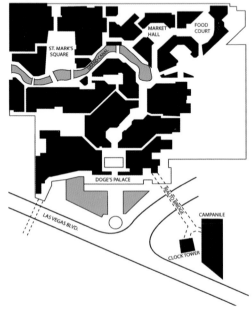

armature, with the Grand Canal, complete with singing gondoliers, on the interior third floor above a 'town square' filled with slot machines and gambling tables, surrounded by cafés. Paris Casino offers a replica piece of Montmartre, complete with interior trees and lanes, while New York Casino fills its 'Central Park' with slot machines.[73]

It is easy to dismiss the contemporary Las Vegas as an exceptional excess, but the casinos demonstrate the power of the metacity and the city as information. The French philosopher Michel Foucault classified casinos as heterotopias of illusion and fast change. Certainly the early casinos along the Strip created a new form of car-based armature that would soon be present as a 'Miracle Mile' in every American city. Given this history, the rapid conversion of parking forecourts into simulacra cities, with new, layered three-dimensional public spaces (albeit owned by global gambling corporations) shows the transformation of the Strip and enclave into a new urban format. Like Disney's plans for a new Disneyland in Shanghai, the casino owners are busy extending their brands on a global scale in Asia. The ex-Portuguese colony of Macao opposite Hong Kong, for instance, houses an even larger replica of the Venetian Las Vegas.[74] This format is not like any previous city: it is layered in unprecedented ways, uses historical urban imagery and collage to hide its novelty. It is possible that in 20 years this new urban simulacra will transform the parking lots of every American city or megalopolis worldwide into new, pedestrian-based urban attractors themed with historic urban images. People might actually live and work upstairs from these images, as they do on vacation now in the hotel towers above the casinos on the Strip (Las Vegas was visited by 37 million tourists in the recession of 2008).[75]

This layered, informational, urban design approach to podium and tower megablocks demonstrates the creation of new, three-dimensional urban spaces that mix uses in previously unforeseen ways, transforming both the enclave and the armature. This layered approach fitted perfectly with the plans of the Seoul city mayor to create a linear park by removing an elevated highway from the centre of the city and opening the street below to reveal the layer of the old riverbed that became the linear Cheonggyecheon Park armature, one level below the city (2005). This design reversed the code of the contemporary High Line Park in New York that recycled the raised railway viaduct. At an important symbolic level this intervention in Seoul, a giant Asian megacity second only to Tokyo according to the UN, created a new multilevel public space and the old river returned, although the actual water that flowed through the artificial streambed was chlorinated to prevent infection.[76]

The layered approach to the city formed a long-time theme of American architect Steven Holl's urban research, encompassing abandoned three-dimensional armatures of the metropolis in the 1980s. One of Holl's first theoretical projects in New York involved an appreciation of the High Line as a raised urban armature that could have new urban elements such as houses attached ('Bridge of Houses', 1981).[77] The continuity of the viaduct formed a basic datum or transept through the city, from which other elements might spring forth, always within a strict, typological, cubic format. Holl's project, with its simple formal vocabulary and respect for the old structure, formed one inspiration for the community group that eventually developed and advocated the designation of the High Line Park.

Cheonggyecheon River Park, Seoul, South Korea, 2005 (photo 2007)
The Mayor of Seoul decided in 2003 to demolish an elevated highway and open up the
covered historic river below. The resultant three-dimensional park armature reverses the
code of the New York High Line Viaduct, excavating a park space inside the city below
ground level. (Photo © David Grahame Shane)

Holl's Linked Hybrid project (2003–9) continued this preoccupation with the layering
of public space in the metacity.[78] In this case the High Line datum became a continuous
band of skybridges on a high floor of several skyscraper apartment towers set in a Beijing
megablock. Holl designed a street-in-the-air as never imagined by Le Corbusier or even
the Smithsons in their Berlin Haupstadt Project of 1958 (see chapter 3). Holl created a
miniature city archipelago of tower blocks set in a private park that he linked with sky
bridges – containing shared facilities for residents, a swimming pool and an art gallery, with
space designated for a sky café and gym – along a continuous circuit within the site. This
high-level skywalk system landed on the top of the lower, circular hotel tower in a small
pavilion, playing with the datum and roofline. Beneath the ground plane of the enclave, Holl
buried the car park, creating a water garden on its roof (reminiscent of the old rice paddies)
with small entry pavilions and a larger cinema complex closing the entry vista. Around the
periphery of the site, Holl partially buried various community functions under green roofs and
landscaped berms, housing a school and a small commercial complex with parkland above.
Underground, the project also housed one of the largest geothermal heating and cooling
plants in the world. Without resorting to the literal, layered urban images of Las Vegas, Holl
transformed what had been a Soviet factory megablock site by his inventive pursuit of themes
from the Deconstructivist layering of a new, three-dimensional public space.

Steven Holl, Linked Hybrid, Beijing, 2003–9 (photo 2009)
In the 1980s, Holl was an early admirer of the disused New York railway viaduct that became the High Line Park. In the Linked Hybrid, Holl continued this research, creating a high-level, semi-public passageway that links the towers. The result is a complex, three-dimensional, urban public space within the megablock development. (Photo © David Grahame Shane)

Conclusion

This chapter has examined the megacity in various formats from Latin America, Asia, Africa, North America and Europe. As the majority of the world's population has moved to cities, the centre of gravity of the world's urban population has shifted to Asia with its megacities and metacities. With the growth of these cities the importance of urban design has increased, but the form of the city has changed. Urban designers work inside widely distributed meshes of different networks and organisations of people, top-down and bottom-up, managing different flows of trade, information and energy, making flexible and heterotopic, sectional solutions much more common.

The next chapter, as well as examining the informal aspects of the city territory and network, will discuss the formal elements of the distributed city spread across networks, including megablocks and meganodes. These urban development hubs combine many mixed uses, creating new urban hybrids, part mall, part railway station, part housing, office and recreational spaces. They have come to symbolise the shift of the global urban centre of population to Asian metacities distributed over vast territories, including agriculture in a new city form.

Asian metacities like Bangkok, Beijing, Seoul or Tokyo can support unprecedented formal, super-dense, layered megablocks and megamall developments with incredibly complex sections dwarfing the Las Vegas casinos, which for the Venturi, Scott Brown and Izenour team

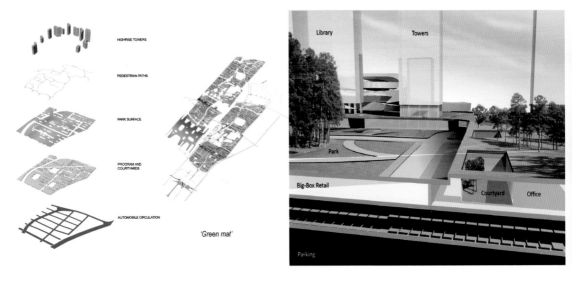

Reiser + Umemoto, axonometric and section, Foshan Sansui Urban Plan, Beijing, China, 2004

In this Beijing megablock proposal, a complex layered three-dimensional street section is cut into a park on the undulating roofs of big-box retail and office buildings that also form a podium for housing and other tower elements above. (Diagrams © Reiser + Umemoto, RUR Architecture, PC)

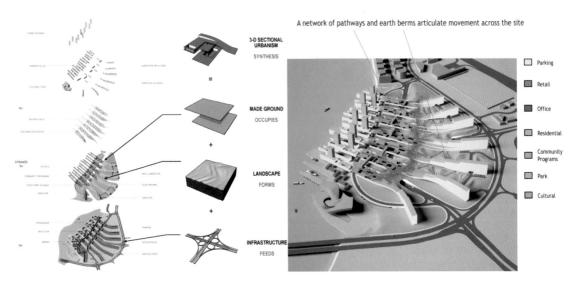

Reiser + Umemoto, Business Bay Three project, Dubai, United Arab Emirates, 2007

Developing the Foshan Sansui section, the undulating roof park conceals large car parks serving the housing and office slabs above. At the water's edge, the three-dimensional spatial matrix opens up to form small coves, with shops, offices and apartments above. (Diagrams © Reiser + Umemoto, RUR Architecture, PC)

represented the epitome of the Pop automobile culture and the megalopolis of the 1960s. The new owners in Las Vegas have installed dense, pedestrian-friendly urban simulacra, promising urban experiences from New York, Paris, Venice or Marrakech, with incredibly complex sections that have in turn inspired mall designers in Asia, as in Langham Place, Hong Kong (2005). These meganodes can be interconnected to form dense urban networks, as in the enormous complex of malls and megamalls that constitutes 'downtown' Bangkok, illustrated at the end of the next chapter as an exemplary Asian megacity.

In these Asian meganodes, as in the desert heterotopias of Las Vegas or Abu Dhabi, strange new layered, three-dimensional urban hybrids are emerging. Jesse Reiser and Nanako Umemoto, for instance, in their Business Bay project, Dubai (2007), create an enormous roof garden lawn in the heat of the sun that stretches as a transept over the top of a large car park, linking up to office and apartment slab blocks above and containing light wells giving down to big-box retail below. As in their earlier Foshan Sansui Beijing megablock project (2004), streets are cut into this landscape, sometimes going below, sometimes appearing above the shifting contour of the undulating landscape datum. Along the water's edge these layers are exposed, forming a modern-day souk or small-scale market, with small stores below village-scaled housing and office facilities above, all overlooking the skyline of Dubai across the bay.

Notes

NB: See 'Author's Caution: Endnote Sources and Wikipedia', towards the end of this book.

1   See: MVRDV, *Metacity/Datatown*, 010 Publishers (Rotterdam), 1999.

2   On the World Urban Forum (WUF-III) megacity critique of cities of 1–2 million population, see: David Satterthwaite, 'Human Settlements at the World Urban Forum, Vancouver 2006', International Institute for Environment and Development website, http://www.iied.org/pubs/display.php?o=G00527 (accessed 2 April 2010).

3   See: Janice E Perlman, *The Myth of Marginality: Urban Poverty and Politics in Rio de Janeiro*, University of California Press (Berkeley, CA), 1976.

4   On *favelas*, see: ibid pp 135–61.

5   On the Mega-Cities Project, see: Mega-Cities Project website, http://www.megacitiesproject.org/default.asp (accessed 12 March 2010).

6   On global urban population, see: *The State of the World's Cities 2006/7*, UN-HABITAT, United Nations Human Settlements Programme, Earthscan (London), 2006, pp 4–12. For megacities and urban agglomerations, see: United Nations Department of Economic and Social Affairs, Population Division, http://www.un.org/esa/population/publications/wup2007/2007urban_agglo.htm (accessed 13 March 2010).

7   See: Janice Perlman, 'The Chronic Poor in Rio de Janeiro: what has changed in 30 years?', in Marco Keiner, Martina Koll-Schretzenmayr and Willy A Schmid (eds), *Managing Urban Futures: Sustainability and Urban Growth in Developing Countries*, Ashgate Publishing (Aldershot, England; Burlington, VT), c 2005, pp 165–85.

8   For UN-HABITAT history, see: UN-HABITAT website, http://www.unhabitat.org/content.asp?typeid=19&catid=10&cid=927 (accessed 2 April 2010); also: Delegation to the United Nations Conference on Human Settlements, *HABITAT, the United Nations Conference on Human Settlements: Report of the Canadian Delegation*, Ministry of State, Urban Affairs Canada (Ottawa), 1977. On the 1976 United Nations Conference on Human Settlements, see: Barbara Ward, *The Home of Man*, WW Norton & Company, 1976. On Barbara Ward, see: http://en.wikipedia.org/wiki/Barbara_Ward (accessed 13 March 2010). On Otto Koenigsberger, see:

http://en.wikipedia.org/wiki/Otto_Königsberger (accessed 13 March 2010).

9   John FC Turner, *Housing by People: Towards Autonomy in Building Environments*, Marion Boyars (London), 1976; see also: John FC Turner, *Freedom to Build: Dweller Control of the Housing Process*, Macmillan (New York), 1972. Bernard Rudofsky, *Architecture Without Architects: A Short Introduction to Non-Pedigreed Architecture*, Museum of Modern Art (New York), 1964.

10 Gordon Cullen, *Townscape*, Architectural Press (London), 1961.

11 See: Fumihiko Maki, 'Some Thoughts on Collective Form', in Gyorgy Kepes (ed), *Structure in Art and Science*, George Braziller (New York), 1965, pp 116–27.

12 On Françoise Choay and 'urban semiology', see: Charles Jencks and George Baird, *Meaning in Architecture*, Studio Vista (London), 1969, pp 26–49.

13 On the Lima, Peru housing competition, see: Fernando Garcia-Huidobro, Diego Torres Torriti and Nicolas Trugas, *El Tiempo Construye: El Proyecto Experimental de Vivienda (Previ) De Lima – Genesis y Desenlace*, Gustavo Gili (Barcelona), 2008; also: Christopher Alexander, 'A Pattern Language: Towns, Buildings', *Construction*, vol 2, Oxford University Press (Berkeley, CA), 1977, p 1130.

14 Terry G McGee, *The Urbanization Process in the Third World: Explorations in Search of a Theory*, Bell (London), 1971. On the *desa-kota* hypothesis, see also: Terry McGee, 'The Emergence of Desakota Regions in Asia: expanding a hypothesis', in Norton Ginsburg, Bruce Koppel and TG McGee (eds), *The Extended Metropolis: Settlement Transition in Asia*, University of Hawaii Press (Honolulu), 1991, pp 3–26.

15 For Angkor Wat, see: 'Map Reveals Ancient Urban Sprawl', 14 August 2007, BBC News website, http://news.bbc.co.uk/2/hi/science/nature/6945574.stm (accessed 2 April 2010).

16 On the history of the Dutch East India Company, see: Els M Jacobs, *In Pursuit of Pepper and Tea: The Story of the Dutch East India Company*, Netherlands Maritime Museum (Amsterdam), 1991.

17 On Mao, Gandhi and Sukarno, see: Clive J Christie, *Ideology and Revolution in Southeast Asia, 1900–1980: Political Ideas of the Anti-Colonial Era*, Routledge (London; New York), 2001, pp 157–74.

18 On urban agriculture in Africa and South America, see: Mark Redwood, 'Agriculture in Urban Planning, Generating Livelihoods and Food Security', Earthscan and the International Development Research Centre (IDRC), 2009, http://www.idrc.ca/openebooks/427-7/ (accessed 13 March 2010).

19 On the 'Green Revolution', see: http://en.wikipedia.org/wiki/Green_Revolution (accessed 13 March 2010).

20 On Dutch delta cities, see: Manfred Kuhn, 'Greenbelt and Green Heart: separating and integrating landscapes in European city regions', *Landscape and Urban Planning*, vol 64, issues 1–2, 15 June 2003, pp 19–27.

21 On Shanghai agricultural land use, see: Christopher Howe, *Shanghai: Revolution and Development in an Asian Metropolis*, Cambridge University Press (New York), 1981, pp 291–5 (available on Google Books).

22 On megacities since 1950, see: 'Fact Sheet 7: Mega-cities', *World Urbanization Prospects: The 2005 Revision*, UN website, http://www.un.org/esa/population/publications/WUP2005/2005WUP_FS7.pdf (accessed 13 March 2010). For megacities and urban agglomerations, see: Department of Economic and Social Affairs, Population Division, Urban Agglomerations, 2007, http://www.un.org/esa/population/publications/wup2007/2007urban_agglo.htm (accessed 13 March 2010).

23 Richard Register, *Ecocity Berkeley: Building Cities for a Healthy Future*, North Atlantic Books (Berkeley, CA), c 1987; Richard Register, *Ecocities: Rebuilding Cities in Balance with Nature*, Berkeley Hills (Berkeley, CA) and Hi Marketing (London), 2001. For early ecology, see: Rachel Carson, *Silent Spring*, Riverside Press, Cambridge, MA, 1962.

24 John Seymour and Herbert Girardet, *Blueprint for a Green Planet: Your Practical Guide to Restoring the World's Environment,* Dorling Kindersley (London), 1987.

25 See: Ecocity Builders website, http://www.ecocitybuilders.org/ (accessed 2 April 2010).

26   For Curitiba, see: http://en.wikipedia.org/wiki/Jaime_Lerner (accessed 13 March 2010).

27   Doug Kelbaugh and Peter Calthorpe, *Pedestrian Pocket Book*, Princeton Architectural Press (New York) in association with the University of Washington, 1989.

28   For ecological footprints, see: Mathis Wackernagel and William E Rees, *Our Ecological Footprint: Reducing Human Impact on the Earth*, New Society Publishers (Gabriola Island, BC), 1996; also: William Rees, 'Revisiting Carrying Capacity: area-based indicators of sustainability', University of British Columbia, http://dieoff.org/page110.htm (accessed 13 March 2010).

29   On Peter Latz's Duisburg-Nord Landschaftpark, see: *Groundswell: Constructing the Contemporary Landscape*, Museum of Modern Art (New York), 2005 (available on Google Books); also: http://en.wikipedia.org/wiki/Landschaftspark_Duisburg-Nord (accessed 14 March 2010).

30   For Milwaukee urban agriculture see: http://www.growingpower.org/ (accessed 14 March 2010)

31   On Slow Food, see: Carlo Petrini and Benjamin Watson, *Slow Food: Collected Thoughts on Taste, Tradition, and the Honest Pleasures of Food*, Chelsea Green Publishing (White River Junction, VT), 2001.

32   See the revised edition: Thomas Sieverts, *Cities Without Cities: An Interpretation of the Zwischenstadt*, Spon Press (London; New York), 2003.

33   Paola Viganò, *La Città Elementare*, Skira (Milan; Geneva), 1999.

34   On Vauban district, Freiburg, Germany, see: Vauban website, http://www.vauban.de/info/abstract.html (accessed 14 March 2010)

35   Philipp Oswalt and Tim Reiniets, *The Atlas of Shrinking Cities*, Hatje Cantz (Ostfildern), 2006; see also: Shrinking Cities website, http://shrinkingcities.com/index.php?id=2&L=1 (accessed 2 April 2010).

36   United Nations Human Settlements Programme, *The Challenge of Slums: Global Report on Human Settlements*, 2003, Earthscan (London), 2003.

37   Mike Davis, *Planet of Slums*, Verso (London), 2006.

38   On vulnerable cities, see: 'On Climate Change and the Urban Poor: risk and resilience in 15 of the world's most vulnerable cities', International Institute for Environment and Development (IIED), 2009, http://www.iied.org/pubs/display.php?o=G02597 (accessed 2 April 2010); also: Gordon McGranahan, Deborah Balk and Bridget Anderson, 'The Rising Tide: assessing the risks of climate change and human settlements in low elevation coastal zones', *Environment & Urbanization*, International Institute for Environment and Development (IIED), vol 19 (1), 2007, pp 17–37.

39   On low-elevation coastal zone (LECZ) urban–rural estimates, see: http://sedac.ciesin.columbia.edu/gpw/lecz.jsp (accessed 14 March 2010); also: CIESIN map, United Nations Population Fund website, http://www.unfpa.org/swp/2007/english/chapter_5/figure8.html (accessed 12 July 2010).

40   On the Nile, see: Madeleine Bunting, 'Confronting the Perils of Global Warming in a Vanishing Landscape', 14 November 2000, *The Guardian* website, http://www.guardian.co.uk/environment/2000/nov/14/globalwarming.climatechange1 (accessed 24 March 2010).

41   David Satterthwaite, *The Transition to a Predominantly Urban World and its Underpinnings*, International Institute for Environment and Development (IIED) (London), 2007, http://www.iied.org/pubs/pdfs/10550IIED.pdf (accessed July 12 2010).

42   On slum upgrading, see: 'What Is Urban Upgrading?' (prepared for the World Bank), MIT website, http://web.mit.edu/urbanupgrading/upgrading/whatis/index.html (accessed 12 July 2010).

43   For SDI and the WSF, see: David Satterthwaite, *The Scale of Urban Change Worldwide 1950-2000 and its Underpinnings*, International Institute for Environment and Development (IIED) Human Settlements Program Discussion Paper, Urban Change 1, London, 2005. On the WSF, See: http://en.wikipedia.org/wiki/World_Social_Forum (accessed 14 March 2010).

44   On Kowloon Walled City, see: Ian Lambot, *City of Darkness: Life in Kowloon Walled City*, Watermark Pub (Haslemere, Surrey), c 1993.

45   Winy Maas, Jacob van Rijs and Richard Koek (eds), *FARMAX: Excursions on Density*, 010 Publishers (Rotterdam), 1998.

46   MVRDV, *Metacity/Datatown*, 1999.

47   William Gibson, *Neuromancer*, originally published by Ace-Berkeley (New York), 1984, now part of Penguin Publishing Group, 2000.

48   Colin Rowe and Fred Koetter, *Collage City*, MIT Press (Cambridge, MA), 1978.

49   On the University of California Berkeley Sim Lab, see: Peter Bosselmann, *Representation of Places: Reality and Realism in City Design*, University of California Press (Berkeley, CA), 1998. On Michael Kwartler's New York Sim Lab, see: David W Dunlap, 'Impact of Zoning is Pretested on Computers', *The New York Times*, 14 June 1992, p 101. See also: Environmental Simulation Center website, http://www.simcenter.org/ (accessed 14 March 2010). On the Sim Lab at University College, London (UCL), see: UCL Centre for Advanced Spatial Analysis (CASA) website, http://www.casa.ucl.ac.uk/about/ (accessed 14 March 2010).

50   On Parc de la Villette, see: Bernard Tschumi, 'La Villette', Pratt Journal of Architecture, vol 2, Spring 1988, pp 127–33; also: Jacques Derrida, 'Point de Folie – maintenant l'architecture', *Architecture Association Files*, no 12, Summer 1986, pp 65–75; also: Bernard Tschumi and Yukio Futagawa, *Bernard Tschumi*, ADA Edita (Tokyo), 1997, pp 32–48.

51   Bernard Tschumi, *The Manhattan Transcripts*, Academy Editions (London) and St Martin's Press (New York), 1994.

52   Sir Patrick Geddes, *Cities in Evolution: An Introduction to the Town Planning Movement and to the Study of Cities*, Williams & Norgate (London), 1915.

53   Ian McHarg, *Design with Nature*, published for the American Museum of Natural History (Garden City, NY), 1969.

54   On maidans, see: James Corner (ed), *Recovering Landscape: Essays in Contemporary Landscape Architecture*, New York, Princeton Architectural Press, 1999, pp 205–20.

55   James Corner and Alex S MacLean, *Taking Measures Across the American Landscape*, Yale University Press (Newhaven, CT; London), 1996.

56   James Corner and Alan Balfour, *Recovering Landscape: Essays in Contemporary Landscape Theory*, Princeton Architectural Press (New York), 1999. For Charles Waldheim's 'Landscape Urbanism' exhibition, see: Paul Bennett, 'The Urban Landscape Gets its Due', *Landscape Architecture Magazine*, vol 88, no 3, March 1998, pp 26, 28.

57   Georgia Daskalakis, Charles Waldheim and Jason Young (eds), *Stalking Detroit*, ACTAR (Barcelona), 2001. Charles Waldheim, *The Landscape Urbanism Reader*, Princeton Architectural Press (New York), 2006.

58   On Freshkills Park competition, see: New York City Department of City Planning website, http://www.nyc.gov/html/dcp/html/fkl/fkl2.shtml (accessed 14 March 2010); also: Robert Sullivan, 'Can Landscape Architect James Corner Turn Fresh Kills Landfill Into a City-Changing Park?', *New York* magazine, 23 November 2008, http://nymag.com/news/features/52452/#ixzz0iFyPD8xQ (accessed 14 March 2010).

59   Bernardo Secchi and Paola Viganò, *Antwerp: Territory of a New Modernity*, Idea Books (Amsterdam), 2009.

60   For the dispersed city, see: Bernard Secchi and Paola Viganò, 'Water and Asphalt: the projection of isotropy in the metropolitan region of Venice', in Rafi Segal and Els Verbakel (eds), *Cities of Dispersal, Architectural Design*, vol 78, issue 1, January/February 2008, pp 34–9. On distributed urbanism, see: Paola Viganò, 'Urban Design and the City Territory', in Greig Crysler, Stephen Cairns and Hilde Heynen (eds), *The SAGE Handbook of Architectural Theory*, SAGE Publications (London), 2011, Part 8.

61   Secchi and Viganò, 'Water and Asphalt', 2008, pp 34–9; P Viganò, *Landscapes of Water*, Edizioni RISMA (Milan), 2009.

62   For European North West Metropolitan Area (NWMA), see: Peter Newman, 'Changing Patterns of Regional Governance in the EU', *Urban Studies*, vol 37, May 2000, pp 895–908.

63   On soft and hard spines, see: Bernardo Secchi and Paola Viganò, *Antwerp*, 2009.

64   For Antwerp, see: Bernardo Secchi, 'Wasted and Reclaimed Landscapes: rethinking and redesigning the urban landscape', *Places*, vol 19, no 1, College of Environmental Design, University of California (Berkeley, CA), 2007, available at http://escholarship.org/uc/item/15q4w442 (accessed 12 July 2010).

65   For the 'city archipelago' 1976–7, see: Oswald Mathias Ungers, Rem Koolhaas, Peter Riemann, Hans Kollhoff, Peter Ovaska, 'Cities Within the City: proposal by the sommer akademie for Berlin', *Lotus International*, 1977, p 19.

66   Rem Koolhaas and Bruce Mao, *S,M,L,XL: Office for Metropolitan Architecture*, Monacelli Press (New York), 1995.

67   Rem Koolhaas et al, *Mutations*, ACTAR (Barcelona), 2001.

68   Matthew Gandy, 'Learning from Lagos', *New Left Review*, no 33, May–June 2005, pp 37–52.

69   Rem Koolhaas, *The Great Leap Forward*, Harvard Design School Project on the City 2, Taschen (New York), 2002.

70   For Hong Kong New Town mall podium with housing, see: http://en.wikipedia.org/wiki/New_Town_Plaza_Phase_3 en (accessed 15 March 2010). For Korea Land Corporation (KLC) and Korea National Housing Corporation, see: Korea Land & Housing Corporation website, http://world.lh.or.kr/englh_html/englh_about/about_1.asp (accessed 11 March 2010).

71   For Bundang, see: http://en.wikipedia.org/wiki/Bundang (accessed 11 March 2010).

72   Robert Venturi, Denise Scott Brown, Steven Izenour, *Learning from Las Vegas: The Forgotten Symbolism of Architectural Form*, MIT Press (Cambridge, MA), 1972.

73   On the new Las Vegas, see: Robert Venturi and Denise Scott Brown, 'Las Vegas After its Classic Age', in Robert Venturi (ed), *Iconography and Electronics upon a Generic Architecture*, MIT Press (Cambridge, MA), 1996, pp 123–8; also: Nicolai Ouroussoff, 'The Lessons of Las Vegas Still Hold Surprises', *The New York Times*, 22 December 2009, p C1.

74   On the Venetian Macao, see: Venetian Macao website, http://www.venetianmacao.com/en/ (accessed 11 March 2010).

75   On the Las Vegas tourist count, see: Andrew Clark, 'Recession Brings ''Las Vegas dream'' to an End', *The Guardian*, 26 June 2009, http://www.guardian.co.uk/business/2009/jun/26/las-vegas-citycenter-recession (accessed 2 April 2010)

76   On Seoul's Cheonggyecheon street, see: http://en.wikipedia.org/wiki/Cheonggyecheon; also: Seoul Metropolitan Facilities Management Corporation website, http://english.sisul.or.kr/grobal/cheonggye/eng/WebContent/index.html (accessed 15 March 2010).

77   Steven Holl, 'Bridge of Houses', in Steven Holl and William Stout (eds), *Pamphlet Architecture*, no 7, Princeton Architectural Press (New York), 1981.

78   On the Linked Hybrid project, see: Steven Holl, *Urbanisms: Working with Doubt*, Princeton Architectural Press (New York), 2009, pp 137–47.

CHAPTER 10

Illustrated Megacity/Metacity

The definition of the megacity/metacity is not only about a scale change in urban design, it also represents a shift in the focus of urban design away from urban fragments and towards the space in between the fragments, their connection in larger networks with important nodes at interchanges. Urban designers sought to connect the earlier fragments and to open them up to new networks and flows of energy and information. They adapted the superblocks and megablocks that formed the basis of the 20th-century new towns in the megalopolis to new purposes, altering the form of the city in the process to include agriculture. Using layering techniques and new computer software, designers sought to extend their control over the city territory through microcodes and landscape techniques, with a goal of rebalancing the city's eco-footprint and including urban agriculture as part of the new mix.

At the same time, designers sought to work across the city territory without making a pre-ordained master plan that would have only one outcome from the top down. Within the megacity/metacity, designers envisioned various scenarios for the evolution of an urban network and the interaction of actors, with different outcomes at various nodes. Personal communication devices and the mass communication systems accelerated this process of decentralisation and extended the range of the city territory, also powering new, hyper-dense nodes for personal meetings, group interactions and mass marketing sales. In these hyper-dense, global nodes and in special heterotopic conditions such as Las Vegas or Abu Dhabi, urban designers were free to experiment with new sectional combinations and imaginative, three-dimensional public spaces, including new media systems and urban images divorced from their original locations. Abandoned factories, urban waterfronts and industrial plant provided another place for experimentation in the shrinking cities of the global north.

This chapter examines the various forms of the megacity as an extended city territory from the shrinking cities of North America and Europe to the relatively stable lower-income megacities of Latin America, and fast-expanding megacities of Africa and Asia. Early megacities did not maintain the strict segregation deemed appropriate by urban designers and planners and state officials often overlooked the self-built housing in shantytowns just as their northern counterparts did not see the expansion in the rural zone around shrinking cities. In both cases, the urban form of the city is changing and requires new tools and urban design mapping techniques to deal with a widely distributed city in the landscape. In both cases, the megablock of the network city is emerging as a new urban form that includes agriculture, in the northern hemisphere in the interstices of shrinking industrial cities, in the south as a remnant of older cosmological and traditional arrangements.

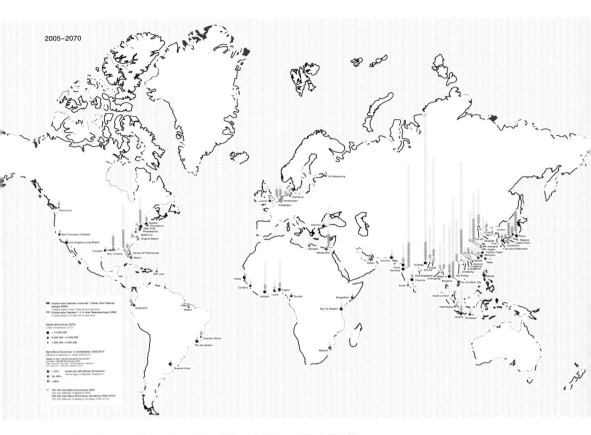

**Philipp Oswalt and Team, Global Map of Megacity Vulnerability to Flooding
at 1 metre and 2 metre (3–6 feet) Water Rise,** *The Atlas of Shrinking Cities,*
Hatje Cantz (Ostfildern), 2006
Oswalt and his team show clearly the vulnerability of Asian megacities on the
coastal plains and in the river deltas. The same pattern can be seen in Europe
and the Americas, while in Africa Alexandria and Lagos are especially
vulnerable. (Map © Philipp Oswalt)

Asian megacities, like their northern-hemisphere counterparts, are often in river deltas
and estuary regions. They are literally archipelago cities located in a river flow. There is a
strong possibility that the resilience and flexibility of the megacity/metacity formulation of
megablock networks and nodes will be tested by extreme climate change, facing either
desertification or floods. As a result, shrinking megacities could appear in the southern
hemisphere, triggering mass urban migrations. The vulnerability of these cities is clear, but
their capacity for change is also enormous, as illustrated by Bangkok as an exemplary Asian
megacity at the end of the chapter.

The shrinking of European and North American cities has often been accompanied by large-scale growth in the megalopolis beyond the official city boundaries, as in the case of Detroit, Michigan or the East Coast corridor from Boston to Washington. The urban actors creating the megalopolis tended to infill new suburbs around the old metropolitan core and along key growth corridors, along railways first, then highways. The urban actors of the megacity in the 1980s and 1990s did not have the same constraints: with cheap oil and widespread infrastructural systems, they could spread more evenly across the countryside, employing modern communication networks to overcome distance. The result was a much more dispersed city in North America and Europe where urban facilities could be spread far more widely, in small towns or villages across a large network.

This small-scale scatter pattern escaped notice for a long time, coming to the fore in the 1990s as an 'ex-urban' phenomenon, beyond even the clusters described by Joel Garreau in *Edge City: Life on the New Frontier* (1992).[1] The New Urbanism movement in North America continued to project large suburban real-estate projects in this period, as described by John A Dutton in *The New American Urbanism* (2000) or advocated by Andrés Duany, Elizabeth Plater-Zyberk and Jeff Speck in *Suburban Nation: The Rise of Sprawl and Decline of the American Dream* (2000).[2] These projects with their large, multicar garages, mansions with vast family rooms on small plots, marketed the symbols of community, but hid the communications revolution powering the network city of which they were a large part. Albert Pope in *Ladders* (1997) and Mario Gandelsonas in *X-Urban: Architecture and the American City* (1999) were amongst the few American architects and urban designers to question closely the structure and geometry of the network city growing beneath the spectacular real-estate bubble of the 1990s.[3]

European urban designers also enjoyed an ex-urban revival and urbanisation of the countryside in the 1990s in the period of cheap oil, cheap credit and the EU 'Blue Banana' (see chapter 6) regional corridor development policies. The loss of empire, difficulties of oil supplies from the Middle East, taxes on oil to protect railways and the governmental regulations protecting agricultural land in many European states made for a different development pattern than the American sprawl. German designers, like the Julia Bolles–Peter Wilson partnership (Bolles + Wilson) in Münster in the mid-1990s, outlined the new, ex-urban format that scattered urban installations at intervals across the countryside, altering the German *Stadtlandschaft* tradition to a '*Eurolandschaft*' scatter pattern.[4] Philipp Oswalt and the *Atlas of Shrinking Cities* (2006) team in Germany were especially aware of the problem of urban shrinkage because of the merger of East and West Germany after the collapse of the USSR in 1991.[5] In former East Germany many cities turned to urban agriculture as a solution, as shown in the landscape urbanism design firm Station C23's design for Dessau (2009).[6]

Xaveer De Geyter in *After-Sprawl: Research for the Contemporary City* (2002) worked with teams from six areas in the European 'Blue Banana' megacity complex to map the different forms that ex-urban network development could take.[7] Local codes and agricultural landscapes in each country and city shaped the generic sprawl response in these 'shrinking cities' expansions. De Geyter included case studies from London, England; Randstad (Ring City), Holland; Brussels–Antwerp–Ghent, Belgium; the Ruhr area, Germany; Zurich–Basel, Switzerland; and the Veneto region, Italy. Within these widely distributed network cities, Deconstructivist urban designers imagined new three-dimensional, layered public spaces that might include the huge media screens seen in MegaTokyo at the dense Shinjuku transportation hub (see chapter 6). The Austrian Deconstructivist architects Coop Himmelb(l) au, for instance, won the Melun-Sénart French New Town Centre competition (1986–7) with a layered three-dimensional, visionary megastructural matrix that was not built.[8] In America the Asymptote Architecture studio won the Los Angeles Gateway competition (1989), employing a similar concept of a new, three-dimensional, layered public space that was open to media and popular events, eschewing the old imperial displays of power and top-down order.[9] Asymptote demonstrated the sculptural potential of the layered Deconstructivist design approach to dense urban nodes. Here, drivers on the highway below and pedestrians at ground level can glance up at the movie screens above, creating a new three-dimensional public space under the belly of the museum.

Asymptote Architects, Steel Cloud, West Coast Gateway Immigration Museum Competition, Los Angeles, USA, 1989
Asymptote demonstrated the sculptural potential of the layered Deconstructivist design approach to dense urban nodes. Here, drivers on the highway below and pedestrians at ground level can glance up at the movie screens above, creating a new three-dimensional public space under the belly of the museum. (Image © Asymptote: Hani Rashid + Lise Anne Couture)

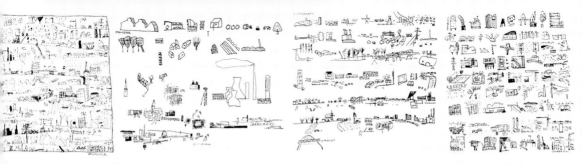

Bolles + Wilson, *Eurolandschaft* sketch, Germany, 1994
Bolles + Wilson noted the shift from the tightly controlled German *Stadtlandshaft* (city-landscape) tradition to a looser, more widely distributed urban network in the 1990s. The drawing identifies the many varied building typologies and functions spaced across the landscape around their hometown of Münster, Germany. (Drawings © Bolles + Wilson)

In 1991, the year of the reunification of East and West Germany, the Ruhr District IBA (International Building Exhibition) held a competition to convert the giant, abandoned and polluted Thyssen-Meiderich Steel Mills in Duisburg, into the Emscher Park eco-park. Peter Latz + Partner's winning design kept the ruins of the abandoned industrial plant as monumental elements of a layered design that used the old industrial structures as walkways and viewing platforms.[10] These giant sculptural elements, their tough, thick walls and rusting steel components became symbols of time passing and memory tokens of now-abandoned industrial processes. In their place, Latz proposed a process of phytoremediation using plants to bioremediate polluted soil (heavily polluted soil was buried in old bunkers). Visitors are encouraged to actively engage with the massive walls of the plant, climbing the walls, sliding down chutes and exploring the multilevel metal catwalks, tanks and gantries. Pools of water and canals provide still spaces of contemplation.

The three-dimensional, layered design approach of Duisburg-Nord learnt from Bernard Tschumi's earlier design of Parc de la Villette, Paris (1982) but introduced natural plantings instead of the abstract geometries of the Paris project.[11] The geometric grids of Latz's tree plantings reflect the controlled grid of red pavilions of La Villette, while the railways replace Tschumi's 'cinematic path', as do the paths on old steel pylons and cut through blast furnace walls. Both parks encourage active play and participation, while also harbouring contemplative spaces associated with reflection and water. Latz acknowledged Richard Haag's Gas Works Park in Seattle, USA (1975) as an inspiration, where old industrial tanks formed monumental sculptural elements in the landscape.[12] Duisburg-Nord demonstrates the power of the layered, Deconstructivist approach to the city and its ability to handle polluted layers of soil, as well as generate exciting three-dimensional public spaces, predecessors of the New York High Line Park (2009, see chapter 2).

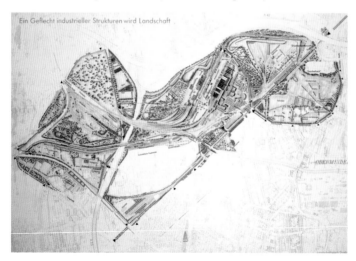

Peter Latz + Partner, plan for Duisburg Nord Landschaft Park, Germany, 1991 (completed 2002)

Latz treated the ruins of the vast abandoned steel mill as a three dimensional matrix that could provide a new kind of public space on many levels, an ecopark with leisure activities. Each part of the site was studied as an ecological patch, with different wild plants and needing different remediation strategies, and then bound together by paths using old industrial structures at many levels. (Plan © Latz + Partner)

Peter Latz + Partner, Duisburg-Nord Landscape Park, Germany, ore bunker park, 1991 (completed 2002)
Latz designed a series of 'playgrounds' for children and adults using the three-dimensional potential of the abandoned industrial structures. A high, central plaza occupied the old blast furnace ruins, climbing walls for adults and slides for children scaled the old ore bunker walls, while skateboarders also found huge sloped surfaces for their enjoyment. (Photo © Harf Zimmermann for *The New York Times*)

Urban designers in Medellín, Colombia used a similar three-dimensional approach in tackling the problem of the isolated *barrios* in the 2000s. Medellín had developed as an enormous, self-built, dispersed Latin American city in the 1950s and 1960s, despite having a master plan for its expansion drawn up in the early 1950s by American planners Paul Wiener and architect José Luis Sert (Gropius's successor as Dean at Harvard University's architecture school).[13] Sert worked with Le Corbusier on the plan for Bogotá.[14] Like many Latin American cities in the age of oil, Medellín expanded along the valley floor, with poorer *barrios* perched on the inaccessible mountainsides as in Caracas, Venezuela (see chapter 6). While Medellín had an economic base in coffee production and industrial base in textile mills in the 1950s and 1960s, the narcotics traffic of the 1970s and 1980s brought wealth and violence culminating in the killing of the drug lord Pablo Escobar in 1993. The election of Alvaro Uribe as president of Colombia in 2002, followed by Sergio Fajardo's election as Mayor of Medellín, brought a drop in crime and increase in the budget for the city, allowing Fajardo to attempt to knit the city back together again.

Medellín's high-altitude location at 1,500 metres (5,000 feet) in the Andes and the steep valley side made a three-dimensional solution to the isolation of many self-built *barrios* essential. A railway system already existed on the valley floor, and after the police and military action Fajardo acted quickly to bring social programmes, gun amnesty programmes, microcredit banking systems and new transportation systems into the poorest *barrios* in 2002.[15] Following the example of Curitiba, Brazil, but in three dimensions, Fajardo built ski-lift-based skytrains up into the *barrios*, beginning with Metrocable Line K in 2004 from Acevedo station to Santo Domingo Savio. At the high-altitude terminal, Fajardo constructed new public terraces with a library and schools, following the social programmes initiated in the *barrios* along with the introduction of the Transmilenio bus system in Bogotá, Colombia in 2000 (see chapter 1).[16]

Map of Metro and Metrocable lines, Medellín, Colombia, c 2009

Acevedo is a valley station on the north–south railway line, with the Skytrain spur shown going up the mountainside to the east (shown on the upper left of this map). The red circle at the end of the Skytrain indicates the location of the Santo Domingo Savio *barrio*, with green indicating new parks created in the valley, purple indicating the new public terrace and plaza, and yellow the public library and school. (Map © EDU Empresa de Desarrollo Urbano)

Skytrain and public plaza beneath Metrocable Line K, Santo Domingo Savio, Medellín, Colombia, 2004
The Metrocable ends in an elaborate public plaza with several levels of public terraces, surrounded by small stores and the old *barrio*. Here the Metrocable passes over the schoolyard terrace of one of the new schools, before dropping down to Acevedo. (Image © EDU Empresa de Desarrollo Urbano)

Park beneath Skytrain Metrocable Line K, Santo Domingo Savio, Medellín, Colombia, 2004
The government built new housing for those displaced by the Metrocable pylons and new plazas. This housing framed the valleys and steep run-off stream courses, creating new parks for the *barrio* inhabitants. (Image © EDU Empresa de Desarrollo Urbano)

In Asia there was a long tradition of mixing the city and the countryside, creating cities that were distributed over a large area, including water supplies, irrigation systems and food production. This *desa-kota* system underpinned the ancient Asian empires that dominated the world economy before the rise of Europe and America in the last two centuries. During the 1990s, the UN-HABITAT sponsored an exemplary 10-year urban design research and planning collaboration between Hanoi University, local municipalities and the Human Settlements Program (ASRO) at Leuven University, Belgium that worked to support this ancient system.

The UN team chose to study Vinh, a town that had been destroyed several times in the last 60 years during the Indochina Wars of Independence, first by the Vietnamese themselves, then by American bombing.[17] The river delta contained an intensively farmed area of fishpond and rice paddies, in an ecology of great natural beauty. The Vietnamese had built a European-style fort at Vinh to defend the river estuary from foreigners in the 1800s. The French colonial regime of the late 1860s had developed a modern grid town around the fort, a beach community on the shore, a plantation system for agricultural exports and an industrial sector producing raw materials with a railway. In the late 1940s Vietnamese resistance to the French colonial regime reduced the city to an empty shell and it only came to life again after the Geneva Accords of 1954 placed it on the southern border of North Vietnam. American forces bombed the reconstructed city in the 1960s as it was the gateway to Vietnamese forces inside South Vietnam. During this period, Vinh was paired by Soviet and Chinese allies with East Berlin, another war-ravaged city. East German and Soviet planners reconstructed the city on socialist realist lines using standardised microraion neighbourhood units and Khrushchev era concrete panel construction slab blocks along the rebuilt highway.

The 10-year UN-HABITAT programme contained three phases: one of research preparation, one of intense on-the-ground project design, and then a follow-up phase advising local authorities. Because of the high water table in the delta area and many lakes, public sanitation arrangements and sewage disposal remained a continuing theme in all phases. The team devoted a huge effort to reconditioning the big Soviet housing estate built beside National Highway 1 to the west of the city, as well as reconnecting the East German central market building to the river's edge right at the city centre. The overall plan proposed to capitalise on the water-based economy of the delta, with more fish farms and rice cultivation and to use water transport systems to link the network together again. Rebuilt roads would connect the widely dispersed urban nodes of the Soviet plan: the airport, beach resorts, railway station, university and industrial districts in a network around the Soviet micraion and central market. This widespread, layered water-and-land network can be seen most clearly in the proposal for the three-dimensional pubic space on the Lam river waterfront in central Vinh. Here, housing and office blocks on pilotis stretch out into the river, forming inlets on the terraces below that shelter a riverside market and quays, some of which are temporary installations subject to seasonal flooding in the monsoon period.

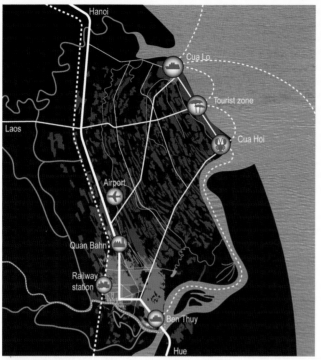

UN-HABITAT, Hanoi University and ASRO team, University of Leuven, Belgium, proposal for Vinh River City Vision, Vietnam, 2000
Vinh was destroyed in the two Indochina Wars of Independence and rebuilt using Soviet models of microraion housing estates, large factories and a central food market. The city sits in a productive river delta with many ponds and lakes that inspired the more widely distributed, 'green' Vinh River City Plan. (Drawing © KU Leuven, Dept ASRO)

UN-HABITAT, Hanoi University and ASRO team, University of Leuven, Belgium, proposal for Vinh, Lam Waterfront Project, Vietnam, 2000
The proposed terraced waterfront development allows for monsoon flooding, while still accommodating market and riverboat transfers.
The raising of the new waterfront development on pilotis protects from flooding while creating a three-dimensional urban space. (Image © KU Leuven, Dept ASRO)

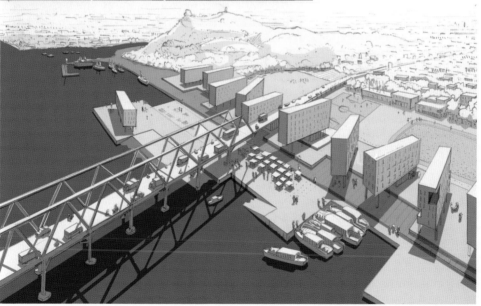

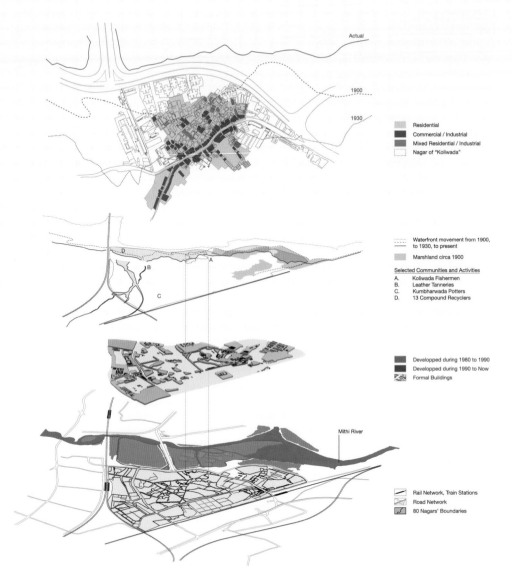

Legend labels within image:

Actual
1900
1930

Residential
Commercial / Industrial
Mixed Residential / Industrial
Nagar of "Koliwada"

Waterfront movement from 1900,
to 1930, to present
Marshland circa 1900

Selected Communities and Activities
A.   Koliwada Fishermen
B.   Leather Tanneries
C.   Kumbharwada Potters
D.   13 Compound Recyclers

Developped during 1980 to 1990
Developped during 1990 to Now
Formal Buildings

Mithi River

Rail Network, Train Stations
Road Network
80 Nagars' Boundaries

Wahid Seraj, layered map of Dharavi, Mumbai, India, 2009
Dharavi began as a series of villages in mudflats on the edge of Mumbai, including the fishermen's village
of Koliwada, effected by the shifting waterfront (top two layers). Leather tanneries, pottery workshops and
recycling compounds sprang up in another series of villages in the 1980s and 1990s (shown in the second
layer up), resulting in the expansion of Dharavi into the present network of 80 'nagars' (microneighbourhoods)
(bottom layer). (Map © David Grahame Shane and Wahid Seraj (www.Dharavi.org))

In the early 2000s, Dharavi came to represent the dark side of the Asian megacity, just like the now-demolished Walled City of Kowloon, Hong Kong in the 1990s. Like that compact three-dimensional enclave, Dharavi's density, lack of water and sanitation threatened lives, but also like the Walled City the network of self-organisation and resilience of the poor inhabitants inspired admiration. The UN described Dharavi as the world's largest slum, with over 1 million people in 2003, and Mike Davis christened it a terrifying 'megaslum' in his *Planet of Slums* (2006).[18] Two years later, Dharavi became famous in Danny Boyle's spirited, hit movie *Slumdog Millionaire* (2008) which did not fail to show the poverty, poor sanitation, inter-faith rivalries and terrible housing conditions as it delivered its message of hope. Inspired by a young man's success in a television quiz show, the movie spotlighted the role of mass media as a place of communal fantasy and way out of the slums in the metacity.

In Dharavi there are a myriad of NGO's and community organisations, like Dharavi.org, that advocate for the inhabitants, organising micro-banking schemes and self-help education.[19] It was no accident that SDI (Shack/Slum Dwellers International), highlighted by David Sattherthwaite at HABITAT III in 2006, began in Mumbai (see chapter 9). The municipality and Indian state have constructed small, single-function, segregated housing estates (chawls) and high-rise apartment blocks beside the main village centres, as slum upgrade schemes. One developer, Mukesh Mehta, wants to 'upgrade' the entire area in his Dharavi Redevelopment Project (2008), as it now lies next to Mumbai's latest corporate business centre, the Bandra-Kurla Complex (started 1977). Dharavi NGOs have proved adept at presenting their case in the global metacity media, and the BBC and the American *National Geographic* magazine have both presented the 'megaslum' in a sympathetic light, as a hive of industry and individual ambition.[20]

Dharavi streets, Mumbai, India (photos 2009)
Dharavi contains village enclaves with highly varied activities, ranging from the market garden by the railway (top right) to the fishermen's market in Koliwada (bottom left), and the pottery workshops, showing ware drying in the sun (top left and centre). The busy recycling compounds (bottom centre and right) confirm the worst fears of Dharavi as a polluted 'megaslum'. (Top three and bottom left photos © courtesy of www.Dharavi.org; bottom centre and right photos © Brian McGrath)

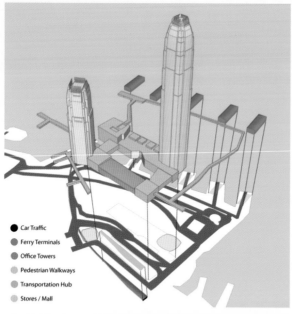

- ● Car Traffic
- ● Ferry Terminals
- ● Office Towers
- ● Pedestrian Walkways
- ● Transportation Hub
- ● Stores / Mall

Uri Wegman, analytic axonometric of Pelli, Clarke, Pelli's International Finance Centre 2, Hong Kong, 2003
The IFC2 tower connects into a meganode consisting of shopping malls, skywalks and an underground transportation hub, linking to the subway system with express rail connection to the new airport. The IFC mall also connects to the new ferry terminals on the waterfront, the Four Seasons Hotel tower and the Mid-Levels (see chapter 11). (Diagram © Uri Wegman)

Planning Department of the Government of Hong Kong Special Administrative Region, design option proposed in the Urban Design Study for New Central Harbourfront, 2008
This photomontage represents one of the several possible urban designs proposed for the public park on the harbourfront around the new Hong Kong Government Centre. The photomontages appeared on billboards and hoardings in the city, as well as in the press and media, as part of the Stage 2 Public Engagement Exercise, evoking an intense public debate in 2008–9. (Designs © Planning Department of the Government of the Hong Kong Special Administrative Region)

MEGANODES: PELLI CLARKE PELLI, IFC2 TOWER, HONG KONG, 2003 AND TRANSBAY TRANSIT CENTER AND TOWER, SAN FRANCISCO, USA, 2007

The 1990s and early 2000s meganodes developed an older morphology of planned transportation hubs, such as Hötorgscity in Stockholm from 1952 (see chapter 4), layering underground rail transportation, bypass roads and car parks, bus stations and shopping levels with office towers above. Hötorgscity also linked by rail to the two Stockholm new towns and suburbs on surrounding islands, forming the key node in the network. The Hong Kong government during the early 1980s developed the Swedish model of new towns connected by public transportation networks, but at far higher densities and with a tower morphology for the housing estates. Shopping malls formed the base of the housing towers at the centre of the new towns, connected by skybridges into a complex, three-dimensional matrix. Bus stations and subway stops were incorporated into these mall structures, creating a new hybrid that was also applied to Central at the heart of Hong Kong.[21]

Caesar Pelli developed this model further, and at a far higher density, in his design for the World Financial Center in 1985, the commercial centre located at the heart of Battery Park City, New York, beside the World Trade Center site. Battery Park City and the WFC were isolated from public transportation networks and the city, like Canary Wharf in London, UK. After the bankruptcy of the developers of Canary Wharf, designers realised that large urban fragments could not be left isolated and needed connection to the host city's infrastructural networks. The Terry Farrell Partnership, for instance, designed the Kowloon Station Complex (1992–8) that was eventually built to include the Elements Mall (2008) with a circle of office and residential towers above (see chapter 11, p 231).[22]

Pelli went on to design several meganodes that connected into the urban transportation networks, fusing mall and subway into a new hybrid, following a pattern first developed in Hong Kong new towns. In Hong Kong, Pelli built the International Finance Centre 2 tower (IFC2, 2003) above an elaborate transport exchange and mall that connected both to the subway and to the new high-speed rail to the airport.[23] Renzo Piano competed against Pelli for the design of the San Francisco Transbay Transit Center and Tower (2007), where Pelli won using some elements from the IFC2 project, again setting the tower to one side from the hub (see next page).[24] Piano proposed the same three-dimensional matrix morphology of layered tower, mall and transport hub in his 2000 Shard tower design above the London Bridge railway station (see chapter 8).[25]

Pelli Clarke Pelli, Transbay Transit Center and Tower, San Francisco, USA, 2007
Like the IFC2 tower in Hong Kong, the proposed tower in San Francisco will connect into a transit hub for the local BART (Bay Area Rapid Transit) subway system and the regional commuter lines, with a local bus station above. Because of earthquake concerns, the tower stands to one side of the terminal and much of the glass-skinned project is above ground level, with a rooftop public garden connecting to street level on the adjacent hillside. (Image © Transbay Joint Powers Authority)

Pelli Clarke Pelli, Transbay Transit Center and Tower, San Francisco, USA, 2007
Layered section showing underground mezzanine leading to tracks for local subway and suburban lines, with provision for the proposed high-speed rail link to Los Angeles. Above the street-level mall, a two-storey bus terminal serves local and long-distance lines. (Drawing © Transbay Joint Powers Authority)

Pelli Clarke Pelli, Transbay Transit Center and Tower, San Francisco, USA, 2007
The view from Mission Square. (Image © Transbay Joint Powers Authority)

Asian megacities already operate using a small fraction of the energy per person compared to North American or European cities. They operate as widely distributed systems mixing urban functions with food production, as in the case of Vinh, Vietnam, with distinct higher-density nodes and interchanges (as in the case of Hong Kong and the Pearl River delta). The megablock system is able to accommodate the *desa-kota* urban village system or a meganode, sometimes both at once as in Bangkok (see p 302).

Faced with this widely distributed, low-energy-consumption, urban model with dense nodes and widespread, semi-rural megablocks, urban designers from the northern hemisphere have been hard pressed to adapt elements from the old imperial system. As part of the original plan for the Shanghai Expo 2010, Arup's 2005 design for the Dongtan 'Eco-City' new town outside of Shanghai, for instance, attempted to merge the Asian city agricultural pattern with the Northern European consensus of the eco-city ideal, as developed in Germany.[26] The result was a town spread amongst lakes, ponds and canals surrounded by streets, forming megablocks containing three neighbourhood units or urban 'villages' and a town centre. These villages represented Northern European preferences for three- and four-storey apartment buildings that raised the density up from the low-rise Milton Keynes megablocks, but would be much lower than Shenzhen at its densest urban village configuration.

Wetlands for migratory birds surround the new town, which is also used for fish farming and rice cultivation. A huge bridge was planned to reach the remote island on the periphery of Shanghai, in the Yangtze delta, all of which would be flooded if the icecaps melt and the extreme 3-metre (10-foot) sea rise takes place as predicted in the worst-case scenarios. It was hoped that Dongtan would provide a prototype for the development of other new towns in China, but its lack of density, remote accessibility and special island conditions made it an unlikely model for the many other Chinese municipalities needing to fast-track development.[27] Instant high-rise megablocks and malls were far more attractive and possibly just as effective ecologically, keeping the city more compact.[28]

Urban agriculture has a long history in Asian cities and its successful survival can be an inspiration to the high-tech designers of the shrinking cities of the northern hemisphere. Many low-tech solutions were proposed in shrinking northern cities for 'green thumb' gardens in abandoned lots (New York, 1970s) or 'street farming' (London, 1970s).[29] The 'Green Revolution' of the 1970s transformed Asian agriculture, introducing petrochemical-based fertilisers and increasing plot yields, while small tractors and gas-powered hand-held machines, like rototillers and weed-trimmers, increased productivity.[30] Enormous global agribusiness corporations also grew in the 1980s and 1990s to take advantage of the cheap global transportation networks and differentials in the cost of labour in different countries. Urban agriculture began to take on some of these high-tech features, growing tomatoes indoors in old warehouses, for instance, in hydroponic systems using artificial light. Urban marijuana growers especially liked this hidden cultivation system that needed no sunlight. Dickson Despommier's 'Vertical Farm' proposal (2007) pushes this logic to an automated, high-tech extreme, proposing an eco-skyscraper to grow food inside the city as a scientific endeavour in the face of the Bangkok banana plantations, Indonesian rice paddies or Shanghai fish farms.[31] This New York skyscraper proposal faces stiff competition from the many small organic farms in New Jersey or further north up the Hudson Valley, selling in New York at sidewalk farmers' markets.[32]

UN-HABITAT, Hanoi University and ASRO team, University of Leuven, Belgium, photocollage by Kelly Shannon, Vinh, Vietnam, 2000
Like many Asian cities, Vinh is a delta city, incorporating water-based agricultural systems of great antiquity and productivity, alongside modern, land-based transportation systems based on cars, trucks and oil. This hybrid Asian *desa-kota* (city-country) system uses a small fraction of the energy consumption per capita compared to European or American systems (for ASRO design see p 293). (Photos © KU Leuven, Dept ASRO)

Dickson Despommier, Vertical Farm, 2007
This variant of the three-dimensional, layered, high-density node proposes to grow food in cities using known hydroponic and other indoor cultivation methods. High-tech informational systems would monitor every plant in order to minimise energy use, but critics argue the 24-hour lighting and heating systems make for a negative ecological impact. (Image © Christopher Jacobs)

Arup, perspective of the South Canal with turbines, Dongtan, Shanghai, China, 2005
Arup's original new-town proposal severely restricted the use of the automobile and grouped three neighbourhood 'village' housing units around the town centre inside a green belt, all connected together by canals. The project, currently delayed, lies on an isolated island in the Yangtze estuary, in an ecologically sensitive area used in the annual flight path of millions of migratory birds. (Drawing © Arup)

Bangkok emerged as a megacity in the early 2000s but had a long agricultural and urban tradition based on canals and irrigation.[33] Bangkok was founded in the 1780s after the fall of the older Ayutthaya Kingdom further north that had begun to cultivate the delta of the Chao Phraya river with fruit in orchards on the west bank and rice paddies and fish ponds on the east bank. The early kings diverted the Chao Phraya river, digging canals and creating a cosmological city based in part on the Buddhist and Hindu models represented by Angkor Wat in Cambodia and the Forbidden City in Beijing. The distinctive feature of the metropolitan design of Bangkok was the location of the central temples and palaces on an island right beside the flow of the river, not at a distance off to one side as at Angkor Wat, Cambodia or in Beijing, China. Thai hydraulic engineers were comfortable controlling the river or building houses on stilts that contained upper levels safe from the monsoon run-off.

The Thai royal family and temples occupied the central island of the city, while merchants and markets were on the surrounding canals to the east. The royal family also engaged in trade, especially with China, while they allied with Islamic merchants to develop links to the Middle East. In the 1800s through a complex and shifting alliance with the British in India, the royal family was able to skillfully remain independent as a buffer state on the edge of the expanding French Empire in Indochina (see Vinh, p 292). Despite their long history of canal building and irrigation, the royal family also sent a team in the late 1800s to examine the modern canal system of the Dutch East India Company's oriental base in Jakarta, Indonesia.[34] Like Amsterdam, the Company's European headquarters, the western half of Bangkok remained in agricultural production during the second half of the 20th century, creating an urban agriculture because of the difficulty of access and river currents. Here, traces of an earlier civilisation survive with houses on stilts above the water level, travelling post offices and stores on boats, with rivers and canals that are clean enough to grow food.

The temple and palace enclaves at the centre of the city have become global tourist attractions in the metacity, marking its symbolic core. The Chao Phraya river links from there to the megahotels for the tourists on the riverbanks. Parts of the old canal system still survive as a ring around the central city, with several cuts through the centre, acting as both drainage system and transportation system, as at the Bobae Market intersection. The canal systems are almost invisible at the city centre and to the east (replaced by pumps and pipes). French urban design and Parisian boulevards influenced the royal extensions of the city in the 1920s and 1930s to the north and east, while American grid planning arrived in the 1960s. Remnants of the earlier agricultural patterning survive in the layout of the Bangkok megablocks and on the periphery in the east, where fishponds and rice paddies once predominated. Within the megablocks, *soi* lanes follow earlier irrigation ditches and land subdivisions, creating cul-de-sacs within the block. The location of skyscraper towers on *soi* lanes creates extreme juxtapositions, such as at the Baiyoke Tower 1 where the small-scale Pratunam fabric market makes a jarring contrast with what was the tallest tower in Bangkok.[35]

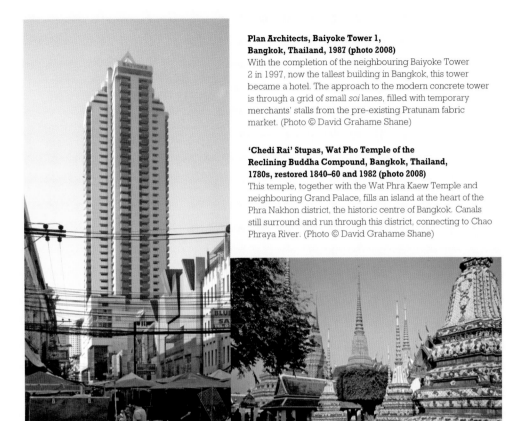

**Plan Architects, Baiyoke Tower 1,
Bangkok, Thailand, 1987 (photo 2008)**
With the completion of the neighbouring Baiyoke Tower
2 in 1997, now the tallest building in Bangkok, this tower
became a hotel. The approach to the modern concrete tower
is through a grid of small *soi* lanes, filled with temporary
merchants' stalls from the pre-existing Pratunam fabric
market. (Photo © David Grahame Shane)

**'Chedi Rai' Stupas, Wat Pho Temple of the
Reclining Buddha Compound, Bangkok, Thailand,
1780s, restored 1840–60 and 1982 (photo 2008)**
This temple, together with the Wat Phra Kaew Temple and
neighbouring Grand Palace, fills an island at the heart of the
Phra Nakhon district, the historic centre of Bangkok. Canals
still surround and run through this district, connecting to Chao
Phraya River. (Photo © David Grahame Shane)

**Bobae Market at the junction of Khlong Phadung Krung Kasam,
Khlong Mahanak and Saen Saep canals, central Bangkok, Thailand (photo 2008)**
A speeding Chao Praya Express canal ferry passes by the towers of the mosque located in the market
at the canal intersection. This ancient market spans four islands at the back of the historic core, filling
the bridges, while the canalside trees provide shade and relief. (Photos © David Grahame Shane)

The Khet Pathum Wan (Lotus Forest Temple) shopping district east of the historic core of downtown Bangkok was named after a temple and royal palace with lily and fish ponds beside the Saen Saep canal. The area also contained rice paddies. The royal family owned the land and laid out a grid of dykes and boulevards, including Rama 1 Road, giving land to the Chulalongkorn University, Military and Police colleges and the Royal Sports Club. During the 1960s the university and crown decided to develop the land along Rama 1 Road, and Siam Square opened as an open-air, drive-through mall with several cinemas in 1965 (serving American soldiers on R & R from Vietnam). This mall was later pedestrianised and houses many language and preparatory schools because of its location close to the university and youth-oriented shopping. The fully enclosed, air-conditioned, American-style, triple-donut mall, the Siam Centre, opened on Rama 1 Road in 1973. The atria of this mall contained Bangkok's first escalators and again it was car-based, aimed at American servicemen and tourists. Tourist hotels developed around this mall, which expanded several times, but was eclipsed in size by the 300-metre-long (1,000-foot) MBK Center dumbbell mall of 1985 next door, at the Pathumwan street intersection.[36] The 89,000-square-metre (1 million-square-foot) mall was the largest megamall in Southeast Asia at that time, until the completion of the rival World Trade Center megamall, hotel and office complex in 1990 at the Ratchaprasong boulevard intersection further east.[37]

In anticipation of the completion of the Skytrain system in 1999, the Siam Discovery Center upscale mall opened beside the Siam Center in 1997, followed by the demolition of the Siam Intercontinental Hotel (2002) at the intersection of Ratchaprasong boulevard, where a Skytrain station connected into the new Siam Paragon mall (2005).[38] The design of Siam Paragon opens out to the street and skytrain, creating a new plaza beside Rama 1 Road. Steps up the Rama 1 facade lead to an elevated plaza connecting to the earlier Siam Discovery Center next door, creating a new megamall complex. The owners of the World Trade Center mall responded to the Skytrain by remodelling their megamall in 2003–6, renaming it the Central World Plaza, doubling it in size with a new hotel tower added later.[39] The open-air Central World Plaza created on Ratchaprasong boulevard became the local version of New York's Times Square with New Year celebrations, connecting at the northern end to the Saen Saep canal ferry stop (the mall was damaged by fire in the aftermath of the civil unrest in Bangkok with the Red Shirts in 2010, and parts may have to be demolished).

The incremental nature and urban evolution of Rama 1 Road and its malls provides a fascinating example of the fragmented metropolis system transforming into a networked urban ecology, tying the fragments together. In part this was due to the Chulalongkorn University and the royal family owning much of the land, partly to the mall developers cooperating with each other, and partly to the arrival of the Skytrain, making the malls turn inside out to welcome the new patrons. The Khet Pathum Wan district replaced downtown as the major commercial and shopping centre of Bangkok within 40 years, coinciding with the massive expansion of the city into an Asian megacity of 11 million.

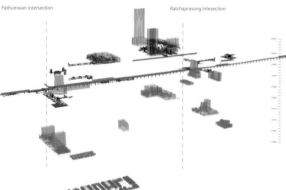

Brian McGrath and Mark Isarangkun, timeline axonometric and street section of malls on Rama 1 Road, Bangkok, Thailand, 2007
During the Vietnam War, the first drive-in shopping centre, Siam Square, opened in 1965 and the enclosed, air-conditioned Siam Center in 1973, with MBK Center following in 1985. Siam Discovery (1997) and Siam Paragon (2005) together created a megamall to rival the World Financial Center/Central World megamall (1990, 2004). (Drawing © Brian McGrath)

Altoon + Porter Architects, Central World Plaza interior, Bangkok, Thailand, 2006 (photo 2008)
The complex, three-dimensional interior organisation of the mall includes a long axial approach to a lozenge-shaped vertical atrium that leads up to a food court and upper-level cinemas. Balconies from the high-level restaurants look down on the exterior Times Square space, while the towers above contain offices and a hotel. (Photo © David Grahame Shane)

Altoon + Porter Architects, Central World Plaza and Spanish Steps, Bangkok, Thailand, 2006 (photos 2008)
After the opening of the Skytrain in 1999, many malls that had been oriented to interior, air-conditioned atria turned to the exterior. The former World Trade Center mall turned itself inside out as the Central World Plaza, creating steps to a high-level plaza and a large public space at ground level that functions as Bangkok's Times Square on New Year's Eve. (Photos © David Grahame Shane)

Bangkok grew from its original foundation, where cosmic diagrams and practical requirements created a palace–temple city surrounded by small canals, making island blocks for traders. While the west bank of the river remained largely agricultural for a long period, the east bank behind the palace–temple island expanded across the rice paddies and fish ponds, remaining true to the dykes and field boundaries. As the chief landowner, the royal family was able to control much of this early expansion into the 1960s, when a new commercial centre began to emerge along Rama 1 Road east of the old downtown.[40] Modern pumps and pipes replaced the old canals and dykes for drainage, allowing the land to be developed for commercial and educational purposes. Old palaces and monasteries remained interspersed amongst the malls, megamalls, colleges and universities.

These megamalls collectively form a meganode comparable to Shinjuku in Tokyo, Japan (see chapter 6), developed in part because of global tourism networks, but also because of local needs in the fast-growing megacity. Further east, beyond the Rama 1 meganode, Bangkok continues to grow out towards the new Suvarnabhumi International Airport, which will be connected to the Skytrain leading in to Khet Pathum Wan new commercial district and shopping centre.[41] Here earlier rice paddies and fish farms are scattered alongside the Saen Saep canal, along with new suburban developments and amongst the agricultural areas are self-built housing, small factories and office parks. Bangkok has one of the most successful outreach programmes empowering self-built housing areas to upgrade their services and public facilities.[42]

The city is also a member of the Large Cities Climate Leadership Group (known as C40) that signed an agreement with the Clinton Foundation in 2006 to join in the Clinton Climate Initiative in planning the reduction of its greenhouse gas emissions and carbon footprint.[43] Already taxis and some motorbikes run on less polluting compressed gas or electricity and there are plans to upgrade the heavily polluting and aged bus fleet. Besides taxis, small motor vehicles, tuk-tuks and motorbike taxis supplement the Skytrains, buses and subway, giving access deep inside the megablocks along the old *soi* lanes. The result is a *desa-kota*-like mix of uses within the megablocks on the periphery and even in the dense Rama 1 megamall area that retains old lily- and fishponds inside temple or royal palace grounds.

Asis Ammarapala, Uri Wegman and David Grahame Shane, layered drawing of Bangkok, Thailand, 2009
The west bank of the Chao Phraya river still remains relatively undeveloped, retaining its canal system for agriculture, transportation and drainage, within the new ring road. On the east bank the old central island and surrounding merchant areas of canals have been replaced by the new commercial and office districts around the malls of the Khet Pathum Wan district that connects via the Skytrain, subways and highways to the later peripheral extensions of the megacity towards the airports. (Drawing © David Grahame Shane and Asis Ammarapala)

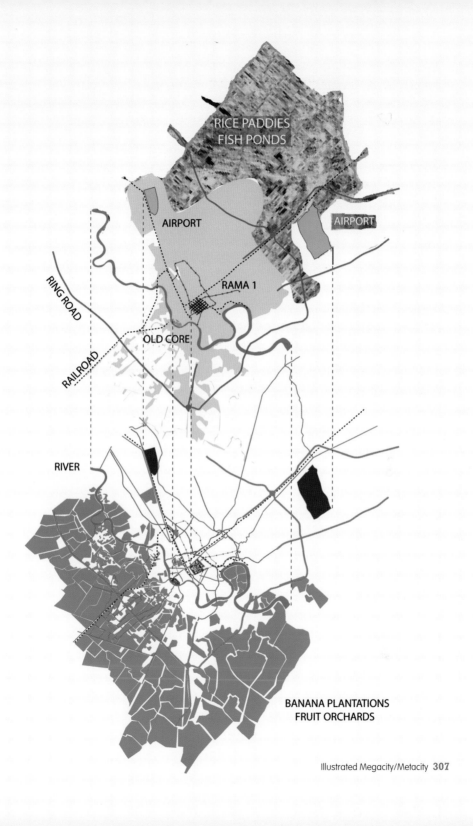

RICE PADDIES
FISH PONDS

AIRPORT

AIRPORT

RING ROAD

RAMA 1

RAILROAD

OLD CORE

RIVER

BANANA PLANTATIONS
FRUIT ORCHARDS

Conclusion: megacities/metacites, networks and nodes

The metacity/megacity with its widely distributed urban networks, personalised mass communications and media coverage provides the background for the emergence of meganodes and megablocks as new attractors at both a local and a global scale. These nodes differ from previous urban fragments in their complex urban sections with new, layered public spaces and their openness to surrounding urban networks and energy flows. Where urban designers had sought to isolate malls in the megalopolis and fragmented metropolis, in Bangkok, and elsewhere in megacities, malls turned themselves inside out to face new public open spaces. These spaces (though often privately owned) connected to public transportation networks and media systems as never before.

Because the megacity/metacity is in part an informational construct and navigation is available through hand-held microdevices, the metacity allows new hybrid, three-dimensional combinations of public space from all other systems, as demonstrated in the meganode complexes of Bangkok and the megacasinos of Las Vegas or Macao (see chapter 9). While the megamalls were often separated from residential developments, in Hong Kong, Las Vegas or Macao they might also provide a model for a multi-use residential future based on a mixed-use, three-dimensional matrix in a base or podium. While the casino cities masked their novelty in historic images of the city, Steven Holl's Linked Hybrid in Beijing showed that such three-dimensional urban imagery could be more subtle, referring indirectly to the lily ponds and rice paddies that once filled the site (see chapter 9).

These high-profile meganodes and megablocks depend on widely dispersed, background urban networks that are almost invisible. The networks consist of service systems and structures that can cover vast areas of city territory, moving with the land, to provide access and support. Cell towers, satellites in the night sky, or common utility poles do not attract attention, nor are cable ducts, canals, drainage ditches, transformer stations or tree plantings normally seen as part of the architecture of the city. The absence of these hidden networks in self-built city extensions like Dharavi remains one of the most difficult problems faced by urban designers and local NGOs alike. The invisible presence or absence of such hidden networks impacts public health, raising issues in stark contrast to the spectacular architecture of a meganode with its megamalls, megablocks, hybrid towers and symbolic skyline.

Urban designers in the megacity have struggled to find a mode of operation that can stretch from mega- to microcode in this complex urban situation with bottom-up and top-down actors. Designers have concentrated on mapping the changing city through layering techniques first developed in landscape architecture and ecology (see chapter 9). After *Collage City* (1978), Deconstructivist architects internalised these layering techniques, opening up the sectional development of architectural and urban design up to new energy flows and informational networks.[44] This development allowed the creation of a new three-dimensional public space, whether in a shrinking city like New York's High Line Park, Duisburg-Nord's Landscape Park, the proposal for the Lam river waterfront in Vietnam or built beneath Medellín's Metrocable.The flexibility of the megacity layer system allows designers to work at multiple scales and in very different locations. It is like a sponge in its ability to absorb, overlay and interact with previous systems. In part, this flexibility stems from its openness as a system, accommodating multiple urban actors in separate layers; in part, it results from the informational nature of the metacity that can link many different actors in different systems and allow people to coordinate with each other in different networks from the bottom up. In addition, the metacity designer can work with the concentrated urban form of the metropolis, the dispersed form of the megalopolis, or with the large urban enclaves of the fragmented metropolis.

Notes

NB: See 'Author's Caution: Endnote Sources and Wikipedia', towards the end of this book.

1   Joel Garreau, *Edge City: Life on the New Frontier*, Anchor Books (New York), 1992, pp i–xix.

2   John A Dutton, *The New American Urbanism: Re-Forming the Suburban Metropolis*, Skira (Milan), 2000; Andrés Duany, Elizabeth Plater-Zyberk and Jeff Speck, *Suburban Nation; The Rise of Sprawl and Decline of the American Dream*, North Point Press (New York), 2001.

3   Albert Pope, *Ladders*, Princeton Architectural Press (New York), 1997; Mario Gandelsonas, *X-Urbanism: Architecture and the American City*, Princeton Architectural Press (New York), 1999.

4   On *Eurolandschaft*, see: Fernando Marquez Cecilia and Richard C Levene, *Architekturbüro Bolles-Wilson, 1995–2001: The Scale of the Eurolandschaft = la scala del europaisaje, El Croquis* (Madrid), vol 105, c 2001.

5   Philipp Oswalt and Tim Reiniets, *The Atlas of Shrinking Cities*, Hatje Cantz (Ostfildern), 2006.

6   For Dessau, see: Station C23 website, http://www.stationc23.de/PROJEKT/teilprojekt-076-iba-stadtumbau-dessau.html (accessed 2 April 2010); also: Sigrun Langner, '2010: The Dessau Landschaftszug – a landscape belt on demolished wasteland by process-oriented design', in N Meijsmans (ed), *2010: Designing for a Region*, SUN architecture (Amsterdam), pp 144–51.

7   Xaveer De Geyter, *After-Sprawl: Research for the Contemporary City*, NAi (Rotterdam) and Kunstcentrum deSingel (Antwerp), 2002 (available on Google Books).

8   On Coop Himmelb(l)au's Melun-Sénart competition design, see: Coop Himmelb(l)au website, http://www.coop-himmelblau.at/ (accessed 22 March 2010).

9   On Asymptote Architecture's gateway competition, see: Asymptote website, http://www.asymptote.net/buildings/steel-cloud-los-angeles-west-coast-gateway/ (accessed 22 March 2010).

10   On Peter Latz, see: Latz + Partner website, http://www.latzundpartner.de/ (accessed 22 March 2010).

11   On Parc de la Villette, see: Bernard Tschumi Architects website, http://tschumi.com/projects/3/ (accessed 14 March 2010).

12   On Gas Works Park, Seattle, WA, see: http://en.wikipedia.org/wiki/Gas_Works_Park (accessed 2 April 2010).

13   On José Luis Sert's plan for Medellín see: Jaume Freixa, *Jose Luis Sert*, Gustavo Gili (Barcelona), 1979, pp 64, 239.

14   On Sert in Latin America, see: Eric Paul Mumford, 'From the Heart of the City to Holyoke Center: CIAM Ideas in Sert's Definition of Urban Design', in *Josep Luís Sert: The Architect of Urban Design, 1953–1969*, Yale University Press (New Haven), 2008.

15   On Sergio Fajardo, see: Daniel Kurtz-Phelan, 'The Mathematician of Medellín', *Newsweek*, 11 November 2007, http://www.newsweek.com/id/69623 (accessed 22 March 2010).

16   For the regeneration of Medellín, see: Jimena Martignoni, 'How Medellín Got Its Groove Back', *Architectural Record*, March 2009, http://archrecord.construction.com/features/critique/0903medellin/medellin-1.asp (accessed 22 March 2010). On Medellín Metrocable, see: Malcolm Beith, 'Good Times In Medellín: a city tainted by violence is experiencing a

renaissance', *Newsweek*, 5 July 2004, http://www.newsweek.com/id/54298 (accessed 22 March 2010). On Bogotá's Transmilenio bus system, see: Transmilenio website, http://www.transmilenio.gov.co/WebSite/Default.aspx (accessed 22 March 2010).

17   For Vinh, see: Kelly Shannon and André Loeckx, 'Vinh – Rising from the Ashes', *Urban Trialogues: Visions, Projects, Co-Productions*, UN-HABITAT (Nairobi, Kenya), *c* 2004, pp 123–51, http://ww2.unhabitat.org/programmes/agenda21/urban_trialogues.asp (accessed 22 March 2010).

18   Mike Davis, *Planet of Slums*, Verso (London), 2006.

19   See: http://www.dharavi.org/ (accessed 2 April 2010).

20   For the diversity of Dharavi, see: 'Life in a Slum', BBC News website, http://news.bbc.co.uk/2/shared/spl/hi/world/06/dharavi_slum/html/dharavi_slum_intro.stm (accessed 2 April 2010); also: Mark Jacobson, 'Mumbai's Shadow City', *National Geographic*, May 2007, http://ngm.nationalgeographic.com/2007/05/dharavi-mumbai-slum/jacobson-text?fs=seabed.nationalgeographic.com (accessed 19 March 2010).

21   For Hong Kong New Town mall podium with housing, see: http://en.wikipedia.org/wiki/New_Town_Plaza_Phase_3 (accessed 15 March 2010). On Hong Kong urbanisation, see: DW Drakakis-Smith, *Pacific Asia*, Routledge (London; New York), pp 163–80.

22   On Terry Farrell & Partners' Kowloon Station project, see: Farrells website, http://www.terryfarrell.co.uk/#/project/0097/ (accessed 19 March 2010). On Elements Mall, see: Elements website, http://www.elementshk.com/eng/index_popup.php (accessed 2 April 2010).

23   On Pelli's IFC2, see: Emporis website, http://www.emporis.com/application/?nav=building&lng=3&id=100614 (accessed 19 March 2010). For Hong Kong waterfront plans and consultation process, see: 'Urban Design Study for the New Central Harbourfront', website of Leisure and Cultural Services Department, Government of the Hong Kong Special Administrative Region of the People's Republic of China, http://www.lcsd.gov.hk/CE/Museum/Monument//form/AAB_134_59attachment2-english.pdf; also: Harbour Business Forum website, http://www.harbourbusinessforum.com/page/file/35/show; also: Swire Properties website, http://www.swireproperties.com/CentralReclamation/english/waterfront/index.html (all accessed 15 July 2010). For Hong Kong NGO, see: http://en.wikipedia.org/wiki/Society_for_Protection_of_the_Harbour; http://en.wikipedia.org/wiki/Victoria_Harbour (accessed 19 March 2010).

24   On Pelli's Transbay Transit Center and Tower, San Francisco, see: http://transbaycenter.org/; also: Pelli Clarke Pelli Architects website, http://www.pcparch.com/ (accessed 19 March 2010).

25   For The Shard, London, see: The Shard website, http://www.shardlondonbridge.com/ (accessed 17 March 2010).

26   For Dongtan, see: Sara Hart, 'Zero-Carbon Cities', *Architectural Record*, March 2007, http://archrecord.construction.com/tech/techFeatures/0703feature-1.asp; also: Roger Wood/Arup, Dongtan Eco-City, Shanghai', presentation at PIA National Congress, Perth, Washington, 4 May 2007, http://www.arup.com/_assets/_download/8CFDEE1A-CC3E-EA1A-25FD80B2315B50FD.pdf (accessed 19 March 2010); also: 'Dongtan: the world's first large-scale eco-city?'. Sustainable Cities website, http://sustainablecities.dk/en/city-projects/cases/dongtan-the-world-s-first-large-scale-eco-city; also: http://en.wikipedia.org/wiki/Dongtan (accessed 19 March 2010).

27   On sea level rise, see: Sea Level Rise Explorer, Global Warming Art website, http://www.globalwarmingart.com/wiki/Special:SeaLevel (accessed 15 July 2010); also: United States Department of Commerce, National Oceanic and Atmospheric Administration (NOAA), Earth System Research Laboratory 'Science on a Sphere' website, http://sos.noaa.gov/datasets/Ocean/sea_level.html (accessed 19 March 2010). For China coast, see: CIESIN (Center for International Earth Science Information Network) map, http://www.unfpa.org/swp/2007/english/chapter_5/figure8.html (accessed 15 July 2010).

28   For critique of Dongtan, see: Martin Spring, ''Masdar: Nice spot for a zero-carbon city...'' *Building Sustainable Design*, issue 22, 2007, http://www.building.co.uk/masdar-nice-spot-for-a-zero-carbon-city/3088039.article (accessed 1 July 2010).

29   On green thumb gardens in New York City, see: Sarah Ferguson, 'A Brief History of Grassroots Greening in NYC', *New Village*, issue 1, September 1999, http://www.newvillage.net/Journal/Issue1/1briefgreening.html (accessed 19 March 2010). For street farming, see: *Street Farmer* magazine, Architectural Association School (London), 1971–2; also: *Mother Earth News*, no 20, March 1973 p 62; also: Stefan Szczelkun blog, http://www.stefan-szczelkun.org.uk/phd103.htm#_ftn2 (accessed 13 March 2010).

30   For the 'Green Revolution', see: http://en.wikipedia.org/wiki/Green_Revolution (accessed 13 March 2010).

31   For the Vertical Farm Project, see: Vertical Farm website, http://www.verticalfarm.com/ (accessed 13 March 2010).

32   On Slow Food in the Hudson Valley, see: Slow Food Hudson Valley website, http://www.slowfoodhv.org/ (accessed 19 March 2010).

33   For Bangkok, see: Brian McGrath, 'Bangkok: The Architecture of Three Ecologies', in Kanu Agrawal et al (eds), *Re_Urbanism: Transforming Capitals, Perspecta 39: The Yale Architectural Journal*, MIT Press (Cambridge, MA), 2007, pp 13–26; Brian McGrath, Danai Thaitakoo, 'Tasting the Periphery: Bangkok's agri and aqua-cultural fringe', in Karen A Franck (ed), *Food + The City, Architectural Design*, vol 75, issue 3, Wiley-Academy (London), 2005, pp 43–51.

34   On the Dutch East India Company, see: Els M Jacobs, *In Pursuit of Pepper and Tea: The Story of the Dutch East India Company*, Netherlands Maritime Museum (Amsterdam), 1991. On Thai agri-urbanism, see: McGrath, Thaitakoo, 'Tasting the Periphery' in *Architectural Design*, vol 75, issue 3, 2005, pp 43–51. On Dutch delta cities, see: Manfred Kuhn, 'Greenbelt and Green Heart: separating and integrating landscapes in European city regions', *Landscape and Urban Planning*, vol 64, issues 1–2, 15 June 2003, pp 19–27.

35   For *soi* lanes, see: Marc Askew, *Bangkok: Place, Practice and Representation*, Routledge (London; New York), 2002, p 12. For Bangkok *soi* as a red-light district, see: http://en.wikipedia.org/wiki/Soi_Cowboy; also: Erik Cohen, *Contemporary Tourism: Diversity and Change*, Elsevier Science (Amsterdam; Boston, MA), 2004 (available on Google Books).

36   On MBK Center, see: http://www.mbk-center.co.th/en/ (accessed 23 March 2010).

37   For a chronology of Bangkok malls, see: Brian McGrath, *Digital Modelling for Urban Design*, John Wiley & Sons (London), 2008, pp 226–45. For the shopping district, see: http://en.wikipedia.org/wiki/Pathum_Wan (accessed 23 March 2010).

38   On the BTS Skytrain, see: http://en.wikipedia.org/wiki/BTS_Skytrain (accessed 23 March 2010). On Siam Center, see: Siam Piwat Co website, http://www.siampiwat.com/php/index.php (accessed 23 March 2010).

39   On Central World Plaza, see: Central World website, http://www.centralworld.co.th/default-th.aspx (accessed 23 March 2010).

40   For the history of Bangkok and royal landownership, see: Askew, *Bangkok*, pp 17–47, and note 11, p 307 (available on Google Books).

41   For the new Suvarnabhumi International Airport, see: Murphy/Jahn website, http://www.murphyjahn.com/base.html (accessed 15 July 2010).

42   For Bangkok slum upgrading, see: Somsook Boonyabancha, 'Baan Mankong: going to scale with slum and squatter upgrading in Thailand', *Environment & Urbanization*, vol 17, no 1, April 2005, http://www.environmentandurbanization.org/eandu_recent.html#april2005 (accessed 2 April 2010).

43   On C40 cities, see: C40 website, http://www.c40cities.org/ (accessed 23 March 2010). For Bangkok ecology, see: UNEP, Bangkok Assessment Report on Climate Change, 2009, http://www.roap.unep.org/pub/BKK_assessment_report_CC_2009.pdf

44   Colin Rowe and Fred Koetter, *Collage City*, MIT Press (Cambridge, MA), 1978.

Urban Ecologies and Urban Design – Future Scenarios

In the last 60 years, the world's urban population has shifted from urban centres, largely in the compact European metropolises powered by coal, to dispersed Asian megacities that include agriculture and meganodes, largely powered by oil. This shift has involved the mass application of petroleum power and engineering to create the megalopolis that severely impacted the old imperial European system, opening the way for the two superpowers of the Cold War (the USA and USSR, 1945–91). The rapid success of the petroleum-powered megalopolis produced its own urban problems, in terms of the abandonment of the metropolis, its dependence on oil-rich supplier nations and the global impact of fossil-fuel dependence on climate change. With just over 50 per cent of the world's population in cities, urban design offers the potential to address some of these urgent questions. Urban designers in the future will have to reckon with this carbon economy, not so much in terms of reducing carbon footprints through ecological interventions, but through altering the shape of cities to ensure human survival on the planet. It is unrealistic to think that carbon emissions can be stopped tomorrow: greenhouse gases from 200 years of industrial production are already in the ecological feedback loop and will mean significant water level rises and desertification. It is also unreasonable to expect any one person or code to take command of such a vast and complex distributive system. Nobody is in control of this global system. Modernising the majority of the world's population in Asia and Africa, as they shift population from the agricultural workers in the countryside to cities, will involve further carbon inputs. This last chapter addresses how urban designers in the unknown future might adjust the existing urban design ecologies examined so far, to deal with this new situation.

Urban actors have created four urban design ecologies that employ enclaves, armatures and heterotopias as organisational and symbolic structures, representing the wishes and desires of dominant actors. In the long term it is becoming apparent that this petroleum- and coal-based carbon economy poses a threat to cities. Greenhouse gases heating the earth's environment mean that icecaps may melt, glaciers disappear on mountaintops, rains will be reduced, rivers run slower, deserts expand and sea levels rise.[1] The only question is the degree of seriousness of this problem: whether water will rise 50 centimetres, 1 metre or 1.5 metres in the next 100 years, causing millions of people to move and cities to change location. Many previous urban civilisations, like ancient Angkor Wat in Cambodia, have died because of water problems.[2] Many contemporary urban civilisations throughout the world will be impacted as most cities sit either in river valleys, near mountain headwaters, on the valley plains or on the estuary and delta. Even without an extreme climate change involving a 3-metre water level rise, water for food production and drinking will be in short supply. Cities might be subject to frequent coastal flooding or will be uninhabitable due to desertification. Urban populations will need to adapt to seasonal floods, as in contemporary Venice, or migrate to new settlements.

The financial collapse of the dominant urban ecology of the megalopolis in 2008 offers opportunities for change. The entire apparatus imploded as oil prices spiked, yielding vast profits, and then crashed as a result of banking deregulation that encouraged risk taking and endangered the entire system, spreading a sense of doom.[3] Subsequently American automobile manufacturers went bankrupt, banks and mortgage brokers collapsed, the house building industry disintegrated with millions of abandoned houses left empty in the American suburbs because of the sub-prime mortgage crisis, while stores closed and people lost their jobs. The collapse of investment company Dubai World followed a similar pattern. After 2008, perhaps some fundamental codes will change to prevent a future collapse, and the global financial model will no longer be based on an infinite extension of the megalopolis around the world. Part of the problem is that cities import not only people and energy, food and water, they are also important legal organisations, involving landownership patterns, codes and regulations, importing capital from profits made elsewhere and stored temporarily as investments in their carbon structures (the new skyscraper towers, apartment blocks, houses that sprang up with easy mortgages).

Cities have traditionally played a role in redistributing income across a wide spectrum of citizens, not just in real-estate ownership and speculation. Cities provided institutional ladders, such as schools and other educational establishments, knowledge-based occupations and new fields, to help people climb out of poverty, and this was part of their historic appeal. The redistributive capacity of the city will be in great demand, hopefully with a new emphasis placed on social equity to prevent the kind of systemic failure and loss of people's homes. In addition, the adaptive and psychological dimension of the city will become more important as the new Asian and African mass migration creates new needs and desires. This chapter will review how urban actors might change the four urban design ecologies of the past 60 years to face up to short-term and long-term scenarios. Urban actors and their designers need to carefully re-examine the carbon economies and structures of each urban design ecology in 'what if' scenarios using enclaves, armatures and heterotopias to probe the future.

The green metropolis

The *New Yorker* magazine's contributing author David Owen argues in *Green Metropolis* (2009) that New York and Hong Kong are fundamentally 'green' eco-cities because they are very densely populated, have good public transportation systems and people can walk to find all their daily needs within close proximity.[4] Owen recounts how, when he moved his family to the American countryside twenty years earlier, the family ended up with three cars, hours of driving, never having time to sit or walk in the country, going miles to get their groceries or see a movie.

Green Metropolis proposes that the true ecological costs of oil should be passed on to American and other consumers through gas taxes and congestion charges, as in Singapore,

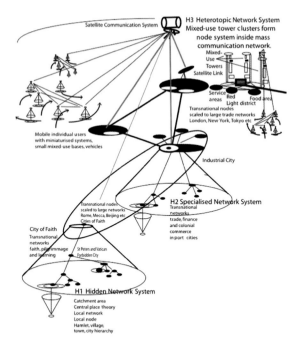

Multilayered city diagram
Here the *archi-città*, *cine-città* and *tele-città* are shown layering up one upon another to form a complex urban system within which urban actors can make multiple choices about how to live their lives. The *tele-città* implies that urban actors are mobile and can communicate with each other no matter which model they inhabit, creating a potentially open system allowing for bottom-up feedback. (Diagram © David Grahame Shane, 2010)

Temporal layering diagram of Munich
A historical study of Munich related graphically by showing successive additions to the historic core by various urban actors. Medieval salt merchants built the old town, while the Enlightenment expansion was planned by Leo von Klenze (shown in black); the later railway company settlement to the west created a new industrial centre (shown in grey) that was captured inside a Weimar Republic ring autobahn, to form the basis for later postwar expansions (shown in red). (Diagram © David Grahame Shane and Angie Hunsaker, 2008)

Stockholm or London. Owen thinks driving in cities should be made very unpleasant, with limited parking spaces and constricted roadways to increase traffic jams and travel times. The goal should be to make street armatures safe and secure for pedestrians by widening sidewalks, planting trees, providing bike lanes and facilitating public transportation systems, as undertaken in some European cities like Copenhagen or Amsterdam. Improving the quality of life and combating crime in the metropolis will make it attractive again. If schools are also improved, then families will not move to the suburbs for their children's safety and education. Old people statistically live longer in cities. Owen argues for very high-density blocks like on the Upper East and West Sides in Manhattan because many services, subways and facilities can then be within walking distance.

Without the skyscrapers or comparable density, the small European city and state capital of Munich, Germany applied many of these eco-ideas during the 1980s and 1990s. Munich began as a small metropolitan city with a single centre at a river crossing. Based on the salt trade, it expanded around that centre in rings, until the European Enlightenment and Napoleon, when the local prince added a grand armature to the city's edge and then a grid (Colin Rowe and Fred Koetter praised this incremental growth in *Collage City* (1978)).[5] The arrival of the railway on the edge of the central city sponsored the growth of a new industrial centre in a cluster further west, at a railway line junction. This was later encircled by the first autobahn ring, passing the village of Dachau (site of a factory that became the first Nazi concentration camp)

and linking to later suburban residential developments, the ill-fated 1972 Olympic Games campus, an out-of-town banking centre enclave with skyscraper towers, the factory campus of the electronics giant Siemens and the BMW works (redesigned by Coop Himmelb(l)au).[6]

Munich city council was unusual in rewriting the central zoning codes to encourage higher densities and development without skyscrapers, creating a green mini-metropolis. The city also retained the famous tramways, pedestrianised the entire city centre, built new subway lines and renewed the historic, war-torn district as a commercial shopping centre with old facades and new interior buildings, courts and glass-covered shopping arcades. The city became an exemplary European eco-city by the 2000s, as a result of Green Party energy codes for solar panels and super-insulation, as well as protections for open countryside and woods (continuing the German *Stadtlandschaft* tradition – see chapter 6). This 'Munich perspective' on energy, city planning, metropolitan shrinkage, dense infill policies and restricting growth drew much praise.[7] Even the small north German town of Münster, where the Bolles + Wilson architectural office had studied the *Eurolandschaft* ecology (see chapter 10), rebuilt its town centre after the war and added an exemplary infill library that completed an urban block and faced out to a bus station and automobile showroom.[8]

The green metropolis was also the theme of French President Sarkozy's planning consultation in 2009 'The Metropolis after the Kyoto Accords'. The idea was to break the old ring-and-radial pattern of the Haussmann metropolis, setting in motion a multicentred

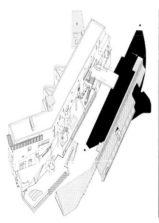

Bolles + Wilson, Münster Library, Münster, Germany, 1993
This axonometric drawing shows the pedestrian street armature cutting through the block, with the library bridge above and the structural layering of the roof that becomes the internal street's facade.
(Drawing © Bolles + Wilson)

Bolles + Wilson, library street armature, Münster, Germany, 1997 (photo 1997)
View of the pedestrian street created through the library block aligning with the back of the nearby St Lamberti Church on the town's principal marketplace. The copper roof is pulled down, to emphasise the perspective cut and form a closed facade to the street.
(Photo © David Grahame Shane)

Parisian megacity. Entitled *'Le Grand Paris de l'agglomération parisienne'* – or 'Le Grand Paris' for short – Sarkozy invited 10 teams including from Britain Richard Rogers, from France Atelier Portzamparc and Agence Grumbach, and from Holland MVRDV.[9] The Secchi-Viganò Studio 09 team expanded on their work for Antwerp (see chapter 9), looking at the porosity of Paris, its organisational structure, street layouts and energy use.[10] The team emphasised the patchy nature of greater Paris, with its valley topography, many streams, rivers, canals, marshes, wetlands, flood lands, parks and wastelands, as well as the suburban green 'drosscape' of low-density, green, private houses and apartment blocks. Haussmann's Paris was only a tiny part of this city territory that the team compared in scale and polycentric structure to the North West Metropolitan Area (NWMA) around Antwerp–Rotterdam in Belgium–Holland, and to Kowloon in Hong Kong and Shenzhen in China.

The Studio 09 porosity study identified areas of the green metropolis that were cut off from the city, often poor immigrant ghettos, ill served by public transport. The study proposed a set of inter-suburban light railways and trams connecting the patches of urbanism and ghettos in the suburbs, so that people no longer had to go via the centre to get to the neighbouring suburb. Studio 09 took sample patches of urban fabric to study in the west and east of the city. The proposal also included designs to retrofit these different urban patches to be more energy efficient, using solar panels, new building skins and geothermal devices, as well as offering single-family house areas (pavilions) bonus floor area if they improved their insulation and energy efficiency.[11] Decaying factory areas could also be converted to mixed use, including housing and solar installations on green roofs. The team also proposed to infill the large open spaces between tall tower blocks (that would also be re-skinned and made energy efficient) with lower blocks also bearing solar panels. The overall result made the existing urban fabric more densely populated, more energy efficient, more flexible and more accessible, breaking the isolation of metropolitan ghettos and bringing public transportation within walking distance everywhere.

Bernardo Secchi and Paola Viganò, Studio09, 'Le Grand Paris' project, Paris, France, 2009
Studio 09 treated Paris as a distributed urban system, ignoring the historic radio-centric pattern. The inset plans and sections study a dying industrial area beside the Seine to the east of the centre, proposing to retrofit the monofunctional enclave as mixed-use, energy-efficient new neighbourhoods with housing, commercial and office uses, as well as residual industrial factories. (Images © Studio09_Bernardo Secchi, Paola Viganò)

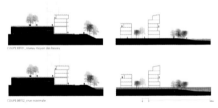

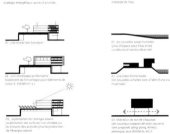

Other teams shared many of the goals of Secchi and Viganò but used different urban elements to achieve their design. The Rogers team, for instance, redesigned the Parisian radial railway armatures as 'green finger' parks on a massive scale, making links across the parks to connect previously disconnected districts with new high-density nodes. The Portzamparc team concentrated on an area north of central Paris, proposing a new business centre enclave to provide a new gateway to London, Frankfurt, Brussels and the Dutch Randstad (Ring City), with educational facilities grouped on either side and parks following the river valleys. In order to break the ring-and-radial structure, new monorail lines circled through the Paris suburbs linking to the new hub. The Grumbach team proposed to turn Paris into a linear city leading down the Seine valley along a new high-speed railway line to Le Havre, transforming Paris into a green megalopolis leading to the Atlantic. Grumbach detected a rhythm in the curves and meanders of the river that set the intervals of the megablocks shaped by two highways, forming parks, forests, residential, agricultural and industrial areas.[12]

The green megalopolis

When the French sociologist Jean Gottmann first proposed the term 'megalopolis' to describe the American East Coast seaboard in 1961, railway lines with coal-fired steam engines still formed the backbone of the transportation network.[13] The American state highways system did not exist. By 1971, when Reyner Banham celebrated the automobile-borne city in *Los Angeles: The Architecture of Four Ecologies* (see chapter 6), the national highway system and airlines had replaced railways.[14] In the meantime Gottmann turned his attention to Tokyo and the *Stadtlandschaft* planning of the Rhine–Ruhr industrial belt (now part of the 'Blue Banana' – see chapter 6). These Asian and European versions of the megalopolis retained railways and state planning that protected agricultural and recreational landscapes, as well as taxing petrol to discourage automobile use. Germany, Scandinavia and then the EU led the way in retrofitting older buildings to new energy codes, and cities like Munich or Copenhagen infilled old city centres to give them new life within the larger urban network. In contrast, Tokyo developed an incredibly dense, widely distributed railway system with enormous three-dimensional commercial and recreational nodes around and above transport hubs, often owned by the state railway system.

Each Western European nation state developed its own characteristic patterns of handling the megalopolis, the highway armatures and megablock enclaves, as demonstrated in the Dutch architect Xaveer De Geyter's editing of *After-Sprawl* (2002).[15] Venice and the Po delta had a different pattern to Holland or Belgium in the Rhine delta, which was different again from London's ring-and-radial system, or Paris's twin development belts along the Seine valley (see chapter 6). Switzerland, with its Alpine valley systems, provided yet another European network pattern of layered linear armature developments over time, beautifully analysed by Swiss architect Franz Oswald and ecologist Peter Baccini in *Netzstadt* (2003).[16] These authors carefully examined the impact of highways and suburbanisation on the delicate Swiss urban design ecology, its growth and surrounding agricultural and forest setting, within the fragile,

Franz Oswald and Peter Baccini, Net City Layered Valley diagram, 2003
Oswald and Baccini separated the forest landscape, the agricultural areas, infrastructure (railways, roads), streams and waterways, and urban villages each in a different layer. The goal was to provide safe drinking water for the valley watershed, identifying development sites or areas that were currently 'fallow', awaiting development (shown in pink). (Diagram © Franz Oswald/Peter Baccini and Birkhauser Publishers, Basel, Berlin, Boston)

Panorama of Federation Square in Melbourne, Australia (photo 2010)
Johan van Schaik's panorama reveals the sloping nature of the pedestrian plaza viewed from the entrance of the
Flinders Street Station. The public plaza includes a Tokyo-style JumboTron public TV screen, as well as metal
fins over the central café block that are part of an elaborate cooling system using the depth of the deck space
above the railway tracks as a natural air-conditioning plenum. (Image © Johan N van Schaik)

natural ecology of the Alpine valleys. The picture postcard fragments of the Swiss villages
were located as precise patches within the flows of water, flora and fauna that made up the
life of the valley, creating a closed ecosystem that was polluting its own drinking water supply.
While many urban designers want to open up hidden rivers or make parks on old industrial
waterfronts, few have calculated so precisely how the ecology of the city, its roads, traffic,
railways, settlements and actors, interact with the surrounding environment.

The Asian and European versions of the green megalopolis are comparatively compact,
with a smaller energy footprint when compared to the American original. The big challenge
for urban designers in America will be reducing the fossil-fuel dependence of this system as
well as making it financially sustainable in the future (paying $4 a gallon for gasoline ruined
this ecology). The conversion of the Las Vegas Strip from isolated pavilions with car parks
and signs to simulated metropolitan fragments (Paris, New York and Venice – see chapter 9)
shows one possible future scenario for the megalopolis where urban imagery and high-rise
residential towers fill mall car parks worldwide, responding to the needs of the metacity and
its informational systems, producing heterotopias of illusion. The latest 'City Center' (2010)
complex on the Strip aspires to be a discrete urban fragment with tower blocks around a
private boulevard cul-de-sac and a shopping mall, designed by Daniel Libeskind.[17]

Most drivers in the American megalopolis travel less than 65 kilometres (40 miles) a
day.[18] Many American southwestern retirement communities and the state of Florida already
allow electric golf carts to be driven on roads, as well as encouraging better insulation,
solar power and hot water installations.[19] Perhaps one day these drivers will run their solar-
powered electric vehicles to new suburban nodes, with public services like libraries and
schools at station stops on high-speed rail or bus lanes, set in 'green finger' parks with urban
agriculture, as in Bogotá's *barrios*. Lab Architecture's Federation Square (2002) in Melbourne,
Australia, opposite the Flinders Street Central Station, provides a vision of an eco-cultural-mall
hub of the future, with its elaborate heating and cooling system sunk in its pedestrian deck,
over the railway tracks, beside the tram lines and the river.[20]

Lab Architecture, site plan for Federation Square, Melbourne, Australia, 2002
Lab Architecture succeeded in creating a sense of enclosure on a platform built over the railway tracks, beside the Yarra river esplanade, in the centre of downtown Melbourne. The plan does not reveal the sloping nature of the plaza surface that is constrained by wedge-shaped pavilions designed to frame views into, and out of, the pedestrian space. (Plan © LAB Architecture Studio)

The urban ecology of the megalopolis might still make sense for oil-rich states where petrol is cheap, like Abu Dhabi and Dubai, Saudi Arabia and Iraq, Venezuela and Brazil, Borneo and Indonesia, Nigeria and Angola.[21] Despite the recent financial collapse, projects that might not be possible elsewhere might be 'sustainable' here. But as in Lagos, Caracas or Jakarta, the oil economy creates its own refugees represented in the Middle East by shantytowns in Gaza or the Lebanon, and in the labour camps in Dubai. Against this shadow city, oil-rich countries project an image of a solar future, making daring investments in a new urban design ecology, like Foster's Masdar, Abu Dhabi (started 2007). This compact, shaded new town with underground transport systems and solar power is planned as a demonstration project in one of the most inhospitable deserts of the world, which will get even hotter by the end of the next century. Such show places, heterotopias of illusion, have always played a role in imagining future scenarios, as at World's Fairs and Olympic meetings. Many oil-rich states are investing in infrastructure, housing and new towns. Ghana, for instance, has awarded a $10 billion contract to the South Korean government agency that built Bundang (see chapter 6) for 200,000 homes and supporting infrastructure, housing perhaps a million people (to be paid for by new-found offshore oil reserves).[22] South Korean conglomerates are also building new towns in Algeria, Kyrgyzstan, Libya, Mongolia, Nigeria, all energy-rich states, as well as Tanzania and Yemen.

The megalopolis and its associated networks of oil wells, refineries, pipelines, tank farms, distribution centres and gas stations, highways, suburbs and mall parking lots makes a huge, global urban design ecology that one day will have to be reformatted and remediated for chemical pollution. In the future Latin American cities, for instance, without major industrial resources will have to retrofit their cities in a 'shrinking city' scenario, reworking the self-built *barrios* and informal settlements. In cities like Bogotá, Caracas, Lima, Medellín, Quito, Rio de Janeiro and São Paolo, the self-built *favela* megalopolis will need adjusting, to bring back urban agriculture for food supplies as the oil and gas run out. These petro-*favelas* might shrink. People might return to villages that might also be updated and linked to global networks. These villages might have better education and informational systems, more open

Weiss/Manfredi, aerial photo of Seattle Sculpture Park, Seattle, Washington, USA, 2007
Seattle sits up on a bluff overlooking the port and harbour. Railways and roads took up the historic waterfront, whose sectional development was always complex. The Seattle Sculpture Park proposes a new model for layered and terraced development from the escarpment down to the shore, weaving ramps and pedestrian access around traditional barriers. (Photo © Benjamin Benschneider)

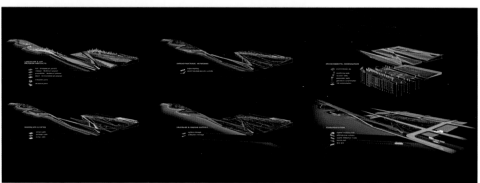

Weiss/Manfredi, layered drawing of Seattle Sculpture Park, Seattle, Washington, USA, 2007
At a small scale, the Weiss/Manfredi Seattle Sculpture Park represents the use of a complex, three-dimensional urban matrix to remediate a polluted waterfront site, providing terraces for artworks and museum pavilions as well as a path that weaves across a highway and railway line down to a restored seaside beach. (Drawing © Weiss/Manfredi)

democratic government and less feudal arrangements than in the past. The same scenario might apply in other oil-rich nations like Nigeria or Angola, Indonesia or Borneo. Teddy Cruz's upgrade work at the US–Mexico San Diego–Tijuana border examines the confrontation of the *favela* megalopolis of the global south and the industrialised megalopolis of the global north, both in oil-powered economies.[23] Cruz proposed to hybridise the two cultures, allowing more freedom within the American Dream of single-family, detached homes with maximal servicing, as well as generous upgrades in the *favelas* in terms of services, public space and private space provision. Cruz is also aware of the macroflows of the stretched armatures, as shown in his analysis of the border as a 'political equator' between the rich northern hemisphere and the poor southern one.

In the northern hemisphere new hybrids are also emerging in the 'shrinking city' scenario. In Germany, for instance, urban designers and landscape designers are already dealing with repurposing industrial plants, wastelands and polluted sites, creating museums and cultural facilities, heterotopias of illusion, as at Duisburg-Nord Landscape Park (1991–2002, see chapter 10). In Asia, Seoul removed an elevated highway and opened up a riverbed to create Cheonggyecheon Park (2005, see chapter 9). American cities like New York have removed elevated, waterfront highways, or made elegant waterfront parks and museums like the Weiss/Manfredi-designed Olympic Sculpture Park in Seattle (2007).[24]

The green fragmented metropolis

The fragmented metropolis, like the green metropolis, should require less carbon input compared to the megalopolis because of its multiple compact centres, but the problem is that they are in an automobile-based network of transportation. Theoretically having multiple dense centres and a good public transportation network could reduce a city's carbon footprint, as in the Vancouver eco-city model. In Vancouver the City Planning Commission, using a complex consultative process, established growth limits at its borders protecting fragile ecosystems, raised density in multiple suburban subcentres and neighbourhoods, and connected these subcentres via greenways and bus lanes to the city centre where dense, high-rise, mixed-use residential development was encouraged. Forty per cent of Vancouver's Downtown and West End commuters now walk or use bicycles.[25] Normally the urban fragments in the megalopolis tended to be single-function enclaves, such as business parks, industrial parks, shopping malls or theme parks. Few were mixed use like the heterotopic casinos as in Las Vegas. Large residential enclaves of single-family houses completed this picture, all connected by highways. Transforming these single-function urban fragments will be difficult as cities shrink and new urban patches develop. There is already a huge inventory of abandoned malls in America listed at deadmalls.com. Recent urban design competitions have involved abandoned airports, such as the old Kai Tak airport in Hong Kong or military bases like the Yongsan Garrison American base in downtown Seoul.[26] American Ken Smith's team's design for the Orange County Great Park (2007) replaced the 800-hectare (2,000-acre) El Toro Marine Corps Air Station in Irvine, California with a 545-hectare (1,347-acre) park and four areas of housing development.[27]

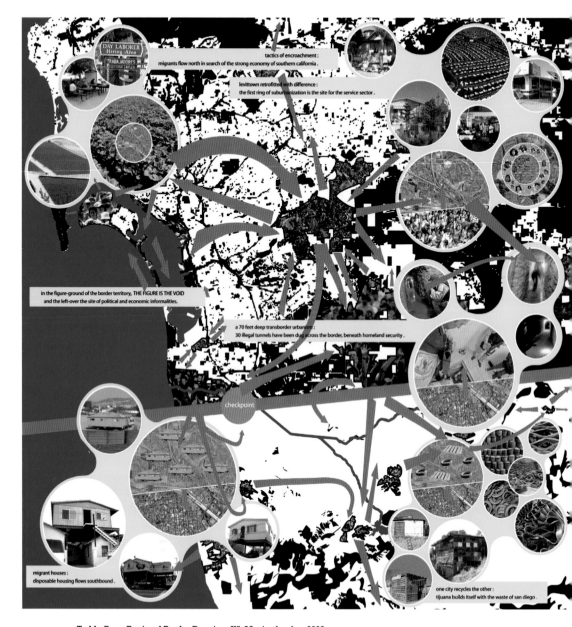

The labels within the drawing read:

tactics of encroachment :
migrants flow north in search of the strong economy of southern california .

levittown retrofitted with difference :
the first ring of suburbanization is the site for the service sector .

in the figure-ground of the border territory, THE FIGURE IS THE VOID
and the left-over the site of political and economic informalities.

a 70 feet deep transborder urbanism :
30 illegal tunnels have been dug across the border, beneath homeland security .

checkpoint

migrant houses :
disposable housing flows southbound .

one city recycles the other :
tijuana builds itself with the waste of san diego .

Teddy Cruz, Regional Border Drawing, US–Mexico border, 2008
The drawing contrasts urban settlement patterns north and south of the US–Mexico border
checkpoint and suggests the possibility of hyrbidisation between the American suburban and
Mexican self-built urban patterns. (Drawing © Estudio Teddy Cruz)

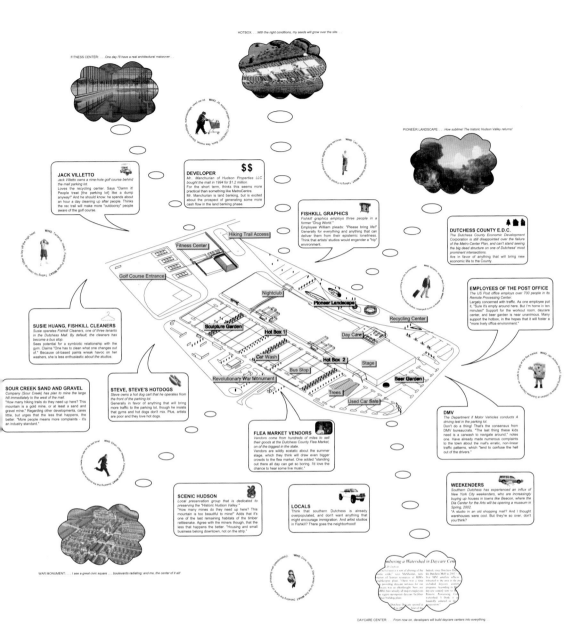

Interboro Partners, proposal for Dutchess County Mall, Fishkill, New York, USA, 2003

This winning entry to Los Angeles Forum for Architecture and Urban Design's 'Dead Malls' competition proposed to transform the dead mall through a series of micro-programmes based on the residual uses already found inhabiting the mall and its vast car park like fleeting, time-based parasites. Selective demolition, repartitioning and creative inserts or new construction would create a space where a new, performative and time-based urbanism might emerge, still based on the automobile, but opening up towards more communal uses. (Images © Interboro (Tobias Armborst, Daniel D'Oca and Georgeen Theodore)

As yet there are few projects that transform malls or single-use fragments such as factory districts into denser mixed-use developments, with solar energy on their roof as proposed by Secchi and Viganò in 'Le Grand Paris'. Interboro Partners' winning entry for the 2002 Los Angeles Forum of Architecture & Urban Design 'Dead Malls' competition attempted to revive an ancient mall by harnessing the micro-activities that took place either on the site or around its boundaries.[28] The proposal did not challenge the use of the car; it included a car sales area and car wash, a gym, a small park associated with a neighbouring golf course, a new pavilion for a dry cleaner who had been operating in the mall, a garden centre selling plants, building on informal uses that already existed on the site's parking lot. As parts of the mall were demolished in the proposal, other parts became a theatre and disco complex using remnants of the large shed of the former department store. Small offices remaining in the mall and a popular restaurant with a separate exterior entrance remained. At the end of the microtransformations the mall was unrecognisable because of new roads, landscaping, lighting and signage.

Malls provided local or regional shopping and commercial services, replacing downtown with a constellation of competing centres. The owners of megamalls sought to replace downtown, sponsoring the Houston Galleria (begun in 1967, see chapter 6). The Galleria formed a modernist megastructure around an interior, street-like armature. These large urban fragments, dense with towers attached, had all the elements of downtown – offices, post offices, coffee shops, department stores and boutiques, plus leisure activities also listed by Foucault as heterotopias of illusion such as cinemas, sports clubs and hotels, even nightclubs – but no residents.[29] Urban designers identified this system of fragments, alternatively as *Collage City* (Rowe and Koetter, 1978) or the *City Archipelago* (Ungers and Koolhaas, 1977).[30] Battery Park City (1978) created a new urban fragment formula with a system of streets and a central mall podium with towers attached inside a special district enclave (see chapters 1 and 7). Alexander Cooper, one of the Battery Park City designers, went on to design the urban village fragment of Celebration beside Walt Disney World in Orlando, Florida (1990s).[31] Despite the pedestrian environments designed here or at Walt Disney World, the global carbon footprint of the some 30 million visitors to Walt Disney World each year hardly makes this a green urban fragment. Besides needing to create mixed use and denser urban fragments, American urban designers need to connect them by new systems of shared transportation (even if people arrive locally by short-distance electric cars in the future).

European and Asian designers learnt to develop new greener urban armatures, creating networks of public transportation that efficiently connect urban fragments in an age of traffic congestion and pollution. OMA's Euralille (1991–4), for instance, with its Jean Nouvel mall, connected to the Eurostar station, highway, car park and regional rail networks with hotel and office towers above.[32] The Battery Park City Authority also rewrote its codes for the special district in the 2000s to include LEED (Leadership in Environmental Energy & Design) environmental certification, attempting to make a green urban fragment via better building materials, windows and insulation with geothermal heating and cooling.[33] During the 1990s, Bangkok and Hong Kong both developed networked urban fragments, linked to public transportation systems as well as highways. Heterotopias of illusion played an important role

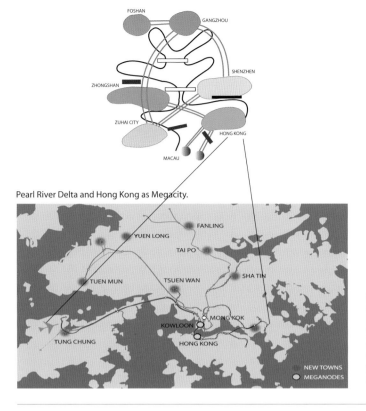

Pearl River Delta and Hong Kong as Megacity.

Pearl River Network Megacity diagram with Hong Kong new towns detail.
The UN identified this region as a 'megacity region' containing 120 million people in 2009. (Diagram © David Grahame Shane, 2010)

in this urban constellation as malls and department stores formed the basis for many urban design projects. Hong Kong acted as a laboratory for experiments in the three-dimensional layering of the city section around malls and public transportation, leading towards Bangkok's megamalls where the arrival of the Skytrain caused malls to turn inside out to face the street (see chapter 10).

Hong Kong planners and urban designers in the 1990s created many green urban fragments, patches of high-density urbanism. The urban design ecology of Hong Kong consisted of a system of dense, high-rise towers on commercial podiums with malls, connected by public transportation and subway lines. Malls shifted with the new railway lines, leaving dead malls stranded. New upper-level walkway armatures linked the malls in Central and around the transport hubs of the new towns. At the back of Central lay a steep sloping neighbourhood called the Mid-Levels, leading up to the Peak mountaintop park overlooking the city (the site of Zaha Hadid's unbuilt Peak Project, 1981 – see chapter 7).[34] Planners long dreamt of running a feeder highway up the hill, but in the early 1990s the highway department inserted a system of escalators down the centre of a street climbing up the hillside. This amazing green escalator armature efficiently carried the morning commuters down the hill, being reversed for the evening flow. The escalators also unexpectedly became a tourist and leisure attraction, bringing bars, restaurants, hotels and condominium developments in tiny sliver buildings.

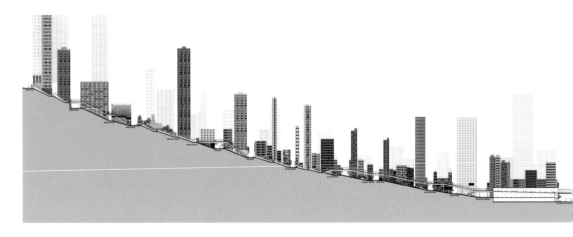

Laurence Liauw, sectional drawing of escalator for Mid-Levels, Hong Kong, 2009
The Highways Department of Hong Kong long dreamt of building a highway up through the Mid-Levels, but in the early 1990s constructed an escalator system for commuters instead. The system consists of several segments, each dealing with very different urban conditions, resulting in the escalators taking many positions in the street section. (Drawing © Laurence Liauw)

Street views of escalators, Mid-Levels, Hong Kong, 2009
The engineers unintentionally produced a tourist attraction that transformed the area, bringing sliver development high-rise towers, bars, galleries and cafés. Development is especially dense where the escalators descend to meet the side streets terraced along the contour. (Photo © David Grahame Shane)

Escalators also act as interior armatures, giving an extreme vertical dimension to Hong Kong malls and creating innovative heterotopias of illusion with complex sections. Langham Place (2005) in Mongkok, Kowloon, designed by The Jerde Partnership with local associates (for section diagram see chapter 2), links at street level into a pre-existing street market and replaced a red-light district around the MTR subway station.[35] The spatial sequence of the mall spirals up through two levels from the subway underground to the street and market. There a second mall continues the spiral up through a conventional, modern Hong Kong mall to a middle level, where a glass-enclosed public plaza on the roof looks down into the street and is wedged between two hotel and office towers, with big public screens as in Japan. Cafés surround this plaza and two super escalators then bypass another smaller mall, leading up to the bars and cinemas stacked on the 12th floor at the top of the mall sequence. From there, a miniature Guggenheim New York-style ramp spirals down past small, speciality boutiques and high-fashion items.

Kowloon Central Station by Terry Farrell (planned 1992–8) forms an even larger commercial meganode above public transportation, part of a green fragmented metropolis.[36] It also flows up through layers, like Langham Place. It is linked to a vast hinterland by the scale of its networks, stretching out across the agricultural and industrial ecologies of the Pearl River Delta. It will be the only stop of the high-speed Chinese railway system in Hong Kong linking via Shenzhen to Beijing and Shanghai. Its skyscrapers match those of the IFC2 at Central across Hong Kong Bay (see chapter 10). The multistorey Elements Mall, with an ice rink, food courts and cinema complex (opened 2007), remains a key heterotopia of illusion above the station. On the roof garden is a park with more restaurants and bars on terraces, overlooked from the circular periphery by office and residential towers. Automobiles and taxis have access to the roof for drop-off purposes. Many architects have designed the various towers, others the roof garden enclave, still others the mall and others the various railway station armatures. The architecture is often commercial and not very distinguished, yet Farrell's overall urban design of the sectional sequence of public spaces, often privately owned and policed, is a gift to the city.

The green megacity: heterotopias of illusion, megablocks and mega-armatures

In the past, heterotopias of illusion provided the impetus for many urban design experiments and displays of future urban ecologies at World's Fairs or Olympic games. General Motors set the pattern in its Norman Bel Geddes-designed 'Futurama' pavilion at the New York World's Fair of 1938, predicting mass car ownership and highways.[37] The Brussels World's Fair of 1958 overlaid the megalopolis and highways on the fading imperial dreams of the European metropolis. Kenzo Tange's megastructure and robots design of the 1970 World's Fair at Osaka reflected the move towards giant urban fragments and personal, electronic communication systems. The design of the Barcelona Olympics of 1991 questioned the fragmented metropolis approach, adding highway and rail connections, as in Beijing in 2008 or London 2012, creating a more complex urban design ecology. The design of the Shanghai 2010 Expo includes a long, megastructural armature, the Expo Axis, stretching down to the Huangpu river, with

Terry Farrell & Partners, section, Kowloon Central Station, Hong Kong, planned 1996–8, completed 2009
In this meganode, the Elements Mall connects the various layers of transportation network up to the circular roof garden, surrounded by residential and office towers. High-speed trains from the Pearl River Delta megacity region, with its 120 million inhabitants, terminate here. (Image © Farrells)

The Jerde Partnership, Langham Place mall, Mongkok, Kowloon, Hong Kong, 2005 (photos 2009)
Visitors to Langham Place, shown opposite, move up on escalators through several malls layered on top of each other, with a public atrium on the roof of one mall looking down into the neighbouring street market. Mega-escalators carry visitors up to the top of the mall to the bars and cinemas, with dramatic views down to the JumboTron screen on the plaza on the roof of the lower mall (see chapter 2 for diagrammatic section). (Photos © David Grahame Shane)

green-themed pavilions alongside forming big enclaves.[38] Each pavilion tells a story, as in the Urban Footprint Pavilion, the Urban Planet Pavilion, Urban Dwellers Pavilion, Urban Beings Pavilion and Urban Dreams Pavilion. These urban and ecological themes reflect the fact that the majority of Chinese citizens still live in rural communes and that China still hopes for an ecological urban future, despite relying heavily on fossil fuels like the USA.

The Shanghai Expo forms a megablock on old industrial land comparable in scale to Disney's EPCOT and expecting twice as many visitors as Walt Disney World in the summer of 2010. The challenge of Asian urbanisation is in part one of scale. In the British industrial revolution of the 19th century, a population of 45 million people had transformed their lives from agrarian to industrial workers by 1945. This British industrial model created a strange urban ecology with a massive, underprivileged working class, creating the global metropolis of London with 7 million inhabitants.[39] In the 20th century, America emerged as a continental, industrial giant with a population of 150 million in 1945 (three times the size of Britain), 32 million of whom lived in the megalopolis of the East Coast in 1961, creating a vast middle class.[40] In China and India a population four times the size of that of the USA is involved.[41] American corporations developed the communication systems and organisational techniques to manage a continental system with a relatively small population. These corporations extended their scale and scope, entering and creating a global market. Now the Chinese and Indian governments face the task of further developing these American organisational techniques to serve their own purposes in Asian megacities and far more densely populated countries and continents. Shanghai, as an Asian megacity with a population of 22 million, represents this quandary, as it also faces potential flooding if even moderate sea level rises take place in the next century. The UN World Urban Forum 4 in Rio in 2010 drew attention to 'megacity-regions', citing the Pearl River delta, with a vulnerable population of 120 million.[42]

Megacity regions imply a dispersed city, where the journey from one end to the other might take three hours or more. This vast expansion of the megacity is made possible by hand-held devices that provide new ways to connect up-close to the city, while satellites provide remote sensing data that will be important in the future as Asian megacities and river delta cities worldwide face the task of possibly moving inland to higher ground. In this scenario the satellite connections and hand-held devices in the *favela* megalopolis, as well as the internet access from new towns and new housing estates, provides a means for people to organise their move (forest fire evacuation alerts in California already arrive via smart phones and internet). Where people will move to is something that urban designers can address as a 'what if' question or design scenario, but people's swarming instincts and personal connections do not always follow such rational paths. While wealthy industrialised nations with strong state governments may build industrial new towns, even there urban villages surface to serve undocumented workers and illicit uses, creating parallel systems. The media dimension of the geography of the city means that when and if the time comes to move major cities, like Chongqing during the construction of the Three Gorges Dam (2008) as shown in Jia Zhangke's movie *Still Life* (2006), people will still be able to find each other and coordinate their moves even as the river rises and the city disappears.[43]

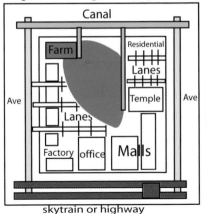

Mega= Extra Large   Mega-Block 1km x 1km

Desa-kota
Mixed-use
Patch

**Asian Megablock Diagram
(based on Rama I, Bangkok)**

A view down into a typical Bangkok *soi* (bottom) includes large buildings on its periphery, medium-sized buildings near its periphery and smaller residential and agricultural compounds nearer the core of the megablock. (Diagram and photos © David Grahame Shane, 2010)

The New Armature Diagram

The diagram shows separate lanes for bikes, cars, buses or light rail, gardens and tree plantings, water management and pedestrians, with reduced car lanes and parking. (Diagram and photos © David Grahame Shane, 2010)

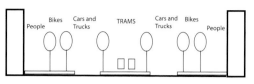

MEGA ARMATURE SECTION

The green megacity needs to be flexible to accommodate rising water, desertification and new migrations or losses of population. The media and communications dimension of the megacity/metacity formulation gives hope for the potential survival of this urban form. At the same time, these new communication systems, combined with new transportation systems, are stretching and expanding the scale of the traditional enclave and armature, creating stretched mega-armatures and megablocks that contain mixed uses, old villages, agricultural settlements, as well as residential, industrial and office patches.[44] Green Asian megablocks in particular also accommodate old canal, irrigation and drainage systems. Mega-armatures are very wide and hard to cross, but include multilane arrangements separating pedestrians, bikes, cars and streetcars in separate lanes, with planting between lanes and on the surrounding sidewalks.[45] These armatures that may also include subways, separate the megablocks, but also make it possible to move quickly from enclave to enclave using navigational and communication systems to coordinate with others in the megacity.

In creating the green megacity, urban designers need to learn from the *desa-kota* patterns of the Asian megacity as a resource, as in Bangkok with its canals (see chapters 8 and 10). This already includes agricultural systems, flood control and irrigation systems that need further development, as in the Han river flowing through central Seoul, with its rice paddies and retention ponds. This scenario of more flexible flood control drives the work of University of Pennsylvania landscape professors Anuradha Mathur and Dilip da Cunha who studied first the *Mississippi Floods* (2001) before Hurricane Katrina.[46] They then studied the water supply system to the Indian garden city of Bangalore (India's IT capital) in *Deccan Traverses* (2006) and the Mithi river that ends in Mumbai in their 'SOAK' exhibition (2009).[47] In SOAK, Mathur and da Cunha imagine restoring to Mumbai the resilience of an estuary with strategies that hold and deflect monsoon waters, working with time as much as with space. They propose the opportunistic use of walls, maidans, infrastructural corridors, and interstitial spaces to recover the filtering and holding rhythms once performed by creeks and mudflats in order to make the city more porous and less liable to flood. They also propose toilet barges that work with biotic technologies for areas where fixed toilets are inadequate and inappropriate, such as for settlements by the sea and areas of Dharavi near the estuarine edge, to alleviate a sewage pollution problem.

Besides such inventions as floating bath houses and toilet barges, green Asian megacities may also involve building in the capacity to move a city, developing new models that include migration and gradual relocation ahead of the rising waters if extreme predictions apply.[48] This is already happening at the mouth of the Ganges in the sinking Sundarban islands, whose 4 million occupants are moving to the self-built shanties of Dhaka, Bangladesh after the cyclone Aila of 2009.[49] Such mass migrations may not happen all at once, but family by family, resulting in new urban patches around the host city. In a fantasy urban design scenario, wise city mayors and powerful urban actors would divert the Asian megacity away from a high-energy-consuming lifestyle, leapfrogging America and Europe to develop attractive, modern, but lower-energy urban design ecology on a massive scale, using solar power. Besides building new towns for the middle class, this scenario would allow the poorer new urban migrants to rehouse themselves in new settlements safe from floods, providing new green jobs.

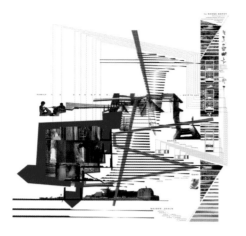

**Anuradha Mathur and Dilip da Cunha,
drawings for 'SOAK: Mumbai in an Estuary',
Mumbai, India, 2009**
In the exhibition 'SOAK', Mathur and Da Cunha
imagine restoring some of the wetlands of the Mithi
up river, reopening multiple channels to the Mumbai
bay to make the city more porous and less liable to
flood. The Sewage Barge diagram is top left, with
views of the Mithi river valley below, on the right are
a series of transept sections of the Mithi valley from
the mountains to the bay. Reservoirs are shown in red.
(Drawings © Anuradha Mathur and Dilip da Cunha)

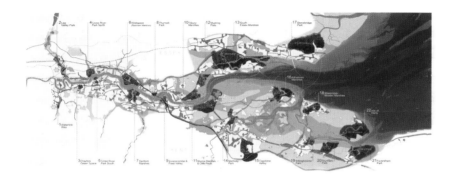

Terry Farrell & Partners, spatial framework for The Parklands Plan, East London, UK, 2008
The masterplan showing all the proposals envisioned for a new national parklands in the Thames Gateway area of East London, including new islands formed on sandbanks in the Thames estuary. Agricultural as well as recreational elements fit within the megablocks of the new high-speed infrastructure associated with the Eurostar line, stopping at Stratford East and Ebbsfleet, shown in this plan. (Plan © Farrells)

This imaginary Asian ascent to a new form of modernity in an attractive green megacity could be matched by a parallel descent to a new, leaner, attractive urban design ecology in American and oil-rich economies. In *Shaping London* (2009), Terry Farrell provides a vision of a green megacity urban design ecology that focuses on the Thames river and its tributaries, the green parks and flood-lands in the west and east, royal parks in the centre, patterns of landownership and development through the centuries, patterns of representation and governance as shown in public ceremonial spaces.[50] The study includes shopping patterns and streets, business centres, village patterns and transportation patterns, including walking, cycles, canals, bus routes, subways and highways. In this study, the memory of the city and its history was always present as the imperial metropolis expanded into the northwest European megacity, including northern France, Belgium and Holland. Farrell's plan drew on many of Mayor Ken Livingstone's visionary projects (advised by Richard Rogers) from the 1990s and 2000s, including the Thames Gateway project.[51] But Farrell highlighted expanding existing parklands and the role of the river as a network in the city, from Hampton Court to Greenwich, combined with Royal Parks, sponsoring valuable open spaces in its flood plain and providing opportunities for opening up hidden streams. Farrell proposed to turn the estuary into a wilderness park, an ecological and recreational resource for Londoners. The vast scheme contained an archipelago of new islands that could help flood control and, in one version, swallow a fifth London airport and new container port to be financed by Abu Dhabi.

Farrell's scenario for a future London retained the memory structure of the past city but opened it to a new life along the length of the River Thames, backed by new transport initiatives like the east–west Crossrail and the high-speed line to France. As people move and migrate, memory plays an increasing role in the psychological geography of the city. In the metropolis people were forced to keep their memory and identity safe in ghettos, like the Chicago slums with their rival gangs: the African American ghettos, Chinatown, Little Italy, German, Polish or Russian Jewish ghettos, and Little Tokyo. The migrants to the *favela*

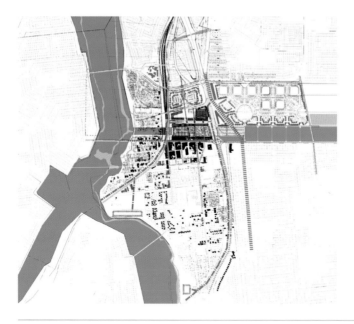

studioMAS, site plan and plan for Freedom Charter Memorial, Kliptown, Johannesburg, South Africa, 2008
Kliptown was a multiracial settlement outside Johannesburg's municipal boundaries where the African National Congress held a rally to ratify its Freedom Charter in 1955. The current plan for the Square includes the preservation of nearby wetlands and renovation of the existing market there, along with the new memorial structures. (Plans © studioMAS)

megalopolis also carried memories of their former homes in agricultural villages in Latin America, Africa or Asia. In the heady days of the American megalopolis, suburban families moved every seven years, fuelling religious organisations and televangelists who offered a portable sense of community away from ghettos. In the new towns of Asia, as in Disneyland in the USA in the 1950s, heterotopias of illusion play their role in helping people adjust to the new world and manage their memories or sense of loss. The difference is that American television systems in the 1950s broadcasted to the masses, whereas now there is a two-way interactive system that allows memories to be stored on a hand-held device or lodged on a Facebook page on the Web, shared and carried everywhere. Even in emergent systems such as connected flash mobs, exploited in the Liverpool Street Station T-mobile cellphone advertisement, there remains a need for the station, for the symbolic place or gateway to the city.[52] Migrants may sublimate this need into their temple, church or mosque, one of Michel Foucault's potent heterotopias of illusion, as a symbol of community.[53] But there also remains a need for secular, political memorials, markers and a sense of history, as in the Kliptown Memorial in Johannesburg by studioMAS (2008).[54] Here a long shed defines a public gathering space on one side, sometimes used for a market, as well as housing a museum and an empty, symbolic, truncated brick cone. The other side of the shed houses a series of market squares, messy and everyday, related to the surrounding townships. The cone in the ceremonial space is placed off centre but is central to the memory of the signing of the anti-apartheid Freedom Charter of 1955 attended by 5,000 people and 2,884 delegates, initiating the birth of democracy in South Africa.[55]

Conclusion: urban design ecologies and the urban future

Urban actors have always projected their hopes, dreams and desires into cities and required memorials. Cities have also always been huge dissipative structures, social organisations that import and redistribute energy and information, creating ladders and networks that citizens can exploit to their advantage. Urban designers have to recognise that there can be no one solution or recipe that fits all urban design situations. Some cities will shrink, some grow, some disappear, some move. Different urban actors will create different urban design ecologies in each situation, ecologies that will include memories and desires for past places of pleasure and meaning. In Montreal the Canadian artist-architect Melvin Charney has created a memorial to the shrinking city that implies that the traditional European metropolis is dead, lingering like a zombie, half alive to be seen from the Canadian Centre for Architecture (CCA) terrace (1987–8).[56] This cemetery for the city contains a number of totems or metaphorical tombs to different urban design ecologies, moving from the east to the west and then taking off in mid-air. The design memorialises shifting urban actors through symbolic intermediaries or sculptures that represent their role in the city's multilayered history of triumphs and disasters. The terrace looks down from a palisade across a highway (which is about to be realigned) to an industrial district beside the 19th-century Lachine canal that was replaced by the 20th-century St Lawrence Seaway. This decaying district houses artists, a farmers' market, new housing developments and a bike path for tourists along the canal, leading to the old metropolitan port centre of the city to the east. The megalopolis stretches out to the west where single-family houses in modern suburbs beyond the ring road lead out to the airport.

On this platform Charney, like an urban shaman, erected a series of totems or allegorical columns representing the different urban actors and their ecologies in the city. The first one represents the first ecology of the hunters and trappers, with a small house or shed for their

studioMAS, aerial photograph of Freedom Charter Memorial, Kliptown, Johannesburg, South Africa, 2008
The long market and museum buildings frame the memorial square where the conical memorial houses 10 tablets containing the ANC Charter. Ten columns on the eastern edge of the square also represent these principles. (Photo © studioMAS, aerial photography by Visual Air)

Melvin Charney, Canadian Centre for Architecture Garden, Montreal, Canada, 1990
This view is taken looking from the Arcade across the Esplanade, showing Allegorical
Columns 6, 7, 8, 10, and 11. (Photo courtesy Collection Centre Canadien d'Architecture/
Canadian Centre for Architecture, Montréal, © Robert Burley)

home. On the next totem column, the giant grain elevators ride on the backs of row houses of the workers. These arrived with the successful farming ecology of the surrounding river plains, producing grain for export and huge silos that still dominate the waterfront of the city. These silos with their stacked elevators and conveyor belts represented the multilayered future city for modernist architects like Walter Gropius or Le Corbusier in the 1910s and 1920s. Next door a Greek Revival temple structure on a column represents the arrival of the banks, or perhaps the church, monumental structures to a fantasy of stability and equilibrium. A further totem celebrates the industrial past of Montreal, with its sawtooth-roofed factories and tall factory chimneys, like those ruins on view below the terrace. This totem is at ground level, while raised up above new row houses a postmodern totem celebrates the skyline of the postmodern city ecology of corporate business towers, as interpreted by the Italian architect Massimo Scolari in drawings from the 1970s. These towers seem to be sprouting wings, like angels about to fly from the city.

The final, western totem sculpture represents the layered, neo-Constructivist or Deconstructivist urban design ecology. The bank's temple front seems to float in the air, held up by diagonal scaffolding that is reminiscent of Constructivist Vladimir Tatlin's Tower project from Moscow in 1917, with an arm stretching out from the scaffolding for Lenin to address the masses (the arm looks suspiciously like a cherrypicker bucket from a JCB construction site backhoe). Here the city seems to be lifting off into the sky as an inaccessible, high arm reaches towards the clouds and the airport to the west. Each urban design ecology has its own totem, tomb or symbolic representation on this terrace. Charney created each symbolic structure and held them all separate, whereas in the city below the terrace urban actors combine and weave together these layers and their symbols in their urban designs.

The terrace presents a memory theatre of urban elements and their recombinations. The design also opens out to the future, the distant horizon with its sky and shifting clouds. Old ecologies and past scenarios are present, while future urban actors, perhaps represented by angels' wings and flying objects, will recombine the floating elements of the final composition, where the urban section is challenged and sectional complexity is symbolised by the irrational diagonal from Tatlin's Tower. Viewed from the ruined walls of the old villa that was once located on the terrace, the totems and flying elements position the urban designer in a present that is never stable and will always involve change.

The terrace represents a sophisticated viewing platform for seeing the ecology, or rather multiple ecologies, of the city. It contains symbolic representations of several urban ecologies whose future should concern urban designers and that need to be addressed with 'what if' scenarios. These towers represent the past performances of earlier urban actors opening up to an unknown future. The design has a rare self-awareness that allows hidden urban ecologies to emerge and each find their own means of expression. None of the totems touch, but a visitor cannot help but combine these potent symbols and imagine new combinations coexisting with the past. Urban design has an opened future and hopefully will co-evolve new urban design ecologies to provide sustainable future scenarios for Asian megacities and shrinking cities alike.

Notes

NB: See 'Author's Caution: Endnote Sources and Wikipedia', towards the end of this book.

1   For Arctic ice melt, see: Mark Kinver, 'Ice Sheet Melt Threat Reassessed', 14 May 2009, BBC News website, http://news.bbc.co.uk/2/hi/science/nature/8050094.stm (accessed 7 April 2010).

2   For Angkor Wat, see: 'Map Reveals Ancient Urban Sprawl', 14 August 2007, BBC News website, http://news.bbc.co.uk/2/hi/science/nature/6945574.stm (accessed 2 April 2010). On Angkor Wat water, see: Emma Young, 'Vast Ancient Settlement Found at Angkor Wat', *New Scientist*, 13 August 2007, http://www.newscientist.com/article/dn12474-vast-ancient-settlement-found-at-angkor-wat.html (accessed 5 April 2010).

3   For the 2008 financial meltdown, see: Joseph E Stiglitz, *Freefall: America, Free Markets, and the Sinking of the World Economy*, WW Norton & Co (New York), 2010; also: Paul Krugman, 'Lest We Forget', *The New York Times*, 27 November 2008, http://www.nytimes.com/2008/11/28/opinion/28krugman.html?_r=1 (accessed 24 March 2010).

4   David Owen, *Green Metropolis: Why Living Smaller, Living Closer, and Driving Less Are the Keys to Sustainability*, Riverhead Books (New York), 2009. See also: David Owen, 'The Risk And Reward Of Manhattan's Density', *The New Yorker*, 11 September 2009, http://www.newyorker.com/online/blogs/newsdesk/2009/09/david-owen-green-metropolis.html (accessed 24 March 2010).

5   Colin Rowe and Fred Koetter, *Collage City*, MIT Press (Cambridge, MA), 1978.

6   For Munich history, see: Franz Schiermeier Verlag, 'stadt – bau – plan: 850 jahre Stadtentwicklung München', http://www.stadtatlas-muenchen.de/stadt-bau-plan.html; also English summary, 'city – building – plan: 850 Years of Urban Development in Munich', Munich official website, http://www.muenchen.de/Rathaus/plan/munich_as_planned/160825/index.html; also: http://en.wikipedia.org/wiki/Munich (all accessed 24 March 2010). For railways, see: Florian Schultz, München U-bahn Album, http://www.robert-schwandl.de/muenchen/ (accessed 24 March 2010). For the BMW museum, see: http://en.wikipedia.org/wiki/BMW_Welt (accessed 24 March 2010).

7   On The 'Munich Perspective', see: 'The Munich Perspective: our city's future', Munich official website, http://www.muenchen.de/Rathaus/plan/stadtentwicklung/perspektive/pm_en_m/41525/index.html (accessed 24 March 2010); also: 'Leicester and Munich prepare cities for a desirable year 2050', Energie-Cités website, http://www.energie-cities.eu/Leicester-and-Munich-prepare (accessed 5 April 2010).

8   For Munster Library, see: Francisco Sanin, *Munster City Library: Architekturburo Bolles-Wilson + Partner*, Phaidon Press (London), October 1994.

9   For 'Le Grand Paris', see: 'Le Grand Paris' website, http://www.legrandparis.culture.gouv.fr/ (accessed 24 March 2010).

10 For Secchi and Viganò's 'Le Grand Paris' project, see: http://www.legrandparis.culture.gouv.fr/actualitedetail/87 (accessed 24 March 2010). On Studio 09's vision of Paris in the future, see: Dan Stewart, 'Sarkozy to Unveil 10 Visions of Future Paris', *Building*, 29 April 2009, http://www.building.co.uk/story.asp?storycode=3139382 (accessed 24 March 2010).

11 For Secchi and Viganò's Paris detail Living retrofit study, see: Studio 09 / Bernardo Secchi and Paola Viganò, 'Le diagnostic prospectif de l'agglomération parisienne', pp 75–80, http://www.legrandparis.culture.gouv.fr/documents/STUDIO_09_Livret_chantier_2.pdf.

12 For Rogers, Portzamparc and Grumbach, see: 'Le Grand Paris' website, http://www.legrandparis.culture.gouv.fr/; also: 'Ten Scenarios for "Grand Paris" Metropolis Now Up for Public Debate,' 19 March 2009, *bustler*, http://www.bustler.net/index.php/article/ten_scenarios_for_grand_paris_metropolis_now_up_for_public_debate/ (accessed 24 March 2010).

13 Jean Gottmann, *Megalopolis: The Urbanized Northeastern Seaboard of the United States*, Twentieth Century Fund (New York), 1961.

14 Reyner Banham, *Los Angeles: The Architecture of Four Ecologies*, Harper & Row (New York), 1971.

15 Xaveer de Geyter (ed), *After-Sprawl: Research for the Contemporary City*, NAi (Rotterdam) and Kunstcentrum deSingel (Antwerp), 2002.

16   Franz Oswald, Peter Baccini, Mark Michaeli, *Netzstadt: Designing the Urban*, Birkhäuser (Basel; Boston, MA; Berlin), 2003.

17   For Daniel Libeskind and Las Vegas City Center, see: Studio Daniel Libeskind website, http://www.daniel-libeskind.com/projects/show-all/mgm-mirage-citycenter/ (accessed 24 March 2010).

18   On US driver mileage, see: Bureau of Transportation Statistics website, http://www.bts.gov/publications/omnistats/volume_03_issue_04/html/figure_02.html (accessed 24 March 2010).

19   On golf carts, see: Damon Hack, 'A Custom Ride, Legal for the Street or the 18th Tee', *The New York Times*, 9 April 2007 http://www.nytimes.com/2007/04/09/sports/golf/09carts.html?pagewanted=print (accessed 24 March 2010).

20   On Federation Square, Melbourne, Australia, see: Lab Architecture website, http://www.labarchitecture.com/ (accessed 4 April 2010).

21   On 'Dutch Disease' and the impact of oil on a host country's economy, see: http://en.wikipedia.org/wiki/Dutch_disease; also: 'Time for Transparency', report in http://www.globalwitness.org/media_library_detail.php/115/en/time_for_transparency (accessed March 24, 2010). On cleptocracy and the impact of oil on Lagos, Nigeria, see: Mathew Gandy, 'Learning from Lagos', *New Left Review*, no 33, May–June 2005.

22   See: 'South Korea in $10bn Ghana Homes Deal', BBC News website, 9 December 2009 http://news.bbc.co.uk/2/hi/africa/8403774.stm (accessed 24 March 2010).

23   On Teddy Cruz, see: Estudio Teddy Cruz website, http://estudioteddycruz.com/ (accessed 24 March 2010); also: Nicolai Ouroussoff, 'Border-Town Muse: an architect finds a model in Tijuana', *The New York Times*, 12 March 2006, http://www.nytimes.com/2006/03/12/travel/12iht-shanty.html (accessed 24 March 2010).

24   On Seattle Olympic Sculpture Park, see: Weiss/Manfredi website, http://www.weissmanfredi.com/projects/ (accessed 24 March 2010).

25   For the Vancouver model, commuting patterns and eco-city planning, see: Vancouver City Planning Commission website, http://www.planningcommission.ca/; also: Vancouver EcoDensity Planning Initiative website, http://www.vancouver-ecodensity.ca/ecodensity_actions.pdf (both accessed 16 July 2010). For cycling/walking, see: cycling statistics, City of Vancouver website, http://vancouver.ca/engsvcs/transport/cycling/stats.htm (accessed 16 July 2010).

26   On Kai Tak airport, see: http://en.wikipedia.org/wiki/Kai_Tak_Airport (accessed 26 March 2010). On Yongsan Garrison base in Seoul, see: GlobalSecurity.org website, http://www.globalsecurity.org/military/facility/yongsan.htm (accessed 26 March 2010).

27   On Orange County Great Park, see: Orange County Great Park website, http://www.ocgp.org/learn/design/ (accessed 26 March 2010).

28   On dead malls, see: http://www.deadmalls.com/ (accessed 26 March 2010). On the 'Dead Malls' competition, see: David Sokol, 'Visions of the Future?', 1 May 2003, *Retail Traffic*, http://retailtrafficmag.com/development/renovation/retail_visions_future/ (accessed 26 March 2010).

29   On mall evolution, see: 'The Architect and the Mall', in *You Are Here: The Jerde Partnership International*, Phaidon Press (New York), 1999. For art galleries, see: David Grahame Shane, 'Heterotopias of Illusion From Beaubourg to Bilbao and beyond', in Michiel Dehaene and Lieven De Cauter, (eds), *Heterotopia and the City: Public Space in a Postcivil Society*, Routledge (Abingdon), 2008, pp 259–74.

30   Colin Rowe and Fred Koetter, *Collage City*, MIT Press (Cambridge, MA), 1978. For 'city archipelago', see: Oswald Mathias Ungers, Rem Koolhaas, Peter Riemann, Hans Kollhof, Peter Ovaska, 'Cities within the City: proposal by the sommer akademie for Berlin', *Lotus International*, 1977, p 19.

31   On Celebration, see: Cooper, Robertson & Partners website, http://www.cooperrobertson.com/ (accessed 26 March 2010).

32   For Euralille, see: Martin K Meade, 'Euralille: the instant city', *The Architectural Review*, December 1994, http://findarticles.com/p/articles/mi_m3575/is_n1174_v196/ai_16561934/ (accessed 26 March 2010).

33   On LEED Local Policy of Battery Park City, see: USGBC (US Green Building Council), 'LEED Initiatives by State', http://www.usgbc.org/ShowFile.aspx?DocumentID=5030 (accessed 26 March 2010).

34   On the Mid-Levels, Hong Kong, see: http://en.wikipedia.org/wiki/Mid-levels (accessed 26 March 2010). For The Peak, see: Hong Kong Extras website, http://www.hongkongextras.com/the-peak.html (accessed 26 March 2010).

35   On Langham Place, see: The Jerde Partnership website, http://www.jerde.com/projects/project.php?id=31 (accessed 26 March 2010).

36   On Terry Farrell Partners Kowloon Station project, see: Farrells website, http://www.terryfarrell.co.uk/#/project/0097/ (accessed 19 March 2010). For the Elements Mall within Kowloon Station, see: http://en.wikipedia.org/wiki/Elements,_Hong_Kong (accessed 19 March 2010).

37   On Bel Geddes' Futurama, see: Richard Wurts and Stanley Applebaum, *The New York World's Fair, 1939/1940 in 155 photographs*, Courier Dover Publications (New York), 1977; also: http://en.wikipedia.org/wiki/Norman_Bel_Geddes (accessed 26 March 2010).

38   On Shanghai Expo, see: http://en.wikipedia.org/wiki/Expo_2010; also: World Expo 2010 Shanghai website, http://en.expo2010.cn/sr/video/shipin2.htm (accessed 5 April 2010).

39   For British population and London population, see: Julie Jefferies, 'The UK Population: Past, Present and Future', 2005, UK National Statistics website, http://www.statistics.gov.uk/downloads/theme_compendia/fom2005/01_fopm_population.pdf (accessed 16 July 2010).

40   For US statistics, see: Historical National Population Estimates, July 1, 1900 to July 1, 1999, US Census Bureau website, http://www.census.gov/popest/archives/1990s/popclockest.txt (accessed 16 July 2010). For East Coast Corridor, see: Jean Gottmann, *Megalopolis: The Urbanized Northeastern Seaboard of the United States*, Twentieth Century Fund (New York), 1961.

41   For India and China statistics, see: United Nations Department of Economic and Social Affairs, Population Division, Population Estimates and Projections Section, http://esa.un.org/unpd/wup/index.htm.

42   For UN megacity-regions, see: John Vidal, 'UN report: world's biggest cities merging into "mega-regions"', *The Guardian*, 22 March 2010, http://www.guardian.co.uk/world/2010/mar/22/un-cities-mega-regions; also: UN-HABITAT website, http://www.unhabitat.org/pmss/listItemDetails.aspx?publicationID=2562 (accessed 1 April 2010).

43   For megacity mapping and navigation, see: Brian McGrath and DG Shane (eds), *Sensing the 21st-Century City: Close-up and Remote, Architectural Design*, vol 75, issue 6, November/December 2005.

44   For Beijing megablock explorations, see: Columbia University's China Lab research, http://china-lab.org/megablock-urbanisms-symposium-video-online; also: Shenzhen & Hong Kong Bi-City Biennale website, http://www.szhkbiennale.org/en/index.php/conferences/2009/12/1565 (both accessed 16 July 2010). For mapping urban villages in megablocks, see: Zhengdong Huang, School of Urban Design, Wuhan University, 'Mapping of Urban Villages in China', undated presentation, Center for International Earth Science Information Network, Columbia University, New York, http://www.ciesin.columbia.edu/confluence/download/attachments/34308102/Huang+China+UrbanVillageMapping.pdf?version=1 (accessed 17 March 2010).

45   For mega-armatures and multilane boulevards, see: Alan B Jackson and Elizabeth MacDonald, *The Boulevard Book*, MIT Press (Cambridge, MA), 2003 (available on Google Books).

46   Anuradha Mathur and Dilip da Cunha, *Mississippi Floods*, Yale University Press (New Haven, CT), 2001.

47   Anuradha Mathur and Dilip da Cunha, *Deccan Traverses: The Making of Bangalore's Terrain*, Rupa (New Delhi), 2006. Anuradha Mathur and Dilip da Cunha, *SOAK: Mumbai in an Estuary*, Rupa & Co (Mumbai), 2009; see also: 'SOAK' exhibition website, http://www.soak.in/ (accessed 26 March 2010).

48   On the global urban mapping programme, see: Brian McGrath and Graham Shane, 'Introduction', *Sensing the 21st-Century City: Close-up and Remote, Architectural Design*, vol

75, issue 6, November/December 2005, p 14. On global flooding, see: Map Large, Inc, Global Flood Map website, http://globalfloodmap.org/ (accessed 26 March 2010).

49   On sea level rising in the Sundarbans, see: 'Sinking Sundarbans: an exhibition of photographs by Peter Caton', 14 January 2010, http://www.guardian.co.uk/environment/gallery/2010/jan/14/ sinking-sundarbans-peter-caton; also: 'Sinking Sundarbans – Climate Voices', Greenpeace website, http://www.greenpeace.org/international/photosvideos/greenpeace-photo-essays/ sinking-sundarbans-climate-v (accessed 28 March 2010).

50   Terry Farrell, *Shaping London: The Patterns and Forms That Make the Metropolis*, John Wiley & Sons (Chichester), 2010; see also: Farrells website, http://www.terryfarrell.co.uk/#/thames-gateway/ (accessed 29 March 2009).

51   On the Richard Rogers report see: Urban Task Force, 'Towards a Strong Urban Renaissance', November 2005, http://www.urbantaskforce.org/UTF_final_report.pdf (accessed 29 March 2010); see also: 'This is why the environment needs to be on the political agenda … what a mess', *Climate Change News*, 24 April 2006, http://climatechangenews.blogspot.com/2006/04/ this-is-why-environment-needs-to-be-on.html (accessed 29 March 2010). On Thames Estuary London Gateway container port, see: http://en.wikipedia.org/wiki/Shell_Haven. On the proposed Thames Estuary airport, see: 'Thames Estuary Airport Feasibility Review', *NCE*, December 2, 2009, http://www.testrad.co.uk/pdf/TEAFRreport.pdf (accessed 29 March 2010); also: http://en.wikipedia.org/wiki/Thames_Gateway (accessed 1 April 2010).

52   On flash mobs, see: Jose Luis Echeverria Manau, Jordi Mansilla Ortoneda and Jorge Perea Solano, (eds), 'Squatting Geometries – Guerilla Barcelona: Technological appropriations of the over-planned city', *Sensing the 21st-Century City: Close-up and Remote, Architectural Design*, vol 75, issue 6, November/December 2005, pp 58–64; also: 'Saatchi & Saatchi Create Dance Mania at Liverpool St Station – Reminding Commuters: Life's for Sharing', 26 January 2009, Saatchi & Saatchi website, http://www.saatchi.co.uk/news/archive/dance_mania_at_liverpool_ st_station_reminds_commuters_lifes_for_sharing and http://en.wikipedia.org/wiki/Flash_mobs (accessed 14 February 2010).

53   See: Michel Foucault, 'Of Other Spaces', in Catherine David and Jean-François Chevrier (eds), *Documenta X: The Book*, Hatje Cantz (Kassel), 1997, p 262, also available at http://foucault.info/ documents/heteroTopia/foucault.heteroTopia.en.html (accessed 29 September 2009).

54   On Kliptown Memorial in Johannesburg, see: studioMAS website, http://www.studiomas.co.za/ wssd.php (accessed 29 March 2010).

55   On the Freedom Charter, see: http://en.wikipedia.org/wiki/Freedom_Charter (accessed 4 April 2010).

56   On Melvin Charney's Canadian Centre for Architecture terrace, see: Melvin Charney, *Parcours de la Réinvention/About Reinvention*, Frac Basse-Normandie (Caen), 1998, pp 119–49; see also: Canadian Centre for Architecture (CCA) website, http://www.cca.qc.ca/en/collection/300-cca-garden (accessed 29 March 2010).

This glossary provides a short guide to the author's terminology employed in this book, explaining key terms that are of relevance to this text. For a more general, witty but very informative glossary of urban design terms, readers are referred to Robert Cowan's *The Dictionary of Urbanism* (Streetwise Press (Tisbury, Wiltshire), 2005) and Cowan's accompanying website http://www.urbanwords.info/.

city model

Urban models represent ideals of what some people think a city ought to be. Kevin Lynch in *A Theory of Good City Form* (MIT Press (Cambridge, MA), 1981) identified and rejected three urban models: the *city of faith*, the *city as a machine* and the *ecological city*. In this book these models are also called the *archi-città*, *cine-città* and *tele-città*, indicating three different sets of relationships between actors, urban elements and the environment. Lynch proposed *city design* as a technique of urban modelling that encompassed many scales of operation and recognised the new landscape scale implied by the automobile as a form of mass transportation. In 1971 the Canadian sociologist Terry McGee proposed a specifically Asian urban model based on the Indonesian *desa-kota* (city–village hybrid) that included urban village agriculture and irrigation systems within the city, greatly expanding Lynch's category of the eco-city.

heterotopia

Michel Foucault defined a *heterotopia* as a real place that facilitated change and research, mirroring in miniature the larger urban system within which urban actors were located (like small cities within cities). Foucault thought that all systems could only become logically consistent by excluding nonconforming items. He proposed to study the logic of systems by looking at the exclusions. In Foucault's theory excluded elements were placed in real, heterotopic spaces, resulting in a strange mixture of disparate elements and people with no apparent overall logic. These real spaces contrasted with utopias – abstract, pure, logical, consistent urban models that Foucault saw as unreal, imaginary, repressive, generic non-spaces. Actors used real spaces, heterotopias, embedded in their systems to accelerate or slow change. Foucault gave as examples of heterotopias 19th-century state-run prisons, hospitals, universities and schools whose design helped bring the modern city and society into being. In the late 20th century many new heterotopias such as world's fairs, shopping malls, theme parks and Olympic events have helped bring a postmodern society into the world. A fuller explanation of heterotopias can be found in Chapter 4 of the author's *Recombinant Urbanism: Conceptual Modeling in Architecture, Urban Design and City Theory* (Wiley-Academy (Chichester), 2005).

fragmented metropolis or city archipelago

The *fragmented metropolis* is a hybrid urban form that arose from the collapse of the metropolis, under the impact of the megalopolis. Where the metropolis lay at the heart of an empire and had a single important centre, with a clear hierarchy of dependent centres, the sprawling megalopolis encompassed many centres with no clear hierarchy. Designers quickly realised they could not control the vast megalopolis, even using Lynch's proposed city design techniques. Urban designers and developers chose instead to control large urban fragments, enclaves where urban design guidelines and controls could shape development. Many authors recognised this urban fragmentation process in the 1970s, ranging from Aldo Rossi in his Analogous City drawing (1976), to Rowe and Koetter in *Collage City* (MIT Press (Cambridge,

MA), 1978) and OM Ungers and Rem Koolhaas in their 'City Archipelago' Summer School in Berlin (1977). The fragmented metropolis implies there are large urban fragments within the city controlled by powerful urban actors who manage their life and design, the city thus becoming a collage of fragments. The city archipelago approach also recognises the large urban fragments but emphasises the interstitial spaces in between the fragments, creating a series of connected urban islands – an archipelago.

metropolis

Metropolis from the Greek means 'mother city', the city from which colonists leave to form a colony. Greek merchants travelling between Aegean islands created a trade bridge between Asia and Europe, colonising the Eastern Mediterranean in the process, with Athens growing as the control centre of the network. Roman, Chinese and Indian trading empires scaled up such small beginnings, producing larger capital cities, such as Rome and Beijing with populations of 1 million in classical antiquity. These cities were often ancient cities of faith as studied by Lynch, centres of a cosmic worldview with a vast hinterland of believers. The metropolis remained at the heart of empire for millennia. As industrialisation replaced slaves as an energy source, the scale of European empires grew to encompass the globe, producing metropolitan centres of 7 million in 1900 in New York and London. From then on the metropolis was linked to global empires. With the decline of European empires after 1945 the ideal of the compact metropolis suffered. Finally the invention of the megalopolis in the 1950s and 1960s seemed to spell the doom of the metropolis within the city-region or network city. Problems with this dispersed urban design ecology resulted in the return of the metropolitan ideal, but fractured and fragmented across the network without a single centre.

megalopolis

Megalopolis from the Greek means 'great city'. Ancient cities were small and compact by modern standards, few having more than 100,000 inhabitants according to Spiro Kostof in *The City Shaped* (Bulfinch Press (Boston, MA), 1991). The French sociologist Jean Gottmann reinvented the term in 1961 to distinguish the urbanisation of the East Coast of the USA from Boston to Washington from the metropolises, the compact large cities in Europe that lay at the heart of empires, with bad housing for the poor, rigid class structures, ghettos and slums. Gottmann argued that never had so many people lived together with such a high standard of living, admiring the urban design ecology of the East Coast corridor and its 32 million inhabitants. In the 1970s urban sociologists studied the new suburban forms while urban designers like the Robert Venturi, Denise Scott Brown and Steven Izenour team detailed the new urban streetscapes sponsored by this vast, new corporate development of housing estates, commercial strips, malls, office parks, industrial parks and theme parks. The oil-shocks of the late 1970s demonstrated the vulnerability of this new petroleum-based urban design ecology, leading to the development of new urban centres and fragments, countering the dispersal of the city that had previously seemed inevitable. As the hidden ecological costs of the megalopolis have become clearer, urban designers have sought to retain its freedom of choice for the individual, sometimes proposing to shrink the city or compensating for its sprawling form through various technological revisions and denser development.

megacity/metacity

The American sociologist Janice Perlman coined the term 'megacity' in the early 1970s to describe the self-built *favela* city extensions of Rio de Janeiro in Brazil, where industrialisation and wealth based on discoveries of vast petroleum reserves spurred the growth of a vast informal city unmapped by the authorities. Perlman went on to found the Mega-Cities Project and act as an advocate for the inhabitants of the *favelas*, leading to the United Nations' acceptance of the term 'megacity' as a city of 8 million, followed by later revisions to 10 million, 12 million and then 20 million. When the UN announced that half the world's population would live in cities by 2007, it also published a report on megacities highlighting their inequalities and problems – although, as critics pointed out, 92 per cent of the world's urban population would live in cities of between 1 and 2 million inhabitants. While some megacities remain in Latin America and a few in Africa, in the future most are expected to be in Asia where the term covers many new urban forms based on the *desa-kota* system, where agriculture is included inside the city. Within these vast networks of mixed-use megablocks formed by armatures of infrastructure, new meganodes provide for the meeting of individuals on a previously unseen mass scale. The latest UN report from the World Urban Forum in Rio (2010) raised the spectre of megacity regions with populations of 120 million, citing the Pearl River delta and Hong Kong as an example. Cities at this scale can scarcely be comprehended except from a satellite or as data artifacts, becoming digital *metacities*, or informational 'data towns' as described by the Dutch architectural group MVRDV in their exhibition 'Metacity/Datatown' (2000).

symbolic intermediary

A symbolic intermediary maybe any person, organisation, information or thing used by urban actors as a token in their negotiations with other actors. The meaning of the symbolic intermediary may change and be renegotiated over time as relationships between urban actors shift. The term is derived from Actor-Network Theory (ANT) as developed by British sociologists such as Nigel Thrift, based on French sociologist Bruno Latour's work on the sociology of knowledge production in scientific laboratories in the 1980s. The changing definition of the megacity described above demonstrates how a symbolic intermediary can shift meaning over time. The memorial at Ground Zero in New York is another example of a symbolic intermediary caught in a discourse amongst many interested actors, who eventually found a consensus around a design, having employed many tactics. These tactics included political pressure from above, street demonstrations from below, media-savvy consultants, utopian design proposals, public exhibitions of designs, public consultations, behind-door negotiations and basic design decisions made by policemen and security consultants at the last moment. The resultant smooth, modernist towers and garden space will be a symbolic intermediary representative of the unequal power of the various urban actors in this messy, discordant, polyphonic design discourse.

urban actor

Urban actors may be individuals or small or large groups who are active and organised to use and manipulate space in the city. They may form associations to achieve common goals, and these organisations may become urban institutions managing a part of the city and beyond. Actors represent their needs and desires in relation to each through the use of urban communication systems to negotiate for space and place in the city. Actors may take many roles in the city, and a single person is not necessarily confined to one role. They may also change roles over time. Examples of urban actors range from interested individuals, NGOs and community groups often called 'stakeholders' to large government organisations and wealthy corporations.

urban armature

Urban armatures are linear organising devices that stretch between two points or attractors. Urban designers of malls discovered that 180 metres (600 feet) constituted the standard pedestrian armature, as in the traditional city street. Armatures could be 'compressed' by being stacked one on another (as in a mall), or 'stretched' by the use of a vehicle, especially an automobile, as in the Las Vegas Strip.

urban code

The term 'code' derives from the Latin *codex*, meaning a written, systematic and logically consistent body of laws and statutes that regulate a situation, activity or place. Many urban actors have defined urban codes over the centuries to govern different aspects of urban models, from the *archi-città*, to the *cine-città* and *tele-città*. In 1945, for instance, American legal codes defined who could live where in American cities, restricting the rights of urban minorities – religious minorities, racial minorities and cultural minorities, like artists or homosexuals. Other legal codes defined zoning restrictions on uses within particular enclaves or in New York required setbacks on skyscrapers to provide light to the street. Modernist urban design codes sought to enforce single-use zoning enclaves. Monofunctional zoning separated housing from work, factories from offices, cultural uses from commercial. Modernist codes also encouraged urban designs with towers or slab blocks isolated from the street, set on a plaza in business centres or in parkland in residential quarters. With the breakdown of modernism and the metropolis, urban designers again sought urban design guidelines based on the street corridor and smaller property plots for developers to work on, where the overall development could be controlled in a large urban fragment. Here urban designers again created new hybrids for mixed uses, yet each use within the city still maintained its own code, enclave and autonomy often in complex, heterotopic urban sections. In the megacity the megablock allowed for this vertical system to expand laterally and still include the Asian tradition of urban agriculture.

urban connector
Urban connectors are visible or invisible armatures, streets, boulevards, highways, telephone lines or cell tower systems that connect mobile or static urban actors in urban patches together into a city archipelago, collage city, network city or megacity/metacity system.

urban cybernetics and urban design ecology
Urban actors construct urban organisations that best serve their needs, usually from the top down but sometimes from the bottom up or in hybrid structures. The dominant actors usually have special privileges within this informational feedback system, but more open systems based on contemporary mass personal communications have the potential to alter these arrangements. In this book, four cybernetic informational structures have been studied in the metropolis, the megalopolis, the fragmented metropolis and megacities. Each of these constitutes an urban design ecology with its own form of informational organisation:

- **organisation 1 – metropolis:** nesting systems place one enclave inside another and value proximity to the centre of the system
- **organisation 2 – megalopolis:** linear sequences, numerical, alphabetical order, sorting devices like streets, boulevards or walkways to numbered airport gates
- **organisation 3 – collage city:** polycentric system, multiple nested fragments, competing centres
- **organisation 4 – megacity:** net city; complex informational systems, multiple organisational capacities, rural–urban hybrid continuum.

urban enclave
Enclaves are organisational devices centred around a single centre. Proximity to the centre indicates importance of the actor or intermediary. Enclaves have perimeter boundaries and gates, with gatekeepers who control entry. Systems of landownership create fundamental enclave systems in cities. Examples of enclaves are urban squares, blocks, malls, superblocks and megablocks.

urban fabric
Urban fabric is built from different building typologies to make a characteristic urban grain or pattern in plan – perhaps a courtyard type, row house type or isolated pavilion type of layout on each lot and block.

urban grain

Urban grain is a property of urban fabric that has to do with its porosity, how space is organised inside the fabric type and at what density or scale. Urban porosity represents a balance between the need for flow and access and the need for privacy and enclosure or stasis.

urban morphology

Morphos means shape or pattern in Greek, and morphology is the logical study of urban shapes and patterns in city plans. Urban designers distinguish between regular and irregular patterns in plan in enclaves, armatures and heterotopias at different scales. Urban actors use urban elements to create and construct different urban morphologies, creating different urban design ecologies.

urban morphogenesis

Urban morphogenesis is the observation of the self-organising properties of how urban actors work over time, how they shift from one spatial organisation or type to another over time through sudden or gradual, non-linear transitions. These changes often involve shifts and recombinations of urban elements to transform an earlier morphology.

urban networks

Urban actors often form networks of relationships inside the city, sharing symbolic intermediaries to create and maintain spaces for their needs and use. These networks may be open and flexible or closed, rigid and hierarchical depending on the structure of the actors' organisation. Actors' relationships may also be channelled into communication or transportation networks, necessitating networks of modern infrastructure.

urban patches or fragments

A patch is a fragment or an area sharing a distinctive urban grain or controlled by a specific urban actor or actors who direct development. The scale may vary from a single block, to an urban village, to a superblock of towers, to a suburban patch like Levittown, New York, to a megablock in a megacity.

urban village

In the classical European urban system based on the metropolis, a descending hierarchy went down from the mother city, to a city, to a town, to a village and then to the lowly hamlet (a village without a church). In this medieval and ecclesiastic definition of the city from Lynch's city of faith, the village formed the bridge between the hamlet and town that might have several neighbourhoods and churches. Serfs were tied to the land and could not travel, the village was their urban unit, with its small market and church or temple, tied to the cycles of agricultural production and a cosmology linked to the circular time of the enslaved vassal. With industrialisation, the slavery of the feudal village receded into the background as the communal aspects of a shared village life became idealised in a faith-based critique of the alienation and anomie of modern industrial society, despite its apparent freedom and promise of plenty. The Garden City movement of the early 20th century reflected this belief in urban villages, and British new town planners often went to great lengths to recognise and preserve villages within new towns. In the Asian megacity, urban villages and their agricultural zones formed a fundamental characteristic of the new hybrid urban form identified by Canadian sociologist Terry McGee in *The Urbanization Process in the Third World: Explorations in Search of a Theory* (Bell (London) 1971).

Author's Caution: Endnote Sources and Wikipedia

Over the years the sources and standards applied to endnotes have changed radically. In the 1960s and 1970s index cards, filing systems in libraries and Xerox copies of information were the rule. With the introduction in the 1980s of electronic databases in libraries, and then in the 1990s of online digital information sources, further expanded with the development of the global Web in the early 2000s, the sources available to scholars have changed and ways of accessing information have also shifted.

In this book, a variety of types of references are given both to indicate the origin of information mentioned in the text, and to point readers towards sources of further information that are as widely available as possible. This broad scope of information and knowledge includes the World Wide Web, embracing both online fee-paying sources of scholarly articles (like JSTOR) and free, easily accessible encyclopedias (such as Wikipedia), presuming students have access to the Internet.

The author has personally checked all the online sources at the time of publication but realises that some may be short-lived and/or unstable on the Net. Whenever possible, hybrid sources are given, including books and articles as well as digital sources. Institutional digital sources have been preferred for their stability.

The author has decided to accept the online encyclopedia Wikipedia because this self-organising collective now has editorial committees that vet the articles and check their content, clearly marking areas of uncertainty. Within this Wikipedia structure the author has carefully chosen sites selected for their clarity of information and relevance to this innovative global survey.

Nonetheless, all readers should be aware that:

- all sources referred to in the notes have been carefully assessed for their validity and accuracy at the time of preparing the book, on the basis of the author's extensive knowledge of the subject
- amateur Internet sources should be treated with caution – especially Wikipedia and related sources which can be edited by anyone, regardless of expertise
- Wikipedia and similar Internet sources have only been included in references when the material concerned offers one of the best sources of information on a subject which is as yet not well covered in English-language publications; but such sources, due to their very nature, may be subject to change at any time.

20 books and idea clusters

- **European history**: Tony Judt, *Postwar: A History of Europe Since 1945*, Penguin (New York), 2006, provides an exhaustive general history of Europe's division in the Cold War, reconstruction and then reunification in the last 60 years.

- **Global history**: Eric Hobsbawm, *The Age of Extremes: The History of the World, 1914–1991*, Vintage Books (New York), 1996, offers a general global history of the Cold War years ending with the fall of the Berlin Wall.

- **The metropolis**: Philip Kasinitz (ed), *The Metropolis: Centre and Symbol of Our Times*, NYU Press (New York), 1994, contains key texts related to the Western European metropolis and American variant.

- **The European modernist view**: Sigfried Giedion, *Space, Time and Architecture*, Harvard University Press (Cambridge, MA), 1941, provides a European modernist interpretation of urban history and the future of urban design based on Le Corbusier and CIAM principles.

- **Postwar reconstruction**: Frederick Gibberd, *Town Design*, Architectural Press (London), 1953, provides a snapshot of urban design theories in the European welfare state reconstruction project of the 1950s.

- **The modernist schism**: Eric Paul Mumford, 'From the Heart of the City to Holyoke Center: CIAM Ideas in Sert's Definition of Urban Design', in *Josep Lluis Sert: The Architect of Urban Design, 1953–1969*, Yale University Press (New Haven, CT), 2008, provides an overview of the end of CIAM and emergence of the Team X group at the end of the 1950s, highlighting Sert's role at Harvard and in Latin America.

- **The metropolis–megalopolis shift**: Kevin Lynch, *A Theory of Good City Form*, MIT Press (Cambridge, MA), 1981, is an essential text on urban modelling, providing a new language for the study of the city at multiple scales, incorporating both the scale of the pedestrian and the automobile over time. See also: Kevin Lynch, *The Image of the City*, MIT Press (Cambridge, MA), 1961; and Donald Appleyard, Kevin Lynch and John R Myer (eds), *The View from the Road*, MIT Press (Cambridge, MA), 1964.

- **The megalopolis**: Jean Gottmann, *Megalopolis: The Urbanized Northeastern Seaboard of the United States*, Twentieth Century Fund (New York), 1961, is a key text. As early as 1961, it identified the USA's East Coast as a new form of linear city network with 32 million inhabitants. Gottmann identified Tokyo as a megalopolis later; see: Jean Gottmann, *Megalopolis Revisited: 25 Years Later*, University of Maryland, Institute for Urban Studies (College Park, MD), 1987.

- **The mall and the automobile**: Victor Gruen, *The Heart of our Cities: The Urban Crisis – Diagnosis and Cure*, Simon & Schuster (New York), 1964, provides the mall pioneer's thoughts on the automobile, urban design and the city.

- **Urban champions**: Jane Jacobs, *The Death and Life of Great American Cities*, Vintage Books (New York), 1961. Jacobs, as defender of the traditional, compact metropolis and urban visionary, had many allies. These included the English architect and urban designer Gordon Cullen, guardian of the picturesque village in London and author of *Townscape* (Architectural Press (London), 1961), and Italian architect Aldo Rossi, author of *The Architecture of the City* (first published in Italian in 1966, MIT Press translation by Diane Ghirardo and Joan Ockman, 1984), whose rationalist approach highlighted the systematic methods employed to make European cities in various periods.

- **Sprawl to megastructures**: Reyner Banham, *Los Angeles: The Architecture of Four Ecologies*, Harper & Row (New York), 1971, Banham's pioneering celebration of the automobile city, is coupled with the demise of the metropolis and the megastructure in his *Megastructure: Urban Futures of the Recent Past*, Thames & Hudson (London), 1976.

- **The urban strip**: Robert Venturi, Denise Scott Brown and Steven Izenour, *Learning from Las Vegas: The Forgotten Symbolism of Architectural Form*, MIT Press (Cambridge, MA), 1972, is the key text on the impact of the automobile on urban form in American cities, creating the new Strip linear city armature.

- **The fragmented metropolis**: Jonathan Barnett, *An Introduction to Urban Design*, Harper & Rowe (New York), 1982. A pioneer of special district zoning and urban design guidelines in New York in the 1960s and 1970s, Barnett is also author of *The Fractured Metropolis: Improving The New City, Restoring The Old City, Reshaping The Region*, HarperCollins (New York), 1996.

- **The collage city**: Colin Rowe and Fred Koetter, *Collage City*, MIT Press (Cambridge, MA), 1978, is a key text, recognising the fragmentation of the modern metropolis under the impact of global changes, the automobile, and the collapse of the modern movement and the metropolis. It enabled designers to consider the centre and edge of the city using the same design techniques. See: John A Dutton, *The New American Urbanism: Re-forming the Suburban Metropolis*, Skira (Milan), 2000.

- **Urban fragments and archipelago city**: Rem Koolhaas, *Delirious New York: A Retroactive Manifesto for Manhattan*, Oxford University Press (New York), 1978, recast Manhattan as a super-dense, commercial urban fragment and model for the global city of the future. The city as a system of large urban fragments also appeared as an archipelago pattern in Atlanta, USA in Koolhaas and Bruce Mau's *S,M,L,XL*, Monacelli Press (New York), 1995, and was extended to Lagos, Africa in his *Mutations*, Arc en Rêve Centre d'Architecture (Bordeaux), 2001 and to the Pearl River Delta, China in his *The Great Leap Forward*, Harvard Design School Project on the City 2, New York (Taschen), 2002.

- **Globalisation**: The rise of the global corporate city is described in Saskia Sassen, *The Global City; New York, London, Tokyo*, Princeton University Press (Princeton, NJ), 1991, while its impact on the American suburbs is described by Joel Garreau in *Edge City: Life on the New Frontier*, Anchor Books (New York), 1992. The resultant mall culture was described in *You Are Here: The Jerde Partnership International*, Phaidon Press (New York), 1999. Global Disney theme parks are in Karal Ann Marling (ed), *Designing Disney's Theme Parks: The Architecture of Reassurance*, Flammarion (Paris; New York), 1997. David Harvey, *The Condition of Post-Modernity: An Enquiry into the Origins of Cultural Change*, Blackwell (Oxford, England; Cambridge, MA), 1989, gave the global financial background and mapped the impact on downtown Baltimore and the harbour.

- **The megacity**: Terry McGee in T*he Urbanization Process in the Third World: Explorations in Search of a Theory*, Bell (London), 1971, first recognised the *desa-kota* (city-village formation) as a typical Asian urban form that included mixed uses and agriculture within short distances of each other inside the city. Janice Perlman is credited with having coined the term 'megacity' during her PhD studies, published as *The Myth of Marginality: Urban Poverty and Politics in Rio de Janeiro*, University of California Press (Berkeley, CA), 1976, and later founded the Mega-Cities Project. John FC Turner, *Housing by the People: Towards Autonomy in Building Environments*, Pantheon Books (New York), 1977, opened architects' eyes to the self-built housing revolution and urban extensions taking place in Latin America. United Nations Human Settlements Programme, *The Challenge of Slums: Global Report on Human Settlements,* 2003, Earthscan Publications (London), 2003, took up the megacity theme, expanding it in scale; and it was amplified still further in Mike Davis, *Planet of Slums*, Verso (London), 2007. The current UN Report highlights megacity regions of 120 million inhabitants. Philipp Oswalt (ed), *Atlas of Shrinking Cities*, Hatje Cantz (Ostfildern), 2006, maps exactly where the probable impacts will be from flooding, desertification and climate change.

- **Eco-urbanism and green enclaves**: William Rees and and Mathis Wackernagel, *Our Ecological Footprint: Reducing Human Impact on the Earth*, New Society Publishers (Gabriola Island, BC), 1996, and Al Gore, *An Inconvenient Truth: The Planetary Emergency Of Global Warming And What We Can Do About It*, Rodale Press (Emmaus, PA), 2006, provide the basic information for an assessment of the planet's urban and ecological future. Richard Register, *Ecocities: Rebuilding Cities in Balance with Nature*, New Society Publishers (Gabriola Island, BC), 2006, provides an idealistic vision of a reformatted American eco-urbanism at still relatively low densities. An argument for far higher densities is provided by David Owen, *Green Metropolis: Why Living Smaller, Living Closer, And Driving Less Are Keys To Sustainability*, Riverhead Books (New York), 2009. For green armatures, see Allan B Jacobs and Elizabeth Macdonald, *The Boulevard Book*, MIT Press (Cambridge, MA), 2003. Terry Farrell analyses London as a network of green enclaves in *Shaping London: The Patterns and Forms That Make the Metropolis*, John Wiley & Sons (Chichester), 2010.

- **Agri-urbanism**: For the distributed city that spreads across the landscape while incorporating agriculture and mixed uses, see: the *città diffusa* in Paola Viganò, *La Città Elementare*, Skira (Milan; Geneva), 1999; Thomas Sieverts, *Cities Without Cities: An Interpretation of the Zwischenstadt*, Spon Press (London; New York), 2003; Xaveer de Geyter (ed), *After-Sprawl: Research for the Contemporary City*, NAi (Rotterdam) and Kunstcentrum deSingel (Antwerp), 2002; or Charles Waldheim, *The Landscape Urbanism Reader*, Princeton Architectural Press (New York), 2006.

- **The metacity**: On the role of information and codes in setting up cities, see: Michael Batty and Paul Longley, *Fractal Cities: A Geometry of Form and Function*, Academic Press (San Diego, CA), 1996; and for their political dimension, see: Rafi Segal and Eyal Weizman (eds), *A Civilian Occupation: The Politics of Israeli Architecture*, Verso (London; New York) and Babel (Tel Aviv), 2003. For the city as information, see: MVRDV, *Metacity/Datatown*, 010 Publishers (Rotterdam), 1999. On media, see: Brian McGrath and DG Shane (eds), *Sensing the 21st-Century City – Close-up and Remote*, AD, vol 75, issue 6, November/December 2005, and Brian McGrath, *Digital Modelling for Urban Design*, John Wiley & Sons (London), 2008.

INDEX